NEO-MARXISM

Recent titles in Contributions in Political Science
Series Editor: Bernard K. Johnpoll

NEO–MARXISM

THE MEANINGS OF MODERN RADICALISM

Robert A. Gorman

Contributions in Political Science, Number 77

G P

GREENWOOD PRESS
Westport, Connecticut • London, England

Library of Congress Cataloging in Publication Data

Gorman, Robert A.
   Neo-Marxism, the meanings of modern radicalism.
   (Contributions in political science, ISSN 0147-1066 ;
no. 77)
   Bibliography: p.
   Includes index.
   1. Communism. 2. Radicalism. I. Title. II. Series.
HX73.G67   335.4′01   81-13404
ISBN 0-313-23264-4 (lib. bdg.)   AACR2

Library of Congress Catalog Card Number: 81-13404
ISBN: 0-313-23264-4
ISSN: 0147-1066

First published in 1982

Greenwood Press
A division of Congressional Information Service, Inc.
88 Post Road West, Westport, Connecticut 06881

Printed in the United States of America

10 9 8 7 6 5 4 3 2 1

To Jesse Paris,
Colin Matthew,
and—especially—dearest Elaine.

Contents

Preface

The familiar question "Does Marxism emancipate or enslave?" summons intense and disparate responses but unfairly presumes that "Marxism" is a cohesive theory and a unified political movement that is either good or bad. I argue, contrary to the shibboleths of the Left and the Right, that—within stated limits—Marxism means different things to different people and hence is a discontinuous movement supporting a heterogeneous clientele. Contemporary neo-Marxism is a living dialogue of antagonistic perspectives, less united than Leftists presume and potentially more attractive than Rightists imagine. In practice, it can emancipate or enslave, depending on the ideas, ideals, and tactics of believers.

Each chapter of this book presents one meaning of Marxism as perceived by those directly involved in its constitution, accenting its rhetorical appeal to sensitive, intelligent radicals. Critical comments are directed at what I perceive to be mistaken or illogical applications of a relevant meaning, or its unresolved problems—not at the meaning itself. Since neo-Marxism today embodies all its historical meanings, I write, where possible, in the present tense, affirming their potential utility for readers interested in radical theory and action.

Marxism is decentered in part because of history's reticence. New meanings gestate as old ones futilely encounter unanticipated events or plaintively await unseen predictions. Moreover, Marx's writings are vague enough on important theoretical issues to entertain a variety of interpretations. Neo-Marxism is therefore practically as well as theoretically motivated. Revolutionaries continually reaffirm Marxism as history and a problematic legacy condition their affirmations. Ironically, each is apotheosized, turning a potentially fruitful dialogue into sectarian hostility. Putative historical and exegetical inconsistencies, to some degree tainting all proffered meanings, are felicitously solved with dialectics, which often turns blatantly contradictory evidence into positive proof. Consequently, dissimilar versions of Marxism are rationalized by the same work (for example, the *1844 Manuscripts*) or phenomenon (for example, working-class conservatism), and everyone discovers a different unifying tendency in Marx's writings and history itself. While dialectics *is* an invaluable method of inquiry, it does not excuse this kind of intellectual fatuousness. Dialectical method can be theoretically justified in different ways and can generate antithetical political strategies. In brief, the intended meaning of dialectics reflects foundational, "meta-dialectical" perspectives. I want not only to describe dialectics as a method, but also to examine its potential meanings and political implications.

This book thus encompasses the entire spectrum of Marxist social theories, examining theoretical links to both non-Marxian philosophy and Marx's own writings, describing significant thinkers, and projecting feasible political strategies. I have selected the important self-conscious representatives of each neo-Marxist meaning, that is, seminal thinkers who purposively formulate original revolutionary social theories. Exceptions are allowed only when unoriginal thinkers have significantly influenced a meaning's evolution. This strategy, unfortunately, excludes legions of important Marxist historians, political economists, sociologists, and anthropologists who productively labor from within a (reflectively or nonreflectively) accepted, established theoretical framework. Moreover, this book examines each neo-Marxist thinker, like each meaning of neo-Marxism, in terms of philosophical preconceptions (where possible, ontology, epistemology, ethics, and methodology), political ideals (particularly freedom and justice), and concrete tactics. Since neo-Marxists have lived in a variety of times, nations, and political conditions—and have formulated strategies dealing with an infinite number of national and local issues, many of which are beyond this book's scope—tactics will encompass general views regarding the proper social role and organization of revolutionary parties. For reasons clarified in chapter 1, epistemology facilely unlocks each total perspective and will guide us through the theoretical and practical thickets.

If this book's ideas are valid and their presentation, here and elsewhere, forthright, then society's move Leftward will be a thoughtful, rational response to economic and political exigencies. But even if they are not, serious readers will have been altered by a liberating spark of reflective insight.

NEO–MARXISM

1.

The Ambiguous Legacy

Social theory is society's conscience. It contemplates the social aspects of individuality and outlines proper limitations by which individuals achieve their potentials in a just and equitable community. It systematically inter-relates the needs of each individual and the requirements of society.

The fulcrum of a social theorist's work is his understanding of the origin, nature, and limits of valid knowledge. To mediate individuality and community effectively, we must know what is real and what isn't. Only then can we build a body of reliable knowledge that is useful in formulating salient principles and concepts. What we call "theory of knowledge," or "epistemology," is therefore implicit to meaningful social theory. Lacking it, we have no rational basis for assertions concerning either individuality or community. There is neither meaningful discourse nor reliable theorizing. Habermas is surely correct when he tells us, "If we imagine the philosophical discussion of the modern period reconstructed as a judicial hearing, it would be deciding a single question: how is reliable knowledge possible."[1]

Epistemology is not an abstract intellectual category, isolated from the world we normally experience. Reflective cognition embodies principles of ontology, epistemology, methodology, ethics, and politics. Each separate perspective is collectively defined by the others. For example, journalists often consider a citizen's reflective decision to protest official policy to be news-worthy. Yet this act's reality comprises far more than the media-image grasps. It expresses a subjectively meaningful procedure for distinguishing right from wrong, a technique for analyzing everyday reality to discern essentials, opinions as to what is real and what isn't, preconceptions concerning humanity's nature and potential, and an apposite strategy. These concepts are as real as the act itself, which merely captures and expresses them at a specific time and place. Meaningful, rational behavior is never isolated in only one category. The Frankfurt School of Critical Theory is obsessed with reflection and theory at the expense of practical political activity, while the New Left sees revolutionary action as an end in itself. Both, however, express very distinct ontological, epistemological, methodological, and ethical beliefs—all vital to a correct understanding of critical theory and New

Leftism. Rejecting political action for reflection is itself a form of action, with obvious consequences. Rejecting theory in favor of spontaneous revolutionary activity is rooted in explicit (perhaps unacknowledged) theoretical principles drastically limiting theory's scope and significance. Meaningfully experienced and reflectively considered reality is, by definition, a unity of theory and praxis. Social reality is far more complex than thirty-second news spots reveal. It is churning, dynamic, and multidimensional, comprising qualities impervious to the naked eye or naive perspective.

Social theory, then, is a totality, including theories of being, knowledge, valid inquiry, and morality, and connected to the institutional world by active, reflective participation. Each dimension nourishes the others. Economic, social, and governmental institutions form an environment that reflects, expresses, and modifies theories, while these are similarly related to concrete institutions. Social theory is therefore initiated and studied from any perspective, theoretical or practical. When effectively consummated, the process propels us directly into the multidimensional totality. Consequently, a theory of knowledge is practical in several ways. It generates a method for valid social inquiry, evolves ethical criteria to discriminate right from wrong, and is realized in meaningful, rational action representing subjectively experienced goals. Epistemology, then, expresses and influences perceptions of being, methodology, and ethics, and permits planned social acts. In turn, it is redefined by these acts as practical consequences confirm or deny the original assertions. Epistemology is thus a central category for understanding social theory and action. It is particularly useful in examining the evolution of Marxist social theory, which is distinguished by its ongoing search for criteria of valid knowledge. Although competing schools of Marxist exegesis reflect different and potentially antagonistic totalities (dissimilar conceptions of ontology, methodology, ethics, and politics), they are originally motivated by epistemological questions, and these determine their exoteric structures.

This interest in epistemology is not surprising. Recalcitrant history has forced Marxism to compete ideologically for the hearts and minds of the discontented, a battle it was ill-suited to wage. Marx never formulated a systematic epistemology. As Marxism was compelled to communicate its own social theory actively, its blatant weaknesses surfaced, and the search began to find in Marx's writings clues for an adequate epistemology.

The first wave of Marxist interpreters includes Engels, Kautsky, Bukharin, and Plekhanov. Theirs is an optimistic scholarship, for they perceived the imminent collapse of Western capitalism and growth of proletariat hegemony. Their literary style, while not exactly inspiring, is relatively clear and forceful, directed both at enlightened intellectuals and the maturing revolutionary masses. They dealt with important epistemological questions but simultaneously anchored these in practical revolutionary strategies, hopefully courting the exploited who would fulfill history's promise.

But Russia's successful workers' revolution was not duplicated in those Western European countries where they were eagerly anticipated. As the likelihood of world revolution lessened, Marxists found themselves questioning their own social theory, seeking causes and remedies for its inability to translate historical necessity into a radical working-class movement. Beginning especially with Bernstein, Labriola, and Lukács, Marxist social theory sought to escape the orthodox vulgarity that Westerners find unattractive but also preserve the essentials of Marx's revolutionary message. This effort shapes neo-Marxist social theory in this century. Unable to provoke a mass revolutionary movement, Marxist social theory questions and requestions itself, looking to understand its failure and reverse its fortunes.

Unanticipated consequences have complicated matters. Neo-Marxism has become disconcertingly inbred. Marxist social theory is now a complex toy reserved exclusively for intellectuals who share an impenetrable jargon and style. Many ideologically sympathetic students hopelessly engage the work of Lukács, Adorno, Althusser, Della Volpe, Sartre, or Kosík—some blatant offenders—and reluctantly retire from the debate. Neo-Marxist journals are often incomprehensible to anyone but contributors, people learned in an arcane terminology that is apparently singularly suitable to revolutionary theory.

This situation has provoked an angry reaction primarily among those linking neo-Marxism's turgid style to its epistemological aspirations. Many now contend that Marxism involves no position on philosophical questions and cite Lenin's condemnation of epistemology as irrelevant to the class struggle.[2] Colletti has recently called methodology "the science of those who have nothing"[3] and accused Marxism of atrophying into a "purely cultural and academic phenomenon."[4] Noting neo-Marxism's incomprehensibility, Perry Anderson blames this "theoretical regression" on epistemology, which accompanied the defeatist mentality associated with a failed revolutionary movement. The goals of Western Marxism, Anderson sadly observes, are "to disengage the rules of social inquiry discovered by Marx, yet buried within the topical particularity of his work, and if necessary to complete them. The result . . . [is] that a remarkable amount of the output of Western Marxism . . . [becomes] a prolonged and intricate Discourse of Method,"[5] a discourse that vitiates Marx's intentions. "When the masses themselves speak, theoreticians—of the sort the West has produced for 50 years—will necessarily be silent."[6]

Obviously, significant historical phenomena have pushed neo-Marxism onto its present path. The triumph of Soviet Marxism, particularly Stalinism, has produced its in-house critics, as has the revolutionary movement's failure in the industrialized West. The restabilization of European capitalism—marked by an economic expansion of Western Europe, the growth of imperialism, and the retreat from classical laissez-faire approaches to economic and social policy—has prompted new, more relevant Marxist theory. The democratization of liberal political institutions, especially the advent of universal suffrage, has complicated the theory and strategy of radical politics in ways Marx did not anticipate. And, of course, factional and personal quarrels within the radical movement itself have promoted a critique of orthodox doctrine. Neo-Marxism has matured in the context of these concrete historical phenomena. Precisely because theory and practice interpenetrate, we must now pay serious attention to Marxism's philosophical motif, which indicates the movement's failure to visualize the origin, nature, and limits of valid knowledge coherently. A superficial, unconvincing epistemology destroys the credibility of Marxist methodology and ethics and minimizes the likelihood of effective revolutionary social action. Epistemology, to repeat, is not purely intellectual; it is expressed in, and defined by, concrete attitudes and actions. The feebleness of revolutionary working-class organizations indicates weakness in revolutionary theory. People simply will not rebel unless convinced it is the "correct" thing to do, based on available "knowledge." Neo-Marxism's concern with epistemology is thus symptomatic of a congenital disease incubated in Marx's own writings. Blindly joining unavoidable philosophical questions with the top-heavy, expendable language Marxists now use is tantamount to discarding the proverbial baby with the bath water.

A brief look at Marx's inconclusive commentary sets the central problematic of neo-Marxism.

MARX AND EPISTEMOLOGY

Aside from Marx's open distaste for extant philosophical idealism and empiricism, his legacy regarding the source, nature, and discovery of knowledge is almost flagrantly ambiguous. He examined philosophical questions primarily in the *Economic and Philosophical Manuscripts* (1844), *The German Ideology* (1846), the 1857 introduction to *Grundrisse,* and the 1859 preface to *A Contribution to the Critique of Political Economy.* Even in these works, however, philosophical positions are suggested but not systematically defined, and nowhere can we find a well-developed epistemology.[7] Marx's attitude toward philosophy in general, and epistemology in particular, is one of indifference, presuming that hotly debated topics, then amusing to bourgeois philosophers who were interested only in scholarship and discussion, were already settled. Residual controversies are purposively shifted onto historical, economical, and political planes, where they are measured with concrete terms and concepts.

The essence of capitalism is its urge for business success, which Marx saw as necessarily based on exploiting and dehumanizing workers. Bourgeois philosophy perpetuates this injustice by flaunting abstract, superfluous concepts, mystifying and confusing people who really need only alter their ways of living together. Philosophy's goal is not enlightenment, but the selfish desires of a powerful ruling class. But science demands a commitment to justified conclusions even if they "little . . . conform to the interested prejudices of the ruling classes."[8] By this criterion, extant philosophy was antiscientific. Since Marx considered himself a scientist, his desire to "settle accounts with our former philosophical conscience"[9] implies spurning philosophy altogether in the quest for revolution and socialist equality. "The philosophers have only interpreted the world, in various ways; the point is to change it."[10]

Consequently, Marx's science unfolds without a clear discussion of mind's relationship to matter, whether the material world is passively "reflected" in mind or is a product of human creativity. These key issues, with which Marx's followers have endlessly struggled, are considered unimportant and meaningless. Questions concerning reality and the quality of truth are "purely scholastic," a consequence of ideological confusion. "The whole problem of the transition from thought to reality, and thus from language to life, exists only as a philosophical illusion: it is justified only to the philosophic mind, puzzling over the origin and nature of its supposed detachment from real life."[11] On the other hand, people have needs to satisfy, and these alone shape relationships to nature and society. The world is an arena where practical needs are fulfilled, not a Pandora's box filled with spiritual profundities. Philosophical dilemmas mean nothing to most people, for the world is only the locus and objectification of their practical activities. "Cognition" means rendering a human sense to things, not grasping at transcendent truths. Knowledge, then, has no "epistemological" value. It is not evaluated independent of practical consequences. "Correct thinking" merely facilitates the satisfaction of needs, allowing us to liberate and fulfill ourselves in nature. "Incorrect thinking," on the contrary, confirms and perpetuates human servility. Thoughts either liberate or oppress by satisfying or denying basic human requirements. This constitutes their truth or falsity. In any case, thoughts occur in and are connected to the surroundings within which we undertake practical activities. Consequently, "truth" and "falsity" become appendages of social systems: Those oppressing and denying humanity generate false images and theories (for example, philosophy), while those that liberate and fulfill yield accurate, true ideas (for example, science).

Marx conflates two distinct problems. The practice of philosophy, including epistemology, is part of bourgeois social theory, a totality comprising all those institutions expressing and supporting it. Marx accurately perceived the close, mutually supportive link between bourgeois philosophy and liberal-democratic-capitalist institutions. Logically, given his unremitting critique of capitalism, he rejected this kind of theorizing. Because liberation is incompatible with capitalist exploitation, bourgeois theory must, indeed, yield to revolutionary action. However, Marx failed to analyze a second issue: how and why oppressed workers will rebel without theoretical justifications for their actions. He apparently assumed, disregarding his own descriptions of humanity's inherent freedom and creativity, that we would automatically, nonreflectively respond to certain material conditions in a revolutionary manner. The presumption is justified only if we conceive oppressed workers as homunculi, naively carrying out historical imperatives or unthinkingly realizing a human essence. Yet, this odious perspective, this definition of men and women as objects manipulated by powerful, uncontrollable forces, he also saw as the essence of capitalism—in response to which he advocated revolution as a release of liberating human energy. The apparent confusion results from Marx's failure to present carefully an alternative social theory that makes cognitive sense, prompts reflective citizens to rebel, and reinforces egalitarian institutions. Marx's eschatological vision of a classless community motivated his critique of bourgeois philosophy and institutions. But rejecting bourgeois theory should not necessarily mean rejecting theory itself. Because it did in Marx's case, his followers developed their own theories to supplement the critique of capitalism and call to revolution, in effect completing the totality which any social theory must encompass.

Marx, ironically, evaluated knowledge and consciousness from an absolute standpoint: the emancipated consciousness of mankind, affirming humanity's liberated potentials—what he called in the early writings "species-essence." This standpoint is presumably indistinguishable from practical reality, which unfolds in predictable patterns reaching a revolutionary dénouement. Marx was neither nihilist nor relativist. He believed that ideology is "false" consciousness while "true" ideas are scientific. His social theory is more than critique. It presumes indisputably positive meanings for "humanity," "freedom," and "justice." In denying the value of epistemology and the need to provide one, he has not, as a mere critic would have, escaped the need to provide epistemological grounds for his own denial.[12] His failure to do so makes judgments regarding both the irrelevance of epistemology and the revolutionary potential of oppressed workers problematic. The unanswered question "why?" keeps cropping up: Why is humanity potentially free and creative? Why does matter shape our freedom and creativity? Why is revolution inevitable and freedom necessary? Reliable answers require systematic analyses of being (ontology), truth (epistemology), science (methodology), and oppression (ethics). Marx felt it unnecessary to spend time on such issues. Marxist social theory has been preoccupied with little else.

When political exigencies in Germany forced Marxists to brew their own systematic social theory in order to compete effectively with bourgeois alternatives, the task was left entirely to Friedrich Engels in *Anti-Dühring* and the posthumously published *Dialectics of Nature*; hence the precedent for neo-Marxists to supply Marx's revolutionary critique with a coherent and explicit philosophy consistent with Marx's own writings. This has been, to repeat, complicated by Marx's philosophical ambiguity. Interpreters discover that despite an antiphilosophical stance, Marx implicitly proffers three philosophical perspectives, expressing three distinct kinds of social theory. Taken together, these are mutually exclusive and contradictory. However, Marx escapes unscathed because he is unwilling even to consider theory as necessary or significant to history's ebb and flow. When students find it historically necessary to expedite a philosophical critique of bourgeois society, they are placed in an awkward and difficult position. Marx's copious writings provide several contradictory insights and ideas, which somehow must be knitted into a systematic philosophy.

This dilemma is starkly framed by a critical reading of Marx's relevant work. Each inchoate social theory is justified by certain specially chosen selections. But a consistent defense of any one would also either ignore or "creatively interpret" sizable chunks of Marx's other writing.

Some of Marx's work, particularly the *Economic and Philosophical Manuscripts,* propound an experiential version of the source and quality of valid knowledge. Marx rejects traditional, static definitions of human nature coveted by bourgeois philosophers. These recognize one immutable quality essential to all humanity and deduce from it principles of social organization. For Marx, on the contrary, each human being, divorced from surroundings, is a bundle of physical, emotional, and intellectual needs demanding satiation. These do not constitute a "human nature" because all living animals, to some degree, share these needs and are similarly compelled to satisfy them. What distinguishes humans is a cognitive awareness of the world as an arena of social discourse, where we creatively interact with neighbors and with nature to fulfill life's primary demands. As sensate individuals, then, we are immediately joined to the insensate natural world and simultaneously perceive the social dimensions of existence. We satisfy needs in nature and society by creatively acting to produce required goods. Our labors, however, modify the world. Since we are primordially worldly creatures, "open" to natural and social environments, needs are ineluctably modified by the consequences of past labors. A new world creates new human demands, satisfied through additional actions. Each productive act fuels history's motor, driving us into a future forever entangled with the present and past. "History . . . on the one hand continues . . . traditional activity in completely changed circumstances and, on the other, modifies the old circumstances with a completely changed activity."[13]

Especially in the early years, Marx defined human life as a process based on praxis. Subjects are inseparably entwined with their environments, each nourishing the other in a perpetual process of transcendence continually reinforced by creative activity. The world in which we live and work is indirectly shaped by human consciousness, mediated through practical activities. Hence, when we talk of "reality," we implicitly mean "human" reality—a world stamped by human intention and meaning. Society's productive apparatus, its means of maintaining and improving the material conditions of life to meet subjective demands, are external, factual representations of conscious experiences, embodied in productive labor. Similarly, human need and reflective activity sculpt the ideologies we use to rationalize and justify economic institutions. In sum, all historically significant human phenomena are explicitly rational and ethical, based on experienced needs and the concomitant praxis. "It is not 'history' which uses men as a means of achieving—as if it were an individual person—its own ends. History is *nothing* but the activity of men in pursuit of their ends."[14] Truth in history is a product of human experience and free action.

Marx evaluated existing institutions by how, and whether, they facilitate our achieving the full dimensions of human potential, our freedom as creative actors. Marx felt that modern society fails miserably. The interpenetration of actor and world has ironically led to our internalizing capitalism's destructive, antihuman qualities. We objectify ourselves by severing connections with nature and society, alienating ourselves from creative activity. History is no longer the product of vital human praxis. Instead, we are passively defined by the very machines and institutions already created.[15] As alienated victims we see truth as something beyond us, belonging to a domineering, uncontrollable reality. Marx insisted, however, that this is an artificial, transitory condition. Human beings can acknowledge oppression and resurrect the hegemony of praxis merely through an act of liberating social transformation. In other words, by consciously experiencing real needs in an unresponsive capitalist society, we reassert history's experiential moment and consequently creatively redefine reality. Marx interprets a priorism and empiricism, both defining reality independent of subjectivity, as symbols of humanity's self-created alienation, symbols that won't survive the reawakening of human autonomy.

Marx's latent experientialism collapses when exposed to other texts written primarily, but not exclusively, after 1850, especially his *magnum opus, Capital.* Here, Marx articulated an a priori version of history and humanity's relationship to the world. Free, creative praxis is replaced by a determinism that defines individuals as mere expressions of an unfolding historical law. Intersubjectively valid knowledge is now located in an objective material reality impersonally shaping history and its human subjects. Truth, now independent of experience, is revealed indirectly through a dialectician's unraveling of history, and directly in the positive correlation between concrete economic development and social change. As an a priori absolute, it "precedes the collection of new empirical data, provides a criterion for their solution, and endows them with a complex meaning which is both intellectual and emotive."[16] While history, for Marx, is still made by human beings, we are now marionettes for preexisting forces.

A priorism is convincingly argued throughout Marx's works, but especially in *Capital,* which talks of economic formations as "process[es] of natural history," developmental laws as "tendencies working with iron necessity toward inevitable results," the "inexorability" of capitalism's demise, and his own ambition to "lay bare the economic law of motion of modern society."[17] It is summed up in a passage from one of *Capital's* reviewers, which Marx approvingly quoted in the "Afterword to the Second Edition," that concludes: "Marx treats the social movement as a process of natural history, governed by laws not only independent of human will, but rather, on the contrary, determining that will, consciousness, and intelligence...."[18]

One can persuasively argue that Marx was always an a priori thinker. His purpose in the *1844 Manuscripts,* from this view, entails reconciling man's existence with his essence as a free actor continually reshaping history. There exists an ideal reality, which defines humanity and is revealed when we consciously recognize labor as praxis. This emancipatory process, however, occurs only under specified economic and social conditions. Marx lacks a phenomenology of subjective freedom. His conceptions of praxis and human potentiality are appended onto his critique of capitalism, thereby establishing an essentiality to human existence derived from an abstract, idealistic universal subjectivity. Hence, Marx's early humanism is generated from a priori qualities that transcend particular subjects. In creative labor we fulfill these universal potentialities and permit truth to reveal itself in practical activity. Scientific knowledge accompanies reflective critique of bourgeois alienation. Theory and praxis finally coalesce in revolutionary activity aimed at concretely realizing the ideal.

This idealistic reading of Marx imposes an epistemological uniformity on his lifework. Both "early" and "late" Marx accepted a priorism. What alters with time is the criterion of scientific validation: What begins as an abstract ideal cognitively experienced only in revolutionary praxis turns eventually into a material law of history, manifest in society's productive apparatus and unequivocally determining human behavior.

Experientialism and a priorism coexist uncomfortably in Marx's writings. Nevertheless, empirical scientists can also find inspiration. No one, of course, will reasonably assert that Marx is an orthodox empiricist. All Marxists, epistemologies notwithstanding, perceive man as a social creature, reject the rigid separation of fact and value, and see history dynamically unfurling into universal justice. These positions are anathema to orthodox empiricists, who reject every assertion or assumption not observed, described, and measured by universally approved standards.[19] Yet empirical Marxists find evidence—especially in parts of *Capital, Grundrisse, Theories of Surplus Value,* and part one of the *Critique of Hegel's Philosophy of Right*—that Marx's revolutionary doctrine is the fruit of accumulated empirical data. Social and historical science is measured solely by its success in explaining and predicting actual events. Its primary goal, in other words, is explaining concrete matter without introducing extraneous experiential or a priori notions. Science must account for itself with confirmable evidence from the empirical world. If the terms "revolution," "class conflict," "surplus value," and so on, have any scientific meaning at all, they must be drawn from actual conditions, not abstract or subjectivistic impressions imposed on reality. Marx's major scientific generalizations are, it is argued, valid in this empirical sense.

Marx, at times, coherently defends empirical verification. He strongly rejects all forms of transhistorical determinism and any attempt to use "as one's master key a general historico-philosophical theory, the supreme virtue of which consists in being super-historical."[20] Social science examines what "is," how it functions, and its developmental trends. *Capital* is Marx's supreme effort at producing science. It explains capitalism in its current (nineteenth-century) empirical form, building its conclusions on the "innumerable different empirical circumstances, natural environments, racial relations, external historical influences, etc.," that yield the "infinite variations and gradations in appearance, which can be ascertained only by analysis of the empirically given circumstances."[21] The various elements comprising base and superstructure will vary according to time, place, circumstance, and human intention. Conclusions concerning relationships between any of these contingent phenomena are derived only from empirical evidence.

This empirical perspective was cultivated in *The German Ideology,* where Marx and Engels demeaned "abstractions" and committed themselves to "real history," which can be verified in "a purely empirical way." Society consists of human beings "not in any fantastic isolation and rigidity, but in their actual, empirically perceptible process of development under definite conditions. . . . " Social scientists must "study . . . the actual life-process and the activity of the individuals of each epoch . . . ," that is, must empirically observe and describe social reality.[22]

Marxism, then, proffers an empirical epistemology and method. By ignoring it, say defenders, we misinterpret Marx's methodological intentions and mistakenly base social science on the twin chimeras of experientialism and a priorism.

In sum, Marx's decision to ignore relevant philosophical questions has the undesirable consequence of integrating three irreconcilable solutions to the problem of locating reliable knowledge and three potentially distinct approaches to political activity. These internal contradictions later turn into competing "schools" of Marxism.

Marxism is thus burdened by an ambiguous legacy, which encourages reasonable people to offer diverse and contradictory interpretations of Marxist theory. When, for example, Marx wrote in the *Eighteenth Brumaire of Louis Bonaparte* that "Men make their own history, but they do not make it just as they please; they do not make it under circumstances chosen by themselves, but under circumstances directly encountered, given, and transmitted from the past,"[23] what exactly did he mean? If we "make our own history," presumably we are free actors shaping the world according to subjectively experienced needs and wishes. But if we "do not make it just as [we]...please," then some uncontrollable force determines the quality of our actions and limits free expression. Nevertheless, if we exist only in "circumstances directly encountered, given, and transmitted from the past," we must first rigorously describe these empirical phenomena to understand human existence and action as historically conditioned. One's understanding of this selection is governed by the phrase accented. Similarly, consider Marx's assertion in the third volume of *Capital* that although laws of history and society function with "iron necessity," they are simultaneously "tendencies" negated or altered by "counteracting circumstances."[24] Can humanity be both the creative subject of history, the "counteracting circumstance," and also the determined product of its laws? Either position is successfully argued by referring to other carefully selected writings. The first rationalizes experiential Marxism, the second a priori Marxism.

In *The Holy Family,* Marx writes that revolution will occur "only inasmuch as it produces the proletariat as proletariat, that misery conscious of its spiritual and physical misery, that dehumanization conscious of its dehumanization and therefore self-abolishing."[25] The strong emphasis on proletariat self-consciousness reflects experientialism's subjectivism. But Marx quickly adds, "The question is not what this or that proletariat, or even the whole of the proletariat at the moment considers as its aim. The question is what the proletariat is, and what, consequent on the being, it will be compelled to do. Its aim and historical action is irrevocably and obviously demonstrated in its own life situation as well as in the whole organization of bourgeois society today."[26] Proletariat consciousness is now "compelled" to realize its own "being," which is "demonstrated in its own life situation...[and] the whole organization of bourgeois society." This apparently steers our original interpretation in an a priori (materialist or idealist) or empirical (stressing the description of bourgeois society) direction, depending on the reader's own predilections. Quotations like these are utilized by theorists as diverse as Sartre, Kolakowski, and Colletti to defend their respective irreconcilable Marxisms.

Nor is the ambiguity limited to Marx's early writings. In volume one of *Capital* Marx emphatically declared, "The life-process of society, which is based on the process of material production, does not strip off its mystical veil until it is treated as production by freely associated men, and is consciously regulated by them in accordance with a settled plan. This, however, demands for society a certain material groundwork or set of conditions of existence which in their turn are the spontaneous product of a long and painful process of development."[27] What would happen if "freely associated men" consciously repudiate the "material groundwork" of existence, or if this alternative is impossible, how are men free? Marx substitutes for the theoretical discussion that could clarify truth's relationship to consciousness the unexamined assumption that they will always correspond under certain material conditions. As to which factor prevails— subjective consciousness, objective truth, or actual conditions—one makes a choice and finds a rudimentary defense somewhere in Marx's work. This theoretical void permits Marx to assert, in a letter to Kugelmann (17 April 1871), "World history . . . would be a very mystical nature if 'accidents' played no part in it. These accidents fall naturally into the general course of development and are compensated by other accidents. But acceleration and delay are very dependent upon such 'accidents,' including the 'accident' of the character of those who at first stand at the head of the movement."[28] Presumably, unique personalities ("accidents of . . . character") do exist and affect history but only by reinforcing its "general course of development," which is impersonal. This may have been a model for Engels's monument to obscurity: "We make our history ourselves, but, in the first place, under very definite assumptions and conditions. Among these, the economic ones are ultimately decisive."[29] For Marx and Engels to declare humans make their own history is tautalogical. Who else can make it? The real issue is whether they behave autonomously, as conscious actors, or are products of impersonal forces.[30] On this, we find in Marx several provocative hints but no systematically defended answers.

The problem is encapsulized in *The German Ideology,* in some ways the most complex and ambitious of Marx's writings. He was trying here to explain scientifically humanity's descent into its present deplorable state of passivity. In a sense, *The German Ideology* bridges his early emphasis on alienation and "species-essence" and his mature economic writings, for in it Marx seeks objective evidence to explain our current disregard of freedom and creativity. This goal is perhaps overly ambitious for one who explicitly rejects philosophical first principles. "Alienation," for example, presupposes active human qualities that fit awkwardly into impersonal, scientific generalizations. If consciousness—alienated or not—is really molded by objective forces, then creative freedom is inconceivable in any case, thereby invalidating the usefulness of the term. This tension rips, unresolved, through *The German Ideology,* but is crystallized in one particular passage that asserts three mutually exclusive ideas: all people are "real" and "active" in the production of their own "conceptions, ideas, etc.," (experientialism), but are also "reflexes" or "echoes"—with "no semblance of independence"— of an overbearing life-process manifest in material production (a priorism), and this life-process is bound to concrete reality and must be "empirically verified" (empiricism).[31] Again, one can interpret the passage in three contradictory ways.[32]

Marxists are thus forced to impose their own preconceptions and preferences, stressing either experientialism, a priorism, or empiricism. Because of Marx's philosophical heterogeneity, they twist his writings into their own frameworks by ignoring or impugning elements that are openly disputacious but won't go away.[33]

NEO-MARXISM'S PROBLEMATIC

The history of Marxist thought, from Engels to the present, is preoccupied with the task of outlining and completing a systematic philosophy that simultaneously promotes emancipatory action. Because of Marx's own inconclusiveness, an element of redefinition is involved in each major interpretation. Marxist social theory, in this sense, has had to create itself in history without abandoning either its radical ideology or its connections with the fountain-source, Marx himself.

A Marxian theorist defends Marxism by interpreting what it means and implies, implicitly assuming it is useful and irreplaceable as a means of social analysis and also self-sufficient for the liberation of humanity. The term "neo-Marxism" therefore symbolizes contemporary Marxist theory, which hermeneutically rectifies Marx's own inconsistencies without muting the revolutionary call for socialist justice.

Each major approach to Marxist theory can justify a range of different political strategies. Occasionally these will overlap: when Sartre, Della Volpe, and Althusser—dissimilar Marxists—defend centralized leadership. At other times, members of the same school may differ: Kautsky, Lenin, and Heinrich Cunow—orthodox Marxists all—offer different views on the political role and organization of the Party. But one Marxist theory can also evolve strategies suitable primarily to itself: "Humanists" defending Western-style democracy; phenomenologists, subjectivity and human initiative; and critical theorists, inactive contemplation. In brief, each brand of Marxism is a totality that embodies a potentially unique approach to politics. Though it is possible for two irreconcilably antagonistic neo-Marxist theories to agree momentarily on one political tactic, such an alliance usually withers in the long run as divergent philosophies pull inexorably in different political directions. Observe, for example, the fickle relationships of Lukács, Sartre, Merleau-Ponty, Colletti, Reich, Korsch, and the "praxis" philosophers to orthodox Party organizations. Studying Marxism by focusing solely on tactics, common among Marxists and non-Marxists, isolates the observer in one naively accepted theoretical perspective and justifies simplistic conclusions (for example, "Marxism and democracy are incompatible" or "Marxism and totalitarianism are incompatible").

Each neo-Marxist "school" selects one of the epistemological threads running through Marx's work to knit a social method as well as a practical guide to action and revolution. Neo-Marxism is therefore a diverse, multifaceted movement, hiding chasms as wide as those separating classical schools of non-Marxist philosophy. Marxists are probably more aware of this than others, and their dogmatic, vicious denunciations of "revisionism," "vulgarity," "hyperempiricism," "idealism," or "scientism"—depending on who does the accusing—indicate the intense incompatibility of competing Marxist social theories. Non-Marxists, on the other hand, are obsessed primarily with Marxism's unquestioned commitment to destroying an unjust, alienating, capitalist system and building in its place socialist equality. Their failure to discriminate subtle theoretical differences has inhibited what can be, potentially, a fruitful convergence of ideas. There are today Marxist social theories philosophically closer to traditional Western values than to Soviet-style Marxism. A neo-Marxist moral and political commitment to human liberation would probably not frighten nonpropertied Westerners aware of the common philosophical bonds uniting them and their "enemy." Radical ideas and policies could perhaps become viable alternatives in a society that now serves the pecuniary interests of a small elite. But first we must abolish the common prejudice that Marxism is a monolithic, homogeneous entity bent on destroying each individual blocking its path to power.

By rejecting formal philosophical discussion, Marx has, ironically, turned neo-Marxism into a vital, self-defining movement, searching for the foundations of valid social inquiry and meaningful revolutionary action. Neo-Marxism encompasses a priori, empirical, and experiential viewpoints, as well as those either rejecting knowledge altogether or inextricably attaching it to history. A priori Marxism includes orthodox materialism and idealism. Experiential Marxism examines the interpenetration of autonomous subjectivity and processes of social and historical development. Empirical Marxism seeks verifiable revolutionary hypotheses. The Frankfurt School of Critical Theory believes that truth probably does exist, but we can neither repossess it from its sociohistorical milieu nor act authentically. Finally, New Leftism denies entirely the existence of objective imperatives, focusing instead on whatever works politically. All neo-Marxists can and do find their roots in Marx's own writings. The following chapters unearth these roots, the theoretical plants they nourish, and the political flowers that bloom in the public eye.

NOTES

1. Jürgen Habermas, *Knowledge and Human Interests* (Boston: Beacon Press, 1971) p. 3.

2. V. I. Lenin, "Statement of the Editors of Proletary," in *Collected Works,* 45 vols. (London: Lawrence & Wishart, 1960–1970), 13: 447. See also Christine Buci-Glucksmann, *Gramsci and the State* (London: Lawrence & Wishart, 1980), p. 10.

3. Lucio Colletti, *Marxism and Hegel* (London: New Left Books, 1973), p. 283.

4. Lucio Colletti, "A Political and Philosophical Interview," *New Left Review* 86 (July–August 1974): 28.

5. Perry Anderson, *Considerations on Western Marxism* (New York: Humanities Press, 1976), pp. 52ff. The quote is on p. 53.

6. Ibid., p. 103.

7. See David-Hillel Ruben, *Marxism and Materialism* (Atlantic Highlands, New Jersey: Humanities Press, 1977), p. 64.

8. Karl Marx, Preface to *A Contribution to the Critique of Political Economy* (1859), in *Early Writings* (New York: Vintage Books, 1975), p. 427. Hereafter cited as *KMEW.*

9. Ibid.

10. Karl Marx, *Theses on Feuerbach* (#11), *KMEW,* p. 423.

11. Ibid.

12. See Martin Selige, *The Marxist Conception of Ideology* (London: Cambridge University Press, 1977).

13. Karl Marx and Friedrich Engels, *The German Ideology* (Moscow: Progress Publishers, 1976), p. 58.

14. Karl Marx, *Selected Writings in Sociology and Social Philosophy,* ed. T. B. Bottomore and M. Rubel (London: Watts, 1956), p. 63.

15. See Karl Marx, *Economic and Philosophical Manuscripts* (1844), in *KMEW,* pp. 279–400.

16. Mihailo Marković, *From Affluence to Praxis* (Ann Arbor, Mich.: University of Michigan Press, 1974), p. 59.

17. Karl Marx, *Capital,* 3 vols. (New York: International Publishers, 1975), 1: 8, 10, 763.

18. Ibid., p. 18.

19. See Charles Taylor, "Marxism and Empiricism," in *British Analytical Philosophy,* ed. Bernard Williams and Alan Montefiore (London: Routledge & Kegan Paul, 1966), pp. 227–46.

20. Karl Marx and Friedrich Engels, *Selected Correspondence* (Moscow: Progress Publishers, n.d.), p. 379. See also Engels to J. Bloch, 21–22 September 1890, in Marx and Engels, *Selected Works* (Moscow: Foreign Language Publishing House, 1951–1958), p. 692.

21. Marx, *Capital,* 3: 792.

22. Marx and Engels, *The German Ideology,* pp. 37–43.

23. *Karl Marx: Selected Writings,* ed. D. McLellan (London: Oxford University Press, 1977), p. 300. Hereafter cited as *KMSW.*

24. Marx, *Capital,* 3: 234–5. The phrase "iron necessity," describing the force of socioeconomic laws, is in ibid., 1: 8.

25. *KMSW,* p. 134.

26. Ibid., p. 135.

27. Marx, *Capital,* 1: 80.

28. Leszek Kolakowski, *Main Currents of Marxism,* 3 vols. (London: Oxford University Press, 1978), 1: 339.

29. Engels to Bloch, p. 692.

30. See Richard Bernstein, *Praxis and Action* (Philadelphia, Pa.: University of Pennsylvania Press, 1971), pp. 62–63.

31. Marx and Engels, *The German Ideology,* p. 42.

32. See S. Stojanović, *Between Ideals and Reality* (New York: Oxford University Press, 1973), pp. 147f., and Z. A. Jordan, *The Evolution of Dialectical Materialism*

(London: Macmillan, 1967).

33. The enterprise of making Marx a consistent philosopher sometimes legitimizes casuistry. See, for example, Ruben, *Marxism and Materialism,* esp. p. 71. Roger Garaudy, on the other hand, openly defends all three positions. See Garaudy, et al., *Initiative in History* (Cambridge: The Church Society for College Work, 1967), p. 18; *From Anathema to Dialogue* (New York: Vintage, 1966), pp. 72–73; *Crisis in Communism* (New York: Grove Press, 1970), *Marxism in the Twentieth Century* (New York: Scribners, 1970), pp. 56–57 and 77; and *Karl Marx: The Evolution of His Thought* (New York: International Pubs., 1967), pp. 196–97.

2.

Materialism

The most influential contemporary approach to Marxism—represented by the Soviet Union and all the so-called "Marxist" states as well as the noncommunist world's "orthodox" Marxist parties—subordinates humanity to uncontrollable historical tendencies that potentially are imposed on the "uneducated." Is Marxism authentically realized in totalitarianism? Or is contemporary orthodox Marxism inauthentic? These questions have generated a lively discussion among neo-Marxists. They cannot be convincingly answered until the devil is given his due.

PHILOSOPHICAL MATERIALISM

To the question "What is social knowledge?" the first systematic answer that Western philosophy offers interprets valid knowledge as pure and eternal. Scientists escape subjectivity and uncover a distinct reality where truth exists in an objective, nonchanging form. What we call a priori knowledge offers rigorous standards for scientific inquiry. Valid knowledge originates in a ubiquitous, nonempirical reality potentially open to all willing observers. Empirical verification reveals only partial, sensate qualities: measurable reflections of absolute truth. Similarly, conscious awareness does not in itself constitute proof of truth's existence, for it exists before cognition and remains despite our ignorance.

For a priori materialists knowledge exists objectively at a level removed from commonsense thinking but is not an ideal abstraction that must be mentally experienced by trained subjects. Materialism, as distinct from idealism, defines reality as a form of "matter," that is, properties that scientific and everyday experience ascribe to physical bodies. Science heuristically interrelates observed facts to reveal their material substratum, which shapes the empirical world we live in and structures our lives. Evidence that ignores these material qualities and relations is, by definition, false.

Though materialism originated in ancient Greece and matured in early Stoicism, its social influence peaked during the Renaissance. Motivated by the needs of industry and government, scholars like da Vinci and Galileo formulated an experimental method emphasizing measurement of observable physical relationships without recourse to primary forms, essences, or divinities. This new thought system was philosophically expressed by Descartes, from whom the modern usage of the term "materialism" is derived.

Although a medievalist in attributing the universal cause and substance of all physical movement to God, Descartes in his philosophical writings described reality as thinking substance (mind) and extended substance (matter), a dichotomy that shaped modern Western philosophy. Henceforth, an idealist is one who denies ontological reality to matter; a materialist to mind. Yet despite Descartes's metaphysical dualism, as a physicist he was a rigid materialist, perceiving organic and inorganic nature as qualitatively identical and relating plant and animal behavior to the functioning of machines. Philosophy from this perspective depends on physics and chemistry. The significance of Descartes's other pillar of reality—mind—is soon obliterated by this material logic. Mechanical explanations are applicable to both mental and social phenomena. Mechanistic materialism, born in Descartes's physics, perceives human beings as nothing more than complex physical mechanisms.

In England, Francis Bacon and especially Thomas Hobbes systematized the materialist study of human and social behavior. Hobbes described the motion of irreducible particles as the prime source of substance and change. Geometry, mechanics, physics, ethics, and politics are scientific to the extent they trace the effects of motion in nature, mind, and society. John Locke asserted that ideas and knowledge are derived from experience and reflection, which Condillac and Helvétius later reduced to sensations. French Enlightenment philosophy, especially Diderot and Holbach, explored how the movement of matter generates consciousness. Diderot in particular argued that the quality or degree of human consciousness is determined by the complexity of material surroundings, in the same manner as sound or light copies the quality and quantity of matter from which it is composed.

Early nineteenth-century materialism strove toward the perfection of man through his reasoned manipulation of nature. This is not surprising, since materialism presupposes that decent, knowledgeable people can be mechanically propagated by apposite conditions. Speaking practically, this means reorienting society toward the people's welfare, initiating concrete reforms to create desirable surroundings. Justice grows from a science of human welfare. First utopian and then scientific (Marxian) socialism appeared as nineteenth-century fruits of philosophical materialism. By the twentieth century, materialism was associated primarily with Marxism, while the non-Marxist, mechanistic brand was gradually absorbed by the methodology of empirical science.

MARX'S MATERIALISM

Ludwig Feuerbach more than anyone else inspired Marx's own materialist inclinations. By the early 1840s, Germany was a hotbed of philosophical and political debate, dominated by Hegelian idealism. From the young Hegelian radicals on the Left of the ideological spectrum, to the more orthodox Conservatives on the Right, Hegel's belief in an abstract world spirit materialized inexorably through a dialectical logic governing the course and content of history is almost universally acknowledged. Still under Hegel's influence, Feuerbach's early work nevertheless tried to loosen the stifling embrace in which abstract ideas—especially religion—held the German populace. By 1848 with the completion of *Lectures on the Essence of Religion,* Feuerbach finally traded Hegelian idealism for a radical anthropocentrism, even though his purpose remained unchanged: to illustrate the reactionary, unhealthy social role of religion. In the context of Germany's unquestioned Hegelianism, Feuerbach became a beacon of materialist rationalism. All human abstractions, he argued, merely reflect our inability to comprehend and control nature. Religion and all forms of idealism are symbols of human ignorance and weakness. As knowledge increases, actions become increasingly rational and abstract symbols superfluous. Rationality liberates humanity from want and social discrimination. With the extirpation of religion and idealistic mystification humanity will experience, at last, the end of poverty, exploitation, and inequality. There is no necessary economic component to social justice. Feuerbach assumed, perhaps naively, that rationality alone ensures peace, equality, and complete freedom.

Feuerbach's influence on Marx was less what he said, than when and where he said it. The materialist critique of German idealism, unexceptional when compared to British and French Enlightenment philosophy, was radical and unexpected in Germany. Marx was, as we shall see, also somewhat infected by Hegelianism, and Feuerbach provided a materialist cure. Though Marx eventually rejected Feuerbach's simplistic assumptions regarding "enlightened" human nature, his writings from 1842 to 1845 expanded Feuerbach's concept of religious alienation and critically examined Hegel's blatant idealism.

These early writings are praised and condemned. Nonmaterialist Marxists claim that their liberating message has been obliterated by the vulgarities of succeeding epigones. Orthodox materialists perceived them as immature and vacillating but significant nevertheless as an inchoate materialist alternative to Hegelianism. Marx's incipient materialism appeared in his earliest published writings, articles in the journal *Rheinische Zeitung* (1842–1843), where for the first time Marx began analyzing matter's influence on social behavior. In the article "Defense of the Moselle Correspondent" Marx noticed the "objective character" of politics, how action is "necessitated by circumstances," and "can be determined with almost the same certainty as a chemist determines under which external conditions given substances will form a compound. . . . "[1] Here Marx began to analyze politics and ideology in terms of concrete economic factors lying hidden in society's material substructure.[2]

In the introduction to *A Critique of Hegel's Philosophy of Right* (1843), Marx criticized utopian socialism (Proudhon, St. Simon, Fourier, and others), particularly its belief in an irresistible ideal that, cognitively experienced, alters consciousness and generates liberating socialist action. Marx also sought reawakened subjects but saw this as fulfilling an actual historical process, making an unconscious historical tendency a conscious one.[3] Rational human will expresses historical necessity, the subject matter of scientific socialism. The proletariat represents universal needs, hence is the wellspring of rebellion. Its emancipation culminates history's impersonal laws and simultaneously emancipates all other classes. The utopian's "irresistible vision" is defined by matter, independent of consciousness. There are no mystical subjective qualities, only material processes bending minds toward history. Social science must expose these concrete forces shaping worldly perceptions. Hence, "In demanding that . . . [workers] give up illusions about their condition, we demand that they give up a condition that requires illusion. . . . The criticism of heaven is thus transformed into criticism of earth, the criticism of religion into criticism of law, and the criticism of theology into the criticism of politics."[4]

Marx continued to emphasize impersonal matter in the *1844 Manuscripts,* although they are mistakenly cited as a source of nonmaterialist Marxism. Marx envisioned communist society as part of history's natural course, not an artificial ideal imposed on humanity. He again excoriated the primitive ideal egalitarianism of the early "crude" communist utopians.[5] They would abolish everything people cannot collectively own, leveling humanity to a base common denominator, eventually abolishing human individualism, talent, creativity, and subjectivity—indeed, civilization itself. In addition to plumbing the depths of capitalist alienation, the *1844 Manuscripts* construed exploitation and alienation as necessary and positive historical occurrences, unavoidable benchmarks in history's evolution to pure communism.[6] His compelling account of human reification obscures the more central goal of describing society at a certain—capitalist—stage of material development. Marx was less concerned with oppressed, debilitated individuals than with capitalism's oppressive, debilitating conditions, which would push us first to rebellion and then communism, "the solution to the riddle of history [that] . . . is aware of that fact"—that is, the culmination of a natural, historical process.[7]

For materialists, the issue is whether the *Manuscripts* are read as lurid journalism or as social science. Marx supported the latter and repeatedly referred to the objective, impersonal matter within which human actors and other natural phenomena function. He stated bluntly, "a being which does not have its nature outside itself is not a natural being and does not share in the being of nature," thereby fixing valid knowledge in an objective realm.[8] Though man is "active" and "sensuous," he is also "a suffering, conditioned and limited creature, like animals and plants. That is to say, the objects of his impulses exist outside him, as objects independent of him; yet these objects are objects of his need...."[9] As "suffering, conditioned, and limited" actors, our ways of life indirectly express impersonal matter. Despite its subjective dimensions, alienation is an impersonal condition equally affecting all exposed subjects. Its meaning exists in material conditions, not in derivative human attitudes. "History itself is a real part of natural history and of nature's becoming man. Natural science will in time subsume the science of man just as the science of man will subsume natural science: there will be one science,"[10] a materialist science.

The Holy Family (1844–1845), rambling and archaic, also signifies Marx's developing materialism. He began to hone his views regarding history's material process by outlining its a priori laws and pictures communism's historical inevitability as being due to capitalism's own internal contradictions. The class of property owners in capitalism needs the labor of propertyless workers, for capitalism could not survive as a productive economic system if everyone were an owner. But it is also the nature of workers in capitalism to be alienated and oppressed by a system that exploits their skills and tears them from the collective products of their labors. Hence, workers eventually self-consciously understand their objective condition and the revolutionary role they are fated to play. "The question is not what this or that proletarian, or even the whole of the proletariat at the moment considers as its aim. The question is what the proletariat is, and what, consequent on that being, it will be compelled to do."[11] History generates a classless society, where the former oppressed class seizes its own products to satiate collective needs. History's material process negates a negation: Each mode of production spawns an exploited class that it cannot do without, assuring its own destruction as the exploited inevitably become exploiters. Moreover, an economic class develops ideas and institutions necessary to rationalize its existence socially and assure its control. Thus, as matter historically unfolds in contradiction and revolution, there are corresponding movements in philosophy and social organization. The history of ideas depends on the history of production.[12]

Marx then illustrates this by historically tracing philosophical materialism. Predictably, he argues that materialism contains its own dynamic leading inexorably—like society itself—to communism. Since materialism presumes that men and women are products of matter, then human potential is realized only when matter (for example, society) is made human. "If man is formed by circumstances, then his circumstances must be made human."[13] And this is possible only in communism, which satisfies real needs rather than the selfish urge for profit. Hence, materialism is an authentic expression of working-class interests.

The Holy Family also broaches an extremely important, and unresolved, methodological issue. Marx interprets post-Cartesian materialism as "one-sided." "Sensuousness lost its bloom and became the abstract sensuousness of the geometrician. Physical motion was sacrificed to the mechanical or mathematical, geometry was proclaimed the principal science. Materialism became hostile to humanity. In order to overcome science the anti-human incorporeal spirit in its own field, materialism itself was obliged to mortify its flesh and become an ascetic."[14] Marx now decried the antihumanism of mechanistic materialism, which is suitable only to the natural sciences, where phenomena are not self-conscious. When materialism is used to explain human history, it can remain mechanistic only by distorting its subject matter. While capitalism treats subjects as impersonal means, mechanistic materialism similarly violates humanity's integrity and freedom— their "sensuous human activity, practice"—with uncontrollable, omnipotent mechanical laws. "The materialist doctrine concerning the changing of circumstances and upbringing forgets that circumstances are changed by man and the educator must himself be educated."[15]

The dilemma is particularly vexing because Marx is certainly in no mood to abandon materialism. He adamantly criticizes idealism, by which he means an interpretation of reality situating objectivity anywhere but in concrete matter. "The essence of man is no abstraction inhering in each single individual. In its actuality it is the ensemble of social relationships."[16] But materialism must, by definition, accept the epistemological priority of objective matter. Marx's project, then, is preserving human autonomy without forsaking materialism, performed, to repeat, without systematically analyzing relevant philosophical issues. The proffered solution, completed in later writings, substitutes dialectical for mechanical materialism.[17] Marx's dialectic interprets subjectivity as one dynamic component of a larger framework of interacting material phenomena. Presumably, this preserves free, creative subjectivity. But the dialectic also remains concrete, composed of and expressed in actual matter. Consequently, the problem is not really solved, simply moved to a new analytical level. Whereas subjects were previously mechanically conditioned by impersonal material laws, now their uniqueness is guaranteed by a dialectic, which itself embodies impersonal material laws. The argument, though palpably ambiguous, tenaciously survives among Marx's orthodox disciples sensitive to the potential dangers of vulgar, mechanistic materialism.

It is difficult to justify Marx's claim in the tenth thesis on Feuerbach of "humanizing" materialism. Consciousness is still determined by matter, as Marx himself will repeatedly stress, and this is what he finds objectionable in mechanical materialism. Materialism leaves no room for autonomous subjectivity, unless we redefine concepts like "autonomy," "freedom," and "subjectivity." Ruben, for example, strains to distinguish "reductive [mechanical] materialism" and Marx's philosophical materialism. The latter presupposes "the irreducibility of human activity" undertaken by "real active individuals," while simultaneously defending the epistemological priority of matter.[18] This argument, however, is less than convincing when Ruben admits it is logically and philosophically unjustifiable.[19] Its defense is political: As the theory of revolutionary Marxism, nonreductive materialism, though philosophically meaningless, supports authentic worker interests. Perhaps Marx is correct in ignoring the issue entirely.

While Marx never satisfactorily solved this problem, *The German Ideology* (1846) indicates he was unwilling to abandon materialism, despite incongruities. This book refutes the argument that mental aberrations cause social injustice and human alienation. In criticizing Feuerbach and the young Hegelians, Marx completed his outline of what has come to be known as historical materialism, Marx's materialist science of history.

Before organized society, men and women lived in and reacted to their immediate sensuous environment, a "completely alien, all-powerful and unassailable" nature to which they related in a "purely animal" manner.[20] In this primitive state we perceive a need to associate with others (our "herd consciousness") and satisfy basic physical, emotional, and intellectual needs. *The German Ideology* quickly entangles nature, society, and humanity in a totality that is rooted in objective matter.

Like other phenomena, humans are extensions of nature. But survival requires that they join together to produce what each single individual cannot. Society is therefore an integral aspect of nature, like clouds or trees. And just as it is silly to presume that trees determine their own shapes and colors, so too for societies, which are similarly conditioned by the same impersonal natural forces.

Though natural, human beings are also in one sense unique, for they alone have the ability to make tools. When battling to survive in inhospitable surroundings we have a distinct advantage over subhumans, who can only find and use nature's own tools. Uniting first into organized groups, then tribes, and finally societies, humans, by creating needed tools, eventually produce more than they consume, generating the possibility of conflict over how to share the surplus. Human history, for Marx, is the totality of those actions by which we produce in the material world to satisfy changing needs. "What . . . [individuals] are . . . coincides with their production, both with what they produce and how they produce it. The nature of individuals thus depends on the material conditions of their production."[21] Oppression originates as one group appropriates the excess goods produced by others. The forms of this appropriation, what Marx calls the "relations of production," characterize society's material base. Obviously, relations of production reflect the technical level of productive forces: as technology—including equipment, productive forces, technical skills, and division of labor—develops, entirely new forms of appropriation become possible. Hence forms of social oppression reflect the level of technological innovation.[22]

Marx and Engels saw relations of production as comprising three interconnected phenomena. First are property relations, essentially the legally protected powers to control raw materials, instruments of production, and products of labor. Second is the social division of labor, separating citizens into one materially productive segment and another involved in functions such as government service, management, entertainment, and so on. Intellectual labor appears in a specific form of productive relations, where appropriation is refined to such an extent that leisure time expands, and materially nonengaged people begin abstractly speculating. The rise of "culture," including the arts, sciences, and philosophy, characterizes a particular form of social inequality. Those defending the autonomy of ideas have lost sight of requisite material factors, even now permitting intellectuals the leisure to ponder first principles. Finally, productive relations comprise the method of socially exchanging and distributing products, the capitalist version of which Marx would later describe empirically. In sum, a base, or substructure, comprises the technical level of productive forces and the relationships involved in production. The latter includes property relations, the social division of labor, and methods of social distribution and exchange.

The position and role occupied in the base determines class, which in turn conditions the way one perceives and understands reality. Class membership, in other words, determines ideas and beliefs.[23] The dominant economic class owns and controls raw materials, instruments, and products of labor, appropriating excess goods and distributing them to maximize their own interests. Because of accumulated excess leisure time and resources, they are theoretically able to rationalize their own material interests. A dominant culture is interpreted broadly as the ideas and institutions by which a society defines itself—in Marx's terminology, the "superstructure." The level of productive forces and relations of production therefore shape society's self-image, its economic, social, political, aesthetic, philosophical, and other institutions and ideas. Consequently, the dominant economic class is society's ruling intellectual force. "The ruling ideas are nothing more than the ideal expression of the dominant material relations, the dominant material relations grasped as ideas."[24]

Marx and Engels apparently meant by "ideology" what Engels later described in *Ludwig Feuerbach* (1888) and the letter to Mehring (14 July 1893): Ideology is false consciousness, people mistakenly asserting the autonomy of logic and intellect, oblivious to real material determinants. Ideology implies ignorance of real causes, hence is nonmaterialist and false. Under Stalin's impetus one hundred years later Marxists began using "ideology" to denote all forms of social consciousness, including those accurately reflecting reality. "Scientific" Marxist ideology, an unsupportable construction for Marx, is nevertheless accepted by contemporary Soviet Marxists.

In *The German Ideology,* the division of labor is prior to private property and hence the first cause, or root, of social oppression. It is endemic to human history (originally "nothing but the division of labour in the sexual act"[25]) and constantly refined as technology matures. Its appearance in history has immediate and dramatic ramifications. Because humans need material products but only some are producers, the division of labor leads necessarily to a system of social exchange. Objects produced by laborers become units of exchange value, or commodities, no longer valued in themselves as crystallized praxis. A worker's connection to the products of labor is severed, and eventually he, too, is transformed into a commodity. Alienation is a direct consequence of the social division of labor. Social institutions become autonomous, uncontrollable, always reinforcing inequality in wealth and property. Human history, for Marx and Engels, is categorized by technological levels of production, and the social forms divided labor and property assume: the "primitive" world, with its tribal property; the ancient world, with communal and state-owned property; the estates and landed property of the feudal world; and private ownership and wage labor in modern capitalism.

Socially divided labor is, therefore, the primary source of private property, inequality, and injustice. Communism abolishes the division of labor, creating workers neither tied to one kind of labor nor estranged from the creative, fulfilling activities of which they are capable. Workers, in other words, control the productive apparatus, ending the reification of material products, private property, and wealth. But seizing the means of production, with its revolutionary impact on the superstructure, occurs only in certain conditions. The increasing impoverishment and oppression of workers creates a disaffected, angry population, eager to initiate social change. But the level of production must be technically mature, so that workers' material needs can be efficiently and effectively met. And the revolution must be worldwide, for communism can survive only in a world market where all countries are economically interdependent. The proletariat, a worldwide class, must mature and rebel collectively. In sum, capitalism's maturing productive capacity produces an increasingly large and volatile class of workers who experience material and cultural exploitation and eventually reject both. Revolution materializes when society's productive forces conflict with its relations of production.

While revolution is a human act performed and suffered by human actors, it also culminates an impersonal developmental process. At certain historical junctures revolutions occur regardless of the actors' unique personalities or feelings. The communist revolution is a natural, inevitable aspect of history, appearing when material productive forces mature and produce necessary conditions. No ethical imperative demands revolution. The proletariat's understanding and evaluation of capitalism is purely practical, inseparably linked to their revolutionary actions. Ethics, then, is part of practical activity, which is part of history's material process, hence Marx's critique, especially in *The Poverty of Philosophy* and the *Communist Manifesto,* of the utopian socialists. They proffer socialism as a normative or moral imperative, not an objective necessity. They ignore the revolutionary role that matter imposes on workers and capitalism's transitory, doomed existence. They naively advocate moral suasion and economic reform to achieve socialism, ignoring history's innate propensities.

Revolution abolishes the division of labor, class conflict, national boundaries, and social injustice, initiating a universal transformation of production and distribution. Subjectivity, facing the impersonal tendencies of scientific materialism, is helpless. The mind, "afflicted with the curse of being 'burdened' with matter," is passive.[26] Although productive forces develop from human energy, "this energy is itself conditioned by the circumstances in which men find themselves, by the productive forces already acquired, by the social form which exists before they do, which they do not create, which is the product of the preceding generation." In brief: "Are men free to choose this or that form of society for themselves? By no means."[27] Objectivity is found in intersubjective matter. "It is not consciousness that determines life, but life that determines consciousness."[28]

Historical materialism, in sum, sees reality unfolding impersonally, determining the quality of subjectivity. Technology determines society's level of productive forces, conditioning relations of production. This base consists of antagonistic classes, which appear historically when human labor is appropriated. Culture reflects the base. Antagonistic economic classes, therefore, produce social classes with opposing interests, expressed in conflicting ideologies. Dominant social institutions and ideas reflect the interests of the dominant economic class. When material conditions ripen, oppressed classes seize the means of production and dissolve existing social institutions—including the state. New institutions represent the new dominant class.

The implications of all this for "active" subjects are ominous. Action is motivated by material interests, which are class-determined. Freedom, equality, justice—like "truth"—are merely verbal disguises for class interests, with no intrinsic meaning. Because governments similarly have no interests beyond the hegemonic classes they represent, the oppressed recognize the futility of all save revolutionary forms of political activity. At this point, one is hard pressed to discern, as Marx did, the advantage of historical materialism over its mechanistic predecessor.

Marx's remedy affords material reality a dynamic quality based on contradiction and incessant change. Dialectical social theory has a long history, beginning in Greece and surviving through the later writings of relatively obscure scholars and theologians.[29] Friedrich Hegel legitimized dialectical thinking in nineteenth-century Europe, and no one, including Marx, could escape the Hegelian tidal wave.

Marx's early work, especially the *Critique of Hegel's Philosophy of Right,* attempted to salvage the dialectic from Hegel's idealism, preserving its "rational kernel within the mystical shell." After 1846 Marx insisted that matter embodies its own dialectical tendency, leading to the "inevitable breaking up" of existing states of affairs.[30] Dialectics, in other words, is an aspect of concrete phenomena as these evolve in history and is accurately defined only by thoroughly describing matter in all its concrete expressions.

Marx's adjectival definition means that dialectics is an aspect of materialism, particularly the contradiction between a society's productive forces and its relations of production. Each mode of production contains the germ of its own dissolution, which grows as the oppressed become increasingly aware of inferior economic, social, and political positions. As bases mature, they exaggerate the inequities between dominant and oppressed classes. The latter cognitively realize misery's concrete, material sources, in a fit of revolutionary pique seize the means of production and become the new dominant class, bringing new social institutions.[31] History has a built-in mechanism of conflict and change, culminating in the abolition of classes altogether.[32] Its locus is the material substructure, and its expression is actual human history. The dialectic, as part of matter, is impersonal and determining, an inexorable law of human evolution generating negation and revolution.[33]

The material dialectic energizes social existence. Empirical reality is a multidimensional material process that explains what is, was, and will be. Dialectics, then, is the appropriate method for scientific inquiry. Each concrete society is a progressive synthesis of past contradictions and a seed of new antagonistic relationships. Similarly, each individual represents a unity of opposites: a reflective subject defined by objective matter. Marx thus salvages active subjectivity from mechanistic materialism: Matter's dialectical quality permits opposites to coexist in dynamic, tense unity. The pesky logical problem of reconciling free subjects and objective processes is solved by abandoning orthodox logic. But the solution smashes into common sense. Marx has equated freedom and necessity without adequately redefining either. If a free subject cannot say "no" to environmental pressures, then how is he free? The question is pertinent even if an impersonal dialectical process makes this negative response impossible.

Grundrisse (1857–1858) shores up what appears, perhaps even to Marx, a weak argument.[34] It describes the social, political, legal, historical, and psychological implications of money as it functions in a capitalist economy. Money is examined as a social relation, not an empirical entity, allowing Marx to analyze its interconnections, exposing the contradictions between and within them, and situating these historically. Capitalism's central conflict or tension is between the freedom and equality of participants in the money marketplace (the "law of equivalence") and capitalists' unending drive for monetary profit—the source of worker exploitation, oppression, and alienation. *Grundrisse* elaborates the multifaceted aspects of this underlying contradiction.

Dialectics now implies a total social process of change, historic (diachronic) and spatial (synchronic), with the features shaped by stages of economic development. Each aspect of society (economic, political, social, aesthetic, legal, and so on) comprises a moment of the total whole, constantly interacting, defining, and influencing others. Hence, concrete levels of social intercourse are neither independent nor identical. In a narrower sense, each aspect of the economy (production, distribution, exchange, and consumption) is similarly defined by its interactions with every other economic aspect, as well as with the noneconomic totality. The emerging picture is multidimensional and alive, where "everything that has a fixed form . . . appears as merely a moment, a vanishing moment, in this [social] movement."[35]

Although ordinarily we see things at rest in a setting that is empirically verifiable, these staid social phenomena are actually in motion. In the first part of *Grundrisse,* called "Money," Marx describes the marketplace: the empirical reality generating liberty and equality, where economic and social differences vanish in impersonal transactions. In this world of liberal freedoms, where a known legal structure is applied universally, "it is impossible to find any trace of distinction, not to speak of contradiction, between them [buyer and seller], not even a difference."[36] This calm surface—what Hegel called, in the *Logic,* a "one-sided immediate unity"— is important in its own right, imposing limits or boundaries within which society can develop.[37] But it also represents one moment of a hidden movement, one aspect of the dialectical process. Money's empirical circulation "is the phenomenon of a process taking place behind it."[38] Marx ventured beyond the empirically obvious in part two of *Grundrisse,* entitled "Capital." Here we find workers transmogrified into units of wage labor, endlessly toiling to produce wealth for capitalists. This "hidden" reality energizes society's contradiction and movement. The "law of equivalence" is properly perceived as only one moment within a whole, which includes capitalist production. Bourgeois liberty, equality, and legalism also express the hideous oppression found in capitalist factories. Eventually the antagonism between worker and capitalist will negate empirical reality, the underlying contradiction will be suspended, and the totality will turn into its opposite—with identities and contradictions at a new, more progressive level.

There are two significant consequences. First, individual categories contain the social totality. A legal or economic "specialist" is by definition a mystifier, reifying an abstraction, turning a dynamic process into a stagnant, self-contained myth.[39] Conversely, the totality is not independent of individual components. Mechanistic materialism's overly simplistic, deductive theories obliterate concrete social reality. Marx's dialectic therefore condemns liberal reformers and utopian socialists, "radical bourgeois democrats" who perfect bourgeois liberty and equality while railing at the market's venality and the tyranny of money, unaware these money and market mechanisms reflect and support the favored freedoms. Dialectics similarly unravels bourgeois economics.[40] The products of labor dialectically express the laboring act, and this constitutes their inherent worth or value. Capitalism mistakenly turns human products into autonomous commodities, their value determined by independent, impersonal laws, the so-called "market forces." The act of labor is artificially separated from actors, and this destructive, alienating process is soon dialectically realized in other facets of social life. By interpreting reality as a tense unity in which social categories mutually interpenetrate, we have, for Marx, an answer to materialism's riddle of primacy. Neither subject nor object dominates: They are interpenetrating, defined by a seamless union.

Like capitalism's "law of equivalence," however, this solution also hides a churning system of contradictions. Examined *dialectically,* Marx's dialectic is incongruous. If neither subject nor object is prior, then we have a sophisticated critique that is politically sterile, lacking guidelines for individual action. Neither objective processes nor subjective initiative is trustworthy. Intentional action would upset the delicate dialectical balance, favoring either subjectivism or reductionism—both false and dangerous. Endless rounds of dialectical critique will lead perhaps to understanding, frustration, and despair, but not rebellion.

This extraordinary attitude is certainly alien to Marx. *Grundrisse,* in fact, identifies dialectics with matter's actual, objective movement, hence generates the epistemological priority of matter. Since production is society's material base, it also determines, in the final analysis, the totality, including its subjective moment. Marx confirmed this: Production, one aspect of society's totality, "is the real point of departure and hence the predominant moment. . . . [It] predominates not only over itself, in the antithetical definition of production, but over the other moments as well."[41] The contradiction of productive means and relationships is, consequently, society's determining moment, defining the whole—the "concrete totality." Revolutionary action is objectively justifiable, an inevitable moment of matter's dialectical process. Economic contradictions "lead to explosions, cataclysms, crises, in which by momentous suspension of labour and annihilation of a great portion of capital the latter is violently reduced to the point where it can go on. . . . Yet these regularly recurring catastrophes lead to their repetition on a higher scale, and finally to its violent overthrow."[42] Far from being a theoretical departure from earlier materialism, *Grundrisse* is a more complex and sophisticated struggle with the same issues undertaken from the same materialist perspective. Nonorthodox neo-Marxism questions this perspective; hence, the shared advocacy of dialectical inquiry obscures fundamental antagonisms.

Capital further examines capitalism's concrete developmental processes, conceptualizing each separate phase within an impersonally functioning totality. Material laws are verified with empirical evidence. Technical economic concepts and terms that explain classical political economy are never severed from the more general principles of historical materialism. The determining material totality, in brief, is Marx's framework for examining capitalism, clarifying what appears to a nondialectical eye as *Capital*'s "contradictory" emphases on particular, factual data and universal, reductive generalizations. Dialectics must grasp the material whole, the dynamic movement within which universals and particulars are only incomplete moments.

MATERIALIST MARXISM

Engels

Marx's friend and collaborator, Friedrich Engels (1820–1895) connected Marx's materialism to contemporary social theory, providing Marxism with the philosophical evidence that Marx himself ignored, that is, drawing ontological and epistemological implications of both historical materialism and dialectics.[43] Scientifically active at a time of pioneering experimentation—yielding dramatic hypotheses concerning human evolution, the conservation and transformation of energy, organic cellular structure, and even the measurement of mental phenomena—Engels was in the mainstream of mid-nineteenth-century European culture, believing the unity of life is expressible in impersonal scientific laws. He based these, however, on materialist, not empirical, evidence.

Engels saw the philosophical dialogue in Europe pitting idealism against materialism, and he explicitly favored the latter. Idealism conjures immaterial principles, spiritual beings that use body organs but are essentially independent of matter. Echoing *The German Ideology,* Engels believed that mind is an attribute of matter (that is, the human body) organized in a specific, materially determined way. All mental functions depend on appropriate bodily organs; hence, intelligence and creativity are qualities traceable to matter via the human body. Mind is therefore the product of a historical process in which animals gradually develop nervous systems that evolve into complex forms of matter we call brains. These allow animals to interpret reflexes meaningfully, and connect disparate physical activities mentally. "Higher" cognitive activities reflect the brain's progressive evolution. Thought merely "translates" matter into the brain's historically developed functions. This form of materialism, known as "monism," rejects the "dualist" assertion that consciousness, though part of matter, is something other than matter. Reinforced by political factors, this subtle distinction is ammunition for Plekhanov's later struggle with Lenin.

Engels defined matter as the physical world directly perceived by the senses, apart from speculation of any kind. All aspects of this world, including space and time, are composed of dynamic, changing matter. Engels felt that matter in motion evolves into ever higher qualities or forms of being. Thus, social movement is qualitatively different—more progressive—than the movement, for example, of plants. Mechanistic materialism, reducing everything to a universal mechanical motion, is therefore ill equipped to reveal life's progressive movement, which marks nature as well as human history and thought. Mind's subjective movement, consequently, merely reflects nature's own objective process, because mind *is* matter that has taken a particular progressive form. Dialectics scientifically explains the movement of matter and the study of that movement. It is thought imitating nature. However, since mind is originally a form of natural matter, dialectical thought—dynamically evolving throughout human history—is an inevitable by-product. "The fact that our subjective thought and the objective world are subject to the same laws, and hence, too, that in the final analysis they cannot contradict each other in their results, but must coincide, governs absolutely our whole theoretical thought. It is the unconscious and unconditional premise for theoretical thought."[44] Truth is a correspondence between ideas and objective reality. Knowledge consists of true ideas. Engels merely fulfills history's promise by assisting in the realization of dialectical human knowledge.

Engels predictably viewed economics as the key to society's material determination. Matter's dialectical movement is expressed in the changing patterns of human productive techniques. Each mode progresses to its own destruction and assimilation in higher productive forms. Class antagonisms are reflected culturally in competing ideas and institutions. Social and economic progress coincide as each successive class seizure of the productive apparatus alters the quality of social life. "Production . . . is the basis of every social order. . . . Accordingly, the ultimate causes of all social changes and political revolutions are to be sought, not in men's brains, but in changes in the modes of production and exchange."[45]

Marx describes matter's dynamic movement concretely, rejecting theoretical discussion of any kind. Engels completes Marx's unfinished picture. Dialectics, for Engels, embodies three universal laws that govern matter in motion: the law of the transformation of quantity into quality, and vice versa; the law of the interpenetration of opposites; and the law of the negation of the negation. These three principles explain reality and generate an apt method of social inquiry.

The first dialectical law, the transformation of quantity into quality, means perceived qualitative changes occur only by the quantitative addition or subtraction of matter in motion. Engels defined quantity as those states that are measurable on the same scale (for example, temperature, pressure, weight, speed, and so on), and quality as those not adequately expressed in figures only. As quantities of matter increase or decrease, they alter qualitatively. A numerical increase in atoms, for example, transforms a molecule into a substance with new properties. A change in temperature produces melting or freezing; the accumulation of cooperative human labor alters the environment; an increase in workers and a decrease in capitalists inevitably yield a qualitatively new form of social life. Engels distinguished his dialectical materialism from mechanism, which defines changes in quality as perceived illusions, mechanically caused by "primary" units to which everything is reduced. Though composed of elementary units of matter, a quality, Engels argued, is also more than the sum of its material parts.

Nature consists of bodies in motion, constantly interacting through attraction and repulsion. From these two subforms of matter—attraction and repulsion, positive and negative—various qualities present in the universe (for example, heat, electricity, light, magnetism, sentiments, and so on) are derived. Motion is therefore a primordial natural substance. It appears materially in the measurable forms of attraction and repulsion, and cognitively as the qualities experienced in life. The world is therefore a unity of opposites, hence the second dialectical principle: the interpenetration of opposites. Each perceived item, and nature itself, is a tense amalgam of antagonistic, interpenetrating motions, which at any one time are empirically invisible. Progress emerges from this opposition and interpenetration. Engels considered this principle to be the decisive refutation of formal (bourgeois) logic, especially its principle of noncontradiction. Since nature, including space and time, is a dynamic unity of antagonistic forms of matter, empirical facts are defined by what they are not, that is, their past, future, and encompassing environments. Revolution, then, is as true and inevitable as a morning's sunrise or a subway ride to work, even though it is empirically nonverifiable at this particular moment in an apparently peaceful society. Everything contains within itself its own opposite which, as a result of laws one and three, emerges and is itself surpassed.

The law of the negation of the negation serves as the linchpin in Engels's system. It is absolutely certain that every object, thought, or condition will turn into its opposite. This "negation" of the original phenomenon is then negated, producing a new reality synthesizing primary qualities of the first two stages and preserving them in a more perfect—or progressive—form. The progressive residue survives in a synthetic unity, which resolves thesis and antithesis. Engels's laws are manifest on every level of life. A seed, for example, develops into a plant (its negation), and the plant produces new seeds and dies. These new seeds, the negation of the negation, propagate the original's most useful or strongest traits but also introduce new ones that increase the second plant's life chances. History is similarly governed: Property relations evolve from common ownership in primitive society, to private ownership in capitalism (the negation), to a newer, more progressive common ownership in socialism (the negation of the negation). Socialism is thus heir to the residual best from both previous stages. Even philosophy begins as primitive materialism, is negated by idealism, and is resolved in the more perfect form of dialectical materialism. The negation of the negation energizes nature and society, where inner contradictions generate quantitative changes that promote ever more perfect qualitative forms. It is "an extremely general . . . law of development of nature, history, and thought; a law which . . . holds good in the animal and vegetable kingdoms, in geology, in mathematics, in history, and in philosophy."[46]

These laws function impersonally. Valid knowledge, natural and human, results from cognitively perceiving and willingly adopting them. But reality, an interpenetration of opposites, is not explained by contemplation alone. Impersonal dialectical laws are defined and expressed by everyday facts, hence the final test of knowledge is practice; in other words, does knowledge help us effectively alter the environment to satisfy real material needs? If so, knowledge is verified. Mental speculation is passive, and therefore scientifically inadequate. Practice is not only a criterion of knowledge but also its source. Real needs propel us to certain fields of scientific inquiry and shape experimental questions. Prevalent forms of scientific inquiry are therefore motivated by the concrete needs of those having the inclination and resources to make science a tool for maintaining privilege, that is, the dominant economic class. Practice is both the purpose and verification of scientific inquiry. If practical consequences—manifest in social practice—satisfy the original, founding need, the science is valid. Knowledge, therefore, is objective (reflecting matter) and practical (satisfying a need), confirming its dialectical character.

Knowledge is dialectical because matter moves dialectically, and this constitutes the epistemological "bottom line." Engels's sophistic critique of "metaphysics" as "a system of natural and historical knowledge which is all-embracing and final for all time [and] is in contradiction with the fundamental laws of dialectical thinking . . . " mystifies rather than enlightens.[47] What are his three "fundamental laws of dialectical thinking" but "all-embracing and final," universally deterministic: "the entire natural world is governed by law, and absolutely excludes the intervention of action from without."[48] Engels's epistemology, in other words, fits squarely in the materialist tradition, with objective, a priori processes governing the entire universe.

Engels never openly repudiated materialism but late in life may possibly have lost the courage of his conviction. In a series of letters written in response to questions regarding the meaning of historical materialism, Engels reclaimed the significance of nonmaterial factors. He admitted that he and

Marx may have overemphasized the historical role of economics.[49] Ideas are, indeed, important: " . . . the various elements of the superstructure . . . exercise their influence upon the course of the historical struggle and in many cases preponderate in determining their form."[50] In sum, crude economic determinists are nondialectical: "They always see only here cause, there effect. That is a hollow abstraction. . . . "[51] Abstraction or not, Engels could retreat only so far before losing credibility among materialists, which he was not prepared to do. The line was quickly drawn: "The ultimately determining element in history is the production and reproduction of real life. . . . There is an interaction of all . . . elements in which, amidst all the endless host of accidents . . . the economic movement finally asserts itself as necessary."[52] "Political, juridical, philosophical, religious, literary, artistic, etc. development-is based on economic development. . . . There is . . . interaction on the basis of economic necessity, which *ultimately* always asserts itself."[53] Engels asserts both the dialectical interpenetration of all phenomena *and* a concrete material process that, "in the last resort," determines. History's dialectic is impersonal, objective matter in motion.

Engels, nonorthodox neo-Marxists argue, vulgarized Marxism with an indefensible metaphysics of nature and history, transforming Marxism into a reductive epistemology that turns humanity into passive, helpless products of autonomous laws. He is atavistic, naively defending traditional bourgeois metaphysics. His tragic misinterpretation, the argument goes, is directly responsible for oppressive Soviet and Eastern European institutions.

Certainly Marx rejected Engels's type of philosophical speculation. But Marx and Engels may have purposely divided their labors to avoid needless repetition.[54] Engels's ontological and epistemological exegesis and Marx's more concrete analysis of historical materialism and capitalism together complete the totality that a materialist social theory must encompass. Marx and Engels jointly believed that matter is prior to thought. For both, the dialectic is an attribute of dynamic matter in history. Engels was probably correct in claiming to have read the entire manuscript of *Anti-Dühring* to an approving Marx, who even collaborated on the tenth chapter. Materialists now also claim that the major themes of *Dialectic of Nature* were discussed by Engels and Marx "many times." "Marx is as ideologically 'compromised' and 'contaminated' as his collaborator."[55]

The situation is actually a good deal more complicated than most Marxists care to admit. Materialist Marxism *has* become reductionist and now rationalizes oppressive institutions. And this *is* traceable directly to Engels. But Engels did not pervert Marxism; he merely expressed philosophically principles that Marx hypothesized in concrete terms. Marxists who condemn Engels do so as nonmaterialists. They, of course, can and do cite potentially anti-Engelsian remarks from Marx. But, we have seen, Marx's invisible philosophy and cursory remarks concerning epistemology are vague and contradictory. Marx confirmed *and* denied Engels's dialectical materialism. Materialists, including the mainstream orthodox movement, approvingly recognize Engels's important contributions to revolutionary social theory. Nonmaterialists see Engels as the first Stalinist. Claiming, however, that Engels distorted or misinterpreted Marx requires that we ignore a significant portion of Marx's work that Engels himself chose not to.

In any case, the Second International eventually recognized Engels as Marxism's official philosopher. "Dialectical materialism," first coined by Engels, became the philosophy of orthodox Marxism, and Party members continually praise *Anti-Dühring* for providing the theoretical analysis that Marx ignored.[56] Significant second-generation materialists—especially Kautsky in Germany and Plekhanov, Bukharin, and Lenin in Russia—are philosophically Engels's children. At the turn of the twentieth century Marxian philosophy is visible only in Engels's brand of materialism.

Kautsky

During those years, the mantle of Marxist orthodoxy passed to Karl Kautsky (1854–1938), the German second only to Engels in influencing contemporary materialism. Active as a Marxist theoretician since the early 1880s, Kautsky also participated in key internecine political controversies that dramatically affected the organization and ideology of Europe's major Communist parties.[57]

Kautsky's materialism is a scientific, deterministic form of inquiry, and his four volumes of historical analysis unflinchingly defend historical materialism. Similarly, his two theoretical volumes adopt Engels's dialectical materialism as the philosophical rationale of proletarian revolution. Kautsky secured his prominent position in history as a systematizer and applicator of Marxist materialism, not as an original theorist. His one original contribution to orthodoxy consists of grafting Darwin's theory of evolution onto Marxism.

Natural and human development, Kautsky stated in *Ethik und material-istische Geschichtsauffassung* (1906), are generated by living organisms interacting with environments. As Darwin unmistakenly proved in his theory of natural selection, the best adapted organisms survive and transmit useful traits to their offspring, assuring a genetically determined movement of history toward ever more progressive, higher developmental stages. The competition for survival among species creates a universal interspecies instinct of aggression and an intraspecies instinct for solidarity. Presumably, then, human beings are aggressive toward lower species and instinctively caring and cooperative with each other. Kautsky connected these theories of biological determinism and universal instincts to a rigidly orthodox rehash of historical and dialectical materialism. Human beings appear in history after an impersonal material process of natural selection, their survival assured because of toolmaking skills and an ability to communicate through language. These same distinguishing attributes, however, lead inexorably to higher social forms and eventually to institutionalized private property. Humanity, then, is propelled by an inner material dynamic toward economic and social inequality, class antagonism, revolution, and finally sublation in higher, more progressive ways of living. The entire process leads to workers seizing the means of material production, eliminating the source of contradiction, and creating democratic socialism, where harmony and peace prevail.

Kautsky's input within the Second International on questions of revolutionary strategy was shaped by this Darwinian Marxism. Predictably, he argued that consciousness evolves like any other natural or social phenomenon, a determined product of objective matter. Hence, scientific socialism reflects and expresses matter and is unrelated to spontaneous working-class perceptions and beliefs. Revolutionary theory is cognitively grasped by historical and social "scientists," who then formulate authentic working-class consciousness. Ironically, Kautsky's analysis theoretically justifies Lenin's closed, dictatorial workers' party, despite the fact that Kautsky, by inclination and argument, was a democrat who later emerged as Lenin's most insistent antagonist. By understanding and accepting dialectical materialism literally, Kautsky believed socialism can appear only after capitalism matures and economic classes polarize. Workers, in other words, can successfully seize political power only in ripe economic conditions. He admiringly repeats Marx's critique of classical political economy, that is, the inevitability of capitalist overproduction, increasing unemployment, and social anarchy. His calm faith in historical determinism indicates the folly of "rushing" history, capitulating to subjectivist schemes for action at any cost. The proletariat, without seeking shortcuts, will carry capitalism to its objective conclusion. They create needed skills and class consciousness and simultaneously exacerbate capitalism's inherent contradictions by working slowly to enact partial economic, social, and political reforms. These, however, are no substitute for the objectively necessary workers' revolution, which may be peaceful or violent depending on concrete conditions.[58] Since base and superstructure are reciprocally linked, effective working-class reformism promotes concrete economic change, even though base is primary "in the last resort"—a phrase borrowed, untouched, from Engels. History's unavoidable workers' revolution will yield a democratic socialist society, where humanity's needs are satisfied. Here, the masses run their own affairs, with the state restricted to coordinating material production and distribution, not ruling people. Although everyone benefits from socialism, history requires the struggle be fought only by workers.

His disagreement with Lenin was primarily strategic, not theoretical, but this dulls neither its intensity nor fury. Kautsky claimed that Marx's "dictatorship of the proletariat" refers to the postrevolutionary government's social content, not its form. Marx used the term, claimed Kautsky, to describe the Paris Commune, which defended basic democratic princi- ples such as free speech, free elections, and open party access to electoral politics. The workers' revolution liberates people to run their own lives, guided by principles of socialist equality. Kautsky questioned whether Russia's revolution should have occurred in the first place, given the unripe, precapitalist surroundings. It certainly could not depend on workers governing themselves, for as a class they were neither skilled nor ideologi- cally mature. Lenin was forced to create a secretive, hierarchical party which, upon reaching power, instituted a new and ruthless dictatorship. Sadly, this would lead to bureaucratic exploitation and a tyranny worse than capitalism's, where workers could at least express divergent points of view. Party dictatorship also increased the likelihood of a strong individual eventually seizing control and subverting Party principles. Finally, Lenin's revolutionary strategy could consume itself by encouraging "Thermidor," a desire by workers for more traditional values and institutions.

Kautsky earnestly contended that no single party should monopolize truth or suppress discussion. Given his theoretical orthodoxy, however, this belief is hollow and naive, built on a boundless faith in history's material laws rather than principle. It was inconceivable to Kautsky that workers in mature capitalism are anything but revolutionary Marxists, and it is similarly inevitable that all nations pass through a capitalist developmental stage. The belief in worker self-government reflects his own assurance that self- governing workers will be Marxists, that is, passively recognizing and following authentic, true needs. Kautsky rejected even the possibility of a conflict between material truth and subjectivity, hence the unhesitating, gullible trust in social scientists. Lenin, as we shall see, shared Kautsky's materialism, but was much more sensitive to Marx's dialectical interpene- tration of subject and object. Historical truth, for him, is actively realized by workers only under constant prodding by his own party's version of Kautsky's "scientists." Allowing history to unfold passively, lacking pur- poseful human action, is nondialectical and untrue, leading finally to worker alienation and reformism. Party dictatorship, for Lenin, is scientifi- cally justifiable.

While Westerners can sympathize with Kautsky's surface democratic sheen, they should also detect a philosophical naiveté. His crude dialectical materialism and simplistic assumption that worker self-government will take only one (socialist) form has had paradoxical consequences for Eu- rope's social democratic parties. Especially after Stalinism, Kautskyite socialists realized that materialism, emphasizing inviolable objective truth, does not necessarily support worker self-expression and democracy and is easily transformed into totalitarianism. Marxist social democracy was burdened with antagonistic legacies inherited from Kautsky. When their reformist tactics effectively altered the most brutal aspects of capitalism, they discarded dialectical materialism as a threat to socialist democracy.

Kautsky's workers' parties remained only superficially loyal by turning his democratic reformism from a means of realizing worker self-government to an end in itself. They are now established participants in capitalist political systems, the same systems that Kautsky felt history—working through his social democratic parties—would obliterate.

Plekhanov

Though Kautsky significantly—even if at times unknowingly—influenced European Marxism, he did little to improve Marxism's sordid reputation among philosophers. George Valentinovich Plekhanov (1856-1918), on the other hand, was a philosopher in the Engelsian tradition. Kautsky and most other non-Russian European Marxists were obsessed with Marxist tactics and strategy and only peripherally with orthodox communist philosophy. Plekhanov, the "father of Russian Marxism," was the first to systematize Marxism coherently in Russia. He differed from European comrades in seeing Marxism as integrally connected to epistemology, ontology, aesthetics, and ethics. His lifework, therefore, embodies a lucid commentary on the total philosophical world view appropriate to revolutionary materialism, a Marxist response to traditional philosophical questions. Though a dogmatic philosopher, Plekhanov was also an excellent publicist, and his books comprised a Marxist catechism for young, disillusioned Russians. Russian Marxism, from its inception, emphasized philosophy in order to distinguish its program from that of other anticzarist revolutionary movements, especially Russian populism.[59] In abandoning philosophical "neutrality"—the haven from which most European Marxists were polemicizing—Russian Marxism produced a crop of important theoreticians, including, in addition to Plekhanov, Bukharin and Lenin.[60] By the second decade of the twentieth century, the philosophical center of Marxism had shifted from Germany and France eastward to Russia.

Plekhanov's most important and influential work is a book originally entitled *In Defense of Materialism* (1894). Though in exile for almost forty years prior to 1917, he managed to publish this book legally in Russia by changing its title to confuse czarist censors. Hence a book with the unwieldy title of *A Contribution to the Question of the Development of the Monistic View of History* surreptitiously became a universally accepted primer for Russian Marxists. Plekhanov traces Marx's philosophical roots through several eighteenth- and nineteenth-century Western European movements: orthodox materialism, especially Holbach and Helvétius; German classical philosophy, culminating in Hegel's idealism; utopian socialism, with its ethical defense of social change; and the French historians of the Restoration period (for example, Guizot, Thierry, and Mignet), who, though idealizing human nature, effectively related social reform movements to material interests. Marx's unique genius, for Plekhanov, was his ability to take the theoretical best from these philosophies and combine it with the idea of historical necessity, the epistemological basis of science. In Marx's science of historical materialism, valid knowledge is shifted from an idealized reality consisting of values and essences to the objective world of matter. Humanity's uniqueness lies in its toolmaking skill, the quality of the tool shaping an era's character and social forms. Technical progress—the historical evolution in toolmaking skills—brings new levels of productive forces and relations of production, which correspond to extant political, ideological, aesthetic, and social institutions. In brief, the economic base molds humanity's self-image and society's institutional character.[61]

Plekhanov castigated critics who derided Marx's inadequate dialectical philosophy. Although Marx wrote few pages on this topic, he nevertheless was able to "think dialectically." Marx always stressed the reciprocal, dialectical interaction of super- and substructures, two aspects of one social process that could not be analytically fragmented. Yet even dialectically interrelated matter must be anchored in concrete reality. Marx's historical materialism serves this function: "In the last resort" social causation lies in the sphere of production; economic factors are determining. Marx's message, for Plekhanov, is that politics, and culture generally, definitely influences a nation's economic policies, but the productive apparatus determines how these cultural structures work. Still, Plekhanov occasionally became mired in the potentially irreconcilable notions of dialectics and economic determinism. When stressing, for example, the immense variety of dialectically interrelated factors involved in historical change, he ambitiously asserted that productive forces are finally determined by geographical conditions, obscuring materialism's professed belief in the priority of economics "in the last resort."[62]

Productive systems evolve dynamically, just as other matter does. They inevitably breed antagonistic classes whose social clash generates higher, more progressive systems, culminating in workers seizing their own productive apparatus. Only the philosophy of dialectical materialism grasps this movement. Plekhanov fully accepted Engels's dialectical laws of matter, which govern human and nonhuman phenomena. Consequently, Plekhanov turned Engels's philosophical reflections into what Jordan calls a "political cosmology," and Colletti a "cosmic systhesis" built on a "single unifying principle, one explanation embracing everything from the most elementary biological level right up to the level of human history."[63]

Plekhanov directly connected the philosophy of dialectical materialism to the science of historical materialism and described the latter as an application of the former to particular historical circumstances. This integration of materialist philosophy and science was passed to Lenin and indirectly to the Soviet state. Plekhanov thus ceded to orthodox Marxism a total and explicit philosophical doctrine of its own, as well as a science of social change. Marxist social theory could now unashamedly consider all traditional philosophical questions and effectively challenge relevant bourgeois answers. One consequence: Plekhanov, with Mehring and Lafargue, was a pioneer in explicating a Marxist materialist aesthetics. Whereas Kautsky outlined and applied Marx's materialism to actual history, Plekhanov consolidated Engels's first principles into a coherent, inclusive "*Weltanschauung*" relevant to all established intellectual disciplines.

Despite this affinity for cosmic speculation, Plekhanov fell easily into the slimy reality of tactical polemics. Until 1903 he was closely allied with Lenin and the Bolsheviks against right-wing revisionists and Mensheviks. He considered the workers' revolution to be the inevitable culmination of capitalism, to which all else—including reformism and liberal democracy—must be sacrificed. By 1905 Plekhanov had colored Lenin an opportunist and withdrawn support from bolshevism. Like Kautsky, Plekhanov's orthodox materialism could not accommodate Lenin's renewed emphasis on the subjective component of history's dialectical totality. Lenin's apparent voluntarism—his hierarchical and centralized party, disbelief in proletariat consciousness, alliance with peasants, and premature workers' revolution—by Plekhanov's standards is nondialectical and nonmaterialist. History's universal material laws should not be short-circuited by power-hungry individuals ignoring concrete circumstances. Proletarian self-consciousness is generated by ripening material conditions. The Party must work with history, not against it; allowing capitalism to mature gradually so that it can be quickly and efficiently annulled by organically aroused workers. These principles guided his participation until 1914 in the Second International. He became a Russian nationalist in World War I, abandoning proletariat internationalism while advocating Russian national defense and unity. But he did so as a materialist: German defeat and Russian victory would hasten the revolutionary potential of both nations. After the February 1917 revolution, he returned to Russia advocating liberal parliamentary democracy and supporting the provisional government. He argued, as it turned out ineffectively, that Russian workers required capitalism as a historical prologue to their own revolution. Defeated by Lenin, his reputation in Russia as the self-proclaimed philosopher of Marxism suffered immeasurably, even though future Soviet primers and texts simply ignore the political controversies that so dominated his last years.

Bukharin

With the philosophy of dialectical materialism formulated by Engels and Plekhanov, orthodox theory comes to a dead end. Except for Lenin's *Philosophical Notebooks,* little of theoretical significance or even interest emerged from materialist Marxism until after World War II. Orthodoxy is represented by polemicists such as D. Ryazanov (born D. B. Goldendach, 1870-1942), a learned and effective historian and publicist. Ryazanov's occasional insights—particularly his prescient, inchoate critique of materialism's "passivity" and the dialectical need to emphasize active praxis within a concrete totality[64]—whet our theoretical appetites but are finally nullified by the ideological dogmatism and obsequious hagiography he shares with his time.[65]

Nikolay Ivanovich Bukharin (1888–1938) epitomizes the plight of trained orthodox philosophers during this period. Faced with near unanonymity of philosophical opinion, they had to decide between parroting an accepted line or, like Bukharin, developing harmless theoretical twists. The energy saved on theorizing is more than balanced by the ferocious personal and tactical struggles staining bolshevism's acquisition and maintenance of state power. This strategic turbulence in Russia often obscures the universal consensus on basic principles. All adversaries accepted the epistemological presuppositions of dialectical materialism and the scientific usefulness of historical materialism. The shared belief in objective material truth makes it easier for orthodox theorists to live with dictatorship, provided it is "scientific." Coincidence or not, anti-Party protest emerged only from those out of power, often from former leaders who had previously advocated stronger Party control. It is unlikely that such disputants were motivated by democratic impulses or moral concerns, other than a self-righteous belief in their own leadership abilities.

Bukharin's work, like that of his peers, is doctrinaire rather than subtle. His two major books, *Historical Materialism* (1921) and, with E. Preobrazhensky, *The ABC of Communism* (1919), remained orthodox primers in the Soviet Union until Stalin, as part of his post-1928 anti-Rightist campaign, declared Bukharin a disreputable "mechanist."[66] They tirelessly, shamelessly repeat the same basic tenets already found in works by Marx, Engels, Kautsky, Plekhanov, and numerous lesser known authors.[67] Historical materialism— Bukharin often calls it "Marxist sociology"—is the only objective, scientific approach to historical and social inquiry. It alone reflects and reveals nature's fixed material laws, which function as predictably as does each separate part of a clock within the whole mechanism. "Both in nature and in society there exists objectively (i.e. regardless of whether we wish it or not, whether we are conscious of it or not) a law of nature that is causal in character."[68] Its qualities are already well known: Beginning with human mind as a function of matter, Bukharin outlined the material origins of productive processes, the determining significance of technology, and the priority "in the last resort" of the productive apparatus.

Bukharin's curious theoretical contribution is his use of the term "equilibrium" in describing Engels's dialectical laws of nature. Society and nature are parts of a dynamic dialectical cycle of change, governed by Engels's three principles. Each successive stage, however, embodies a new level of temporary stability, a state of equilibrium where potential internal contradictions live but are not yet manifest. As they mature quantitatively, they disturb the equilibrium and produce a new qualitative level. History is reducible to a constant process of disturbing and restoring social equilibrium, Bukharin's "law of equilibrium."[69] In the revised terminology, proletarian revolutionary forces mature and destroy capitalism's equilibrium, bringing forth a new proletariat state, which owns and controls production, exchange, and distribution. When pure communism is realized, social equilibrium is permanently restored, and a liberated society finally achieves its full material potential.

Though Bukharin's focus on social equilibrium permits him, more than predecessors, to appreciate the accomplishments of capitalism and bourgeois social science calmly, his belief in an objective material dialectic never wavers. Because "the basis of all things is . . . the law of change, the law of constant motion,"[70] capitalism is merely transitory and Bukharin's sanguine evaluation of its merits evokes a hangman's kiss. His reputation is unrelated to revised jargon, but rather to membership in the doomed Right opposition to Stalin: defending Kulak rights, advocating an evolutionary approach to accumulation and industrialization, opposing Party despotism and terror, and favoring an open culture and free social science. He was increasingly anointed a forerunner of European social democracy and reformism, despite the fact that before 1921 he strongly advocated proletariat state control over all economic and political matters, including coercing peasants and militarizing workers. As the true historical representative of the working masses, with an absolute knowledge of history's objective laws, the Communist Party is justifiably sovereign. Directing workers to their own liberation is certainly, for Bukharin, not exploitation. His apparently contradictory behavior before and after 1921 is explained by the inner dynamics of materialist Marxism. With truth defined impersonally, democracy—worker self-government and social freedom—is merely a potential tactic in its concrete realization. Bukharin's early position was that if the Party actually is controlled by scientists, then democracy is expendable, a subjectivist deviation. If, however, the Party falls to a demagogue, as he later contended, then history's laws are better realized through the free actions of a mature working class, well fed by independent farmers and eager to govern themselves. There is an inner unity to Bukharin's tactical vacillations, just as there is to Trotsky's and those of most other orthodox theorists during this period of Soviet history. Dialectical materialism, the philosophy of materialist Marxism, can justify democracy only as one replaceable means of realizing an absolute truth. It can similarly justify dictatorship. By dialectically evaluating Party leadership, one determines the appropriate path.

Lenin

Lenin, better than anyone else, illustrates how dialectical materialism generates a plethora of tactics and strategies oriented solely toward realizing truth in changing circumstances. Vladimir Ilyich Ulyanov (1870–1924), who after 1901 wrote under the pseudonym "Lenin," was converted to Marxism after 1890 by reading Marx and Plekhanov. By 1893–1895, when his first professional writings appeared, he shared with Plekhanov a strong belief in the scientificity of historical materialism. He honed these views until 1901 in critiques of Russian populism, "legal Marxism," and "economism"— three anticzarist movements rejecting Marxist materialism. Only in 1914, however, did Lenin theoretically reconsider the dialectical materialism of Engels, Kautsky, and Plekhanov. Though he never abandoned materialism, the dialogue between Lenin's early and mature philosophies holds the key to understanding what many have interpreted as his "voluntarism" or "opportunism." Lenin, his own standard comments notwithstanding, directly confronted fundamental epistemological problems that others ignored.[71] *Materialism and Empirio-Criticism* (1908) and the *Philosophical Notebooks* (1914 ff.) illustrate both the contradictions and underlying unity in Lenin's philosophical peregrinations and also clarify the conundrum now preoccupying post-Stalinist Marxist materialism.

Philosophy's problematic, described in *Materialism and Empirio-Criticism,* is the relationship of mind to matter. In criticizing empirio-criticism, Lenin contended that there can be only two answers: idealism and materialism. Extant philosophical "schools" are variations or consequences of these two themes, which are irreconcilable. Each has practical consequences: Idealism upholds the interests of the bourgeoisie, materialism those of workers. Empirio-critics, like many other nonmaterialist philosophers, improvise a vague language to hide their idealism. Despite bloated ambitions, they merely intellectually justify bourgeois hegemony.

Lenin defined idealism as epistemological subjectivism, the mind creating ideas and using them to evaluate and explain reality.[72] There is no objective criterion of truth because it is, by definition, a subjective idea. Idealistic philosophies proliferate and clash, but the final arbiter regarding "right" or "wrong" is public opinion. Since reality is defined subjectively, idealistic science consists of whatever most people *think* is real. Yet this glossy public dialogue of ideas has onerous consequences. In capitalism, idealism stresses the priority of subjectivity both epistemologically and practically. Individuals are legally free to speculate and choose the most attractive world view. The apparent battle of ideas is really a unanimous consensus on bourgeois values and institutions, for these intellectual freedoms are also necessary to preserve liberal democracy and capitalism, and to reinforce elitism. Idealism engages in an endless series of subjective intellectual games whose sole practical purpose is to maintain class domination.

Materialism, on the other hand, defines human cognition as the mental reflection of actual objects which exist materially, independent of mental counterparts. Lenin's so-called "copy theory" of perception presumes all sensations are photocopies, imitations of the real thing. Objective matter exists outside the mind, determining what we perceive but not coextensive with mental processes. Sensations, for Lenin, are "images" or "reflections" of real things, "the direct connection between consciousness and the external world."[73] The mind is a correlative of matter: The latter exists only in relationship to mind. Lenin's "dualism" presupposes two realities, the objective material world and its cognitive mirror image. Plekhanov, and the orthodox school generally, are "monists" because they define mind in material terms only, as matter determined by the physical world. Mind, in other words, is complex matter that is part of material reality in the same way that trees, stars, or subhuman animals are. The external perceived object *is* the content or data of perception. Since mind is passively determined matter, there is no intervening mode of cognition which reflects or mirrors reality. Dualism absurdly argues that physical processes occurring in the mind are in some strange way the same as outside events, and even this justifies only knowledge of perception rather than of reality itself.

Lenin's early epistemology has been roundly criticized by Marxists and non-Marxists but with particular sarcasm by other materialists.[74] In his defense, however, Lenin was a self-proclaimed and ardent materialist. Indicting dualism as idealist belies Lenin's own arguments in *Materialism and Empirio-Criticism*. He never doubted the reality of "objective law in nature and objective causality," inexorably "reflected ... in the mind of man ...."[75] The entire dispute between monists and dualists has been blown out of proportion, a perfect example of supposedly nonphilosophical Marxists' philosophical nit-picking. Both defend the same materialist epistemology: Knowledge exists objectively in matter, determining individual and social behavior. Lenin's cognitive reality, conceptually, is matter's determined effect, just as it is for monists. Why, then, did Lenin diligently accumulate Engels's scattered comments on cognitive "reflection" and construct a potentially confusing concept, which from his own materialist viewpoint is superfluous? Lenin, it seems, was a materialist who was unwilling to accept the passive, noncreative role assigned to social actors. By describing a subject's cognition as "reflecting" matter, he implicitly condemned orthodox Marxism for denying mental reality altogether. If everything, including mind and its contents, is reducible to physical properties, then Marxian materialism is indistinguishable from the vulgar non-Marxist predecessor. Our role in history requires meekly awaiting the inevitable revolution, which will appear independent of unique desires or intentions. This attitude was obviously unsuitable to Lenin's temperament and the circumstances of a decaying czarist Russia. Lenin's dualism, then, is a backward, ineffective materialist defense of ideas and intentional action, resurrecting subjectivity and simultaneously denying its autonomy. It is not nearly as sophisticated as the still unpublished *Grundrisse*, which Lenin could not have known. In all fairness, however, Lenin was at least more bothered than Kautsky, Plekhanov, or Bukharin by orthodox Marxism's hapless view of humanity. And despite theoretical shortcomings and a strident, inflexible style, materialists still consider *Materialism and Empirio-Criticism* an important philosophical work—perhaps even the final philosophical word. Stalin and his successors have naively concluded that all bourgeois philosophy is merely a variation on the empirio-critics, Mach and Avenarius. *Materialism and Empirio-Criticism* is Russia's last systematic work of philosophy dealing directly with an issue of interest to non-Marxists.

Encouraged by his reading of Hegel during the war years, Lenin continued searching for a revised, subjectively relevant dialectical materialism. The *Philosophical Notebooks,* published posthumously in the Soviet Union as volume thirty-eight of the *Collected Works,* consists of speculative writings completed after 1914. Its quality is uneven, occasionally rambling incoherently, sloppily blending commentary and description. Still, it is a tantalizing prologue to later orthodox attempts at reinvigorating the dialectic with a clearer sense of subjectivity. It is also invaluable for understanding Soviet domestic tactics. For a brief time in the 1930s, when Stalin was purging Bukharin and others in the Right opposition, the *Notebooks* even emerged as a seminal work in orthodox Marxism-Leninism. Stalin's decision, however, was purely tactical. Obviously more comfortable with the direct, polemical style of *Materialism and Empirio-Criticism,* Stalin's success relegated the *Notebooks* back to official obscurity.

His goal in these essays was to examine Hegel's dialectic and salvage what could fruitfully be applied to materialism. The *Notebooks* do convey reality's intricate dialectical complexity but too often at the cost of clarity. *Materialism and Empirio-Criticism* argues reflection is a mirror image of concrete objects, conceptually separating mind and matter and then resuscitating the former. Lenin probably sensed his failure. The new jargon cannot rescue subjectivity from its servile relationship to matter. With Hegelian inspiration, he attacks again in the *Notebooks,* adopting Hegel's concepts of "universality" and "individuality" to "open up" the perceptual process. All phenomena, including material objects and human minds, embody universal (abstract) and particular (material or concrete) qualities. Hence, perceived objects are never completely understood, for they express an infinite number of meanings that can appear to us only through an infinite number of perceptions. A desired mate, for example, expresses not only the beliefs and values endemic to his/her role in the production process, but also sensuality, social acceptability, psychological dependence or dominance, intellect, moodiness, strength or weakness—the possibilities are endless because the object manifests abstract as well as concrete meanings. In perceiving this object, I also express abstract and concrete meanings. I cognitively experience him/her not only in the light of my socioeconomic conditioning, but as a sexual object, a symbol of conquest, a communicant, a lover, an intellectual equal, a rejected parent—again the possibilities are endless. This same complexity marks every perceptual act and perceived object. The world, as Lenin sees it in the *Notebooks,* is infinitely complex, with all of its parts interconnected and interrelated. "The universal exists only in the individual and through the individual. Every individual is (in one way or another) a universal. Every universal is (a fragment, or an aspect, or the essence of) an individual. Every universal only approximately embraces all the individual objects. Every individual enters incompletely into the universal."[76]

Since absolute truth requires perceiving reality's infinite dialectical linkages—an impossible task—human knowledge is always fragmentary. Each particular cognitive reflection is incomplete and exhibits internal contradictions between universal and particular elements, the variety of abstract and concrete meanings it simultaneously expresses. As knowledge increases, these contradictions are surpassed and replaced by new ones. This cycle continues endlessly: Incomplete and contradictory knowledge is resolved by continued learning but reappears at more advanced levels and pushes us to learn even more. Truth, never absolute, is generated by this process of resolving contradictions. It reflects "the universal, all-sided, vital connection of everything with everything and the reflection of this connection . . . in human concepts, which must likewise be hewn, treated, flexible, mobile, relative, mutually connected, united in opposites, in order to embrace the world."[77] It is, in sum, "the totality of all sides of the phenomenon, of reality and their (reciprocal) relations. . . ."[78]

Lenin emphasized the dialectical complexity of subject and object as separate entities and implied that, when perceiving, neither is absolutely primary. In *Materialism and Empirio-Criticism* he unequivocally rejected idealism as false, misleading, and oppressive. By now, Lenin had mellowed somewhat. Idealism merely overemphasizes or absolutizes truth's abstract component at the expense of its particularity. Idealism, in other words, has gnoseological roots and cannot be ignored or simplistically dismissed. There is some truth in all knowledge, including idealism. It, too, is "one of the shades of the infinitely complex knowledge (dialectical) of man."[79] "Metaphysical materialists," on the other hand, exaggerate the particular, material component of knowledge. They, for example Plekhanov and the monists, mistakenly turn reflective knowledge into an automatic, passive product of dynamic matter. Lenin's intense dislike of Plekhanov as well as his new-found Hegelianism propelled him to the brink of orthodox heresy: "an intelligent idealism is closer to an intelligent materialism than is a stupid materialism"; "man's consciousness not only reflects the objective world, it also creates it."[80] Lenin meant, apart from overly zealous polemics, that reflective knowledge is constituted by abstract and particular aspects of both material objects *and* perceiving subjects. Knowledge is never a product of only object *or* subject.

The *Notebooks* courageously analyzed the reciprocity of subject and object, reality's dialectical complexity. Were it not for its awkward, fragmented style, it would surely be more widely acknowledged as a major work of Marxian theory. In understanding dialectics it parallels Lukács's *History and Class Consciousness* and is certainly the equal of Kosík's *Dialectic of the Concrete,* which has recently created a stir among European Marxists. Yet it is plagued by the same irrepressible dilemma that is endemic to all Marxist materialism: the necessity of explaining concretely—materially—nature's "flexible, mobile, relative, mutually connected" dialectic. By rejecting a priori materialism and idealism, Lenin is bereft of epistemological moorings. His theory is not scientific. The notion that everything in nature is interconnected may be analytically useful, but we also need an objective pattern or law or idea to prevent being immobilized in an endless, circular word game. Nature's dialectic must manifest an absolute truth or we have no rationale for intentional action of any kind, no insight whatever into social or historical necessity, and no basis for prediction. A dedicated Marxist revolutionary, Lenin obviously cannot survive in this epistemological limbo. Like Marx in *Grundrisse,* Lenin disguised rather than eliminated materialism. He enumerated sixteen "elements of dialectics," the underlying motif being the conflict and unity of opposites.[81] These dialectical qualities include Engels's three laws as well as Hegelian concepts and terminology taken from the *Logic.* What matters most, however, is Lenin's palpable reversion to dualism, now called "*Bildertheorie.*" Dialectical truth is again securely anchored in nature's matter: "the laws of logic are the reflections of the objective in the subjective consciousness of man"; "all scientific (correct, serious, not absurd) abstractions reflect nature"; "logical forms and laws are . . . the reflection of the objective world"; "knowledge is the reflection of nature by man"; "cognition is the eternal, endless approximation of thought to the object"; and "life gives rise to the brain. Nature is reflected in the human brain. By checking and applying the correctness of these reflections in his practice and technique, man arrives at objective truth."[82] Lenin's revised dialectic takes us back to Engels. It is a property of reflective knowledge *and* an objective trait of nature. History and society are therefore governed by nature's dialectical laws, which exist prior to human perception or will. Capitalism dissolves into its opposite as surely as did feudalism; proletarian revolution inevitably resolves bourgeois contradictions. Incontrovertably, Lenin remains a dialectical materialist.

In retrospect the *Philosophical Notebooks* transforms dialectical materialism from a frozen formula into a dynamic process. Lenin reactivates subjectivity as a complex unity of abstract and concrete processes rather than, as before, stuffed bodies manipulated by impersonal forces. Yet these incredibly complex human agents also express and reflect objective universal laws governing all human and nonhuman phenomena. He is defending the integrity of irreducible subjects as well as the epistemological priority of an objective material dialectic. This project is nurtured by orthodox Marxists, many of whom are troubled by the numbing consequences of their own materialism. Other than abandoning the latter altogether, however, no satisfactory resolution is possible. Lenin's epistemology is either warmed-over materialism or philosophical legerdemain. Neither justifies an irreducible subject.

Whether Lenin's unrealized philosophical dream is a cause or consequence of his revolutionary tactics, Leninist theory and practice are mutually supportive. Unlike Plekhanov and Kautsky, he is not willing to await history's dénouement passively. Social actors are more than automatons. History's dialectical process includes real live subjects reflectively perceiving and creatively altering the world. But history is not arbitrary. "Everything that takes place in history takes place of necessity, that is elementary."[83] History unfolds dialectically; society passes through developmental stages leading inexorably to workers' revolution. History's truth, in other words, is expressed in creative activity by reflective, knowledgeable people. However, only "correct" actions are justifiable. Here is the rationale for Lenin's voluntarism. While Leninist tactics are shaped by concrete circumstances, they also express his unique epistemology. Successful revolutionary strategies embody creative, goal-oriented actions by knowledgeable agents generating history's objective process. By having it both ways epistemologically, that is, defending irreducible, innovative subjects and a determining, objective dialectic, Lenin can creatively modify historical materialism's reductionism and impose a rigid dictatorship of scientists.

Lenin's unity of theory and practice is vividly illustrated in the functioning of Leninist Parties. As a materialist, he never doubts that there are fundamental, objective class interests defining the workers' role in history. In their oppressive environments, however, they develop neither the initiative nor the desire to decipher history intellectually and discover authenticity. They become everyday equivalents of what Plekhanov and the monists represented within the Bolshevik Party: nonreflective, passive reductionists, simplistically defining reality with ready-made social recipes. "The history of all countries shows that the working class, exclusively by its own effort, is able to develop only trade-union consciousness. . . . The theory of socialism, however, grew out of the philosophic, historical, and economic theories elaborated by educated representatives of the propertied classes, by intellectuals."[84] Worker spontaneity ignores scientific historical evidence and violates history's objective evolution. Spontaneity is nondialectical, untrue. Workers, perverted by environment, live inauthentically, reinforcing myths that deny history and hinder objective liberation. "Hence our task, the task of social-democracy, is to combat spontaneity."[85] Leninist Parties actively intervene in history to aid the oppressed. But this active, reflective intervention is part of dialectical reality; it *is* history expressing itself through human agents. The belief in subjects reflectively mirroring objective history is philosophically clarified first in Lenin's dualism and later his revised dialectic. *What Is to Be Done* concludes that parties must be small, centralized, and tightly controlled by professional revolutionaries who, because they reflectively perceive the inevitability of proletarian revolution and are prepared to act forcefully, are society's scientists.

Lenin equates revolutionary success with the concrete realization of history's dialectical laws. Both are expressed by scientists actively intervening in history. Revolutionary parties are therefore truth incarnate: There can be no limits on activities and policies, hence his somewhat unorthodox strategies regarding the peasant and national questions and the issue of permanent revolution. The historically "correct" approach to each is whatever promotes a successful workers' revolution. Russia's Bolsheviks, composed of scientist-revolutionaries, are history's reflective agents. Their reading of concrete facts proves peasants are a potentially useful ally for overthrowing the czar. They support peasant land demands even though the orthodox— "reductionist"—rule intimates that this is always counterproductive, creating a large, mollified group of reactionary small landowners.[86] Similarly, the Party recognizes nationalism as a bourgeois value but also as a tactic that, in some conditions, serves the revolution. Decisions regarding the support of nationalist movements are made on an individual basis rather than by one static, overarching principle.[87] Any national movement improving the tactical position of internal revolutionary forces, or corroding the imperialist sinews of Western capitalism, is historically valid. Finally, the bourgeois stage of history is not sanctified. In some instances the Party may guide workers in controlling the bourgeois revolution and directing it immediately to socialism, telescoping both historical phases into one. Even Marx, in letters to the editor of *Otechestvennye zapiski* (1877) and Vera Zasulich (1881), implied that *Capital* did not prohibit Russia from finding its own path to proletarian revolution, perhaps even by avoiding the evils of capitalism. Presumably, Parvus (A. L. Helfand) and Trotsky (L. D. Bronstein) had already proven that the success of Russia's permanent revolution depended on its spreading to the more developed capitalist states. But, for Lenin, the theory of permanent revolution also should not ossify, for this would handcuff Party members, turning them into passive victims of orthodoxy. Lenin's vacillation—he rejected this theory until 1905, adopted it until 1917, and later modified it by muting the necessity of an international workers' revolution—is historically correct because it worked first to establish and then to preserve Russia's revolution. The policy changes reflect history's dialectical movement, expressed in shrewd, calculated Party actions.

Lenin, like Marx in *Grundrisse,* tried to reassert the subjective moment of matter's objective movement. In one of history's more grotesque ironies, materialism's latent anti-individualism is unintentionally realized by one who rejected orthodoxy's antihuman vulgarity. Leninist institutions, once established, are entirely acceptable to orthodox dialectical materialists, even those who would have preferred a more systematic, evolutionary approach. Lenin's impetuosity may have rushed history but not substantively altered its objective patterns. Leninism itself eventually hardens into an inflexible reductionism, a ruthless Party dictatorship, which pulverizes subjectivity beyond recognition.

Stalin

The recrudescence of reductionist dialectical materialism occurred under Joseph Stalin (born Yosif Dzhugashvili, 1879–1953), who sought ironclad rules to justify and support his personal power. As a political theorist, Stalin's contributions are miniscule. In 1938 *The History of the Communist Party of the Soviet Union (Bolsheviks), a Short Course* was edited by an anonymous Soviet commission. Stalin was initially credited with writing the fourth chapter, "On Dialectical and Historical Materialism." He later claimed to have written the entire volume.[88] For fifteen years, the *Short Course* was an article of unhesitating truth that literate Soviet citizens read continually. It lauds everything Lenin and Stalin did to foment and preserve the workers' revolution and labels their theoretical and political opponents people's enemies.

"On Dialectical and Historical Materialism" smoothly rehashes basic orthodox principles of Engels, Plekhanov, Bukharin, and, of course, Lenin. Conceived as a catechism of what Stalin calls "Marxism-Leninism," it is written in very simple language with each idea numbered—presumably to facilitate memorization. Under the unacknowledged influence of Plekhanov—a man elsewhere ridiculed—Stalin described dialectical materialism as the general laws governing matter and historical materialism as a special case referring particularly to history and economics. He delineated four unoriginal laws governing nature's dialectical movement (for some unexplained reason ignoring Engels's "law of the negation of the negation") and three already popular principles of materialism, and concluded by unimaginatively describing the primacy of material production, the interaction of base and superstructure, the class struggle, ideology, the role of technology, and history's progression of socioeconomic systems. Stalin was neither innovative nor prepared for philosophical subtleties: He adopted, for example, Lenin's reflection theory of knowledge but ignored the important issues raised in the *Notebooks*. Praxis is unquestioningly determined by fixed historical laws.

Stalin's unrivalled, absolute power in the Soviet Union made theory of any kind expendable. He did whatever he wished and later found appropriate quotations; hence, his significant contributions to Marxist materialism are policies enunciated while consolidating power. The principle of "socialism in one country" is partially intended to raise Party and worker morale at a time of unfulfilled expectations regarding world proletariat revolution. Appearing in *Concerning Questions of Leninism* (1924), only two years after *The Foundations of Leninism* (1922) confirmed the necessity of proletariat revolution in the West, "socialism in one country" also legitimated the brutal suppression of those, like Trotsky, who were dissatisfied with Stalin's policies promoting world revolution. Preceding the violent purge of the Left opposition in July 1928, Stalin declared that maturing Soviet communism had intensified the class struggle, making Party violence a necessary and acceptable tactic. As purges continued, Stalin declared (12 January 1933) that dialectics required the proletariat state to evolve first into a state of maximum power before finally "withering away." These Stalinist "principles" were obviously premeditated excuses for an unprincipled reign of terror. During this period, Stalin published articles on a variety of scientific and artistic topics, none innovative or theoretically significant. Collectively, they comprised an official "line" and determined what Soviet scholars were permitted to write about. Stalin emerged as head of Lenin's Party, world communism's chief scientist. His actions were objectively justifiable. Potential critics, *ipso facto,* reject history's valid laws—and Stalin did not tolerate such arrogance. A priori materialism slid headlong into totalitarianism not because it is inherently antidemocratic— Kautsky, for one, considered himself a democrat—but because it theoretically emasculates subjectivity, leaving the masses unwilling and unable to defend themselves actively against unscrupulous scientists. Trotsky, in public office, unhesitatingly employed violence to defend historical truth and revolutionary justice.[89] When expelled, he virulently attacked Stalin for doing the same thing and implored workers to cleanse bureaucratic sycophants from the Party apparatus.[90] His last words, like his severed head, fell meekly, unacknowledged by passive subjects who were now the tools of men as well as history.

Kosík

Stalin's unspeakable horrors and the chill of cold war diplomacy effectively nullified what little non-Soviet popular appeal orthodox Marxism retained. Revisionists soon dotted Eastern Europe, dedicated to "humanizing" dialectical materialism by reinjecting praxis and tempering the Party's authoritarianism. Faced with an unyielding Communist bureaucracy, many either abandoned revolutionary Marxism for Kautskyist social democracy or rediscovered roots in nonmaterialist Marxism, already blooming in the works of Lukács, Korsch, Gramsci, and the Frankfurt School. Those remaining inside orthodoxy saw two options. They could philosophically acknowledge orthodox dialectical materialism, evaluate Stalinism as unfortunate but historically necessary, and work at purging Communist Parties of Stalinist hacks. De-Stalinization erased potentially authoritarian personalities but left theoretically untouched principles already proven vulnerable to the likes of Stalin. Alternatively, theorists could reformulate dialectical materialism to represent a revitalized, active, and free working class, henceforth unwilling to endure calumnies of self-styled dictators. This, however, leads us back to the pesky chore of reconciling free subjects and impersonal material laws. In brief, contemporary "neo-orthodox" theorists intellectually restructured materialism with high hopes and a new, heady jargon but ended up replicating questionable arguments from *Grundrisse* and the *Philosophical Notebooks.* The Czech Karel Kosík (b. 1926) is an important and influential contemporary neo-orthodox theorist, and his *Dialectic of the Concrete* (1963) proffers a representative point of view.[91]

Kosík calls the commonsense world we normally experience "pseudo-concrete." Everyday perceptions submerge reality in an ocean of isolated, disconnected empirical facts, obscuring the "essential" dialectical process energizing matter. Philosophy must systematically and critically catch this essence ("thing-in-itself") and generate valid knowledge of nature's objective patterns. It must, in other words, be dialectical. Dialectics reassembles the real world that everyday perceptions artificially fragment, unpacking hidden interrelationships governed by matter's essential movement. Though disguised in nonreflective empirical consciousness, matter in motion governs all experienced objects and events. Dialectical method, which generates essential truth by emulating it, is therefore expressed in practical actions, not merely contemplative abstractions. History's material dialectic has already been adequately described in *Capital,* where Marx proved that dialectical method is an explanation that takes the concrete form of working-class revolutionary praxis. Theory, truth, and revolutionary practice are separate moments of one dialectical unity, anchored in dynamic matter.

Real essences, hidden by empirical phenomena but also expressed in them, comprise concrete human praxis—a unity of object and subject. This world is not—as in vulgar, or reductive, materialism—fetishized, an impersonal predetermined reality molding helpless subjects. Instead, it includes the activity of reflective subjects, creatively laboring in material conditions. Dialectical knowledge embodies dynamic processes instigated and realized by human beings, whose personal lives are infected with what Kosík calls "transparent rationality." Reflective actors live the truth. By dialectically destroying pseudo-concreteness, we escape dead abstractions and begin actively shaping the world. Because authentic social reality is a unity of opposites, dialectics simultaneously liberates "subject" and "object," avoiding abstract idealism and mechanistic materialism. Dialectical theory scientifically describes a subjectively meaningful, authentic, essential life-style and also prescribes apposite revolutionary activity. Knowledge therefore represents one manner of appropriating the world.

Like an automobile driver with extraordinary peripheral vision, consciousness actively moves ahead, guided by surroundings. In Kosík's terminology, subjectivity is one element in the totality's grand horizon, which includes historical, social, and natural objects. In normal, nonreflective states we are unaware of these. However, as authentic actors we reflectively experience them in everything we do. As aroused actors, consciousness has two aspects. First, it is theoretical and practical: cognitively experiencing reality, rationally planning a life strategy, and acting appropriately. But second, it is pre-predicatively, precognitively defined by the material totality. Authentic consciousness is thus a dialectical unity of opposing forces. It is "ambiguous," part "reflection" and part "projection." Existentialism or idealism "instantiates" creative activity, ignoring the determinate whole we are in. Conversely, vulgar materialism reduces consciousness to objective components and ignores subjective experience. Essential reality dynamically mediates concrete whole and abstract part; objectivity is expressed in and through subjectivity. This is what Kosík calls "the concrete totality."[92] Methodologically, the concrete totality interprets individual facts as artificial abstractions, naively isolated from matter's dynamic movement. The whole, on the other hand, remains analytically useless independent of facts: "the dialectical understanding of the totality means not only that the parts are internally related and connected amongst themselves and with the whole, but also that the whole cannot be fossilized in an abstraction foisted upon the parts, since the whole *creates* itself in the interaction of the parts."[93] Reality vacillates from fact to totality and back again, both analytical poles moments of a unified process. "[T]he totality itself is concretized, and such a concretion is not merely the creation of the content but the creation of the whole as well."[94] Consequently, unilinear causal explanations are invalid. No single factor (for example, economic) determines others, because all factors interact with each other and the concrete whole. Each reflects and expresses the others and the whole. Dialectical social inquiry begins anywhere and leads inexorably everywhere.

Kosík, like Lenin, broaches apostasy. If we take his delicate subject-object dialectic literally, it lacks criteria of scientific verifiability. Dialectically interpenetrating objects and events, if separated from objective first principles, justify pure contemplation and moral relativism. Everything is related to everything else, and nothing is true absolutely. Since neither history nor action is objectively justifiable, historical and social science as well as goal-oriented action disappear. This is not Kosík's position. He, like Lenin, is a revolutionary and a social scientist, perceiving practice and theory as aspects of one objective material law. Though the latter is realized subjectively, it is also foundational in an epistemological sense: Action is one moment of the concrete totality, which is prior to and includes subjectivity. Kosík's materialism describes objective social patterns. "Reality comes to be interpreted not by means of reduction to something different from itself, rather, by explaining it in terms of reality itself, through the development and the illustration of its phases, of the moments of its movement."[95] Matter, expressed in reflective activity, exists intersubjectively. Man, an "objective socio-historical subject"[96] is "subjective" in an "objective" sense, consciously realizing essential, interpersonal matter. Hence economic base, the process of material reproduction, is still prior to other social factors. Despite disclaimers, Kosík's materialism leads, hesitantly, to this conclusion: Though base and superstructure interpenetrate, "the base retains a decisive role."[97]

Philosophically reconciling active, intentional subjects and materialism without merely redefining subjectivity to eliminate the problem, haunts contemporary materialists. The editors of *Telos,* admirers of Kosík, see "praxis," man's "real freedom," "determined" by a synthesis involving an "a-historical universal."[98] Freedom, in other words, expresses a universal material dialectic. Meaningful actions deviating from universal necessity are, by definition, false and unfree. "Activity" involves consciously experiencing universal determinants of consciousness. Dick Howard talks of socialism as a "theoretical necessity which assumes that mankind is rational and human," and then describes praxis as rational, free action. Freedom, then, expresses matter's necessity. Though "neither the individual nor the collective can be given logical (or historical) priority," still, authentic knowledge and action represent "the formal, a priori structures which govern the relationship between the individual constitutive acts and the plural social structures they constitute, and which in turn reconstitute them."[99]

CONCLUSION

Beginning with Marx, materialist Marxism exhibits an internal tension that shapes its history. Vulgar, orthodox, reductive materialism postulates objective matter impersonally determining natural and human phenomena. It is a systematic, internally consistent philosophy stressing the priority of base over superstructure, the socially determining influence of material production. Unfortunately, it also ignores common sense and empirical reality, both indicating the enormous social and historical roles of ideas and noneconomic institutions. Moreover, it defuses humanity's revolutionary impulse by making actors impotent tools of history, precluding revolutionary protest save in the most extreme, "mature" circumstances. Hence Marx, Lenin, and Kosík enhance subjectivity's historical role by transforming reductive materialism into reflective materialism, what Colletti aptly calls an "objective object-subject process." Thoughtful social actors are significant in their own right, values and ideas reemerge in history, and revolution is a reflective, critical reaction to dehumanizing capitalism. But revitalizing reductive materialism generates impotent philosophy. If neither objective matter nor subjective reflection are foundational or determining, then Marxism is no longer scientific, critical contemplation replaces praxis, and a workers' revolution is problematic. Thus, reductive materialism surreptitiously resurfaces even in its materialist critics. Dialectically interpenetrating ideas and institutions are determined, "in the last resort," by material productive processes. Base determines superstructure even while the latter is historically "autonomous."

All materialist Marxists, reductive or reflective, define subjectivity impersonally and freedom as realizing objective laws. In the reductive version, this is blatant. Engels, for example, interprets free will as "nothing but the capacity to make decisions with knowledge of the facts. Therefore the *freer* a man's judgement in relation to a definite point in question, the greater the *necessity* with which the content of this judgement will be determined." Freedom appears with knowledge of nature's impersonal laws. Concrete actions are materially determined whether or not we exercise free will.[100] Plekhanov concurs: Subjective freedom is an awareness of objective (material) necessity. Free action is "the activity of men in conformity to law in the social process of production."[101]

Reflective materialism, on the other hand, postulates a unity of subject and object within a material totality. Freedom still reflects matter, but actively rather than passively. Since free actions, active or passive, reflect the same material dialectic, presumably they are, in identical circumstances, identical. If not, for example, during internecine Party struggles, someone is being "unscientific"—an accusation usually leveled by all sides. Thus, reflective materialism's prime advantage is tactical, advocating more spontaneous, nondogmatic revolutionary activities—potential ammunition for dictators and democrats alike. Philosophically, it echoes reductive materialism, but imprecisely, with confusing language. Reductive materialism, despite its crudeness, avoids the impossible.

Timpanaro

His training in linguistics sensitizes Sebastiano Timpanaro to materialism's limits regarding subjectivity. He calls nonreductive materialists home: "those who have embarked on a 'Marxism without Engels' have arrived, coherently enough, at a 'Marxism without Marx.' "[102]

Neo-orthodoxy is a cure worse than materialism's malaise. Timpanaro reverts to basic principles, purified of avant-garde idealist excrescences. Materialism must reacknowledge "the priority of nature over 'mind' . . . of the physical . . . over the biological, and of the biological . . . over the socio-economic and cultural . . . both in the sense of chronological priority . . . and . . . conditioning. . . . " Timpanaro fearlessly asserts the ontological primacy of material nature and the unavoidable "element of passivity in experience."[103] Materialism is either true or history, external reality, and other people are no longer intersubjectively verifiable.

Contemporary Marxist materialism unnecessarily transgresses a straight, narrow, and necessary philosophical path. The "decisive primacy" of base over superstructure—the heart of Marxism—is applicable only to social events occurring since humans have populated nature in their present physical form.[104] Historical materialism concretely explains social change *within* the current natural epoch of human history. But materialism also transcends the class struggle. Humanity is, in the last instance, dependent on and conditioned by nature and biology, although today we are decisively conditioned by the base. The latter occurs in the former and is its determined consequence. Moreover, even in capitalism, material nature conditions us in noneconomic ways, for example, natural calamity, death, disease, and so on. Hence, we cannot escape nature, even when it temporarily allocates priority to economics.

For Timpanaro, humanity's biological and natural conditioning are mediated by a "second nature"—a naturally evolved ability to labor and experience social life subjectively. Only this is explained by historical materialism. Postrevolutionary communism is emancipated and free (that is, a "third [human] nature") but is also mediated by nature's more fundamental conditioning, hence unavoidably limited. Marxism promises an end to economic and social oppression, but progress in nature "will always be reformist, and not revolutionary. . . . Man's biological frailty cannot be overcome, short of venturing into the realm of science fiction."[105]

While human beings are active, intentional, and cognitive, this "must be accounted for, both historically . . . and presently. . . . " What we know, and how we know it, are scientific problems for neurophysiology, biochemistry, and cybernetics. By explaining material nature's influence on the evolving human nervous system, and—within this constraint—the "enormous importance of class relations in determining the [current] 'environment,' "[106] we grasp the source and quality of human cognition. Subjectivity is real but is also a passive consequence of matter. Similarly, humans intentionally act to achieve desired ends, but this capacity is itself a product of biological evolution, and the ends we seek are materially determined. "Freedom" exists "within the causality" of nature.[107]

Timpanaro admits that Marxism exhibits "a lack of clarity that goes right back to the origin of Marxist theory and was perhaps never completely overcome even in Marx's mature thought."[108] While recognizing the "decisive primacy" of the base, the early Marx presumed that physical and biological nature predate human history, and praxis is humanity's sole link to nature—obscuring nature's determination of thoughts and actions. Marx's distaste for philosophy meant that post-1846 writings, though materialist, never clarified the early confusion. Consequently, Marxism requires Engels's "brilliant attempt to fuse 'historical materialism' with the materialism of the natural sciences,"[109] despite his affinity for superfluous cosmic laws. Lenin's *Materialism and Empirio-criticism* is the seminal twentieth-century work on materialism, continuing Engels's quest to integrate human development and nature philosophically.[110]

The Soviet Union since Stalin, and to some extent Mao's China, are bureaucratic dictatorships.[111] Though materialism generates a revolutionary party of scientists, it also requires democracy at all party levels, so that truth—not myth—triumphs. Stalin's brutality, in this sense, was mistaken. But even mistakes are necessary parts of material nature, in this case Russia's backwardness and Stalin's own psychological and biological makeup. While another person might have been less authoritarian, given the primitive milieu, some authoritarianism was necessary.[112] Hence "involuted bureaucracies" are necessary mistakes in nondeveloped Marxist states, leaving thoughtful materialists at a loss to do anything but rationalize the status quo and hope for less psychopathic leaders. Western Parties, on the other hand, must democratize, de-Stalinize, so strategies become effective, reflecting actual matter. Once in power, however, the very success of demagoguery becomes its own justification, for democracy is necessary only when matter causes it.

With Timpanaro we return to pure, unadulterated·materialism: impersonal, determining, potentially authoritarian—but philosophically consistent.

NOTES

1. Karl Marx, "Defense of the Moselle Correspondent," in *Selected Writings,* ed. D. McLellan (London: Oxford University Press, 1977), p. 24. Hereafter cited as *KMSW.*

2. See his "The Law on Thefts on Wood," ibid., pp. 20–22.

3. Karl Marx, *Early Writings* (New York: Vintage Books, 1975), pp. 256–57. Hereafter cited as *KMEW.*

4. Ibid., pp. 244–45.

5. Karl Marx, "Economic and Philosophical Manuscripts," ibid., pp. 345ff.

6. See esp. ibid., pp. 322–34.

7. Ibid., p. 348.

8. Ibid., p. 328.

9. Ibid., p. 329.

10. Ibid., p. 355.

11. Karl Marx, *The Holy Family,* in *KMSW,* p. 135.

12. Ibid., pp. 140–41.

13. Ibid., pp. 149–55.

14. Ibid., p. 152.

15. Karl Marx, *Theses on Feuerbach,* ibid., p. 156. The earlier quote is from the first thesis. This one from the third.

16. Ibid. (sixth thesis), p. 157.

17. However, Marx never used the term "dialectical materialism."

18. David-Hillel Ruben, *Marxism and Materialism* (Atlantic Highlands, New Jersey: Humanities Press, 1977), pp. 116, 79, and 75.

19. Ibid., pp. 107–9.

20. Karl Marx, *The German Ideology,* (Moscow: Progress Pubs., 1976), pp. 49–50.

21. Ibid., p. 37.

22. The priority that was given to technology, Marx's early "technological de-

terminism," is muted somewhat in Marx's later description of the dialectical interpenetration of all modes of social life, especially in *Grundrisse* (New York: Vintage Books, 1973) and *Capital,* 3 vols. (New York: International Pubs., 1975).

23. Marx did not adequately define the notion of class. His discussion in the last chapter of *Capital* volume three remains incomplete. The implication, systematically developed by Kautsky in his *Die materialistische Geschichtsauffassung,* 2 vols. (Berlin: Dietz, 1927) is that the major determinant of class is ownership of the means of production and the surplus value created therein. Consequently, in capitalist society there are two inclusive classes: owners, including industrialists who directly own the factories and the surplus value created by workers, and landowners, who indirectly benefit from them; and workers, including those selling their labor power, and small artisans, craftsmen, and peasants who own means of production but do *not* own and benefit from surplus value created by others. Within each class are groups whose interests may conflict on short-run issues (for example, industrial capitalists versus financiers, skilled versus manual workers).

24. Marx, *The German Ideology,* p. 67.

25. Ibid., p. 50.

26. Ibid., p. 49.

27. Karl Marx, "Letter to Annenkov" (1846), *KMSW,* p. 192.

28. Marx, *The German Ideology,* p. 42.

29. Leszek Kolakowski, *Main Currents of Marxism,* 3 vols. (London: Oxford University Press, 1978), 1: 7-39.

30. Karl Marx, *Capital,* 1: 19-20. See also idem, *The Poverty of Philosophy, KMSW,* pp. 196 and 202.

31. After 1848 trying to balance the urge for revolutionary action—especially among many of his followers—with the necessity for capitalism to mature, Marx vacillated regarding the precise economic and social conditions making a capitalist society ripe for revolution.

32. In the *Critique of the Gotha Programme* (Moscow: Progress Pubs., 1971), Marx recognized the need for an intermediary period between the proletariat revolution and the advent of true socialism. In this transition period economic rights are proportionate to labor, and the proletariat organize themselves into a "dictatorship of the proletariat" to abolish class distinctions forcefully and develop the economy. The full promise of communism is realized only when productive forces are fully developed.

33. See Karl Marx, preface to *A Contribution to the Critique of Political Economy, KMEW,* pp. 425-26.

34. *Grundrisse der kritik der politischen Ökonomie* (English translation by Martin Nicolaus, *Foundations of the Critique of Political Economy*). The three volumes of *Capital* and *The Theories of Surplus Value,* the major works published after *Grundrisse,* are merely fragments of an unrealized original plan expressed in *Grundrisse.*

35. Marx, *Grundrisse,* p. 712.

36. Ibid., p. 241.

37. See, for example, ibid., pp. 270, 324-25, 334-35, and 405-23.

38. Ibid., p. 255.

39. See ibid., p. 106.

40. Applied to historiography, the dialect justifies inquiry that proceeds from

abstract to concrete *and* vice versa. *Grundrisse* defends both. See ibid. pp. 100–08 and 881.

41. Ibid., pp. 94–95.

42. Ibid., p. 750.

43. Engels's major works include: *Der deutsche Bauernkrieg (The German Peasants' War)* (1850); *Herrn Eugen Dührings Umwälzung der Wissenschaft* (known as *Anti-Dühring*) (1878); *The Origins of the Family, Private Property and the State* (1884); and "Ludwig Feuerbach and the End of Classic German Philosophy" in *Die Neue Zeit* (1886). In the early 1870s, Engels began writing a critique of "vulgar" materialism based on a dialectical approach to knowledge. The finished material, some incomplete, was first published in Moscow (1925). Its English title is *Dialectic of Nature.*

44. Friedrich Engels, *Dialectic of Nature* (New York: International Publishers, 1940), p. 266.

45. Engels, *Anti-Dühring* p. 343. See also *Ludwig Feuerbach and the End of Classical German Philosophy* (Moscow: Progress Pubs., 1969).

46. Friedrich Engels, *Anti-Dühring* (Peking: Foreign Language Press, 1976), p. 179. See also pp. 27ff, 150–63, and 165–82.

47. Ibid., p. 30.

48. Friedrich Engels, introduction to English edition of *Socialism: Utopian and Scientific* (1892), in Lewis Feuer (ed.), *Marx & Engels: Basic Writings on Politics & Philosophy* (New York: Anchor Books, 1959), p. 51.

49. "Engels to Conrad Schmidt," ibid., p. 396.

50. "Engels to Joseph Bloch," ibid., p. 397.

51. "Engels to Conrad Schmidt, ibid., p. 407.

52. "Engels to Joseph Bloch," ibid., pp. 397–99.

53. "Engels to Heinz Starkenburg," ibid., p. 410. See also "Engels to Conrad Schmidt," ibid., p. 396.

54. See John Hoffman, *Marxism and the Theory of Praxis* (London: Lawrence & Wishart, 1975), pp. 48–56, and Sebastiano Timpanaro, *On Materialism* (Atlantic Highlands, New Jersey: Humanities Press, 1975), p. 83.

55. George Novack, *Polemics in Marxist Philosophy* (New York: Monad Press, 1978), p. 193. See also Bertell Ollman, *Alienation* (New York: Cambridge University Press, 1971), pp. 53–64.

56. Including Kautsky, Riazanov, and even Max Adler. See Maurice Cornforth, *The Theory of Knowledge* (New York: International Publishers, 1963), for a current analysis of diamat that parallels Engels's.

57. Major works include: *Ökonomische Lehren* (1887) (*The Economic Doctrines of Karl Marx),* a summary of *Capital,* volume one, which served for many years as a primer in Marxist economic theory; four historical works applying his brand of Marxism to a historical analysis of political conflict and ideology; and two theoretical works: *Ethik und materialistische Geschichtsauffassung* (1906) (*Ethics and the Materialist Interpretation of History*), which integrates Darwinism and Marxism; and *Die materialistische Geschichtsauffassung* (1927) (*The Materialist Interpretation of History*), a summary of his mature ideas. He also wrote numerous polemics as well as three critiques of the Russian Revolution.

58. This is Kautsky's "centrist" solution to the reformist and Leninist extremes, begging the question of what the precise role of the proletariat party should be and

avoiding the problem involved in a reformist party maintaining working-class revolutionary intensity.

59. See George V. Plekhanov, *Socialism and the Political Struggle* (1883), and especially *Our Differences* (1885).

60. There were also in Russia strict mechanists who believed theory was superfluous, including Ivan I. Skvortsov-Stepanov, Arkady K. Timiryazev, and Lyubov A. Akselrod.

61. George Plekhanov, *The Development of the Monist View of History* (Moscow: Progress Publishers, 1956), pp. 123–24. See also pp. 124ff and 155, and idem, *Fundamental Problems of Marxism* (New York: International Publishers, 1969), pp. 21 and 57–62.

62. Plekhanov, *Fundamental Problems of Marxism,* pp. 44 and 48ff, and editor's note on pp. 129–30. See also *The Development of the Monist View of History,* pp. 127ff. and 216–18.

63. Z. A. Jordan, *The Evolution of Dialectical Materialism* (London: Macmillan, 1967), pp. 206–7; and Lucio Colletti, introduction to *KMEW,* pp. 8–9. These themes are repeated in Plekhanov's two polemical works, *The Role of the Individual in History* (1898) and *Contributions to the History of Materialism* (1896).

64. See D. Ryazanov, *Karl Marx and Friedrich Engels* (London: Martin Lawrence, 1927), pp. 57–58.

65. See ibid., pp. 60–62; "Explanatory Notes to a revised (1922) Russian edition of *The Communist Manifesto* of K. Marx and F. Engels," pp. 170–76; and D. Ryazanov, *Karl Marx—Man, Thinker, and Revolutionist* (London: Martin Lawrence, 1927), esp. p. 282.

66. Bukharin's other major 'volume is *Imperialism and the World Economy* (1918), based on the pioneering work in political economy done by Hilferding. Bukharin introduced the notion of "state capitalism" into the Communist lexicon. Imperialism and the battle for world markets would force national bourgeoisie to coordinate internal production. As a result, Bukharin claimed that periodic economic crises would occur *between* nations, on an international scale.

67. Including A. M. Deborin, G. S. Tymyansky, I. K. Luppol, V. F. Asmus, N. A. Karev, I. I. Agol, Y. E. Sten—most of whom were caught in Stalin's battles and failed to survive the purges.

68. Nikolai Bukharin, *Historical Materialism* (Ann Arbor, Mich.: University of Michigan Press, 1969), p. 30.

69. See ibid., pp. 74f.

70. Ibid., p. 72.

71. "From the standpoint of Marx and Engels, philosophy has no right to a separate, independent existence, and its material is divided among the various branches of positive science." V. I. Lenin, *Collected Works,* 45 vols. (London: Lawrence & Wishart, 1960–1970), 1: 418.

72. V. I. Lenin, *Materialism and Empirio-Criticism* (Peking: Foreign Language Press, 1972), pp. 34f and 47f.

73. Ibid., pp. 33 and 44.

74. See, for example, Neil McInnes, *The Western Marxists* (New York: Library Press of New York, 1972), pp. 42–43. Kolakowski, *Main Currents of Marxism,* 3: 154; and Jordan, *The Evolution of Dialectical Materialism,* pp. 220–23.

75. Lenin, *Materialism and Empirio-Criticism,* pp. 154–55. See also pp. 38, 48, 106, 133–42, 191–92, and 268–69.

76. V. I. Lenin, *Philosophical Notebooks* (Moscow: Progress Publishers, 1972), p. 361.

77. Ibid., p. 146.

78. Ibid., p. 196.

79. Ibid., p. 363.

80. Ibid., pp. 258 and 212.

81. Ibid., pp. 221–22.

82. Ibid., pp. 183, 171, 180, 182, 195, and 201.

83. Lenin, *Collected Works,* 21: 120. This statement was made in 1915.

84. Ibid., 5: 375.

85. Ibid., p. 384.

86. Ibid., 6: 134ff and 397f.

87. Ibid., 15: 195, and 19: 116 and 501.

88. Joseph Stalin, *Dialectical and Historical Materialism* (New York: International Publishers, 1940).

89. See Leon Trotsky, *In Defense of Marxism* (New York: Pathfinder Press, 1970).

90. See Leon Trotsky, *The Revolution Betrayed* (New York: The Pathfinder Press, 1972).

91. Karel Kosík, *Dialectic of the Concrete.* Two key chapters, from which most of this material is taken, are in *Telos* 11, no. 2 (Fall 1968): 21–37; and 11, no. 3 (Winter 1968): 35–54. Others who share Kosík's project include Robert Havemann (East Germany), the "Petofi Circle" (Hungary), and the "Telos School" (USA), especially Dick Howard, Pier Aldo Rovatti, and Paul Piccone.

92. See *Telos* 11, no. 2 (Fall 1968): 36.

93. *Telos* 11, no. 3 (Winter 1968): 43.

94. Ibid., pp. 49–50.

95. *Telos* 11, no. 2 (Fall 1968): 35.

96. *Telos* 11, no. 3 (Winter 1968): 44.

97. Ibid., p. 51.

98. "Introduction to Karel Kosik," *Telos* 11, no. 2 (Fall 1968): 19–20.

99. Dick Howard, *The Development of the Marxian Dialectic* (Carbondale, Ill.: Southern Illinois University Press, 1972), p. 167; and idem, "Existentialism and Marxism," in *Towards a New Marxism,* ed. B. Grahl and P. Piccone (St. Louis, Mo.: Telos Press, 1973), p. 107.

100. Engels, *Anti-Dühring,* p. 144. See also *Ludwig Feuerbach,* pp. 104–5.

101. Plekhanov, *Fundamental Problems of Marxism,* p. 168. See also pp. 142–46; and *The Development of the Monist View of History,* p. 220. Bukharin concurs; see *Historical Materialism,* pp. 37–39.

102. Sebastiano Timpanaro, *On Materialism,* p. 132. See also idem, *The Freudian Slip* (London: New Left Press, 1976), pp. 173–76.

103. Timpanaro, *On Materialism,* p. 34.

104. Ibid., pp. 43–62.

105. Ibid., p. 62.

106. Ibid., pp. 55–56, 57. See pp. 34 and 80.

107. Ibid., p. 105.

108. Ibid., p. 40.

109. Ibid., p. 69. See pp. 100ff.

110. Ibid., p. 41. Though Lenin was always a materialist (p. 118), the *Notebooks* show an "enthusiasm for certain Hegelian propositions [that] is excessive...." (p. 251)

111. Ibid., p. 23.

112. Ibid., pp. 111–12.

3.

Hegelian Idealism

Despite the efforts of its best theorists, Marxist materialism remains anti-individualistic, denying autonomous subjectivity. This complex issue, however, hides very practical, nonacademic consequences. Marxism in Western Europe responds to perceived evils of maturing capitalism; hence, its practical success depends on successfully wooing intellectuals and workers from a culture that cherishes and procedurally guarantees human autonomy. Materialism effectively explodes the myth that capitalism, *in fact*, secures everyone's basic individual freedoms. However, the factors generating this critique also inhibit Westerners from supporting the materialist alternative. Even oppressed individualists will not readily accept a theory defining subjectivity and freedom passively, molded by uncontrollable matter—trading one form of oppression for another that rejects the foundational ideals of modern Western life. No wonder, then, that orthodox Marxism has unintentionally propelled critical thinkers back into liberalism, where they reform an imperfect system rather than embrace a potential Stalin.

For Marxists this situation is disastrous. Liberalism, despite rhetoric, is elitist, but in advanced capitalism orthodox Marxism actually retards the revolution by frightening workers and intellectuals with talk of "inevitability," "necessity," and "dictatorship." Materialism, threatening all vestiges of personal uniqueness and creativity, seemingly makes liberal democracy worth salvaging. Surprisingly, it works better in economically nondeveloped lands lacking a bourgeois tradition.

In response, Marxists return to Marx, searching for new beginnings. If Marx was a materialist, if truth is objective matter impersonally determining nature and society, then nothing can rescue Marxism from its current predicament. On the other hand, if Marx's truth is an abstract quality—not concrete matter—experienced by thoughtful subjects in propitious material conditions and generating revolutionary activity, then Marxism may be a social theory that reflective Westerners can live with, asserting the primacy of the dialectic's subjective moment. Reflective creativity now mediates concrete and abstract: Thought is now important in itself, not merely as a determined moment in a precognitive material process.

Idealism, as the epistemology of revolutionary Marxism, touches the nerve pulse of Western philosophy, actively involving reflective individuals in the unfolding dialectic. Only human beings can intellectually grasp history's essential structure and act appropriately. Social progress occurs actively, reflectively, without ineluctably sucking in helpless, predetermined conglomerations of matter.

PHILOSOPHICAL IDEALISM

A priori idealism finds social knowledge firmly anchored in abstract, nonmaterial objectivity. Social scientists accumulate knowledge that is real, distinct, and verifiable—subjective intimations of universality. It has taken several different forms in history, depending on its criteria of valid inquiry: intellectualism, where properly trained, rational minds identically cognize universality; spiritualism, where faith, not intellect, taps universality; and instinctualism, where precognitive primal forces generate truth irrespective of ideas or faith.

But idealist Marxism bears the indelible imprint of Friedrich Hegel (1770-1831), whose philosophy spawned the group of radicals from which Marx himself appeared. Hegel questioned the validity of sense perceptions, which glean the appearance of things, not their truth, and chose to reconstruct them critically with the aid of a new logic. The mind's logical concepts are epistemologically prior to empirical experiences, which by themselves supply only false images. However, mind is transpersonal and universal—that is, "Mind"—existing independent of empirical subjectivity as a sum product of absolute truth. This objective, nonmaterial "subject" governs the world's development, including human history. Hegel's idealism thus posits an a priori truth that must and will be cognitively perceived as Mind dynamically materializes in history. Truth, therefore, though cognized by reflective subjects, is *not* a product of subjectivity. The standard materialist critique of Hegelian idealism as "subjectivist" misrepresents Hegel's theory of knowledge and severely distorts the essential contours of idealism.

Hegelianism answers Immanuel Kant's assertion that mind understands the world through a set of categories that organize cognitive experiences, permitting us to experience the world as determinate qualities and relations. Mind's structural categories are fixed and unchanging, an a priori foundation of valid knowledge. Reality, subjectively apprehended, is not reality itself. We never know what things-in-themselves ("noumena") are, because knowledge is what mind conceptualizes ("phenomena") based on its structural constitution.

Hegel rejects two of Kant's basic principles. Since we can't know reality-in-itself, then reality *is* what we experience, and the exotic noumenal world is superfluous. Correlatively, concepts that Kant thinks cannot be experienced (for example, God, the minds of others) *do* exist because we know them as integral parts of the experienced world. Once noumena are discarded, we realize that abstract concepts must be real if cognized. Hegel then rejected Kant's timeless, static, unalterable categories of mind. The history of thought exhibits constantly changing structures for perceiving and understanding the world, each age developing its own. None represent abstract thought as such. The essential structures of thought *are* history's evolving forms of cognition. As humanity becomes conscious of cognitive modes, it understands, criticizes, and eventually transcends them. Hence, essential forms of thinking are expressed by the historical growth of human consciousness into self-consciousness. By rationally comprehending the whole of cognition and history, we constitute a new Reason, an absolute knowledge never before achieved. Hegel's writings tell us how Reason becomes conscious of itself.

Hegel takes the universe that Hume, Kant, and others had analytically split into pieces and reconstitutes it as one dynamic totality in which separate parts are defined by the whole. Fact and value, for example, each express one unifying idea determining the quality of empirical phenomena and the methods used to understand and evaluate them. Although facts are incomplete and empty, Hegel does not deny the reality and wonder of the empirical world. Similarly, though absolute truth is real and determining, he does not believe that subjectivity is passively conditioned. Hegel preserved the richness and variety of both the empirical universe and human subject, but neither is prior and both represent a unifying absolute.

The synthesis is accomplished by allowing Mind to perceive itself in objects, freeing it of the contingency that objects usually impose on subjects. Philosophy, for Hegel, is at home in the world. With Mind including objectivity, each empirical subject can finally abolish alienation from nature and society by experiencing subjectivity and objectivity as moments of Mind's delicate, totalizing unity. A unity that assimilates objective phenomena into universal subjectivity without arbitrarily destroying them. Mind's negation of objectivity is therefore an assimilating negation, what Hegel terms "*Aufheben,*" or "sublation." It preserves objective Being even while assimilating and surpassing it. Hence the "*Aufheben*" is performed not by simply defining Mind to include objectivity, but by an elaborate history disclosing civilization's generation of Absolute Mind. Reason, in other words, describes humanity's historical passage from integration (the original awareness of Mind) to alienation (life influenced by the Judeo-Christian dichotomy of spiritual and secular) and back again. As Reason unfolds, as we become self-conscious of it, alienation ends, and we actively participate in the world as free citizens. With Reason comes freedom, the ability to see truth. Freedom is thus the rational goal of human history, the culmination of Mind's historical journey to self-consciousness.

The Phenomenology of the Spirit traces the history of consciousness from pure self-awareness to absolute knowledge by arguing every historical, human, or natural reality is merely a phase of Mind's development. Mind winds through history toward the realization of its own potential, its existence for itself as absolute self-knowledge. In other words, Mind objectifies itself in history, so that it can eventually eliminate its objectivity and become a sublated object, assimilated by its own self-knowledge. Human reason, like other phenomena, is part of this process. Objective phenomena as well as subjective thoughts are moments of Mind's evolution, hence are rational. Since thoughts are part of the world we think about, truth and meaning are understood only in relation to reality's total process.

The truth of every single being is contained in its concept, realized only when that being unfolds the fullness of its potential and expresses history's hidden meaning (that is, Mind's self-realization). Individual things actualize their own particular truths by realizing their natures or potentials, assimilating their concepts. Seeds evolve into trees, babies to adults, sunlight to warmth, and so on, and truth in each case is the dynamic process of realizing its nature, carrying forward the single process of Mind's historical self-realization. As particular empirical occurrences and/or social theories rise and fall in history, this process is constituted. Presumably, if a movement or idea or object survives, it is reasonable or rational, while its failure indicates the opposite.

Just as each particular being realizes itself in its history, in other words, conforms with its own concept, the Being of Mind (history itself) conforms with its own concept: the self-consciousness of its being. Mind therefore surpasses its objectivized forms and returns to itself as self-awareness, once again conscious of its own truth. Absolute knowledge marks history's origin and culmination, but Mind has not merely reverted to an aboriginal state. Its self-awareness is now part of the process leading to it. It historically objectivizes itself, and then reassimilates (negates) its own objectifications. Each new negation leads Mind to a new developmental stage, preserving what has appeared while absorbing and transforming (synthesizing) it into higher stages. Mind is continually mediated, or differentiated, by its many partial expressions, which are all sublated by the whole process. Hegel's *Logic* studies Mind's categories in their development and interrelationships and sets out the logic by which reason, through a dialectical process of negation and synthesis, culminates in absolute knowledge.

In the *Phenomenology,* Hegel traced Mind's evolution to conscious self-awareness through five historical stages. Beginning with a slave's externalization or alienation of consciousness in objects he is forced to make, Mind unfolds chronologically as: human consciousness apprehending itself as infinite and freeing itself by ignoring external reality (for example, Stoic values); consciousness comprehending the external world through its own idealized concepts (for example, Renaissance values); consciousness becoming reasonable in the narrow sense of recognizing truth in external reality, perceiving the objective world's rational character (for example,

Christianity); and consciousness assimilating Mind, producing absolute knowledge. In this final stage, truth and the understanding of truth unite, bridging intellect (subjectivity) and world (objectivity). Human consciousness has overcome its contingency and finitude through Mind's concrete social mediations, the actual civilizations humanity has lived through. Consciousness is progressively less estranged, until it finally sees the object in itself and itself in the object.

The *Lectures on the Philosophy of History* describes stages in the historical maturation of consciousness, each one expanding human freedom: from the ancient Orient where only a despotic ruler was uncontrolled and hence free, to contemporary Christian-Germanic life where Mind has merged with human cognition, universalizing freedom. As Mind is mediated through human civilizations, each individual can participate in history's rationality only by actively enjoying his particular culture, especially the arts, religion, and philosophy. Only in modern times, however, does Mind self-consciously realize itself, and what distinguishes our civilization is the nation-state. Consequently, the state manifests Mind. Only in and through the state do individuals reconcile themselves to Mind's universal Idea. *The Philosophy of Right* describes the state appearing in history to assimilate progressively, or sublate, the antithetical forces of individuality and community. Representing and surpassing the best of each, the state is the essence of individual liberty and social justice: Its laws objectify Mind, hence unify subjective freedom and objective necessity. The state's civil servants mediate Reason and the everyday affairs of social life. Their decisions and the impersonal state laws that guide them express the collective good. While others maintain private lives, state officials are truth incarnate, immediately representing universality. Public decisions are Mind's concrete pictures and hence reasonable. Although they must be obeyed, Hegel is not willfully advocating totalitarianism. A state predicated only on terror and violence is not a true mediation of subject (citizen) and object (community), not a valid, reasonable ending for history. The state's moral authority indicates humanity's intellectual maturity, generated by history's rational movement. As a reasonable synthesis of individual and community, the state assimilates both, which is impossible in circumstances of unremitting fear and oppression. However, in situations where public and private interests conflict, the former necessarily prevails. Humanity, in other words, is now synonymous with Mind, which is concretized in the state. Good citizens are crystallizations of necessity and truth, reflectively willing freedom by obeying the law.

Personally, Hegel was a conservative and nationalist, but his philosophy can be interpreted in several ways. The *Logic*'s dialectical categories, logically and temporally preceding actual experiences, outline a world whose very existence makes it rational. This translates, then and now, to reverence for the state and the status quo generally, as well as passive obedience to public officials. Conservative Hegelians, emphasizing the *Logic* and the *Philosophy of Right,* include Bossanquet, the Oxford Idealists, and twentieth-century theorists of fascism. But there is another ideological side to Hegel, especially in the *Phenomenology*'s description of dialectics as part of human experience. Although logically prior, the dialectical sublation of concrete reality through negation and synthesis is realized by actual human beings in actions, thoughts, and institutions. The young, or Left, Hegelians emphasized negation, Reason's creative transformation of reality. Reason is never static and congealed. Reasonable citizens think and act decisively, realizing history's potential for universal freedom. Left Hegelianism generated a radical critique of politics and culture, eventually justifying communism.

Prominent members of the Hegelian Left included David Straus, Bruno Bauer, Arnold Ruge, and Moses Hess. Ideologically, it concentrated primarily on religion, penetrating Christian dogma with dialectical reasoning. Bauer, for example, perceived Christianity as absolutized Spirit, totally subordinating subjective will and freedom. Potentially creative individuals are alienated by a deterministic spiritual law, which must be negated. Humanity must return to itself, so that free actions meaningfully express Spirit—in Hegel's terminology, we must recognize the objective in our subjectivity. The negation will cleanse Christianity from public life, permitting free individuals to manifest Spirit voluntarily. Once "Mind" replaces Christian "Spirit," Bauer rejects Christianity altogether. Left Hegelianism eventually abrogated religion from public life, presaging Marx's systematic defense of atheism.

The Left Hegelians eventually extended the critique to politics. Ruge, for example, matured from a Hegelian Protestant and nationalist into a radical pitting dialectical Reason against empirical reality, demanding revolution as the sole means of realizing Mind in the subjective perceptions of German citizens. Living in an authoritarian, religious environment, Left Hegelians as a group desired social activism, the establishment of a republic, universal suffrage on the basis of political equality, civil freedoms— particularly of press and speech—and representative government. Through enlightened education and political freedom, they felt the masses would voluntarily identify public and private interests. A free and open society, in other words, generates universal consciousness in each separate person, history's Reasonable ending. They were not socialists. Like eighteenth-century republicans, they believed that enlightened public policy and political liberties solve all society's problems. Wealth need not be redistributed if Reason rules rich and poor alike.

Moses Hess single-handedly carried Left Hegelianism to socialism. In two major works, *The Sacred History of Mankind* (1837) and *The European Triarchy* (1841), Hess used Hegel's dialectic to justify economic and social equality. As a Hegelian, Hess saw thought and action, freedom and necessity, coalescing when Spirit manifests authentic social agents, each representing a transpersonal essence, a oneness with nature and other people. Nineteenth-century Germany, on the other hand, cultivated artificial boundaries between people, rationalized by religion, private property, and money, which engender isolated, selfish individuals, and symbolize the irrationality of contemporary life. Reason negates this decadent reality through revolutionary activities of enlightened, rational citizens who perceive the identity of personal freedom, social necessity, and perfect human equality. The ensuing state has no rational use for institutionalized religion, private property, money, even politics. Alienation becomes irrelevant when essence and existence are one, when human cooperation is Reasonable. Hess saw this utopia's concrete beginnings in the Germany of his day, particularly in the polarizing of rich and poor. He speculated, well before Marx, that the worsening conditions of impoverished workers would enable them to evaluate reasonably the dominant social myths justifying religion, property, and money. Poverty and exploitation breed rational self-consciousness. By violently rejecting social irrationality, workers act Reasonably and hence are free. The working class, for Hess and Marx, concretizes Reason in institutions of absolute equality and freedom.

Marx's debt to Hess is enormous. Concepts like alienation, species-essence, revolutionary self-consciousness, the unity of theory and practice, and the historical necessity of communism are all in Hess's work, awaiting sophisticated packaging and apposite social conditions. The two collaborated for a time after 1841, but split when Hess rejected *The German Ideology*'s non-Hegelian materialism. Idealist Marxism, by excavating its Hegelian origins, continually rediscovers the revolutionary implications of Hess's idealism.

MARX'S HEGELIAN IDEALISM

Marx's education, after 1835, as a law student at Bonn University included lectures by Eduard Gans, a liberal Hegelian who believed that Mind's ineluctable evolution in history would propel society to socialism. Marx's own early position, as we shall see, falls somewhere between that of the Left Hegelian emphasis on Reasonable critique and the conservative Hegelian glorification of the status quo. The latter was represented, at this time, by Friedrich Karl von Savigny, a professor at Bonn University who stretched conservative Hegelianism into a theory of positive social customs and rules as valid sources of law. Influenced by Gans and Savigny, Marx decided that Mind's permanent negativity simultaneously preserves and expresses empirical reality.

This synthetic project is evident in Marx's doctoral dissertation.[1] Left Hegelians were already interested in post-Aristotelian Greek philosophy, feeling its rejection of classical Panhellenism and Aristotelianism was analagous to their own critique of Napoleon's failure in Europe and Hegel's universal philosophy. The Left Hegelians, especially Bauer, argued that Epicureanism, Cynicism, and Stoicism elevate critical intellect over empirical reality, hence are reasonable in the Hegelian sense. Marx's dissertation compares Epicurus's naturalism and Democritus's atomism and reflects Hegel's logic. Its romantic, sentimental style is not unusual among Left Hegelians but still shocks readers who expect the scientificity of *Grundrisse* or *Capital.*[2] The style and Hegelian content are not unique to the dissertation. Marx also argued, in *Rheinische Zeitung* (1842-1843), against government censorship of the press, declaring "the essence of a free press is the rational essence of freedom in its fullest character,"[3] and then distinguishing "real" states—reflecting essence or nature—and "empirical" states maintained only by force and repression. Only the former guarantee "freedom," the true essence of the state. When states defend only the wealthy, they violate their idea, contradicting and invalidating themselves.

Marx's work during this period from 1839 to 1842, though plainly idealistic, also introduced a significant new theme: Mind transcends empirical facts but is not independent of them. When realized, Mind is inseparably linked to the concrete world. Marx did not, therefore, parrot Hegel or the Left Hegelians, alienating the latter, for example, by arguing that Epicureanism rejects politics and social activism and hence is escapist. Similarly, he parted with Hegel in articles defending freedom of expression as an absolute, without which a state never attains perfection. Reason, in other words, congeals in concrete action based on praxis. In the early writings, praxis is still an abstract ideal, emphasizing universality more than particularity. However, in the *1844 Manuscripts* Marx refined praxis to a point where it becomes the primary receptacle of Reason, Mind's outlet in the concrete everyday world. Through praxis, Marx pulls Spirit into individual subjects, obliterating Hegel's separation of thought and action, knowledge of history and history itself. Marx was dissatisfied with Hegel's overly abstract essentialism. Without rejecting idealism, he turned essence into a subjectively relevant quality consciously perceived and expressed by people living in real economic and social conditions. Rational empirical conditions coincide with the liberated consciousness of history's human agents. Praxis is rational in reflecting both the empirical life-world and universal truth.

In the *Introduction to a Critique of Hegel's Philosophy of Right* (1843) and *On the Jewish Question* (1843) Marx upbraided Hegel for starting from abstract rather than concrete categories and ignoring links between the "political" state (that is, the sphere of universal, shared interests, "Reasonable" in the Hegelian sense) and "civil" society (the everyday work world). As the concrete expression of Reason, the state epitomizes universal freedom. Marx favored democratizing political life, including disestablishing state religions, equalizing citizens' rights, and universalizing suffrage— allowing everyone to participate meaningfully in political activities and hence realizing the state's essence. But Marx quickly emphasized, especially in *On the Jewish Question,* that political emancipation that ignores economic and social realities produces only an illusory and rhetorical sense of universality, invalidating the state's historical purpose. Political freedoms mean little to people struggling in oppressive, dehumanizing conditions. They are concerned with material survival, not rationality as an essence embodied in the state. In these conditions they cannot think and act reasonably and are denied their promised freedom. Oppressive economic and social conditions make humanity selfish and irrational, deflecting history's natural evolution toward universal freedom and making praxis inconceivable. Real emancipation requires that the state's universality simultaneously be expressed in actual everyday conditions. Praxis appears historically when concrete conditions become Reasonable, reflecting humanity's collective interests. Our essential nature, or "species-essence," is then realized politically as well as economically. Freedom is finally achieved only when politics and civil society become two inseparable aspects of one essential historical truth. While Marx rejected private property in civil society, in 1843 he did not yet argue explicitly for its abolition. Nor did he describe class struggle as the distinguishing feature of bourgeois civil life or the concrete expression of Reason's march in history. Like Feuerbach and the utopian socialists, Marx still believed that truth is self-evident to reflective people, generating a utopia where essential humanity is expressed in equitable economic, social, and political institutions. Emancipation, in all spheres, appears only when "the lightning of thought has struck deeply into this virgin soil of the people."[4]

The *1844 Manuscripts* analyzes alienation as being due to irrational concrete conditions of bourgeois civil society, which block praxis. Marx distinguished Hegel's "objectification" (*"Vergegenstandlichung"*) and "alienation" (*"Entfremdung"*). The former describes human subjects producing artifacts or ideas that represent a historical stage of self-consciousness and presumes the separation of subject and object. Culture is the accumulation of human objectifications, the self-conscious preconceptions of an entire people. Objectifications thus represent finite indications of Mind's development as it passes through qualitative stages, each negating itself and being sublated by a higher one. In sum, labor "objectifies" an actor in produced objects, and these express Mind's materialization in history. Labor is therefore mental or intellectual, encompassing self-consciousness as part of Mind's historical process. Alienation, for Hegel, is identical to objectification and hence an existential necessity. To be known, self-consciousness must objectify itself in ideas and things. It is observed only in its creations, which are outside of subjectivity. Culture is therefore necessarily estranged from subjective creators. Alienation ends when objectification is self-consciously surpassed, Mind fully realizing itself in history and subjects recognizing self-consciousness in the unfolding layers of objects and ideas. When we reflectively perceive historical Reason, when subject and object merge in absolute Mind, we sublate both objectification and alienation. Objects and ideas become aspects of Mind and subjectivity. At this historical moment the objective world—including nature—is reabsorbed into human essence, a sublation accomplished in an abstract, intellectual sphere not directly related to concrete civil conditions.

Marx cut the link connecting objectification and alienation. Men and women cannot survive without objectifying themselves, that is, creatively laboring in nature to satisfy basic needs. However, labor is a sensuous physical interaction with nature, not an abstract mental activity, producing the civil conditions within which we self-consciously perceive human essence. The concrete phenomena we need to perfect ourselves—tools, land, other people, technology, energy, and so on—exist in nature independent of subjectivity. Laboring makes natural things serve human needs, in this sense only transcending them. Contrary to Hegel, we cannot transcend objectivity itself. Labor, or objectification, is not necessarily alienated. Since it is a practical, physical praxis involving a needy subject and an objective environment—not merely abstract self-cognition—we are integrated with objective reality when it satisfies practical needs and do not intellectually assimilate or sublate it. Objectification becomes alienation only when society prevents us from realizing human essence. Alienation, in other words, occurs in historical and social settings which hinder Reasonable actions, eliminating labor as praxis. Marx's alienation is a social condition produced by active human beings, terminated merely by rationalizing these alienating civil conditions. The *1844 Manuscripts* describes the circumstances under which objectification turns into alienation, and the civil requisites of fulfilling, nonalienating objectification. Like earlier writings, the *Manuscripts* anchors Hegel's abstract Mind in concrete economic and social factors. However, Marx, like Hegel, contended that humanity dialectically perfects itself in history through labor, and more importantly, that human essence culminates history's dialectical process. This essence expresses an unfolding Idea or Reason. Though cognized only in rational conditions, it is still an abstract, idealized quality transcending and defining these conditions.

In the *Manuscripts,* humanity exists neither outside the world, isolated from it, nor as a homogenized, passively predetermined remnant of nature. Labor, the distinctive human attribute, keeps us always in contact with nature, creating, satisfying needs, modifying reality to produce life's necessities. But the objects of human need, those natural things we work on, exist independently. Humanity, in other words, actively creates and passively receives objective nature; is dialectically open to the world, defining and simultaneously being defined by it. Perception combines objective nature and subjective praxis. Similarly, consciousness creatively reflects an objective, nonreflective world. Truth, neither objective nor subjective, is generated by free subjects bending an independent, inescapable world to suit real needs. Marx calls this a "naturalist" and "humanist" epistemology.[5]

Despite reviling fixed "human natures," what Marx called in the *Theses on Feuerbach* "internal, dumb generalit[ies]," Marx's naturalism is clearly Hegelian to the extent that humanity's "openness" to nature is endemic to human "being." Humanity's "essence," or "species-being," is an ideal or pure state where subjects relate to environments creatively, via labor. Indeed, it is not "fixed," for it materializes only when we live in rational conditions, which evolve dialectically according to Reason's own logic. Every era defines humanity based on its stage of development. Humanity self-consciously recognizes itself as "open" to nature and capable of praxis only at a certain developmental stage. Though essence is not fixed, its reality transcends subjective cognition and concrete sociohistorical conditions. It exists as human potential—the purest stage of human self-realization —in every era, patiently awaiting inevitable cognition and relevant actions. "Species-essence" is therefore an a priori category subjectively realized when history's rational evolution is complete. Marx alters Hegelianism by emphasizing the concrete aspects of freedom, but leaves untouched the idealist belief in a human essence evolving in history dialectically and necessarily cognized by reasonable people.

There are two aspects to Marx's "spiritual essence" ("*Wesen*").[6] First, humans are essentially conscious, cognitive creatures reflectively perceiving and creatively modifying nature. We fashion ideas and institutions to suit experienced needs. "Man makes his life activity itself an object of his will and consciousness. He has conscious life activity. . . . Conscious life activity directly distinguishes man from animal life activity. Only because of that is he a species-being. Or rather, he is a conscious being, i.e. his own life is an object for him, only because he is a species-being. Only because of that is his activity free activity."[7] Second, humanity is essentially "open" to nature and society, arenas where we pursue projects and satisfy needs by laboring. Nature and society are "in" humanity, and humanity is "in" them. As self-realized, perfected, essential human beings, we embody independent worlds, which we "humanize" by reflection and labor. Hence, social actors recognize their needs as identical to those of nature and of other actors: Humans are essentially "communal" and "natural." By satiating "personal" interests, we also meet the needs of all humanity and realize nature's splendor and promise. Marx illustrates this by describing man's essentially "natural" connection to woman. The quality of this relationship is a barometer of empirical society's freedom and humanity, for crystallized, it "demonstrates the extent to which man's *needs* have become *human* needs, hence the extent to which the *other*, as a human being, has become a need for him, the extent to which in his most individual existence he is at the same time a communal being." In a nonsexual sense, (wo)man, as species-essence, exists for other (wo)men, and they for him (her).

Society is therefore the perfected unity in essence of man with nature, the true resurrection of nature, the realized naturalism of man and the realized humanism of nature. ... My *own* existence *is* social activity. Therefore what I create from myself I create for society, conscious of myself as a social being. ... My *universal* consciousness is only the *theoretical* form of that whose *living* form is the *real* community, society. ... universal consciousness—as activity—is my theoretical existence as a social being.[8]

Essential humanity is "particular individual" and "ideal totality," a unity of opposites that realizes both. Marx leaves little doubt this unity is an abstract, idealized category of being. Man's "feelings, passions, etc., are not merely anthropological characteristics in the narrower sense, but are truly *ontological* affirmations of his essence. ... "[9]

Though ideal, Marx's species-being appears in history only when concrete conditions are oppressive, generating reflective thought and action. Moreover, the most economically deprived group stands to gain the most from this critical reevaluation and hence is likely to initiate it. Consequently, by improving social conditions and satisfying needs, workers represent the whole of society. Human essence materializes in authentic proletarian self-consciousness.[10] A society meeting workers' needs is universally free. Only communism subordinates narrow self-interest to the objective requirements of humanity and nature. It is "the true *appropriation* of the *human* essence through and for men; it is the complete restoration of man to himself as a *social,* i.e. human being. ... "[11]

Alienation, for Marx, distinguishes populations that have not yet become species-beings. Since communism supplies propitious surroundings for authentic self-consciousness, noncommunist societies are all, to some degree, alienated. Although species-being appears in precommunist society as critical reflection, only united class action will generate apposite, nonalienated communist conditions.

There is a material component to species-being, but it also represents an abstract, cognized ideal. Moreover, capitalism does not cause alienation: "although private property appears as the basis and cause of alienated labour, it is in fact its consequence. ... It is only when the development of private property reaches its ultimate point of culmination that this its secret re-emerges: namely, that it is a) the *product* of alienated labour and b) the *means* through which labour is alienated, the *realization of this alienation.*"[12] Alienation is not, for Marx, a predetermined state caused by matter. A materialist, on the other hand, interprets abstractions like "essence" and "reflective" cognition as gibberish.

Though essentiality precedes matter, Marx also recognizes that capitalism's relationship to alienation "later ... becomes reciprocal."[13] Maturing capitalism autonomously reinforces the imperfect condition from which it arose. The material component of alienation, in other words, increasingly perpetuates oppression. Hence the individualism, self-interest, and greed of the capitalist marketplace mold bourgeois ideology, and are Marx's themes, especially in the *Manuscripts,* for understanding humanity's distorted connection to nature and society.

Alienation grows simultaneously in several dimensions. Since commodities are transformed through market mechanisms into money, we slowly lose contact with created products, which are transformed into autonomous objects whose value is independent of the labor they embody. They are isolated or estranged from creators. Species-beings labor to fulfill themselves and satisfy needs: Objectification unifies subject and object, creativity and objective necessity. As capitalist wage labor, however, objects are autonomous and we, the creators, observe helplessly as "natural laws" of the marketplace turn them into profit. "The object that labor produces, its product, stands opposed to it as *something alien,* as a power independent of the producer. . . . [T]he more powerful the alien, objective world becomes which he brings into being over against himself, the poorer he and his inner world become, and the less they belong to him."[14] The laboring act itself is soon vulgarized into impersonal activity, justified only by the money it generates. Labor "is therefore not the satisfaction of a need but a mere *means* to satisfy needs outside itself." Human activity, whose product belongs to an employer, is estranged from the actors. By purchasing workers' productive time with wages, employers now own both the commodity and the labor producing it. Consequently, "the spontaneous activity of the human imagination, the human brain, and the human heart detaches itself from the individual and reappears as the alien activity of a god or of a devil, so the activity of the worker is not his own spontaneous activity. It belongs to another, it is a loss of self."[15]

The dismal effects of estranged labor pervert our essential openness to nature and society. Existence becomes static and closed, isolated individuals doing whatever is necessary to survive. This invariably includes selling oneself as a worker-commodity, which only accelerates the original process of estrangement. Actors are transformed into objects without the unique traits distinguishing humanity from other living forms. We adopt salaried social roles and the appropriate dress, language, demeanor, and expectations. Dynamic species-being is mutilated by internalized personality packages. We inauthentically, naively *become* a social role and then helplessly agonize over our inability to sustain meaningful relationships of honesty, communication, and love. Moreover, alienated self-abusement further isolates us from neighbors, friends, and family: "when man confronts himself he also confronts *other* men. What is true of man's relationship to his labour, to the product of his labour and to himself, is also true of his relationship to other men, and to the labour and the object of the labour of other men."[16] Natural connections between people are severed. We view others as competitors or enemies, vying for the wages everyone seeks. We are immune to human suffering because we fear care's consequences in a society based on self-interest. "Looking out for number one" and "doing my own thing" rhetorically justify a life-style turned in on itself, where workers either win or lose as individuals and compassion is tantamount to defeat. In a world like this everything and everybody are tools for self-advancement. We choose friends and lovers as one might a flattering neck-tie. Nature is also an enemy or opponent, an autonomous realm awaiting conquest and exploitation. We dispassionately rape it of resources, generating profit without considering the devastating ecological consequences, which are noticed only when threatening to undermine the rampant, uncontrolled industrialization that is their source. In nature and society "the intention to plunder, to deceive, inevitably lurks in the background for, since our exchange is self-interested on . . . [both sides] we must necessarily strive to deceive each other."[17]

Alienation, for nonidealist Marxists, is humanity's subjugation by its own material products and institutions. Capitalism, a concrete social and economic system, conditions alienation. Marx, even in the early years, recognized this. The *Manuscripts,* for example, critically analyzes profit, accumulation, rent, production, division of labor, and money as alienating features of bourgeois life. *On the Jewish Question* and particularly *Excerpts from James Mill's "Elements of Political Economy"* (1844) focus on the alienating consequences of money (a "veritable God," "the economic judgement on the morality of man"), wage labor, credit, and banking. Estrangement, Marx implies, is expressed in actual human relationships and concrete material conditions of capitalism. However, Marx also suggested that alienation is more than its material capitalist features. It is conceptually measured by idealized species-being, as the negation of human potential in concrete material conditions. Materialist Marxists entirely ignore two salient and obvious points. First, alienation precedes capitalism and causes it. Second, humanity's essential state, or "objective being," is open to nature and society.[18] The former implies that reflective self-perceptions mature in history and cause new social and economic forms. The latter interprets capitalism as inhibiting self-realization and fulfillment. Oppression is measured by the extent that capitalism inhibits our subjectively perceiving essential, nonmaterial truth. Together, they express the Hegelian notion of Reason historically realizing itself in reflective self-consciousness.

After 1844 Marx abandoned Hegelian terminology to analyze the material components of alienation fully. This represents a change in emphasis, not substance. He had already acknowledged, explicitly in the *Manuscripts* and implicitly in several earlier works, the reciprocity of bourgeois institutions and human alienation. The decision to stress matter is probably the result of his desire to separate scientific from utopian socialism, which propagates a moral ideal associated with enlightened interclass cooperation. Marx now believed that socialism appears only from the revolutionary clash of social classes, which occurs in history when workers self-consciously recognize common objective interests. He rejected utopian sentiments that obscure revolution's necessity and advocate political reformism. Reasonable proletarian action precludes interclass cooperation. However, alienation always remains a central feature of Marx's work because he continually presumed that humanity is "truly" something beyond its alienated, empirical being. Without this ideal standard alienation is a meaningless term, and it is impossible to make any sense of Marx's references to bleak, oppressive, unfulfilled lives in capitalism. Working-class life would be "natural" in the same sense in which Marx had earlier used this term: objectively, impersonally real, and hence justified by its very existence. Writing for the *New York Daily Tribune* (14 July 1853) well after what materialists term his misguided infatuation with Hegel, Marx lauded the "spirit" of the revolutionary masses, which lifts them from a normal working-class life as "apathetic, thought-less, more or less well-fed instruments of production . . . a heart-broken, a weak-minded, a worn-out irrestible mass whose self-emancipation would prove as impossible as that of the slaves of Ancient Greece and Rome."[19] Marx referred to humanity's "emancipation" from alienation to authenticity, now being squashed by capitalism. The concept of species-being, if not the words, is a necessary premise of Marx's comment. Materialists naively ignored the subtlety of Marx's dialectic, focusing entirely on the one-dimensional, nonspeculative terminology from the post-1844 work. Pre-dictably, Marx's revolutionary spark was eventually snuffed out entirely as materialism evolved into Kautskyist reformism. The dialectical tricks of Lenin, Kosík, and others are futile substitutes for Marx's belief in the reinvigoration of human spirit. Marxism, a social theory expressed for tactical reasons in several idioms, is always faithful to its Hegelian heritage.

Marx's later writings substantiate this. *The German Ideology* outlines the undesirable consequences of an unnatural division of labor on worker consciousness. As work becomes specialized, we conjure an impersonal and indomitable history, tyrannizing its creators. Marx and Engels want us to abolish the division of labor and create a society where individuals are not locked into one form of work, where they intellectually and emotionally fulfill themselves while producing needed social goods. This is possible when workers self-consciously manage the productive apparatus, reasserting their control of history and subjecting social and economic development to human authority. "Only at this stage does self-activity coincide with material life, which corresponds to the development of individuals into complete individuals and the casting-off of all natural limitations."[20] The *Communist Manifesto* (1848) describes the "selling" of workers "piecemeal . . . like every other article of commerce." Workers are asked to replace capitalism with an association "in which the free development of each is the condition for the free development of all,"[21] the distinctive trait of what Marx earlier called species-being and later—in *Wage-Labour and Capital* (1849)—"the manifestation of . . . [human] life." The latter analyzes capitalism as a concrete productive process that estranges humanity from creative labor, our "life-activity."[22] *Grundrisse,* which typifies Marx's seasoned outlook, concentrates on the interpenetrating processes of capitalist production and the loss of authenticity. The old themes of alienation, man as a social being, communism as humanity's fulfillment, and reflective perception generating history's dialectical movement are all clearly reasserted.

Marx was unhappy with the labor theory of value, which represents the best of classical bourgeois political economy. Value is determined, according to classical theory, by the average labor time embodied in a commodity. Marx felt that the underlying presupposition, which unknowingly shapes this theory, was the bourgeois principle of individual equality. Value is determined by labor time rather than real workers because there is no reason to distinguish between workers. What is problematic for bourgeois economists, however, is the value of labor itself. Two explanations emerge. One equates the value of labor and wages. But in capitalism, labor's product obviously has more value than wages; hence, the value of labor as output is greater than the value of labor as wages. There must be some source of value other than labor. The familiar triumvirate of "land, labor, and capital" is capitalism's solution to this vexing problem of value. Marx was dissatisfied because it exalts abstract, impersonal productive forces as sources of value, further estranging workers from the world they create. The second theory equates the value of labor and the product's value. However, the implication—damning for capitalists—is that workers are not paid the value of their labor. Few self-respecting bourgeois economists (Ricardo is one exception) acknowledge such a blatant defense of worker exploitation. Marx felt that neither proffered theory adequately explains capitalist accumulation or the growth of commodity exchange value, forcing bourgeois economists to avoid altogether questions of value and concentrate instead on market forces and the fluctuation of commodity prices.

Grundrisse surpassed bourgeois alternatives by striking directly at the concept of commodity. Classical political economy justifies capitalism by assuming that all things by nature are commodities, and all commodities by nature are "things." When applied to labor these assumptions transform workers into objects to be used and discarded like any other commodity. Marx claimed that labor is not a thing: "it . . . [does] not exist as a thing, but as the capacity of a living being."[23] When sold as a commodity to capitalists, labor is human power and creativity. The question "what is the value of labor?" is misstated. Labor is activity; it creates value and is itself invaluable, measurable only by time. The commodity that workers sell to capitalists is the "right of disposition" over labor power, enabling them to determine how it will be used.[24] While working, we are slaves, and employers are masters. Capitalism, whose labor theory of value rhetorically postulates human liberty and equality, in practice brutally denies these principles. Marx replaces the term "labor" with "labor power," preserving the bourgeois principle of the determination of value by working time, while simultaneously explaining capitalist accumulation (that is, labor power produces "surplus value"[25]). As capitalists grow wealthier from the surplus value produced by labor power, the relative condition of workers deteriorates to the point where revolution becomes the only rational response.

Alienation, in *Grundrisse,* is based on the inhuman consequences of commodity labor, workers selling labor power to 'the highest bidder. "It is clear, therefore, that the worker cannot become rich in this exchange, since, in exchange for his labouring capacity as a fixed, available magnitude, he surrenders its *creative power,* like Essau his birthright for a mess of pottage. Rather, he necessarily impoverishes himself . . . because the creative power of his labor establishes itself as the power of capital, as an *alien power* confronting him."[26] Marx devoted the following pages in *Grundrisse,* as well as most of *Capital'*s three volumes, to delineating the empirical processes involved in capitalism's exploitation of labor.[27] By juxtaposing alienation and capitalist production, Marx emphasized their dialectical interpenetration, the unity of subject and object. However, Marx's dialectic was grounded in a Hegelian idea: the essential human quality, lost in alienation, that is realized first in reflective proletariat consciousness and then in revolutionary action. Were this ideal lacking, the concrete processes of exploiting labor power could not "impoverish" workers, destroying their "creative powers." The notion of species-being is implicit in *Grundrisse.*

But Marx opted for revised terminology that downplays latent Hegelianism. *Grundrisse* replaces "species-being" with two types or styles of human existence: "private individual" and "social individual."[28] The former is alienated: Private individuals own things rather than act dynamically, and have a matching life-style. Capitalists, for example, own factories and live only to maximize profit. Workers own labor power and strive to sell this commodity for the highest available wage. Private individuals are free to pursue business, but this freedom is distorted and perverse and is "at the same time the most complete subjugation of all individual freedom, and the most complete subjugation of individuality under social conditions which assume the form of objective powers, even of overpowering objects—of things independent of the relations among individuals themselves."[29] It is, in other words, inauthentic freedom generated by dehumanizing capitalism. Private individuals will not survive the abolition of private property. "Social individuals" are emancipated, exhibiting an authentic, universal humanity. They are well developed in terms of laboring skills and sensitivity to the needs of others, recognizing the essential "mutual interconnection . . . the social connection between persons." As self-realized human beings, they are open to nature and society and free to act creatively. Freedom, therefore, manifests human labor; the social individual appears as "the full development of activity itself . . . [T]he absolute working-out of his creative potentialities." Real freedom requires grasping truth, not merely earning money, and hence is a "most intense exertion" that transforms us into nonalienated, creative subjects.[30] It replaces capitalism with humane institutions that work for the common good. Communism thus realizes essential humanity. Whether one calls this "species-being" or "social individual" is less important than recognizing the philosophical unity of the *Manuscripts* and *Grundrisse*.

Marx continued, in *Capital,* to emphasize the material aspects of alienation. Labor power alone produces value. Commodities, therefore, represent the value of the labor power that goes into producing them. To gain a profit, capitalists employ human labor and pay them less than the value they produce. Workers oblige by selling labor power in the marketplace, turning human labor into a commodity. *Capital* defines two modes of laboring: abstract and concrete. Labor is abstract when it produces commodities that generate a profit for the capitalist in the open market. Marx called this laboring to produce "exchange value." Labor is concrete when creating products needed by humanity, producing "use value." Capitalism is motivated by the drive to constantly increase exchange value. Hence human activity is nonhuman, creating things that satisfy capitalists' self-interest, not real human needs.

From the back door of material process we thus enter the *Manuscripts'* alienated reality. Wage labor reduces workers to dehumanized commodities whose market worth is determined by impersonal laws of supply and demand. Behind the rhetoric of universal freedom and equality, bourgeois society drains its working citizens of uniqueness. Like ham hocks and Harlequins, workers are bought and sold at predetermined prices. Because they are the property of others, at least for the duration of the working day, the laboring act is beyond worker control. They perform as directed or forfeit their means of subsistence. Creativity is, for most of us, an abstraction relevant only to the commercial art and theater markets. Commodities reflect the pecuniary needs of an elite rather than social prerequisites for a decent, humane existence. They are, in this respect, antisocial. Workers suffer a similar plight. They perceive each other as competitors only, vying for an adequate means of material subsistence. They produce without knowing or caring what is socially needed, unaware that their separate labors yield products that society needs to sustain itself. Because, as *Capital* puts it, individual labor is part of social labor, the time spent producing exchange value is time denied humanity. The workers' product, in sum, is transformed "into value that sucks up the value-creating power, into means of subsistence that buy the person of the labourer, into means of production that command the producers."[31]

Despite frequent use of the word "alienation," Marx continued in *Capital* the post-1844 project of purposely minimizing abstract terms. Hence, we search vainly for descriptions of praxis, human essence, species-being, fulfillment, and so on. He even abandoned the concept of "social being,"

Grundrisse's substitute for species-being. What we find, instead, is the introduction of yet another term, "fetishism" or "reification" ("*Versachlichung,*" "*Verdinglichung*"), which is conceptually identical to alienation. In laboring to produce commodities, "a definite relation between men . . . assumes . . . the fantastic form of a relation between things. . . . This I call the Fetishism which attaches itself to the products of labour, so soon as they are produced as commodities. . . . " Since the fetishism of commodities originates in "the production of commodities," the social character of labor in capitalism, alienation has again been pulled from the Hegelian heavens back down to matter. All noneconomic, that is political, religious, aesthetic, emotional, and similar aspects of alienation are rooted in the debilitating consequences of our social roles as wage labor. As long as these remain constant, advances in science, technology, or administration will only further bury us in misery.

Commodity fetishism encompasses the dehumanized world of the *Manuscripts,* despite emphasizing its connections to actual economic processes. It describes, like the *Manuscripts,* our loss of control over a world we create. Capitalism ossifies the social character of individual labor and the labor theory of value, severing humanity's natural connections to, and control over, the external world. Estranged from produced commodities and productive acts, we perceive these as autonomous social entities governed by impersonal, uncontrollable market forces. We become "mechanical automatons," helplessly confronting instruments of production that take the form of capital, "dead labour that enslaves the power of living labour and pumps it dry." Machines become masters while human beings are replaceable commodities, dutifully, unthinkingly producing surplus value for capitalists. In a brutal reversal of priorities, capitalism is historically realized as "material relations between persons and social relations between things. . . . Commodity fetishism, then, is the inability of human beings to see their own products for what they are, and their unwitting consent to be enslaved by human power instead of wielding it."[32]

The theme of alienation in the young Marx was consistently developed and refined in later, more empirical works, including *Grundrisse, Capital,* and *Theories of Surplus Value.* For tactical reasons, the mature Marx emphasized its concrete aspects, especially capitalist economic processes that transform creative laborers into dead commodities. This is less a change of direction than a shrewd emphasis on one moment of a dialectical totality, whose importance is explicitly acknowledged well before the publication of *The German Ideology,* considered by some a watershed in Marx's thinking. His lifework is a unity that emphasizes one or another of many interrelated factors in order to meet changing exigencies. The Hegelian foundation of alienation is therefore an unspoken but unavoidable and necessary component of all of Marx's writings. Unless an a priori ideal measures actual conditions in bourgeois society, we can never be certain what we are alienated from, and the term is superfluous. Had this been Marx's intention, he surely would have abandoned it altogether rather than making it a primary, lifelong theme. "How," in other words, "could Marx use (in *Capital*) the concept of the 'crippled man' if he did not have a concept of a 'model of human nature' which could be crippled."[33] Marx's answer is clear and forthright to anyone willing to think dialectically:

Modern industry, indeed, compels society, under penalty of death, to replace the detail-worker of today, *crippled* by the life-long repetition of one and the same trivial operation, and thus reduced to the *mere fragment of a man,* by the *fully developed individual,* fit for a variety of labours, ready to force any change of production, and to whom the different social functions he performs, are but so many modes of giving free scope to his *natural* and acquired *powers.*[34]

If capitalism makes us "fragments" of "natural" selves, then when "fully developed," we realize an existence that transcends capitalism as an ideal or essential "telos." Though suppressed by capitalism and nourished in communism, these material processes do not "cause" its disappearance or emergence. As "telos" it is realized cognitively before practically. The economic laws of capitalism that Marx studied so extensively in later works allow workers to cognize human potential and act rationally. Revolutionary praxis is the dialectical expression of human reason. It is an autonomous moment in the process of social change.

The epistemological foundation of Marx's dialectical social theory is an idealism whose roots are Hegelian. Several significant developments in the style and content of Marx's mature work have misled most Marxist scholars into chopping Marx's ideas into chronological stages and naively degrading the early ones. Through a new idiom (including phrases such as "labor theory of value," "labor power," "surplus value," "abstract and concrete labor," "wage labor as a commodity," "social being," "fetishism," "exchange value," and "use value") Marx refines ideas that originated before 1846 as "praxis," "species-being," "essence," and "alienated labor." Marx also changes the locus of activities that are a function of the term "labor." In the early writings, labor is a creative act that characterizes (potentially) all human activity. Later, especially in *Grundrisse* and *Capital,* labor becomes synonymous with the alienated work of capitalism, not the creative freedom we are promised in communism. *Grundrisse,* for example, promises the "abolition of labor" among social individuals, and *Capital* sees freedom beginning "where that labour which is determined by need and external purposes ceases; it is therefore, by its very nature, outside the sphere of material production proper."[35] What remains constant, however, throughout these changes in emphasis, idiom, and definition is a belief in humanity's essential connections to nature and society. In appropriate, historically conditioned material conditions—which Marx described at great length after 1846—we perceive the interpenetration of subject and object, and rebel against capitalism's institutionalized inhumanity. History, therefore, is evolving toward human freedom, realized in the revolutionary praxis of reasonable actors. Its tool is the working class, for their tragic suffering is the impetus to correct thinking and apt revolutionary action. Freedom and necessity coalesce in an essential truth cognitively experienced by reasonable workers at a mature stage of capitalist development.

HEGELIAN IDEALIST MARXISM

Hegelian idealist Marxism flourished in the 1920s among Marxists opposed to the mechanistic determinism of the Second International. They attacked orthodox materialism for incorrectly separating matter and spirit, transforming the latter into a mechanical reflection of the former. Materialism had become a metaphysics of nature and society, defining workers as homunculi whose thoughts impersonally reflect economic processes. Humanity and nonhuman natural phenomena are both conditioned by matter's universal dialectical laws. Revolution occurs when capitalism's economic base experiences the first tremors of instability, causing workers to recognize objective interests and socialism's inevitability. Orthodox Marxism, in other words, dehumanizes workers even while advocating their emancipation. In the aftermath of World War I, when worker solidarity dissolved into national patriotism and proletariat revolution into reformism, Marxists began searching for a new identity. Orthodoxy blindly ignored a trite but basic truism: the working-class revolution cannot materialize without workers. By resurrecting spirit and human essence and emphasizing subjective cognition, idealist Marxism aspired to winning workers' allegiance and strengthening the proletariat revolutionary movement throughout industrialized Europe.

Labriola

The origins of idealist neo-Marxism go back to the work of Antonio Labriola (1843–1904). A professional philosopher whose early work shows no traces of Marxism or socialism, Labriola's later years yield an unorthodox brand of orthodox Marxism, which vacillates between materialist determinism and Hegelianism.[36] His dissatisfaction with materialism was probably the result of his cultural background. Because of the church's pervasive influence in Italy, bourgeois reformers and socialists were allied in struggling to secularize society. This opened each side to the other's values and produced a Marxism more atuned to liberal traditions and more sympathetic to Italian patriots such as Garibaldi and Giordano Bruno. Italian philosophy generally has always rejected scientism in favor of global thinking that combines spirit, existence, and history into a universal theory. Labriola, like most Italian philosophers, related social phenomena to grand historical totalities, and his mature concern with worker oppression and social injustice was probably popular with non-Marxian reformers as well.

Labriola viewed praxis in a Hegelian light. Human history consists of free action self-consciously reflecting history's rational evolution. Praxis, in other words, is reflective, reasonable action simultaneously expressing subjective contingency and historical necessity, a unified totality encompassing object and subject: "in speaking of praxis from the integral point of view we imply the overcoming of the opposition between theory and practice as it is vulgarly conceived."[37] The significance of subjectivity in this grand historical totality generates a critical assessment of orthodox materialism. Because actual history is "the work of man," not an impersonal, determining process, there are no valid universal historical laws. History is marked by progress and regression, depending on the reasonableness of human activities. Although progress is effectively catalogued by Marx's science of historical materialism, Marxism is interpretive rather than inherent in history, which is lived and created subjectively. Labriola's Marxism is not "a great plan or . . . design, but it is merely a method of research and of conception." Though evidently socialism will follow capitalism, the future is basically undecided and unpredictable as long as people are capable of praxis. The arrogance and self-assuredness of Engels, Kautsky, and Plekhanov had no basis in the recent factual history of European workers. "The whole course of human events . . . represents neither the tendency to realize a predetermined end nor the deviation of a first principle from perfection and felicity."[38]

Labriola saw history unfolding organically, as a total whole or unity of opposites generating reasonable praxis. He rejected the orthodox dichotomy of reality into base and culture. Each historical factor (for example, economics, politics, religion, and so on) exists only conceptually. History's organicism means "economics" cannot be the prime "cause" of historical progress because it doesn't really exist autonomously. Knowledge cannot be fragmented into isolated facts or disciplines without distorting the reality it explains. Dialectics illustrates the complex mediations comprising each artificial discipline that facilitates inquiry. Hence we can't simply follow "the deductive road from the economic situation to all the rest."[39]

This provocative form of dialectical inquiry generates two principles that are anathema to orthodoxy: nationalism and religion. Labriola was an ardent Italian nationalist and a strong advocate of establishing a Polish homeland. The emotionalism surrounding the national issue was an irreducible and important component of Italian working-class self-consciousness. If naively reduced to economics, it would distort reality, which is epistemologically and tactically foolish. Moreover, there is nothing inherently regressive about nationalism. It can, at times, be useful for organizing workers into an effective strike force. Labriola is more ambiguous about the social role of religion. He adamantly refuses to believe, however, that it is solely an instrument of class mystification and illusion. This orthodox simplification, by substituting materialist reductionism for dialectics, violates history's subjective component and, like capitalism, dehumanizes workers.

Despite morsels of apostasy, Labriola exhibited neither the inclination nor perhaps the ability to inflate his theory into a viable alternative to materialism. His remarks on dialectics, religion, and nationalism were meant to correct orthodoxy, not replace it. Surprisingly, Labriola also described dialectics as depicting the complex social mediations by which underlying economic structures determine society. Although epistemologically inaccurate, factor research leading to unilinear causal explanations is often useful and necessary. Religious, intellectual, moral, and political ideas are, "in the last resort," determined by concrete matter. Though the future is undetermined, capitalism sets the stage, and socialism reflects a tendency inherent in history itself. There are "objective causes of every [human] choice" located outside the actor. Praxis, therefore, is determined by material production. Indeed, all "historic facts [are explained] by means of the underlying economic structure." Labriola eagerly consecrated a dialectical universe in which impersonal material laws are mediated by, and expressed in, praxis—preserving the best of both materialism and idealism but producing an epistemological nightmare. He concluded, as he must, with the following enigma. "Reasonable and well founded is the tendency of those who aim to subordinate the sum total of human events in their course to the rigorous conception of determinism. There is, on the contrary, no reason for confusing this derived, reflex and complex determinism with the determinism of the immediate struggle for existence which is produced and developed on a field not modified by the continued action of labor."[40]

Although Labriola's Marxism is philosophically immature, it was nevertheless well received by materialists openly thirsting for an alternative to Engels's metaphysics. The notion that all historical phenomena are "reciprocally interrelated" means that subjectivity is important in its own right, an attractive idea for disenchanted advocates of a doctrine for which subjectivity itself is problematic. His influence on Lukács and Gramsci is obvious. However, even in his own lifetime Labriola had a significant impact on Marxism. The work of Émile Vandervelde, for example, a leading theoretician in the Parti Ouvrier Belge and the chairman of the Second International from 1900 to 1914, bears the distinct imprint of Labriola's incipient idealism. His L'Idéalisme dans le marxisme (1905) drew some disturbing implications of Labriola's revised dialectic. Vandervelde argued that economic change does not necessarily precede social change, implicitly opening the field of Marxist social inquiry to noneconomists. He suggested that intellectual activity can shape technical progress, moral factors may serve to initiate social change, and demography and geography may be independent variables in history's evolution. The gist of Vandervelde's case is that historical materialism is a useful tool for perceiving general trends but is not necessarily the sole or even primary explanation of social progress. The theoretical gap separating this type of Marxism from orthodoxy prompted Plekhanov's·accusation that Vandervelde is not even a Marxist—despite chairing the Second International!

Luxembourg

Idealism would not fully bloom as an independent approach to Marxism until Lukács's *History and Class Consciousness.* However, this is merely the last mile on an intellectual path already blazed by unhappy materialists like Labriola and, especially after 1917, Rosa Luxembourg (1870-1919). Luxembourg was primarily a strategist and political economist, not a theoretician. In retrospect, her philosophy is indeed blemished by the same indecisiveness and temerity we noted in Labriola. Yet her tactical influence on the European working-class movement was enormous, and certainly no reasonable observer can deny the magnitude of her personal courage and commitment to proletarian democracy, a commitment that led to murder by German reactionaries who resented her support of the Spartacus uprising, against which she had voted in caucus. *Die krise der Sozialdemokratie* (1915), commonly known as the *Junius Pamphlet,* became an ideological signpost for the Spartacus League and, through the league, the future German Communist Party (KPD). *Die russische Revolution* (1922) graphically presented the outrage that democratic socialists experienced as Leninism turned dictatorial. The ensuing condemnation and rejection by Lenin, more than any other single factor, doomed Luxembourg to a secondary position in the litany of Marxism.

Capitalism, described in *Die Akkumulation des kapitals* (1913), can survive only as long as it has noncapitalist markets—internal and external—to support it. It ineluctably breeds the accumulation of surplus value and the continual increase in constant capital (that is, the reproductive apparatus). Surplus value, however, must be changed into money by selling commodities. The inevitable increase in accumulation means that new markets are continually needed, for workers cannot consume enough to keep up with the incessant drive for accumulation. Capitalism is thus pushed into a frantic search for backward lands and rural economies to assimilate economically. Ironically, this expansion sucks dry the lifeblood by which capitalism survives. When accumulation becomes impossible because new markets can no longer be found, then capitalism itself becomes unfeasible. Imperialism is the last-ditch struggle among capitalists to gain control of untapped markets. It marks the final stage in capitalism's development.

The Accumulation of Capital defines the precise economic circumstances under which capitalism becomes untenable. Luxembourg condemned Marx's ambiguity on this subject, his vague assertion that capitalism's increasing concentration of capital and worker impoverishment would precipitate a revolution. Hers is, therefore, a scientific elucidation and verification of Marx's economic theories. *The Accumulation of Capital* proves, at least to its author, that capitalism will self-destruct because of inherent material processes.[41] The inexorable tendency toward compound accumulation means that capitalism reflects impersonal matter, independent of human intention. This work establishes Luxembourg's materialist credentials. Her Marxism in 1913 was deeply rooted in the epistemology of Engels and Kautsky. As a result, she firmly, some might say inflexibly, defended the orthodox condemnation of reformism and nationalism, holding both to be reactionary and unjustifiable in any circumstance.

There is, however, another side to Rosa Luxembourg, one that dominated the later years and is effectively expressed in *The Russian Revolution* (1922) and *Leninism or Marxism* (1904).[42] Though revolution is necessary and inevitable, it actually occurs only when the prediction itself becomes part of history, that is, when workers self-consciously realize it. Luxembourg maintained that revolutionary theory had already been promulgated by Marx, Engels, and the others. What was needed now was proletarian revolutionary consciousness, which occurs spontaneously, without coordination or prior direction. A revolutionary party is unable either to launch or to prevent revolution because it cannot control human cognition. It must cooperate with workers, for they *are* the working-class movement. The Leninist Party emasculated this group by depriving them of responsibility and initiative. Revolutionary tactics fall meaninglessly on deaf ears when formulated by this kind of insulated Party bureaucracy.

Luxembourg was convinced after examining the Russian revolution of 1905 and other workers' uprisings that mass strikes are the most useful form of revolutionary action. They are spontaneous, uncoordinated, leaderless outbreaks, not controlled by parties. Revolutionary organization is a product of spontaneous action, not its source, so in the course of its struggle workers will spontaneously unite and form needed organizations and institutions. Through such actions, workers realize their objective and collective interests, and proceed to a full-scale revolution. The Party's role is to help cultivate a collective revolutionary consciousness. If successful, it becomes superfluous, and workers complete their project as independent, free, unguided actors. A Communist Party, therefore, should consist only of active workers who easily slip back into battlefront positions. They must transform scientific theory into revolutionary action by encouraging spontaneous worker strikes. Theory and action blend in the thoughts and actions of workers spontaneously realizing the truth.

The Bolsheviks correctly seized power in Russia, but were now misusing it by casting, from above, a uniform revolutionary consciousness. By destroying democratic institutions in Russia, Lenin and Trotsky eliminated the only means by which workers could act collectively to support their revolution. Lenin did not understand that socialism lives not by administrative fiat but in workers themselves, through free self-expression. Workers control their revolution only in circumstances of unlimited democracy, which includes basic liberal freedoms of election, speech, public opinion, press, association, artistic expression, and so on. "Dictatorship is not a matter of abolishing democracy but of applying it correctly."[43] While a Leninist-type dictatorship of the proletariat is justifiable under adverse conditions as a temporary means of survival, its success is measured by how quickly it dissolves into a workers' democracy. By this criterion, bolshevism is a dismal failure.

Luxembourg's mature writings indicate that she was aware of the theoretical links between materialism and Bolshevik tyranny. Her pamphleteering, however, never surpassed livid critique, and her assertions regarding revolutionary spontaneity are philosophically unsupportable. She was driven, in other words, to the untenable position of defending materialist orthodoxy while denying the one institution (the Leninist Party) charged with realizing it. She believed in both the materialist predetermination of history and the essentiality of working-class spontaneity. Epistemologically, this is inconsistent and unconvincing. Materialists simply overlook the sincere but naive emotionalism with which she measured Lenin's revolution. However, in terms of the historical reemergence of Hegelian Marxism, Luxembourg perceived materialism's inability to explain worker oppression effectively and mobilize working-class support. Her critique of bolshevism lifts subjectivity above material process. Workers possess an innate, collective essence which must and will be realized consciously before the revolution can succeed. This spiritual renewal is generated by spontaneous strikes, unplanned collective activities that galvanize oppressed workers into authentic consciousness and assure democratic working-class institutions. Though material conditions must be ripe for such a transition to occur, Luxembourg suggested that workers consciously experience a transcendent historical truth that simultaneously manifests practical action. Luxembourg's Hegelianism shines through despite a credulous philosophy.

Pannekoek

Anton Pannekoek (1873–1960), a member of the "Council Communists" that actively opposed Lenin during the interwar years, was strongly influenced by Luxembourg. Like her, Pannekoek strained the limits of materialism, unable or unwilling to part company philosophically, but also sensitive to its limitations regarding human subjectivity. He believed that materialism is an adequate epistemology and social science is predicated on the causal priority of base over superstructure. But he also saw the class struggle as a struggle of consciousness. Workers must be liberated from bourgeois attitudes and beliefs, for the "spiritual power of the bourgeoisie" is as dangerous as its power of economic exploitation. Capitalist values emasculate workers' critical potentials and enslave them to machines and institutions. Hence, workers must be emancipated theoretically as well as materially, primarily through mass actions that instigate a unified collectivity from which new, objective working-class ideas will gestate.[44] Institutionally, emancipation generates workers' councils, self-governing groups that run factories and administer the state. "Council socialism" is worker democracy in both economic and political spheres, that is, workers simultaneously taking control of factories and government. Pannekoek felt that mass actions, including wild-cat strikes and forcible factory seizures, inevitably produce collectivist ideas and workers' councils. Marxist parties are analogous to temporary "think-groups," guiding discussion and provoking spontaneous protest actions (what he calls "the Task"), but immediately surpassed by the councils. Leninism has turned into "state capitalism," where an elite bureaucracy now runs the economy and state, prohibiting worker democracy. Neither "Party Socialism," the label given Soviet-style democracy, nor capitalism is democratic. Worker self-government awaits the historical appearance of a consciously unified collectivity from which council socialism will arise.[45] The incipient, but theoretically undeveloped, connection to Hegel is obvious.

Brzozowski and Jaurès

Labriola, Luxembourg, and Pannekoek bent orthodoxy to accommodate a revived subjectivity. Their work appealed to unhappy materialists but lacked the power, subtlety, or ambition to transform orthodoxy successfully. On the other side are Stanislow Brzozowski (1878–1911) and Jean Jaurès (1859–1914), idealists who entered Marxism from the back door of Hegelianism.

An eclectic philosopher, borrowing from Nietzsche, Sorel, Bergson, and the Russian empirio-critics, Brzozowski's major work of theory—*Ideas* (1910)—posits a metaphysics of absolute freedom and creativity based on a "philosophy of labor." Reality is a function of humanity's practical connections to the world, epitomized in our inherent ability to labor. This creative action that produces needed goods is praxis in the true Hegelian sense: More than subjectivism or voluntarism, it embraces objective tendencies of economic and social development. It is, in other words, an essential unity of subject and object expressed as human creativity. Truth is manifest in authentic freedom, which always takes the form of praxis. History is produced by human action rather than preexisting laws (for example, materialism) and therefore is not predetermined. Yet, truly free action fulfills history's objective tendencies.

Brzozowski's philosophy of labor metaphysically rationalizes socialism.

Since praxis is the essence of authenticity for everyone, a just society is realized through the collective labors of authentic workers. Free labor, not arbitrarily guided by bureaucrats or dictators, generates dignity. Brzozowski's Marxism demands the proletariat's spiritual rejuvenation, which means worker self-government and labor as praxis. This will accompany their seizing a capitalist productive apparatus that is objectively decaying anyway; hence, an undetermined act of praxis culminates capitalism's historical tendency toward dissolution. Socialism is thus a human adventure in which workers confront and conquer nature and actualize an essential, idealized humanity. When Brzozowski, in his last years, added strong doses of Polish nationalism and Catholicism, he was less a Marxist than a speculative, idealist metaphysician calling forth a spiritual or emotional worker's revival. Just as orthodox Marxists flirting with idealism become second-rate materialist theoreticians, Brzozowski's frantic efforts to ground abstractions in matter was, as he eventually realized, self-defeating and futile.

Jaurès was a professional philosopher who skipped nimbly from Kant to Hegel and Marx. His path to socialism, therefore, lay in pre-Marxist bourgeois theory, and he did not hesitate to refer to philosophers as diverse as Proudhon, Blanqui, Fichte, Lasalle, and Rousseau in addition to Kant and Hegel. Jaurès interpreted Being as a universal whole, encompassing every level of physical and social organization, that evolves into a pervasive harmony and oneness. When historically mature, Being unifies thought and external reality. This highest stage defines everything that has preceded, determining their specific roles in the totality. What a particular phenomenon means, in other words, is determined by its part in Being's grand design. The universe is neither spontaneous nor haphazard, but determined by the highest unity of Being and Truth, a unity unfolding gradually in history. Thus, each level of reality is defined not merely in relation to other levels, but by its part in Being's progressive historical flowering. Reality is Being unfolding historically, the Absolute temporally realizing itself. Human beings perceive this reality, act, and help cause it. Truth is not prior to Being. They coexist as the former realizes itself. All natural phenomena and cognitive experiences of Being are equally valid and important, for they embody the historical process of perfect unity at specific temporal moments. Jaurès calls this unity God. Faith, therefore, is the subjective experience of true knowledge.[46]

Socialism is the final, mature unity of Being and Reality—history's goal, defining all preceding political and economic struggles and social forms. Orthodox Marxism abstracts the material processes of social evolution and applies them to scientific social inquiry, hence is scientifically valid and useful. However, it is neither sufficient nor autonomous. Material reality is only one aspect of historical Being, which includes and determines everything in the Universe, material and nonmaterial. Marx's historical science is one fragment of a universal soteriology of Being. It complements faith rather than rejects it. Although economics shapes social institutions, both these phenomena reflect, and are defined by, Being's progress in history. Society embodies both mechanical laws of matter and abstract processes. Marxism indicates the material prerequisites for socialism, but socialism itself is built on the people's will to live truthfully in universal freedom. Socialism realizes humanity's material potential, but also culminates history's essential, absolute Truth. It is "necessary" in an idealistic sense quite foreign to orthodox materialism, even though God—Truth—also lives in those mechanistic economic laws that now fascinate Marxists. Socialism is concretized only when an exploited humanity experiences God's will and actively fulfills its revolutionary historical role. Orthodox materialists mistakenly ignore this subjective component of history.

An active, willful, revolutionary proletariat culminates history's universal progress. Properly informed and motivated, workers will perceive socialism not as the negation of bourgeois civilization, but its progressive completion. Socialism, for Jaurès, is an extension of liberal republicanism, nationalism, religion, and so on, preserving and perfecting their progressive, historically significant features. The proletariat, history's "progressive" class, represents Being's universal moment. Its struggle has a universal character. Its interests are divine, not narrowly self-motivated. Hence, workers will unite with all mature, knowledgeable groups—peasants, petit bourgeois, even capitalists—in perfecting social institutions and values. Their revolution is also humanity's and God's and can therefore be accomplished without violence or hatred. Jaurès's pantheistic metaphysics describes individuals with antagonistic material interests living blissfully together under God's historical will. He was a revolutionary who preached nonviolence and devoted thirty years to electoral politics in France. As a Marxist with unbreakable connections to bourgeois culture, Jaurès "rectified" orthodox materialism by substituting orthodox Hegelian idealism, including its naively optimistic view of the bourgeois state's moral leadership in achieving universal justice. Jaurès's synthesis of idealism and Marxist materialism, like Brzozowski's, is one-sided and unconvincing from any but a Hegelian perspective.

Lukács

The movement to revitalize the Hegelian moment of Marxism systematically, tentatively initiated by disillusioned representatives of both orthodoxy and Hegelianism,[47] finally congealed in Georg Lukács's *Geschichte und Klassenbewusstsein* (1923), a watershed in the development of Marxist theory generally as well as the professional life of Lukács (1885-1971). The essays comprising *History and Class Consciousness* were written from 1919 to 1922. Prior to this, Lukács had written two major philosophical works,

History of the Development of Modern Drama (1911) and *Theory of the Novel* (1916), both reflecting an early infatuation with Kant, the German Romanticists, and the Heidelberg School of intuitionism (including Dilthey, Rickert, and Windelband).[48] The major problematic of the early writings concerns Kant's dichotomy of reality into coexisting but independent realms, the abstract, value-laden world of subjective freedom (noumena) and concrete objective necessity (phenomena). Kant proposed that moral decisions are based on sensually unverifiable qualities cognitively grasped as absolute ideas, or moral imperatives. Whereas the human mind experiences objective phenomena through sensually verifiable categories (for example, space, time, density, and so forth), there are no such obvious criteria to guide human action. The ultimate questions regarding truth, beauty, goodness, and the like are solved only through creative intuition. Answers exist as ideas subjectively realized in thought. Lukács's early work proffers a subjectivist, idealist approach to aesthetics based on a hypothesized transformation of man's inner life. While objectivity is not ignored, man's search for truth, beauty, and authenticity ends in the subjective world of thought.

Ironically, Hegelianism actually pulled Lukács down to objective matter and into Marxism's magnetic field. Hegel's dialectical unity of subject and object opened up the entire spectrum of economic and social inquiry to Lukács. He proved to be a sensitive, even prescient, student of Marxism. The essays in *History and Class Consciousness* were likely written before Lukács had access to the *1844 Manuscripts* or *Grundrisse*.[49] Insights into human reification and dialectical method—undoubtedly the most lucid modern work on these issues, comparable to Marx's own writing in terms of clarity and impact—are therefore all the more impressive. One can, then, justifiably term Lukács's social theory in *History and Class Consciousness* either a Hegelian synthesis of materialism and Romanticism (what Lukács disparagingly calls his "third way"[50]) or Marxist materialism mediated by Hegel, the Romantics, and the young Marx. Lukács courageously explicated the idealist moment in Marxism, basing history's economic and social trends on an a priori truth that must and will be subjectively realized.

This synthetic project did not please orthodox materialists, who reacted swiftly and viciously to the publication of *History and Class Consciousness*. The sharp critiques by Zinoviev (1924) and Bukharin (1924) confirm that since Engels, Marxism had become a closed materialist system. While people like Labriola and Luxembourg were ridiculed but tolerated as misguided theorists, Lukács's break with orthodoxy was penetrating and compelling enough to be dangerous. *History and Class Consciousness* quickly disappeared from official Communist libraries throughout Europe and was rediscovered by the Party only after Stalin's death. Lukács was soon confronted with the choice of renouncing either idealism or Marxism. If the latter, he simultaneously forfeited any realistic opportunity to influence Hungarian history on the eve of an expected workers' revolution. This probably influenced his decision, as Lukács implied in published confessionals. Karl Korsch, on the other hand, attributed his capitulation to an insidious lack of character, a fear of standing up for truth and integrity— and being read out of the movement. Some idealist Marxists, including Kolakowski, saw inchoate Stalinism staining the essays of *History and Class Consciousness,* making it relatively easy for Lukács to slither into an orthodox snakeskin. There is convincing evidence for each position. Indisputably, however, *History and Class Consciousness* is a crossroads in Lukács's professional development. Prior to its publication, he was an outright Romantic idealist. The book itself represents a Hegelian approach to Marxism. After 1922, Lukács recanted and apparently willingly submitted to Stalin's orthodoxy, abrogating any hopes he or others might have had for an intellectually comparable sequel. After restating familiar themes in several relatively minor publications preceding Stalin's accession to power,[51] Lukács was angrily repudiated by Béla Kun and the Third International for penning vaguely critical phrases in the so-called "Blum Theses" (1928)—a document published by émigrés and written by Lukács, providing theoretical guidance to Hungarian Communists. By 1933 Lukács explicitly repudiated both the theses and the major hypotheses of *History and Class Consciousness,* and by so doing maintained Party membership. However, he also withdrew into an orthodox shell, spurning any type of potentially antagonistic political activity or theorizing. His later writings are theoretically insignificant for Marxists. They comprise, in short, conventional, Stalinist presentations of historical materialism and familiar critiques of empiricism. Two of his major philosophical works during this period, *Existentialism or Marxism?* (1947) and *The Destruction of Reason* (1954), are rigidly, almost embarrassingly Stalinist, and neither is ever repudiated. Although he professed ideological independence, he occasionally altered opinions to accommodate Stalin's whims and policies. After Stalin's death, Lukács shifted gears and became increasingly critical of Stalinist distortions, particularly in Eastern Europe. He joined the "Petófi Circle" of intellectuals in Hungary and later was minister of culture in the Nagy government before the 1956 Soviet invasion. His final, unfinished theoretical work, *Zur Ontologie des gesellschaftlichen Seins,* evokes the intellectual vitality and creativity that many Western Marxists thought had long since dissipated.

History and Class Consciousness pierces the heart of orthodox dialectical materialism by questioning the authority of its great priests. Materialist Marxism, for Lukács, hangs on the arguments of Engels's *Anti-Dühring* and Lenin's *Materialism and Empirio-Criticism,* both misinterpreting the universe as an objective reality impersonally determining attitudes and behavior of human and nonhuman phenomena. The resulting social theory emulates the "methods of the natural sciences" by reducing human subjects to "purely quantitative essences."[52] What began in Marx as emancipatory philosophy culminates in an all-powerful antiphilosophical metaphysic that defines humanity in material terms equally suitable to the scientific description of organic excrement. Engels's dialectic of nature and Lenin's theory of reflection obliterate the distinctly human aspects of life, denying masses of oppressed workers the joys of subjective thought and emotion that enliven their everyday lives. Orthodox Marxism unintentionally affirms the impersonal identity that capitalism foists on workers, who are now told by oppressors and liberators alike that they lack dignity as human beings.

Reality obviously consists of objective matter as well as subjects who cognitively live and work. Although Marxists distort this basic truth, Marx himself certainly did not. For Lukács, the essence of Marxism is dialectical method, that is, a way of looking at society that properly relates subjective and objective moments in an unfolding, inclusive totality. This method is an irreplaceable tool for social inquiry, not—contrary to Engels and the entire orthodox movement—an objective material law. "Orthodox Marxism" really means returning to Marx's method, derived from Marx's own written analyses of the reciprocal interpenetration of all of life's aspects.

Lukács's understanding of "totality," constant from 1919 to his death, is the analytical key to his social theory. Marx's dialectical method presumes the priority of the social whole over parts. Each of these, isolated from the totality, is an empty, meaningless abstraction, radiating a physical presence but devoid of real life—like a flower plucked from the earth, torn from life nourishment and negated by rootlessness. Each part of the social totality, each empirical fact, is defined by its relationship to the whole, and is properly understood only when perceived in this relationship. We understand social facts by relating them to a reality not directly given or empirically verifiable. This totality is dynamic, comprising social trends rooted in the past, expressed in current institutions and values, and fully realized only in the future. In brief, empirical facts must be interpreted in the light of the global totality they express. However, just as a flower's connection to the clouds is mediated by rain and earth, observed social facts are mediated by subordinate totalities within which they fit and make sense. The concrete historical and social totality, then, consists of levels of dynamically interrelated partial totalities, each expressing and defining lower level mediations of which it is composed and higher level mediations within which it fits. All the mediations, taken together, comprise the rhythm and movement of the totality. Thus, a factory worker's relationship to global trends is mediated by the partial totalities of family, class, nation, religion, sex, genetic makeup, neighborhood, and so on. Each level interpenetrates with the whole, which, as the quality defined by and expressed in sublevels, ultimately determines its parts.

All levels of society, in other words, are dialectically interrelated. Analysts overemphasizing a single level or mediation or part, in effect plucking it from the totality's nourishment, distort the phenomena they pretend to explain. This is precisely what empirical scientists do when they artificially isolate social phenomena and treat each sensually experienced and verified datum as an autonomous quality. Empirical facts accumulate into tomes of computer readouts, but we still aimlessly search for causes and cures of social problems that seemingly defy explanation. As long as social scientists ignore the empirically nonverifiable interrelationships defining each problem, this hopeless situation will continue. Similarly, reformists naively isolate government from its total surroundings instead of recognizing it as one important mediation in a global movement. Incremental political reforms cosmetically disguise problems whose roots lie in the totality and whose solution awaits more foundational change affecting society's interrelated mediations. On the other hand, orthodox Marxists ignore particular social phenomena and overemphasize the totality. By lumping significant aesthetic, intellectual, political, and psychological factors into one undifferentiated whole, materialists vulgarize the dialectic and propound a theory that in its own way is as misleading as empiricism. They don't understand that life's mediations are real and important to reflective actors, an essential component of all social situations. Materialists, in sum, believe in a dialectics that unfolds without mediations, which is no dialectics at all. The form of Lukács's eventual repudiation of Stalinism was conceived before 1922, though apparently not the will to carry it out.

Economic determinism, which Lukács called economism, is the fruit of nondialectical Marxism. When Marx said that social being determines consciousness, he meant only to explain the determining connection between the social whole (totality) and individual consciousness (mediation), the general determination of each part by the whole. This is the fundamental relationship, not that of the parts to each other, which, though important, are also mediations of the determining totality. Lukács condemned vulgar Marxism for postulating a direct, causal connection between base and ideology. Consciousness is determined by the totality, mediated not only by the mode of production, but also the political, social, aesthetic, religious, and other forms of social activity. Consciousness is determined only in the most general sense by humanity's social being, the totality of social life.

Dialectical method, a tool for social inquiry, is not, however, independent of social life, to be picked up and used by anyone for any purpose. It is part of human cognition, and inconceivable apart from reflective subjects.[53] As part of humanity's connection to nature and history, dialectics is actively involved in the social reality it is applied to as a method. Since it is simultaneously an aspect of humanity and an expression of the social and historical totality, it manifests the theoretical and ideological consciousness of history's agent of transformation. Put differently, the social group that perceives itself in historical terms (born in and bound to the past, oppressed now, liberated in the future) is aware of the totality and, by definition, expresses and realizes history's dialectical complexity. For Lukács, as for Marx, this group is the proletariat. Dialectical method is therefore suitable only for observers who share the political perspective of, and commitment to, proletarian liberation. The dialectic does not exist apart from the proletariat's revolutionary struggle. They alone can grasp the totality: the determining influence of the whole and the transformations by which this influence will be realized. In this sense, they are a "universal class," destined to assimilate the past while creating the future.

Though Lukács equates the movement of totality with Marx's class struggle, his is not an "objective" description of reality. Marxism *is* the theoretical consciousness of a maturing, revolutionary class of workers. Their revolutionary consciousness does not "reflect" objective conditions but rather constitutes the revolutionary process itself. Reflective subjectivity is an integral part of the totality that is shaping the future. All prior revolutionary classes in history have worked only for themselves, fulfilling partial interests. They lacked the universal perspective necessary to cognize the totality. Consequently, their revolutions invariably fell victim to myth and unsatisfied promises. Bourgeois revolutions are doomed because the class interests of capitalists, the desire for profit and negative freedom, conflict with the means by which they are realized (that is, capitalist productive techniques). Capitalist factories, in other words, are inadvertently socializing workers to their own objective interests, assuring capitalism's destruction. Proletarian revolutionary success hinges on how well workers do what the bourgeoisie couldn't: cognitively perceive the totality, clearly understanding their position in society and their revolutionary historical role. Empirical social science is both an epistemological symbol of bourgeois self-interest and a form of theoretical consciousness that, by obscuring social knowledge, blinds capitalists to their fate. Proletarian self-consciousness, on the other hand, is equivalent to knowledge of the historical and social totality. The process of workers comprehending the world is therefore the same as transforming it. Knowledge and action coincide. Theory and practice are one. The proletariat is the identical subject and object of history, for it cognitively realizes history's objective total movement. Man, a cognitive subject, is "the objective foundation of the historical dialectic." He freely and reflectively expresses historical necessity. History's objective totality, and proletarian awareness of it, are identical.[54]

Historical materialism is worker "self-knowledge of capitalist society," revealing the dialectic of history and society and also unmasking capitalist exploitation. It is, therefore, a science and a "weapon of war," though both these qualities are defined from the proletariat's standpoint. Bourgeois (empirical) science is also valid, epistemologically and tactically, from a capitalist perspective. Truth, then, can "only achieve an 'objectivity' relative to the standpoint of the individual classes." Historical materialism, as a historical and social science, is the same as what Lukács calls "ascribed" ("*zugerechnet*") or authentic, proletarian self-consciousness. That it is now defined by materialists as the "primacy of economic motives in historical explanation" shows how far the concept has strayed from its original meaning.[55]

Historical materialism, proletarian social science, uncovers the totality of society's dialectical processes. When applied to capitalism, it reveals the immensely significant role played by "reification" ("*Verdinglichung*") in mediating totality and proletarian self-consciousness. Lukács's analysis of reification is not really conceptually innovative. Although not yet aware of the *1844 Manuscripts*, he was familiar with the chapter in *Capital* on commodity fetishism and relied heavily on it. What distinguishes Lukács's work on reification in *History and Class Consciousness* is the role that this concept plays in his Marxism: He was the first neo-Marxist to treat worker alienation as the distinguishing feature of capitalism, rather than an epiphenomenon of the base. Since the dialectic is inconceivable apart from reflective human subjects, the social forms that temporarily ensnare workers in a web of inauthenticity—inhibiting correct perceptions of history's essential movement—emerge as the vital connection between worker and totality. Capitalist productive relationships, dialectically expressed in reified existence, will change only when subjects reassess authenticity by willfully abrogating reification. In this sense, society's base reflects the historical evolution of authentic worker self-consciousness, what Hegelians call objective Mind.

Lukács defined reification by describing a capitalist world where labor is a commodity bought and sold in the marketplace, transforming people into objects.[56] Social relationships between laborers are stripped of sentiment and understanding. The work process, including its commodities, are controlled directly by capitalists and indirectly by "laws" of supply and demand. Workers passively do as told, producing exchange value rather than use value and hence enriching their overseers. There is apparently no choice. Economic laws governing commodities—including human labor—seem to fall from the heavens as impersonal dictates determining what is produced, what price it commands, and what salaries employees receive. In capitalism, workers become spectators to uncontrollable social forces that enrich the few at their expense.

Reification is a necessary condition of capitalism. Only when people are ignorant of life's true dimensions, that is, its transhistorical and social character, can they tolerate isolated, objectified, and enslaved life-styles. Only when workers ignore their true universal role in the dynamic totality, that is, their emancipated futures, can they tolerate economic exploitation. Every aspect or level of capitalist society reinforces this ignorance by rationalizing reification. Capitalist social and economic "progress," for example, increases mechanization and bureaucratization (what Lukács called "mechanized rationalization"), treating each laborer as one isolated work unit whose productive role is impersonally determined solely by criteria of efficiency and profit. "Progress" brings with it workers' intellectual and spiritual death. The legal system, dressed in glittering liberal aphorisms, actually reinforces reification by defining actors as isolated juridical units whose "rights" are protected regardless of social, economic, or political consequences. Bourgeois philosophy takes either of two forms: vulgar idealism, propelling us into mystifying flights of abstraction, ignoring the everyday reality in which we live and work; or, more commonly, empiricism, the philosophical expression of reification. By systematically cutting the social world into manageable, independent units that interact like moving billiard balls, empiricism intellectually destroys the historicity of human existence. Truth is generated from empirically verified social relationships—autonomous, impersonal, determining, exactly like the market laws of capitalism. Capitalists then apply knowledge to maximize efficiency and profits, guaranteeing society's economic and social "progress." Bourgeois society naively justifies itself through its own workings, not the reflective evaluation of its people.[57]

Capitalism, in sum, embodies a fatal contradiction. It functions properly when workers naively sever connections to nature and society. Workers perform most efficiently when reified, impervious to real needs and unquestioningly obeying market "laws." Capitalism and reification are thus two aspects of one reality. In contrast, authentic subjectivity is no longer an individual "I." In comprehending the totality, reflective actors are open to history and other people, and "infer the thoughts and feelings appropriate to . . . [their] objective situation."[58] The authentic "I," in other words, is a "we" simultaneously aware of history and capable of realizing history's objective trends. This contradiction between empirical and authentic self-perceptions is mediated by the material productive process. Capitalism, by virtue of material mechanisms that Marx explored thoroughly in *Capital,* generates class polarization and proletarian immiseration. As its productive capacity grows, which it inevitably must because of the never-ending urge for increased profits, workers are increasingly exposed to a socialized work place. Their heightening exploitation and alienation starkly contradict the material conditions in which they work. The tantalizing specter of interpersonal cooperation begins haunting workers who are laboring as isolated units despite crowded surroundings. Concrete economic development provides the motive and means for social change by creating production alternatives that potentially are more beneficial to producers.

Materialism notwithstanding, however, material production cannot *cause* this change. Revolution depends on workers cognitively realizing the standpoint of the totality. Only identical subject-objects understand the unity of thought and action as aspects of a dialectical, historical whole. This reflective attitude, not a specific stage of material development, is the immediate spark igniting revolution. "To become conscious is synonymous with the possibility of taking over the leadership of society." Authentic consciousness breaks the spell of naive, uncritical thinking that supports reification. Conscious rebellion also emancipates men and women from objects into self-conscious subjects, and creates socialist institutions that serve true needs of "authentic humanity." "When the worker knows himself as a commodity, his knowledge is practical. That is to say, this knowledge brings about an objective structural change in the object of knowledge." Lukács referred to the early Marx to support his belief in the priority of objective proletarian self-consciousness. In a letter to Ruge (1843), Marx declared in true Hegelian style: "The reform of consciousness consists in no more than causing the world to become aware of its own consciousness, in awakening it from its dream about itself, in explaining its own actions to it. . . . [I]t will then be seen that the world has long possessed a dream of things which it has only to possess in consciousness in order to possess them in reality."[59] The workers' revolution is nurtured by concrete processes of production and oppression, but is initiated reflectively when workers recognize universal subjectivity.

Lukács's disagreements with Engels and Lenin are now crystallized. The materialist dialectic of nature reinforces reification by positing an objective reality, independent of subjective cognition. We behave socially by passively receiving and following matter, as workers do in capitalism's market economy. Engels destroys the essential unity of subject and object, negating the dialectic. Lenin's reflection epistemology also assumes that we passively receive external stimuli and are materially programmed. We are reality's "objects," which is another way of saying we are reified. Lukács wanted workers to reassert subjective control of the world. From a dialectical perspective, correct thinking is the irreplaceable premise of revolutionary action. The unity of thought and action is impossible in Lenin's materialism, and the *Philosophical Notebooks* indicate that Lenin himself recognized this deficiency.[60]

Despite stressing consciousness, Lukács supported Lenin's conception of the function and organization of Communist Parties. His reasoning reflects the critique of empiricism. In capitalism, the proletariat's empirical consciousness is not identical with its ascribed, true class consciousness. Trusting popular opinion is therefore equivalent to abstracting one fragmentary level from the whole social totality. Examined alone, it tells us what many people appear to want. But placed in the totality, it indicates only the distorted perceptions of enslaved objects who, at this point, are not aware of their own interests. Communist Party members are nonreified historical subjects, correctly perceiving the totality—including the universality of proletariat class interests. This is the criterion for Party membership. The Party, therefore, embodies authentic proletariat class consciousness. By comparing workers' empirical attitudes to authentic ones, the Party recognizes the actual extent of worker reification and formulates apposite

strategies. The Party, then, is a mediator between workers and the historical totality. It guides workers to self-conscious awareness of historical
objectivity, thereby performing a necessary historical activity.[61] In "Tactics
and Ethics," Lukács.justifies Party loyalty even when an individual leader
(Stalin?) is proven wrong. His study of Lenin advocates a dominant postrevolutionary role for the Party, in effect equating Marx's dictatorship of
the proletariat with Lenin's dictatorship of the Party. Workers' councils, or
Soviets, useful before the revolution to properly funnel worker energy,
must later cede power to the Party.[62] While Hegelian Marxists often advocate dismantling bureaucratic, omnipotent Party structures, it is painfully
evident, at least to democrats, that a priorism—material or ideal—can
potentially justify a dictatorship of Party-scientists.

Lukács's idealism postulates that the "duality of thought and existence"
can be conquered, history's objective necessity can unite with a nonmaterial,
nonempirical essence realized in authentic proletarian consciousness. Although thought and existence do not correspond or reflect each other,
"their identity is that they are aspects of one and the same real historical
and dialectical process." This totality is manifest in. capitalism's historical
maturation, but clearly is prior to concrete matter. It is an abstract universal force, dressed in historical and social forms but fully realized only in
correct thought. Real knowledge generates a reflective awareness of the
necessity of revolution and also the will to rebel. Thus the antinomy
between subject and object is transcended by real proletarian self-
consciousness: "Only if the true were understood not only as substance,
but as subject, only if the subject (consciousness, thought) were both
producer and product of the dialectical process, only if as a result the
subject moved in a self-centered world of which it is the conscious form
and only if the world imposed itself upon it in full objectivity, only then
can ... the antitheses of subject and object, thought and existence, freedom and necessity, be held to be solved."[63]

Hegel was unable to discern the true subject-object of history, asserting,
instead, an abstract myth. The proletariat, a class born in the material
conditions of capitalism and subjectively maturing along with its material
environment, provides Lukács with a suitable substitute for Hegel's myth of
nationalism. Lukács, more than Hegel, recognized the importance of history and material development in the total scheme of things. Nevertheless,
History and Class Consciousness draws heavily from its Hegelian source,
particularly the notion of Absolute Mind as a unity of subject and object
realized in liberated self-awareness. The working class, Lukács's identical
subject-object, is a material representation of Hegel's Mind that realizes its
own essentiality in socialist revolution. Lukács never recanted the dialectical
method outlined in *History and Class Consciousness,* especially the unity
of subject and object, the identification of theory and practice, cognition
as a revolutionary activity, and reification. Yet he explicitly reneges his

Hegelianism, calling it an "extravagant . . . distortion," which grossly under-estimates the significance of "objective societal conditions."[64]

Lukács's own actions and words render his significance in the history of Marxist theory problematic. It is entirely possible that he remained intellectually a Hegelian Marxist and opted for pragmatic self-renunciation in order to maximize his political influence. But his later theoretical work and post-Stalinist self-criticism are dressed in the strong, dogmatic rhetoric of authentic materialism. He probably could have survived politically with a less stinging recantation. Hence, Lukács may have honestly believed that he could justify a dialectical unity of subject and object, theory and practice, with a materialist epistemology. The essays in *History and Class Consciousness* are motivated by futile orthodox efforts to do just this. His concepts of mediation and totality, the core of *History and Class Consciousness,* are emasculated if, in the last resort, "irreducible" ideas reflect economics. It is difficult to believe that such a sophisticated and articulate philosopher could seriously devote himself to an argument, resembling Lenin's in *Materialism and Empirio-Criticism,* that makes philosophical sense from neither an ideal nor a material point of view.

Whatever Lukács's motivations after 1922, *History and Class Consciousness* stands on its own as the classic modern work of idealistic Marxism, a subtle braiding of Hegelian epistemology and orthodox Marxist economics. It culminates a trend in Marxist theory originating in Labriola's fulminations on subjectivity, and blossoms into a popular twentieth-century Marxist alternative to materialism. Lukács's reputation as a social theorist ultimately rests on this one work.

Korsch

Karl Korsch (1886–1961) is in some ways Lukács's alter ego. A writer whose creative potential is far below Lukács's, he also courageously resisted intellectual compromise and consequently suffered the indignities of Party expulsion and forced emigration from his German homeland prior to World War II. Korsch eventually became an intellectual pariah as well, an embittered man whose work was received quietly in Europe, prompting him to question and abandon his own philosophical principles. He was at various times in his professional career a Leninist, a Hegelian Marxist, and a critical theorist. His major work of theory, *Marxismus und Philosophie* (1923) is ambiguous enough perhaps to encourage such intellectual meanderings. Still, its basically Hegelian critique of orthodoxy makes it a seminal document in the evolution of idealist Marxism.

The success of Lenin's Bolshevik revolution disillusioned Korsch. Ever since Engels, orthodox Marxism had interpreted the unity of theory and practice to mean the conformity of ideas with objective material needs and actions. Human reflection passively assimilates a preexisting, impersonal, determining reality. Scientific materialism is no real improvement on ideal-ist metaphysics, for both perform identical functions of reducing cognition to an automatic reflection of omnipotent objectivity. True Marxism is not a "science" in the orthodox sense. There is no objective material reality independent of living human beings. Knowledge, therefore, does not pas-sively reflect, but actively constitutes a complex, interpenetrating world. A true idea expresses a real human struggle, not an objective datum.

The underlying presumption of *Marxism and Philosophy,* like *History and Class Consciousness,* interprets society as a totality, an indissoluble whole where each element reinforces and reflects all others. Base and superstructure are reciprocally interconnected, and knowledge is incon-ceivable as an independent, passively determined epiphenomenon. Bour-geois society comprises a mystified, alienated consciousness and an exploitative, oppressive economic system. It "can only be abolished in thought and consciousness by a simultaneous practico-objective overthrow of the material relations of production themselves, which have hitherto been comprehended through these forms." If Marxism is to be revolution-ary, it must offer not only a doctrine of political and economic rebellion, but also a philosophical critique intellectually destroying an alienated bourgeois world view. This critique aims at abolishing ("*Aufhebung*") phi-losophy "as part of the abolition of bourgeois social reality as a whole, of which it is an ideal component."[65]

Marxism "transcends" philosophy, in other words, is truly scientific, recognizing theory and practice as integral parts of one total whole. Bour-geois philosophy ignores this, perceiving itself eternally valid, independent of social activity. Ironically, however, in annihilating bourgeois philosophy, Marxism cannot ignore or abandon philosophy altogether. Orthodoxy is unaware that philosophy dialectically expresses historical trends and processes, and this ignorance isolates workers from their own revolution. A working-class revolution requires participants to experience revolutionary ideas cognitively as part of the actual disrupting act. The material ripening of capitalism, accompanied only by bourgeois values, increases the severity of exploitation without producing the impetus for change. Orthodox Marx-ism abdicates its philosophical responsibilities, is "untrue," by ignoring the actual plight of those it represents. Marxism embodies a unity of theory and practice, realized as a philosophical critique of capitalism that is simultaneously part of a total revolutionary process. In this sense Marxism has philosophically inherited the dialectical interrelation of theory and practice characterizing Hegelian idealism, although stressing—for the first time—matter.[66]

Common Hegelian roots make similarities with Lukács unavoidable. Dialectics, for Korsch and Lukács, is not an objective method that anyone can use to study any subject. It expresses the proletariat's revolutionary movement and is inseparably part of that movement. Thus dialectics is effectively applied to social inquiry only in revolutionary proletarian practice. Workers comprise a "universal" class in being uniquely capable of cognizing history's total movement. Of course, this cognition is dialectically expressed in the revolutionary act, which culminates history's objective "telos." The proletariat is, in Lukács's terms, the identical subject-object of history.

Hegelian Marxism prescribes an a priori totality encompassing past and future, marked by polarizing class struggles corresponding to the developmental level of material production and culminating in workers subjectively cognizing their objective revolutionary functions. *History and Class Consciousness* draws appropriate conclusions regarding the priority of authentic, not empirical, class consciousness. Korsch, however, is uncertain of Hegel's idealism, despite its logical connection to his own totalism. He argues that philosophical truth changes with history; hence, Marxism is a science to the extent that it adequately articulates the consciousness of revolutionary workers at the time that this consciousness peaks. As events change, so will Marxism's validity and usefulness. A philosophy that is true now because it adequately represents proletarian self-consciousness will turn false when workers' perceptions change. Marxist philosophy must take different forms in different historical eras, the implication being that, when no longer relevant to worker consciousness, it will disappear. "Marxist ideologies must . . . be seen in a historical, materialist and dialectical perspective *as products of a historical evolution. . . .* [The] development of Marxist theory . . . was always a *theoretical reflection of the latest practical experiences of the class struggle* which was reawakening in various ways." There is no such thing as a purely theoretical, "objectively valid" Marxism.[67]

Natural science also expresses human interactions with nature mediated by productive forces. As the latter change, as we find more advanced ways of satisfying material needs, we relate differently to nature. The "validity" of present empirical "laws" is predicated on their adequately expressing common perceptions of nature. In bourgeois society, these alienate humanity from nature and postulate a belief in objective, impersonal, unilinear causal laws. Empirical natural science is valid because it reflects bourgeois alienation. After the proletariat revolution, however, the perceived relationship to nature will change as we socialize the productive apparatus and work cooperatively. External reality, no longer only a tool for personal aggrandizement, will be the natural context of history's totality, hence the environment for multifaceted human fulfillment. Nature will be humanized. Socialist natural science will analytically reflect and express this new cognitive dimension.[68]

Korsch's "relativism" or "historicism" is useful in criticizing abstract idealism and dogmatic materialism. By eliminating the a priori rationale of history and society, he theoretically negates Lenin's dictatorial party of scientists. Marxism is scientific to the extent that it expresses an empirical proletarian world view and cannot forcibly impose objective truth on ignorant workers. History is constituted by empirical phenomena that shape perceptions. There is no organic, total process based on either a generic essence or an objective material dialectic. It is not surprising that Korsch gravitates toward the Frankfurt School of Critical Theory.

Socialist revolution abolishes bourgeois economic, social, and ideological categories that now shape proletarian self-consciousness—not only bourgeois philosophy and institutions, but the natural sciences as well, including mathematics, physics, chemistry, and biology. Socialist forms will reflect a nonalienated humanity, where individuals realize potentials by becoming part of history's dialectical movement. As the working class matures in capitalism, it becomes conscious of its exploitation and revolutionary function. "Socialism . . . is a struggle to realize freedom."[69] Korsch presumed that this socialist utopia is possible and historically imminent because the materialist mechanics of capitalist development imply qualitative transformation. Marxism is therefore "progressive," expressing the revolutionary mentality of enlightened workers. But here is the problem: From a purely historicist perspective, we can presume neither an objective human "potential" nor a historical trend leading inevitably to proletariat revolution. The necessity and desirability of smashing the bourgeois totality and realizing freedom, which Korsch strongly advocates, are based on a priori preconceptions regarding an ideal, fully realized human nature, which simultaneously expresses history's total movement. The dialectical unity of subjectivity and objectivity, praxis and theory, is foreign to epistemological relativism, which denies historical objectivity. A consistent relativist cannot define capitalism as "oppressive" and "alienating" or socialism as "liberating," nor advocate and work for revolution. Such definitions and actions presume objective historical and human categories. Korsch wants the substance of Hegelian Marxism without adopting the relevant epistemology. Philosophically, he lacks the courage of his convictions.

When Korsch applies dialectics to the history of Marxism itself, the argument is clouded by this philosophical confusion. Marxism has evolved through three distinct stages, each corresponding to a phase of worker self-consciousness.[70] In stage one (1843-1848), Marx's early writings reflect workers' inchoate fury, their slow but tangible realization of a dehumanized life in capitalism. The class struggle is just emerging in the minds and hearts of people hungry for freedom. Marxism, at this stage, is romantic—even idealistic—overemphasizing history's subjective component and ignoring concrete material conditions. Stage two (1848-1900) encompasses the period of capitalist expansion and consolidation. Worker self-consciousness is stunted. Workers adopt bourgeois values and participate in bourgeois institutions. They no longer perceive exploitation and seek instead success according to capitalist standards. In the context of retarded worker consciousness, Marxism becomes pure theory: dogmatic, positivistic, metaphysical. Vulgar materialism is the form that Marxism takes in this time of worker reaction, its roots found in utterances of Marx—taken out of context—and in Engels. Marxism is an ideology, cut off from reality and congealed in an inflexible body of objective material laws. Stage three (1900–) corresponds to the emergence of trade-union reformism, syndicalism, and bolshevism, all indicating the reawakening of proletarian consciousness. Marxism must now account for subjectively perceived class dynamics by philosophically recapturing history's totality, including reflective proletarian praxis. This is Marx's original intention, and the essence of dialectics as a method of inquiry. Korsch repudiates the Third International for reverting to stage two: defining consciousness as passively reflecting reality and defending a Party forcibly injecting truth into workers' minds.

Korsch has backed into an awkward position. The analysis of Marxism's history, published in 1923 and reiterated in the "Anti-Critique" (1930), generates an inescapable question: Is there a total historical movement culminating in reflective, revolutionary authenticity? If so, if we accept the consequences of Hegelianism, then neither of the first two stages is dialectical. Korsch is then describing the history not of Marxism, but of nondialectical idealist and materialist philosophies, which falsely claim Marx's legacy. In this case, Korsch cannot claim that Marxism changes form with each change in proletarian self-consciousness. Revolutionary social theory is part of history's total movement, awaiting proletarian thought and action. It appears in history with correct thinking; it is not continually changing forms, ostensibly separated from the historical and social whole. If, on the other hand, there is not a priori totality, then no objective criteria exist for condemning capitalism or becoming a revolutionary. Now Korsch's assertions regarding capitalist oppression, revolutionary praxis, and socialist freedom are problematic. From this second perspective, vulgar materialism accurately reflects the current empirical consciousness of the masses and hence is historically correct. Its political success depends on outwitting the capitalist enemy and manipulating workers, both facilitated by a hierarchical, inflexible, and secretive bureaucracy. Korsch, of course, rejected Leninism. But historicism dishonors the noblest of democrats.

In the years immediately following *Marxism and Philosophy,* Korsch was unclear on these matters. However by 1935, it was increasingly obvious that orthodox Marxism would survive his critique, capitalism remained vital and more flexible than anticipated, and workers in Western Europe were subjectively committed to capitalism. Stage three of Korsch's historical division would not likely experience the dialectical recovery of subjectivity. With all this depressing empirical evidence at hand and with Korsch entering the Frankfurt School, the issue was finally decided against Hegelianism. In "Why I Am A Marxist" Korsch delineated his nonidealist Marxism, which now merely performed a critical social function—spurning a positive epistemology and aiming to verify all claims empirically.[71] Marxism deals with specific situations, not generalities, and is particularly useful in critically explaining capitalism's vertiginous transformation into fascism. Moreover, although Marxism must change, not merely contemplate, the world, it should not speculate on absolutes such as justice and freedom. Korsch had jettisoned not only Hegel's idealism but also apparently the notion of dialectics as an interpenetration of social phenomena. He isolated specific events and institutions, and verified all assertions empirically. How this can be reconciled with the commitment to revolution is unclear. This article, like Korsch's early writings, is built on philosophical quicksand. Though never comfortable with one epistemology, he also never convincingly worked out his problems. In retrospect, his eclecticism lacks philosophical rigor. Though his principled, inflexible rejection of Stalinism shows an impeccable character, his theoretical work is less admirable.

Gramsci

Antonio Gramsci (1891–1937) borrowed from both Lukács and Korsch, adopting the former's Hegelianism and the latter's hesitancy to abandon the everyday world for idealism's heavenly abstractions. This synthesis is formed, speaking generally, by emphasizing the active moment of the a priori totality, while always assuming that praxis reflects and expresses a universal pattern of historical development. Rational subjectivity is therefore objectively necessary even if uncaused. Marxism, which describes the plight of workers from oppression to revolution, is a "philosophy of praxis" in depicting workers' subjectively relevant actions. This term, originally used by the imprisoned Gramsci to trick censors, aptly represents the flavor of his idealism, the constant awareness that, while philosophy must be theoretically pure, Marxism must also cater to workers living and working in the everyday life-world.

Gramsci's personal life was stained by unusual suffering. A leader of the Italian Communist Party when Mussolini gained power, Gramsci was arrested in November 1926 and spent almost all his remaining years imprisoned, writing feverishly under trying conditions. He became fatally ill in prison, was temporarily released in 1934 at least partially because of international pressure on his behalf, and succumbed in 1937. His reputation as a Marxian theorist is based primarily on the posthumously published documents, notes, and letters from prison (1929–1935), which total more than 3,000 pages and 7 volumes, the most significant of which is probably the *Prison Notebooks*.[72] Like Labriola, Gramsci's Marxism is uniquely colored by his national heritage, particularly the idealism that traditionally characterizes Italian thought. As a student, Gramsci was already an ardent follower of Benedetto Croce's brand of Hegelianism, especially Croce's critique of positivism, and eagerly anticipated an idealist "renewal of . . . [Marxism] in our day."[73] Only much later, in prison, is Gramsci concerned with Croce's own festering anti-Marxism and the possible reactionary implications of Crocean idealism. The emphasis Gramsci accorded the subjective moment of Hegel's totality is surely a response to his mentor's move Rightward.

Gramsci interpreted human behavior, ideas, and symbols in relation to their historical environments and the transhistorical patterns they manifest. The criteria and content of truth, then, vary with historical time and place. This historical relativism, not orthodox material determinism, is the essence of Marxism. "Matter," for Gramsci, is epistemologically insignificant. In any given time and place, knowledge expresses social relationships rather than objective matter. It is entirely possible that under generally similar material conditions, two societies will have significantly different cultures. Matter must be studied only as a connection between the way we think and the way we organize means of production. Though capitalism cannot appear in feudal material conditions, these do not necessarily "cause" noncapitalist productive modes. A feudal productive apparatus reflects material conditions only through nondetermined mediations such as cultural beliefs and institutions. Marxism is therefore "true" only by expressing current historical forces better than any other doctrine. An "objective" social science, in fact, cannot exist because the very concepts we use to define science express dominant historical patterns. As early as the critique of Bukharin's *Theory of Historical Materialism* (1921), Gramsci interpreted historical materialism, like religion, as a sign of weakness exhibited by oppressed peoples having little hope for immediate change. It is "true" only because commonly believed, but this won't qualify it as science. Orthodox Marxism is stuck with a doctrine that "becomes a cause of passivity, of idiotic self-sufficiency. . . . The claim, presented as an essential postulate of historical materialism, that every fluctuation of politics and ideology can be presented and expounded as an immediate expression of the structure, must be contested in theory as primitive infantalism . . . ."[74]

When oppressed workers are reflectively self-conscious and actively seek change, ideas concerning objective, deterministic historical laws fade. Humanity takes history into its hands and shapes the future. Or so it seems. Gramsci, unlike Korsch, was aware that historical relativism can neutralize any call to action that a social theory sounds. Leading a revolutionary Party, he obviously rejected such bourgeois nonsense. Consequently, Hegelianism reappears in Gramsci's version of totality. The common practices of isolating different historical epochs from each other and different empirical facts from the social whole, reflect Western Europe's dominant culture. Empiricism, like historical materialism, has no objective foundation independent of its naive acceptance by vast numbers of people. It is equally naive to assume that individuals are ahistorical empirical entities free to do whatever they like. Strong forces, in fact, inhibit change and limit what people can accomplish. Individuals can and do cognize oppression and actively rebel. Although this action is not caused by economics, it is part of history's total process, which weans out historically "incorrect" acts. In other words, history is a product of practical activity, human will. But effective action is rational, not arbitrary, expressing dominant developmental patterns, the nuts and bolts of universal history. Although action at any one time represents only a single actor, its rationality is confirmed when assimilated in commonsense thinking, that is, when it becomes part of culture. The "correctness" of an idea is confirmed when it historically prevails over competing ideas, integrating itself into history's total movement.[75] The economic evolution of capitalism, generating worker immiseration and institutional inequity, is the historical context for praxis. Within it, only certain actions are "rational," that is, aspects of history's universal development subjectively relevant to society's masses. Marx correctly perceived the necessity and rationality of proletarian revolutionary action. Today, praxis *is* worker revolution. This is the "truth" of Marxism. It simultaneously describes our contemporary self-creation and history's progressive, universal development.

We find here a component of any Hegelian approach to Marxism: the dialectical interpenetration of subject and object, Lukács's identical subject-object of history. Praxis is "correct," "necessary," and "real" when expressing history's total movement by living in reflective perceptions. Historical progress occurs at "the point at which the conception of the world, contemplation, philosophy, become 'real,' since they now aim to modify the world and to revolutionise praxis. One could say therefore that this is the central nexus of the philosophy of praxis, the point at which it becomes actual and lives historically (that is socially and no longer just in the brains of individuals) when it ceases to be arbitrary and becomes necessary-rational-real." The universality of history is itself an idea that must be reflectively realized and expressed in rational action. Since rational praxis expresses universal history, Gramsci, like Korsch and Lukács, saw practice and theory as two moments of a dialectical unity. We cannot learn the "truth" of history and later pass it on to workers. Social change occurs as class consciousness develops. History evolves through praxis, not theorizing, but rational praxis is the realization of historical truth. "The identification of theory and practice is a critical act, through which practice is demonstrated rational and necessary, and theory realistic and rational."[76] Marxism is not "science," "sociology," or "philosophy." It expresses history's evolution in proletarian self-knowledge, which appears as revolutionary praxis. Marxism is both a theory of reality and an act altering it.

Base and superstructure are reciprocally interconnected, two cultural aspects of unfolding history. Both play important historical roles. The base provides a material context for everyday reality. In the superstructure, we consciously experience life and act appropriately. Neither "causes" the other. Marx's so-called "laws of social development" are really only "laws of tendency," illustrating in concrete terms the general trends of history that must be subjectively realized in praxis. When revolutionary change takes place, base and superstructure are altered, indicating their irrationality and obsolescence. The common distinction between "science" and "art" is artificial, for both are dialectically interconnected aspects of a historical whole, with important practical roles to play in preserving culture. Intellectuals, conceived very broadly to include "artists," "scientists," "philosophers," and others concerned with ideas and institutions, are as historically significant as politicians. They work to create that moment of simultaneous awareness and praxis by which history expands. Philosophers are thus politicians, and politicians philosophers. When studying society, we also actively participate in the examined social process. Cognition, like other aspects of social reality, temporally and spatially represents history's universal process. It can never be, as empiricists claim, "objective" or "disinterested." Consequently, there is no qualitative distinction between "is" and "ought." An accurate, rational social analysis advocates proletarian revolution. The "correctness" of intellectual effort and praxis is confirmed by historical success.[77]

Gramsci separates his epistemology from classical idealism by denying the reality of an absolute human "essence," or unchanging nature. Self-concepts are derived from historically variable social relationships. He implicitly assumed, however, that rational praxis in a capitalist era appears as proletarian revolution. Workers' reflective subjectivity culminates universal historical development, and is therefore objective or necessary. While rejecting a transhistorical human essence, Gramsci described a transhistorical pattern or idea that rational people necessarily express in authentic self-knowledge and praxis. Gramsci's Marxism finds its roots in Hegel and Lukács, not in the orthodox materialism of the Second International.

This Hegelianism is the skeleton of Gramsci's more accessible and well-known body of social theory. Each dominant culture maintains itself in the commonsense attitudes and behavior of its population. Culture, in other words, lives in human praxis, which expresses human beliefs. It survives by exerting "hegemony," or control, over people's ideas. Capitalism, for example, thrives through bourgeois control and manipulation of a massive network of cultural institutions—schools, churches, parties, newspapers, media, and private associations—which incessantly propagate cultural ideas supporting the extant mode of production. A successful revolutionary movement in Western Europe must fight bourgeois hegemony in a long and complex "war of position," whose goal is a new hegemonic apparatus to replace the old. Revolutionaries working only as trained cadres preparing to seize political power will fail miserably. The state itself is far more than a simple political apparatus by which a dominant class coerces enemies, although it is certainly this. It is also an "equilibrium" between "political" and "civil" societies, that is, a hegemonic apparatus that molds ideas as well as instruments of direct coercion. A state's power includes all those cultural institutions through which power relations are mediated, "the entire complex of practical and theoretical activities with which the ruling class not only justifies and maintains its dominance, but manages to win the active consent of those over whom it rules."[78] Gramsci's "integral state" thus comprises coercive (political) and hegemonic (civil) apparatuses. This expanded notion of the state is the hub of Gramsci's social scheme. History evolves through the progressive transformation of states, each representing a particular dominant economic class as well as the entire coercive and hegemonic apparatuses through which civilizations are propagated. The workers' state will, therefore, represent a unity of theory and practice, its rationality entwined with those working-class beliefs and behaviors it cultivates. It is truth manifest in concrete working-class praxis. Before workers can successfully rebel against capitalism, they must defeat both the political and civil components of the bourgeois state.

Intellectuals serve the distinctly political function of legitimating culture, making it accessible to everyone and universalizing its dominance. In maintaining class rule, therefore, they play as important a role as government officials charged with enacting and executing public law. They are the fuel of hegemonic structures, generating ideas, values, and beliefs that are repeatedly cranked out in books, journals, classrooms, pulpits, and air waves. They are disguised soldiers for the status quo. Their work represents society's cherished features, the basic, emotion-laden institutions and attitudes that we unthinkingly internalize as children and that later define us as members of a particular culture—what Gramsci calls a "historical bloc." Each historical bloc, because it survives and proves its rationality, has its own experts in legitimation who have successfully performed their allotted task. A historical bloc is an integral state rooted in an organic relationship, not merely an alliance, between leaders and masses.

Not surprisingly, Gramsci foresaw intellectuals playing a vital role in the imminent revolution. Revolutionary intellectuals demystify contemporary culture, showing the masses how bourgeois words and symbols represent the interests of the small group of capitalists dominating our historical bloc. In winning working-class minds, intellectuals prove their own rationality and necessity. The fruit of their intellectual labor is authentic worker self-consciousness, dialectically expressed in revolutionary praxis. Workers cannot be told, from above, to rebel. The impulse is subjectively experienced; working-class unity only emerges from a reflective identity of interests that smashes the bourgeois myth of autonomous individualism. "An historical act can only be performed by 'collective man,' and this presupposes the attainment of a 'cultural-social' unity through which a multiplicity of dispersed wills with heterogeneous aims, are welded together with a single aim, on the basis of an equal and common conception of the world. . . . "[79] This dramatic and complex project requires direct channels of communication connecting workers and intellectuals. Members of the intelligentsia perceiving themselves as "better" or "above" the average and working in an excessively abstract mode forfeit their proper historical function. They engage in irrational symbol games generating mystification and amusement. Authentic revolutionary intellectuals, on the contrary, share an identical life-world with workers. By manipulating universally accepted words, symbols, and emotions, they reflect the subjective side of workers' lives while implanting a critical attitude toward it. They are, in Gramsci's terminology, "organic," arising from and reflecting the objective needs of real working people. They come "directly out of the masses, but remain in contact with them to become, as it were, the whalebone in the corset."

The Party carefully organizes this transformation of proletarian consciousness and ensuing cultural renewal. It is a voluntary organization uniting intellectuals and workers in an "organic relationship" that generates proletariat hegemony. Through a coordinating or mediating role, it helps workers emancipate themselves and create a classless society of socialist justice. In brief, it actively organizes that "collective will" that intellectuals are slowly cultivating in workers' consciousness by systematically orchestrating the workers' movement prior to the revolutionary act, funneling new human energies in appropriate, rational directions. A spontaneous revolution could easily spin out of control in a churning, chaotic atmosphere. Party members must organically reflect subjective needs and ideas of the entire nonentrepreneurial population, including workers and peasants. When composed of self-styled "scientists" who know what to do regardless of workers' empirical attitudes, a Party becomes inbred and elitist, losing touch with the human forces that sculpt history into new blocs. But if haphazardly organized, a Party's effectiveness is neutralized. While avoiding a mindlessly inhuman structure, it must be run efficiently and hierarchically according to principles of "democratic centralism." The Party, in sum, is a complex unity of worker praxis and planned, conscious guidance, "the result of a dialectical process in which the spontaneous movement of the revolutionary masses and the organized and directive will at the centre converge . . . ."[80] It consciously directs worker and peasant activities into historically "correct," rational paths. When proletariat hegemony is finally established, it will have guaranteed "its own disappearance" as workers become educated in the art of self-management.

The Party's major problem is formulating institutions that propagate worker authenticity and also train workers in economic self-management. Undoubtedly influenced by Sorel, Gramsci speculated that the factory council movement, which flourished for a time throughout postwar Italy— especially in Turin—was appropriate.[81] When workers actively participate in running factories, even while still privately owned, they will likely recognize the historical necessity of complete worker self-management. Capitalism will become, in the minds of its workers, increasingly irrational.

The Party promotes these councils and taps the ensuing revolutionary fervor. Councils will remain after the Party dissolves, as the rational form of organizing free workers in communism.

Gramsci's idealist Marxism enticed disillusioned Westerners. It unequivocally rejected orthodox materialism as just another unverifiable metaphysics. But Gramsci emphasized the subjective moment of Hegel's dialectic more than predecessors. Proletarian self-consciousness is a voluntary, subjective expression of historical forces that, though evolving in concert with matter, are directly influenced by society's image makers. Proletarian praxis reflects a long process of learning to think differently, abandoning outmoded bourgeois ideas for more relevant socialist ones. Gramsci-ism generated principles that rushed gently, reassuringly on the ears of Western democrats. He was no raging ideologue whose doctrine trampled the emancipated: "It seems necessary to leave the task of researching after new truths and better, more coherent, clearer formulations of the truths themselves to the free initiative of individual specialists, even though they may continually question the very principles that seem most essential." Reflective public opinion is the guarantor of truth. "Mass adhesion or nonadhesion to an ideology is the real critical test of the rationality and historicity of modes of thinking." Freedom, then, "should not be conceived of in the administrative and police sense. . . . " Gramsci lauded basic civil liberties—individual freedoms of thought, press, speech, and association—as hallmarks of historical rationality. Just as the minds of individual workers must be won through the open interplay of competing ideas, each nation must respond in its own manner to capitalism's challenge. National Marxist Parties mold strategies to their workers' cultural beliefs. The alternative, imposing an absolute formula on all peoples regardless of subjective peculiarities, vitiates history's goal of establishing worldwide proletariat cultural hegemony. "The line of development is towards internationalism, but the point of departure is 'national'—and it is from this point of departure that one must begin."[82] Parties themselves are voluntary, organically reflecting actual, subjectively perceived proletarian needs, and council democracy is nonbureaucratic and nonhierarchic.

But Gramsci's epistemology is Hegelian, and the other dialectical shoe must eventually fall. Although human will—praxis—is the basis of philosophy, "it must be a rational, not an arbitrary, will, which is realized in so far as it corresponds to objective historical necessities, or in so far as it is universal history itself in the moment of its progressive actualization."[83] Gramsci's open society is no excuse for capriciousness. Praxis and historical necessity must and will correspond. The give and take of social freedom will result in Marxism's victory, its voluntary adoption by the masses. Revolution is historically necessary and inevitable, and this will be proven in worker praxis. Reformists are objectively wrong, and reformism is an irrational approach to capitalist exploitation. Like Rousseau's General

Will, Gramsci's Marxism presumes that subject and object, praxis and theory, freedom and necessity, will never conflict. This is also Lukács's presumption, but confronted with unaccommodating empirical conditions in Hungary and Western Europe, he reaffirmed the universal moment, first in the "scientific" Party and later by capitulating to orthodox materialism, which despite imperfections is apparently the current historical expression of universal truth. Ironically, Gramsci's tragic incarceration prevented him, as the acknowledged leader of the new Italian Communist Party, from dealing with similar problems in Italy. Had he avoided Mussolini's grasp and faced the probable conflicts between Party (universal) survival and actual (subjective) attitudes and conditions, he probably would not have stressed subjectivity to the extent he did when isolated in prison. On the other hand, if as head of the Italian Party he remained loyal to subjectivism, Stalin's henchmen would swiftly and surely have terminated both conflict and leader. In retrospect, Gramsci might view his own miserable fate, with its unspeakable physical pain as well as fruitful intellectual yield, as historically rational — universal truth dripping from a tyrant's bloody hands.

Kojève and Hyppolite

The two purest recent examples of Hegelian Marxism are Alexandre Kojève (1902-1968) and Jean Hyppolite (1907-1968). Both were Hegelians straining to prove that Marxism is merely an elaboration of themes that Hegel had already formulated primarily in the *Phenomenology of the Spirit*. Kojève, in particular, proffered a Marxist reading of Hegel. Although well known among French intellectuals as a professor at the École Pratique des Hautes Études (1933-1939), Kojève actually published very little.[84] The roots of Kojève's dialectical materialism were contained in Hegel's philosophical anthropology. In Hegel's dialectic of master and servant, Kojève saw the origins of Marx's revolutionary proletariat and the idea that labor is the motor of historical change. His was, therefore, a concrete, materialist Hegelianism.

Hegel rejected the bourgeois premise that individuals are rational, autonomous subjects always calculating self-interest and protecting property. Men and women are indelibly *in* history. What one does and how it is done are questions answered by the sociohistorical milieu, which is bound to universal processes. The first historical "moment" of human reality is a simple, non-self-conscious, passive awareness of external objects — the world of sensation, perception, and primitive consciousness. At this stage of history subjectivity is not yet constituted. Eventually human beings recognize in themselves a distinctive conscious humanity and the need for others to acknowledge it. We are constituted as human beings by interacting with, and being acknowledged by, other people. "Real and true man is the result of his interaction with others," the original impulse by which history and nature are humanized.[85] As actors quest for recognition and affirmation of autonomous humanity, they are thrown into social relationships. Thus begins the next developmental stage, marked by wars of prestige. In risking our physical lives to gain others' respect and recognition, we implicitly acknowledge the humanity of competitors, and they of us. Human history now is struggle and war, battles to the death where humanity rises triumphantly from the ashes.

While some perish, these struggles terminate by establishing permanent relations between combatants. The victor is powerful, controlling, autonomous consciousness; the slave, vanquished and dependent. Civilization consists of societies of rulers and ruled, kings and serfs. Like all of history, this stage also generates inherent conflicts and contradictions. Master and slave define each other, shaping the other's consciousness. Ironically, the master's humanity is recognized only by the slave who, in the eyes of others, is unworthy. To everyone else, the master is merely a "slave owner," an objectified, dehumanized role. Thus, the master continually searches for an autonomous individual to acknowledge his humanity. The fruits of victory are frustration and anguish. The slave, acknowledged by no one and defeated in battle, is angry. In the terror of his master's oppression, the slave discovers his humanity as something denied and strives for the freedom to develop. This he achieves through labor, or praxis: actively humanizing nature and society, bringing them under his own willful control. Through labor and its products, slaves recognize their objective humanity. History's universal process culminates in mankind's authentic freedom. Each laborer eventually perceives himself as " 'incarnated' Spirit, . . . historical 'World,' . . . 'objectivized' History."[86]

Hegel was the first to accord labor an immanent, rather than instrumental, value. It is the vehicle for humanity's evolution to autonomous consciousness and hence the essence of humanity. Through labor, the masses (that is, the working class) create a productive apparatus that satisfies material needs and facilitates control of nature and society. Marx merely described the concrete forms that this struggle takes, actual material stages in the universal progression from exploitation and alienation to revolutionary freedom. Hegelianism, therefore, generated revolutionary Marxism. Historical materialism describes universal history in the contemporary era of humanity's liberation from masters, extending Hegel's analyses of historicity and dialectical logic. Marx's proletariat revolution culminates a total human movement from nonreflective passivity to "fully conscious consciousness," where workers cognitively will universal truth.[87] Hegel's World Spirit works itself out in the concrete praxis of workers.

Hyppolite, more than Kojève, was descriptively faithful to Hegel's texts.[88] He is interested in discerning a common theme rather than justifying a Marxian interpretation of the *Phenomenology*. This he found in the distinguishing trait of both Hegelianism and Marxism: the historicity of Reason.

Because Reason is realized in and expressed by actual history, human progress toward "rationality" requires a heightening awareness of existing social forms of cooperation. Authentic self-consciousness, in other words, occurs only in community, where existences for and with others congeal into history's total movement. This is Hegel's meaning in depicting the master-slave relationship. Hyppolite believed that Marx and Hegel shared a deep concern for capitalist alienation and dehumanization. People must function as more than nonreflective commodities if they are finally to realize potentials as free, rational actors. Marx's economic and social critique of capitalism concretely expressed Hegel's more general belief in the historical necessity of reason and freedom. Proletariat revolution is reasonable in the Hegelian sense, reflectively expressing history's global tendencies. Hyppolite, as well as Kojève, conveniently ignored Hegel's *Philosophy of Right,* which equates rationality and freedom with the preservation of dominant bourgeois institutions.

Kojève and Hyppolite were professional philosophers, not social theorists, elucidating and defending Hegelianism. They rekindled in postwar Europe the Hegelian impulse that motivates idealist Marxism, that is, proletariat revolution as a subjectively experienced moment in history's abstract objective totality. Hence they reaffirmed for contemporary Marxists the relevance of Lukács, Korsch, and Gramsci.

Kolakowski

Leszek Kolakowski (b. 1927) is a Polish national whose professional career spans the eras of Stalinist orthodoxy and post-Stalinist revisionism. He is, understandably, a difficult person to pin down philosophically. His early work was synchronized with the orthodox materialist Party line. After the intellectual thaw accompanying Stalin's death, he proffered a basically anti-Party, critical social theory eclectically borrowing from orthodoxy, the Frankfurt School, humanist socialism, and Hegel. Obviously motivated both to condemn the Marxist totalitarianism he had experienced firsthand and to preserve Marx's sense of proletariat justice, Kolakowski defends ethical individualism ("only individuals and their actions are subject to moral elevation"), social determinism ("moral judgments are socially conditioned"), and the absolute right to judge existing institutions morally. Here is an impassioned plea for nonoppressive, humane institutions in Eastern Europe that is also philosophically weak—coming, as one commentator puts it, "dangerously close to syncretism."[89] It is one thing to condemn totalitarian social theory, quite another to redefine Marxism through a pastiche of incompatible ideas.

In recent work, Kolakowski finally comes clean: "There is no discontinuity in Marx's thought . . . it was from first to last inspired by basically Hegelian philosophy." Kolakowski's Marxism postulates that "the historical process and the free development of consciousness will be one and the same." In his usual eloquent style, Kolakowski philosophically joins hands with Lukács, Korsch, and Gramsci.[90] However, Kolakowski's background makes him extraordinarily sensitive to the potentially heinous consequences of absolute historical laws—material or ideal—mediated by Party scientists. He therefore is Hegelian in perceiving the revolutionary significance of reflective proletarian self-consciousness but wary of its dialectical correlate: objective universality. Kolakowski emphasizes the sanctity and necessity of free, subjective praxis, even in revolutionary and postrevolutionary situations. His angry critique of Marxist theoreticians, institutions, and ultimately Marxism itself, is generated by this subjectivism. Kolakowski is thus philosophically vulnerable, for without an a priori foundation he risks solipsism. He lauds the Hegelian origins of Marxism, and then shamelessly attacks Lukács and Luxembourg for the Stalinist sin of defending a non-empirical, autonomous reality manifesting "authentic" freedom. Historical materialism, he declares, describes "mass phenomena which are not consciously willed by anyone but which obey social laws that are as regular and impersonal as the laws of physical nature," and concludes "in the fullness of time the economic factor will prevail." Then he recants: social life derives "its creative forces from . . . [no] other source than . . . personal, subjective existence." He surmises that historical materialism explains broad trends, not individual acts, but also criticizes Engels for ambiguous comments concerning the priority of economics "in the last resort." Finally, he continually discusses proletarian praxis as realizing human essence, but castigates "the dilemma of utopianism."[91]

Kolakowski solves his problems somewhat disingenuously.[92] Notwithstanding the Hegelian wellspring of Marxism and his own sympathy for Marx's moral exhortations, he equates Marxism solely with its orthodox Stalinist practitioners. Dialectical materialism, in this vulgar materialist form, is a threat to everyone's liberty ("negative freedom"), hence incompatible with proletariat justice. Methodologically, Marxism's emphasis on the priority of economics is self-defeating: Carried to one extreme, it is absurd; to the other, commonplace. As ideology and method, Marxism is a dead letter in humanity's struggle for social justice. Perhaps projecting his own intellectual plight, Kolakowski contends that all Marxists interested in authentic subjectivity have already, or will eventually, discard Marxism in favor of reformist democratic socialism, which values liberal freedoms. In the end, Kolakowski's unpleasant experiences in Poland overwhelm the concern for dialectical subtleties. Subjects must be protected at all costs, even by naively positing an unbreakable connection between Marxism and Stalinism.

The entire history of Hegelian Marxism illustrates its potential compatibility with Marx's major hypotheses. As part of that history, a bit of critical self-reflection should have muted Kolakowski's emotional condemnations, which negate an entire body of respected literature as well as his own Marxist reputation. Perhaps the guilt of an ex-Stalinist who lived through the hellish nightmare of his own beliefs has overwhelmed Kolakowski's impressive intellect and sensitivity.

NOTES

1. The dissertation was completed in 1841. Parts of it were published by Mehring (1920), and it first appeared in toto in 1927. English translations are in N. Livergood, *Marx's Philosophy of Action* (The Hague: Martinus Nijhoff, 1967) and David McLellan, ed., *The Early Texts* (Oxford: Oxford University Press, 1971).

2. See Karl Marx, *Doctoral Thesis,* in *Karl Marx, Selected Writings,* ed. David McLellan (London: Oxford University Press, 1977), p.15. Hereafter cited as *KMSW.*

3. Ibid., pp. 17-18. See also pp. 20-22.

4. Karl Marx, *Introduction to A Critique of Hegel's Philosophy of Right,* in Karl Marx, *Early Writings* (New York: Vintage Books, 1975), p. 257. Hereafter cited as *KMEW.*

5. See Karl Marx, *Economic and Philosophical Manuscripts,* in *KMEW,* pp. 327-28 and 345-58. See also Z. A. Jordan, *The Evolution of Dialectical Materialism* (London: Macmillan, 1967).

6. This is Marx's terminology (*Economic and Philosophical Manuscripts,* in *KMEW,* p. 329).

7. Ibid., p. 328.

8. Ibid., pp. 347-50.

9. Ibid., p. 375.

10. See especially Marx, *Introduction to A Critique of Hegel's Philosophy of Right,* p. 254.

11. Marx, *Economic and Philosophical Manuscripts,* p. 348.

12. Ibid., p. 332.

13. Ibid.

14. Ibid., p. 324.

15. Ibid., p. 326.

16. Ibid., p. 330.

17. Marx, "Excerpts from James Mill's *Elements of Political Economy,*" in ibid., p. 275.

18. Marx, *Economic and Philosophical Manuscripts,* in ibid., p. 352.

19. Leszek Kolakowski, *Main Currents of Marxism,* 3 vols. (London: Oxford University Press, 1978), 1: 302-3.

20. Karl Marx, *The German Ideology* (Moscow: Progress Pubs., 1976), p. 96.

21. Karl Marx, *Communist Manifesto,* in *KMSW,* pp. 226 and 238.

22. Karl Marx, *Wage-Labour and Capital,* in ibid., esp. p. 250.

23. Karl Marx, *Grundrisse* (New York: Vintage Books, 1973), p. 323.

24. Ibid., pp. 284 and 293.

25. See chapter five.

26. Marx, *Grundrisse,* p. 307.

27. See chapter five.

28. See Marx, *Grundrisse,* pp. 161–62, 172–73, 325, 487–88, 540–42, 611, 652, 706,

708, 712, 749, 831–32.

29. Marx, *Grundrisse*, p. 611.

30. The quotes are in ibid., pp. 611, 157, 162, 488, and 611.

31. Karl Marx, *Capital* 3 vols. (New York: International Pubs., 1975), 1:571.

32. Ibid., pp. 72 (see pp. 71–83), 419–23, and 73–77. See also *Theories of Surplus Value* 3 vols. (Moscow: Progress Pubs., 1969–72), I, pp. 389–90, 392; and *Results of the Immediate Process of Production,* 2 vols. (1865; Reprint ed., Moscow: Arkhiv Marksa i Engelsa, 1933), vol. II, pt. 7, pp. 197f and 213ff.

33. Eric Fromm, "The Application of Humanist Psychoanalysis to Marx's Theory," in *Socialist Humanism,* ed. Fromm (New York: Anchor Books, 1966), p. 242. See also Kolakowski, *Main Currents of Marxism,* 1: 132–33; and R. Dunayevskaya, *Marxism and Freedom* (London: Pluto Press, 1971), pp. 103ff.

34. Marx, *Capital,* 1: 488. Emphasis added.

35. Marx, *Grundrisse*, p. 325; and *Capital,* 3: 934. See also *The German Ideology,* p. 224. ("Labour is free in all civilized countries; it is not a matter of freeing labour but of abolishing it.")

36. See Antonio Labriola, *Essays on the Materialist Conception of History* (1896) (New York: Monthly Review Press, 1966); *Various Writings on Philosophy and Politics,* ed. B. Croce (Bari: Laterza, 1906); and *Socialism and Philosophy* (1897) (St. Louis, Missouri: Telos Press, 1980).

37. Labriola to Sorel (10 May 1897), in Kolakowski, *Main Currents of Marxism,* 1: 190–91.

38. Labriola, *Essays on the Materialistic Conception of History,* pp. 135 and 123.

39. Ibid., p. 153.

40. Ibid., pp. 124, 111, and 124. See pp. 98, 110–24, and 135–55.

41. Her economics, today, is generally condemned, even by Marxists. It misrepresents, for example, the will of capitalists to sacrifice compound accumulation for simple accumulation when its survival is at stake. It ignores the potential role of the government in regulating production and consumption, and the safety-valve function of the armaments industry. It wrongly predicted the quick disappearance of non-capitalist underdeveloped markets. In addition, it underestimated capitalism's ability to survive by raising wages and increasing domestic markets via commercial advertising.

42. See Rosa Luxembourg, *The Russian Revolution* and *Leninism or Marxism?* (Ann Arbor, Mich.: University of Michigan Press, 1976), and *Selected Writings,* ed. D. Howard (New York: Monthly Review Press, 1971), esp. pp. 368ff.

43. Luxembourg, *The Russian Revolution,* p. 78.

44. Anton Pannekoek, *Workers' Councils* (Melbourne: Southern Advocate for Workers' Councils, 1950), p. 29. See also Stanley Aronowitz, "Left-Wing Communism: The Reply to Lenin," *The Unknown Dimension,* ed. Karl Klare and Dick Howard (New York: Basic Books, 1972), pp. 169–94, and Richard Gombin, *The Origins of Modern Leftism* (Baltimore, Md.: Penguin Books, 1975), pp. 87–97.

45. See Pannekoek, *Workers' Councils,* esp. chap. 1 and pp. 69, 85, 201–2, and 225.

46. This metaphysics is outlined in Jean Jaurès, *De la réalité du monde sensible* (doctoral dissertation, Toulouse Univ., 1891). The following argument is found in Jaurès, *Oeuvres,* 9 vols. (Paris: Rieder, 1931–1939), esp. 4: 94ff.

47. Other idealists reaching toward Marxism include P. B. Struve, S. N. Bulgakov,

and N. A. Berdyaev. See George L. Kline, "Kolakowski and the Revision of Marxism," in *European Philosophy Today,* ed. Kline (Chicago: Quadrangle Books, 1965), pp. 117-66, esp. pp. 130-36; and idem., "Changing Attitudes Towards the Individual," in *The Transformation of Russian Society,* ed. C. E. Black (Cambridge: Cambridge University Press, 1960), pp. 618-23.

48. See Georg Lukács, *The Theory of the Novel* (Cambridge, Mass.: MIT Press, 1971), pp. 12-13.

49. *Grundrisse,* lost for many years, was first published in the original German in 1953. Limited editions had been published by Foreign Language Publishers in Moscow in two volumes (1939 and 1941, respectively). Lukács read Marx's *1844 Manuscripts*—still unpublished—when at the Marx-Engels-Lenin Institute in 1930-1931.

50. Georg Lukács, *Existentialisme ou Marxisme?* (Paris: Nagel, 1948), p. 48.

51. For a complete bibliography see G. H. R. Parkinson (ed.), *Georg Lukács* (New York: Vintage, 1971), pp. 238-43.

52. Georg Lukács, *History and Class Consciousness* (Cambridge: MIT Press, 1971), p. 5.

53. Lukács thus separates natural and technological science, presumably governed by objective laws that determine the interrelationships between nonhuman phenomena and social science based on dialectics.

54. Lukács, *History and Class Consciousness,* p. 19. See also pp. 189ff. and 271.

55. Ibid., pp. 229, 224, 189, 51, and 27.

56. Ibid., p. 87. See also p. 103.

57. Ibid., p. 7.

58. Ibid., p. 51.

59. Ibid., pp. 268, 136, 169, and 259. See also pp. 197ff.

60. The orthodox reaction to Lukács's critique of Engels and Lenin was fierce. In "Mein Weg zu Marx" (1933), Lukács hesitatingly withdrew his critique. In "The Significance of *Materialism and Empirio-Criticism* for the Bolshevization of Communist Parties" in the Hungarian journal *Pod zumenem Marksizna* (1934), he more explicitly criticized himself and *History and Class Consciousness* as hopelessly idealistic and praised Stalin for preserving the best of Marxism-Leninism.

61. Lukács, *History and Class Consciousness,* pp. 68-81 and 295-339.

62. Ibid., pp. 79-80.

63. Ibid., pp. 204 and 142.

64. Lukács, Preface to the New Edition (1967) of ibid., pp. xvii-xx, xxiv, and xxiii.

65. Karl Korsch, *Marxism and Philosophy* (New York: Monthly Review Press, 1970), pp. 93 and 68.

66. Ibid., pp. 49-50.

67. Karl Korsch, "The Present State of the Problem of 'Marxism and Philosophy'—An Anti-Critique" (1930), in ibid., pp. 98-144. The quotes are on pp. 104-17.

68. See ibid., pp. 133-39.

69. Ibid., p. 144. See also pp. 94-97.

70. Ibid., pp. 44f.

71. Karl Korsch, "Why I Am a Marxist," *Modern Quarterly* 9, no. 2 (April 1935): 88-95, esp. p. 89.

72. These include, in addition to the *Notebooks: Il materialismo storico e la filosofia di Benedetto Croce* (1948), *Gli intellettuali e l'organizzazione della cultura*

(1949), *Il risorgimenti* (1949), *Note sul Machiavelli, sulla politica e sullo Stato moderno* (1949), *Letterature e vita nazionale* (1950), and *Passato e presente* (1951). Useful secondary works include John M. Cammett, *Antonio Gramsci and the Origins of Italian Communism* (Palo Alto, Calif.: Stanford University Press, 1967); and Christine Buci-Glucksmann, *Gramsci and the State* (London: Lawrence & Wishart, 1980).

73. Antonio Gramsci, *La Città futura* (Milan: Feltrinelli, 1959), p. 4.

74. Antonio Gramsci, *Selections from the Prison Notebooks* (New York: International Publishers, 1971), pp. 337–407. See pp. 381–472 and 12.

75. Ibid., esp. pp. 352–54.

76. Ibid., pp. 369 and 365. See also pp. 356–57, 395–402, and 425ff.

77. Ibid., pp. 3ff, 169–72, 351–66, and 434–36.

78. Ibid., p. 244. See also pp. 12f, 259, 264–65, 366–67, and "Letter to Tatania" (9 July 1931) in *Lettere dal Carcere* (Turin, Italy: Einaudi, 1947), pp. 479–83.

79. Gramsci, *Selections from the Prison Notebooks,* p. 349. See also pp. 3–23, 201–2, and 323–80. The following quote is on p. 340.

80. "Letter to Togliatti" (2 September 1924) in John Merrington, "Theory and Practice in Gramsci's Marxism," *Western Marxism,* (London: Verso, 1978), p. 171. See also Gramsci, *Selections from the Prison Notebooks,* pp. 147–57 and 196–200. The following brief excerpt is on p. 152.

81. Many of Gramsci's articles for the Italian journal *L'Ordine Nuovo* focus on the Turin experiment in worker democracy. See Antonio Gramsci, *Political Writings 1921–1926* (New York: International Publishers, 1978), pp. 109–13, 142–46, and 260–64.

82. Gramsci, *Selections from the Prison Notebooks,* pp. 341 and 240. See also p. 350.

83. Ibid., p. 345.

84. Kojève's best known published work is actually a compilation of his students' notebooks, collected and edited by Raymond Queneau. The English edition is *Introduction to the Reading of Hegel* (New York: Basic Books, 1969).

85. Ibid., p. 15.

86. Ibid., p. 25.

87. Ibid., p. 35. See also pp. 130ff.

88. See Jean Hyppolite, *Introduction à la philosophie de l'histoire de Hegel* (1948; Reprint ed., Paris: M. Rivière, 1968); *Genèse et structure de la phénoménologie de l'esprit de Hegel* (Paris: Aubier, 1946), esp. pp. 35, 235, 246; *Logique et existence: essai sur la Logique de Hegel* (Paris: Presses universitaires de France, 1953); *Études sur Marx et Hegel* (1955), English translation by John O'Neill, *Studies on Marx and Hegel* (New York: Basic Books, 1969), esp. pp. 13 and 162f; and *Marxisme et existentialisme* (Paris: M. Rivière, 1962), esp. p. 46.

89. Kline, "Kolakowski and the Revision of Marxism," p. 153. The earlier quotes by Kolakowski are on p. 152. Kolakowski's early works include *Toward a Marxist Humanism, Marxism and Beyond,* and *The Alienation of Reason.*

90. Kolakowski, *Main Currents of Marxism,* 1: 263, 322. See also pp. 222–24, 402–3, and 304.

91. Ibid., pp. 341, 340, 312, and 304. See also 3: 253–307; 2: 61–97; and 1: 223 and 343–44.

92. Ibid., 3: 487ff.

4.

Non-Hegelian Idealism

Lukács, Korsch, and Gramsci so effectively plumbed the Hegelian foundation of Marxism that by the end of World War II, except for the more ephemeral work of Hyppolite, Kojève, and Kolakowski, there was little left to say. Idealist Marxism therefore turned to classical idealism. Hegelians view humanity historically, and define freedom as a merging of subjectivity and universality that occurs only at a certain stage in society's material development. Human nature is inconceivable apart from the global movement of history. Classical idealists, on the other hand, define essentiality as an objective, ahistorical quality transcending temporality. Human nature is static: It never changes even though humanity lives through various historical stages of ignorance regarding its real dimensions. There is a clear sense in which essentiality—including objective human nature—takes primacy over human evolution in history. Classical idealists evaluate the truth or falsity of cultures on their approximating a timeless ideal. This is somewhat different from the Hegelian position, which recognizes the "truth" of all cultures and putative views of human nature as partial manifestations of an increasingly self-evident universal process. Of course, both forms of idealism define truth as an a priori abstraction subjectively realized in thought, related to matter but not its epiphenomenon. The postwar evolution of idealist Marxism exhibits both tendencies, but moves steadily in a non-Hegelian direction.

By vulgarizing idealism, Marxism opens itself to the entire range of bourgeois philosophies. Materialist and Hegelian idealist Marxism are inherently antithetical to bourgeois ideas, defining them as transitory developmental stages in a global movement leading to socialism. However, when Marxism is dehistoricized, verified by static and timeless principles just like bourgeois antagonists, accommodation is possible. Marxists accepting a bourgeois idealized view of human nature "radicalize" it by demonstrating first its resemblance to Marx's early ideas concerning species-being, and then capitalism's negative impact on its realization. Ensuing possibilities are vast: humanist, structuralist, even Freudian Marxism. All three schools are particularly interesting because their major representatives have enormous followings among academic, activist, and lay Westerners.

HUMANIST MARXISM

The fears and pressures afflicting Kolakowski are endemic to an entire school of predominantly Eastern European philosophers. The so-called "humanist" Marxists flowered first in postwar Yugoslavia, already revising orthodox communism with workers' councils that meaningfully influenced the central Party's economic decision making. In this relatively decentralized environment, cultural and artistic debate swelled. From 1964 until its forced closing in 1975, a journal called *Praxis* carried thoughtful discussion of significant issues of Marxist epistemology, ethics, and aesthetics. Contributors, many of whom had been partisan fighters during the war, informally organized themselves and convened annual meetings attended by international scholars. The *Praxis* group thus had immediate and direct access to the non-Communist West and became quite popular among many politically active students and intellectuals. They comprised the spirit and body of humanist Marxism.[1] They also increasingly irritated Yugoslav state and Party authorities. Most were eventually expelled or forced to resign from the Party and by 1975 were also relieved of university positions.

Humanists rescued praxis, the subjective moment of Lukács's and Gramsci's Hegelian dialectic, from heavy-handed materialism, but their Stalinist backgrounds had sensitized them to the potential dangers of a priori totalities. Hence, they were idealist Marxists wary of the objective moment of history's global movement. Unlike Kolakowski, rather than abandoning Marxism as inimical to subjective autonomy, humanists absolutize Hegel's idealism by dehistoricizing it, transforming it into a transcendent truth immanent to humanity at every stage of human development. Marx, remember, believed that capitalism occludes human nature. Indeed, Marx's work, early and late, is unified around idealistic, ahistorical preconceptions regarding pure being. Humanist Marxists believed it "a simple matter to establish beyond dispute that from his youth to the very end of his life Marx thought and wrote about man as man, and labored to give the fullest possible definition to human essence."[2] Revolution is *not* caused by objective material laws, for these are philosophically unjustifiable. Workers rebel after subjectively realizing that capitalism obliterates essential humanity, transforming people into something they are not. Socialism is justifiable only when institutionalizing these same essential qualities.

The distinctive essence of humanity is praxis, "a structure of being peculiar to ... [us] which is common to all really human properties and activities." Humanists adopt the early Marxian notions, from the *Manuscripts,* of individuals laboring in nature to satisfy needs and cognizing a natural world that they are subjectively engaged in. However, they freeze this active moment and absolutize it. Praxis is undetermined and autonomous, an act "by which man changes his world and himself ... [and] determines his deed by himself."[3] Human essence is "the potential to achieve self-realization through the process of self-creation."[4] The distinguishing trait of men and women, the quality that always has and will separate us from other creatures, is the essentiality of creative labor. Human action is subjectively generated, expressing "profound internal needs" that manifest the "unconstrained development of all of one's abilities."[5] Humanist Marxism presumes that humanity's inherent ability to interact creatively with nature and society will translate, practically, into cooperative social behavior. Actors, in other words, are naturally "total" beings, open to others. Capitalism and Stalinist socialism repress this potential, fractionalize personalities, and alienate citizens from essential selves and fellow human beings. Whether enslaved by the market or Party bureaucrats, people are denied their potentials, forced into subhuman, determined lives. Social justice, in such circumstances, is inconceivable. However, when emancipated into authenticity, we live creatively and cooperatively in socialist equality. Neither bourgeois philosophy nor orthodox dialectical materialism correctly perceives *"true* human needs and *basic* capacities, *positive* freedom . . . and human *emancipation."*[6] An aroused international citizenry must create a socialist ideology based on worker autonomy and self-government, a cooperative, planned economy realizing subjective freedom.

Humanist Marxism establishes the difficult, perhaps impossible, task of demonstrating how the historical evolution of concrete economic and social forms emanates from constant, ahistorical, essential structures of being. This is also existential Marxism's project, but people like Sartre are better equipped with a carefully formulated ontology open to history and matter. Humanists, on the other hand, unceremoniously assume essential structures that apparently lie in an ideal, ahistorical reality approached only by self-determined acts of will. The dialectical link between history and revolution is severed. There is no way of telling when or where proletariat revolution will occur, because praxis is a spontaneous subjective expression of a constant truth. As a philosophy of history, therefore, it is neither scientific nor particularly revolutionary, emphasizing an a priori realm theoretically realizable in any institutional surroundings. This prompts Petrović, for example, to admit even non-Marxist bourgeois philosophy is valuable for scientific inquiry.[7]

Most Praxis philosophers, however, are less conciliatory, seeking humanism and Marxism in the traditional sense. Adam Schaff, who from 1945 to 1950 was the chief Polish spokesman for orthodox Marxism, was transformed in the post-Stalinist thaw into a humanist who still believed that Marxist philosophy is revolutionary and "scientific." His solution: redefine essential subjectivity to include nature, matter, and self-determining praxis. We labor creatively, even though praxis is impersonally determined by society and nature. "When a Marxist talks of autonomous anthropology, he means that the world as a product of social man's self-creation is independent of any superhuman factors; he is far from asserting the individuals autonomous existence. . . . "[8] "Objective laws of historical development" lead inevitably to revolution, realized in self-determined, "autonomous," purposeful praxis. Schaff explicitly rejected materialism, idealism, and proposed syntheses (for example, Lenin and Kosík, Lukács and Gramsci). He outlined a new humanism in which the essential quality of praxis is also essentially historical and revolutionary, diluting the meanings of relevant terms. Most humanist Marxists are situated philosophically somewhere between Petrović and Schaff, advocating either abstract intellectualism or some incoherent synthesis of idealism and materialism.

Humanist Marxism denies materialist objectivity, critically rejects hierarchic, centralized Party bureaucracies run by self-proclaimed scientists, and advocates worker self-government. Briefly, it supports socialist democracy based on worker praxis rather than Party dictatorship. In post-Stalinist Eastern Europe, where humanist Marxism began, it is a radical, even revolutionary alternative, sufficiently threatening to justify suppression by hegemonic elites. Humanist dissidents in Hungary, Czechoslovakia, Poland, and the Soviet Union have confirmed orthodoxy's worst fears. However, humanist Marxism's role in Western liberal democracies is not as clear. As a theory of capitalist exploitation and proletariat revolution, it is weak and ineffective. Its idealized version of humanity guarantees subjective autonomy and emphasizes reflection, hence is unusually attractive to liberal intellectuals. Although socialist, humanism's indeterminism blunts its revolutionary impact. Western humanist Marxists usually write books rather than organize workers. While others actively realize history's immanent movement, humanists describe the essence of life and illustrate capitalism's artificiality. Whether the concrete effects of this strategy are radical is, to say the least, problematic.

FREUDIAN MARXISM

Like humanism, Freudian idealism strikes a sympathetic note among many liberals. Predictably, its radicalization has provoked interest and support, especially among Western scholars and professionals. The school's major representatives—Reich, Marcuse, and Fromm—provocatively iterate the sexual aspects of capitalist exploitation.

Reich

Wilhelm Reich (1897–1957), who died a recreant in Lewisburg, Pennsylvania, federal prison, spent his professional life examining the social function of psychological processes. A student and admirer of Sigmund Freud, Reich also perceived a basic, precognitive impulse in human beings generating the physical release of inherent sexual energy. Other aspects of the psyche—unconscious or conscious—are derived from this quantifiable sexual energy and the dynamics of sexual instincts constantly pressing for discharge. Freud argued that sexual repression was inherent to civilization and potentially healthy if properly channeled into alternative means of symbolic expression. Reich contended, to the contrary, that blocked sexual energy led inevitably to neuroses. When sexual blockage is eliminated, inner psychological conflicts dissolve. This is not a matter of just engaging in genital orgasm but also requires a more general emancipation of psychic and physical forces, "the capacity of surrender to the flow of biological energy without any inhibition, the capacity for complete discharge of all damned-up sexual excitation."[9]

Reich's Freudian preconceptions and his intellectual and political commitment to Marxism (1927-1936) are reconciled in the dialectical connection between psychic impulses and concrete social forms.[10] He claimed that the sex drive is one of several material human needs that Marx implicitly recognized—analogous to hunger, thirst, and labor. Just as humans must eat, drink, and actively produce, so too must they discharge sexual energy. For most people, especially Westerners, living socially means, in effect, that we are at least minimally fed and quenched and are producing needed goods. Sexual impulse is apparently not directly related to physical survival. Indeed, there are subcultures that reward abstinence, and members will survive as long as nonsexual needs are satiated. But this fact obscures the pervasive influence that sexual instincts have on the quality of experienced life. By blocking release of physical energies, we emasculate psyches, producing environments that feed mental disorder and encourage perverted, nonhuman life-styles. Since the advent of patriarchal society, these unnatural inhibitions are precisely what humankind has been engaging in, building elaborate institutions designed, subliminally at least, to control active sexuality. Economic and social institutions, in other words, mediate sexual instincts and humanity's nearly universal fear of uninhibited sex. Marx's analysis of the dialectical interpenetration of base and superstructure is entirely consistent with Reich's self-styled Freudianism. Concrete social and economic factors affect and express the manner in which sexual instincts are dealt with. In capitalism, as Marx has shown, the dominant economic class exploits workers by expropriating surplus value. Culture reinforces this relationship, obfuscating material reality with a barrage of bourgeois rhetoric. Sexual attitudes are part of this rhetoric, and therefore a tool for maintaining capitalism. However, sexual energy is also inherent to all humanity, irrespective of historically conditioned social forms. Capitalism is merely the current social means for coming to terms with this vital force. Like prior forms of patriarchal society, it is motivated by fear and ignorance. Capitalist production, which Marx analyzed so precisely, aids in repressing sexual energy. While capitalists exploit workers and create potentially self-destructive revolutionary conditions, they also formulate ideas and institutions that perpetuate an age-old bias against unfettered human sexual discharge. Socialism, a mode of production encouraging free, uninhibited self-expression for everyone, is a necessary material precondition for sexual emancipation. In postrevolutionary socialist equality there is no longer an elite to profit from sexual repression. Economic and political democracy are dialectically expressed in liberated attitudes toward all human relationships. Capitalism is inadvertently pushing us toward socialist justice and sexual liberation.

The dialectical interpenetration of sexuality and economics is central to Reich's Marxism and is originally based on the priority of materialism— transforming psychoanalysis into a branch of orthodox dialectical materialism. At this early point, Reich was "clearly aware that the unconscious structures which are . . . reacting irrationally are themselves the product of historical-socio-economic processes, and that, therefore, they cannot be ascribed to unconscious mechanisms as opposed to economic causes, but viewed as forces mediating between social being and human modes of reaction." The human psyche evolves dialectically, mimicking nature. Hence psychic evolution depends on economic and social conditions, which impersonally channel instincts into predetermined avenues: "the libido process is secondary to social development and dependent on it. . . ."[11] Sexual practices are "in the last resort" economically conditioned. Freud's "super-ego" (our impulse to be "good"; ethics and morality) is a social product, the determined consequence of matter influencing instincts.

Later, recognizing the obvious incongruity between orthodox Marxism and psychoanalysis, Reich became idealist, joining other Marxists who were uncomfortable with the Engelsian tradition.[12] The libido's historical development, though entwined with matter, now autonomously conditions human "working capacity," that is, the quality and forms of labor in history. Psychoanalytical social inquiry is useful independent of dialectical materialism. Clearly, the "essence" of humanity is perceived as an ahistorical ideal in which sexual energy is uninhibitedly discharged. The dialectical interpenetration of economics and sexual instincts takes place under the aegis of an a priori ideal only partially manifest in concrete matter.

Instincts and social conditions are mediated by what Reich calls "character structures": naively internalized rules depicting "normal" behavior in "typical" everyday conditions.[13] We generate character structures by life-long formal and informal processes of education, socialization, and peer pressure. Personal identity, "the specific way of being an individual," is defined by character structure. Gestated in infancy to protect against external punishment (for example, from parents, teachers, clergy), character structure protects adults from internal antisocial impulses. Throughout life we hide in "normal," "expected" behavior to avoid social and psychic dislocations. The actual quality of character structures depends on the particular class we belong to and on membership in class society. Personalities, in other words, are both class-determined and class society-determined. We become, for example, "typical" workers, with emotional, intellectual, and physical traits admired in working-class neighborhoods and factories. In class society generally, the hegemonic ruling class uses an ideology that, intergenerationally, perpetuates character structures that reinforce the existing social order. Capitalist ideology emphasizes qualities like individualism, self-interest, competition, patriotism, religion, and family—epitomized by the "typical" bourgeois entrepreneurial personality: a disciplined, hard-working, family-oriented businessman, guided by eternal spiritual and market principles. The "typical" worker in capitalism aggressively competes with peers in non-work-related activities, identifies with successful professional sports and entertainment personalities, provides for his family even at the cost of uninspiring, tedious workdays, and loves God and country. Both character structures—employer and employee—reinforce and perpetuate capitalism and bourgeois culture.

Character structures perform the important functions of producing "good" citizens and reinforcing class rule. Their prime purpose, however, is to repress humanity's inherent sexual instincts by absorbing a portion of libidinal energy and legitimizing the acquisition of private property. Humanity long ago recognized that accumulating property is inconsistent with free and natural sexual discharge. Men needed wives and children to survive physically as well as to protect and exploit land. Permanent and stable family units, however, could not survive in an atmosphere of uninhibited sexuality. Thus, the origins of sexual repression are in the birth of patriarchal social arrangements. These generated unique character structures, which drove men and women into permanent monogamous family units and rewarded husbands with a dowry of land and/or other resources needed to accumulate fortunes. Henceforth, character structures worked to reinforce property rights by blocking sexual fulfillment with rules and prohibitions that "normal" people unquestioningly accept. In capitalism, they embody the bourgeois rejection of profligacy and admiration for self-sacrifice, discipline, marriage, and family. These modern character structures inhibit full sexual orgasm and promote social attitudes that explicitly reject unfettered sexuality but implicitly encourage sex-oriented institutions based on fantasies and repressed libidinal drives. The unhealthy confluence of libidinal energy and bourgeois asceticism generates a dull, uncreative, uncritical, passive, irrational mass population—precisely the qualities that a society geared toward commodity rather than use value requires. It is certainly not coincidental that capitalism degenerates to fascism, populated by frustrated, fearful, guilt-ridden, and anxious citizens. In sum, the social (that is, to reinforce capitalism) and psychic (that is, to repress inherent sexual energy) functions of contemporary character structures overlap. Reich's theory explains the origin and survival of capitalist alienation, "bridging the gap" between actual working-class inauthenticity and exploitative material conditions.

Psychoanalysis transforms character structure to reflect the actual essence or truth of being. Since capitalism needs sexual repression to support institutions of patriarchy and monogamy, as well as its sub- and superstructures, psychoanalysis is, by definition, revolutionary. Liberated sexuality survives only if private property is abolished, eliminating the *need* for sexual repression. Humanity's need for sexual fulfillment is met only in societies committed to satiating all human needs, that is, socialism. Hence the Freudian, nonmaterialist Reich fervidly believed in proletariat revolution, although indicting orthodox revolutionaries as insensitive, inflexible materialists. Respect workers, he pleaded, understand the psychological as well as material sources of capitalism, and create a revolutionary class by encouraging workers to cognize essential being and capitalist repression. In 1929 Reich established the Socialist Society for Sex Hygiene and Sexological Research to aid in problem solving among young men and women. It also sought to abolish marriage and patriarchy, which translates into political and economic radicalism. Reich felt that the workers' revolution would emerge from self-conscious attitudes of sexually liberated young people.

Reich's idealist Marxism satisfied neither Freud nor Comintern officials. The former, in *Civilization and Its Discontents,* argued that civilized society is inconceivable without a degree of sexual repression because the impetus for cultural progress is generated by sublimated sexual energy. Reich's sexually liberated utopia would, from Freud's perspective, stagnate and eventually perish in unrestrained concupiscence. Moreover, psychoanalysis is a process of personal discovery for individual patients, devoid of political or social implications. Orthodox Marxists, on the other hand, saw psychoanalysis as a bourgeois tool reintegrating the alienated and discontented back into capitalism. Prior to 1934, Reich could nevertheless find some intellectual encouragement in postrevolutionary Soviet society, where legal restrictions surrounding marriage and divorce went unenforced, and revolutionary authorities cooperated with sexually unrestrained couples. Sexual freedom grew, particularly among the young. Abortion was available free of charge to any woman who wanted it. A potential competitor of Lenin's proletarian state, families were systematically weakened through government policy and a new revolutionary mentality questioning all czarist institutions. Reich exultantly observed what he assumed was empirical confirmation of his theories, even uncovering an inchoate philosophy of sexual liberation: Alexandra Kollontay's theory of proletarian sexual freedom in socialism, and I. D. Yermakov's synthesis of Freud and Marx. Even Trotsky advocated psychoanalytic therapy, though he always carefully rejected its "reactionary" theory of knowledge. Despite Soviet cynicism of Freudianism, Reich could still be optimistic in 1929 regarding the postrevolutionary fate of Freudian idealist Marxism.[14]

After Stalin's barbaric consolidation of power, Reich realized that these enlightened policies and ideas were tolerated only when they reinforced

Party dominance. After 1934 traditional sexual and family mores were reinstituted, and intellectuals were again restricted to echoing the Stalinist Party line. Reich was unceremoniously expelled from the German Communist Party. His own confidence in the tenuous dialectical balance of id and economics flagged badly, as the drastic economic and social transformation he advocated was not accompanied by sexual liberation. Faced with an apparent conflict between institutionalized materialism and human instinct, Reich's idealism obliterates the dialectical synthesis. Rather than condemning orthodoxy as "anti-Marxist," as Hegelians and Humanists do, Reich bowed subserviently to Freudianism by abandoning Marxism altogether. Henceforth, all references to Marxism were carefully cleansed from revised publications. Reich retreated to his orgone box, preaching the virtues of genital orgasm as the ultimate remedy for social injustice.

Reich's contribution to Marxist theory was an analysis of the sexual aspects of capitalist alienation. Capitalism isolates humanity from natural sexual proclivities, even as it enriches the few. Its social conditions, institutions, and values are disguised in self-righteous rhetoric, demanding "discipline," "character," "self-control," "duty," "perseverance," while materially and sexually repressing its victims. The market's reification of workers resembles capitalism's objectification of sex, which is unnaturally depersonalized and mystified by superstition and fear, and sold like any other commodity. Capitalism sexually objectifies men and women, perversely generating widespread prostitution as well as the simple-minded chauvinism of one sex toward the other. Capitalism has denatured a physical process inherent to all living animals, the ultimate source of life itself.

Reich's eventual disenchantment with Marxism, however, was the result of a nondialectical idealism that presumes that sex alone defines humanity. There are two necessary corollaries: Terminating sexual repression generates authentic freedom; and social justice necessarily manifests complete sexual liberation. The latter was disproved by the unanticipated Stalinist turn of Russia's socialist revolution, prompting Reich to abandon social theory altogether. The former is now dissolving in contemporary Western society, where a liberated attitude toward genital sex blatantly serves the ends of capitalist oppression and alienation.[15] Orthodox Freudians argue that this submissive attitude is the source of encroaching social disintegration and anarchy. Reich's mistake, Marxists and Freudians agree, is equating historical progress and sexual indulgence.

Marcuse

Herbert Marcuse (1898–1979) cavalierly dismissed Reich's vulgarization of Freud in one brief paragraph, accusing him of "a sweeping primitivism" which foreshadowed "the wild and fantastic hobbies of . . . [his] later years."[16] But Marcuse also believed that Marxism must be revivified with Freudian idealism. Despite Marx's compelling critique of political economy, the working masses as a whole are quiescent, unwilling or unable to radicalize everyday attitudes. These are imprisoned in the technologically reinforced borders of capitalism, incapable of transcending one-dimensional, ahistorical bourgeois values. Even sporadic revolutionary outbursts are assimilated into mainstream society through the combined efforts of advertising media, social scientists, and politicians—sickeningly transformed into harmless new products, reformist ideas, or slogans. Materialism cannot explain the contradiction between material oppression and worker inauthenticity because it lacks a social psychology. Freudianism provides Marxists with the analytical tools to measure a transfixed workers' movement, by describing the psychological processes of human repression. It therefore explains why workers identify with oppressors while suppressing real needs and how to sensitize workers to history's inevitable socialist revolution.

Marcuse began with Freud's reality principle, the belief that social order depends on directing libidinal energy into necessary culture-producing activities. Without denying libidinal instincts, Marcuse argued that whether they are repressed, and the possible forms this repression takes, are both influenced by concrete institutions representing specific stages of human development. Humanity has always lived in conditions of economic scarcity—less goods and services available than humanity needs—and this has necessitated both labor and a system of controlled distribution. Uninhibited sexuality is obviously impractical when actors must struggle to satisfy nonsexual material needs. Hence, a "basic" amount of instinctual repression has always been necessary to establish and maintain civilization. The actual forms this repression takes, the distribution of resources and the organization of work, are determined by an era's level of technical development. Instinctual repression, in other words, is historically synchronized with the incessant class struggles that accompany material progress. In any historical era, the material forms of instinctual repression reinforce the power and influence of one class. By commanding the superstructure, the elite secures mass acknowledgment that their social domination is justified by reality. *How* workers perform their social tasks becomes the measure of virtue and social usefulness. In "reality," of course, our performance, the social hierarchy, the distribution of resources, and the quality of work all reinforce the ruler's needs. The dominant class introduces forms of instinctual repression "over and above those indispensable for civilized human association. These additional controls arising from the specific institutions of domination are what we denote as 'surplus-repression.' " While some "basic repression" is required by civilized people in economic scarcity, most citizens are repressed more than necessary in order to stretch the elite's power. This distortion is tolerated because they have internalized the proffered "performance principle," and now are eager to excell as workers. The performance principle has become "the prevailing historical form of ... [Freud's] reality principle."[17]

Marcuse reduces human history into two stages. The first, pretechnological period required an extraordinarily high level of basic repression. Social domination was required to wipe out scarcity and establish the economic and social prerequisites of material abundance. This phase was marked by regimented, often brutal social structures rationalizing mass slavery and poverty. With the advent of industrialization humanity enters a new developmental stage in which scarcity begins to fade. As social wealth and resources proliferate, as technological progress makes scarcity less of an obstacle to cultural development, social repression becomes surplus, serving primarily to support and maintain existing elites. Libidinal instincts are repressed more than civilization's survival requires. Capitalism desexualizes humans, molding them into compliant, passive, noncreative, nonerotic instruments of labor, mindlessly performing the routinized tasks of modern factory production. This unnecessary work negates libidinal energy and benefits the few. But by internalizing the performance principle, we inauthentically experience "freedom" in slavery and are "happy" in our misery.

Reich had equated libidinal energy and genital orgasm and defined freedom as unrestricted, nonsublimated access to the physical act of sexual release. Marcuse's libido is broader, reflecting Freud's mature metapsychology depicting warring instincts of "Eros" (love or life) and "Thanatos" (aggression or death). Libidinal energy is generated by the human body as a whole. When released, it is experienced not only genitally but also as a pleasurable sensuality enervating the entire organism—what Marcuse terms "Polymorphous-Perverse sexuality." Humanity is capable of experiencing this total bodily enjoyment. In a rational, nonrepressive society of material abundance, liberated sexuality is channeled, or self-sublimated, into "free Eros," the force of life or love that "binds" destructive instincts. Contrary to Freud's warnings, unfettered sexuality—nonrepressively sublimated into Eros—"does not preclude lasting civilized societal relationships."[18] The destructive orgy of sexual debauchery that many associate with sexual liberation is unwarranted, created by alienated personalities, like Reich, who equate the libido solely with genital orgasm. Capitalist sexual repression—manifest in controlled, monotonous work and monogamous relationships—is no longer a prerequisite for maintaining civilization. Bourgeois society is constructed on surplus repression, with material exploitation of workers reinforced by the performance principle. Marcuse seeks a "revolt of the instincts," a nonrepressive civilization governed by aesthetic (libidinal or sensual) rationality, liberating sexuality and sublimating it into Eros. The *Essay on Liberation* finds this "biological foundation for socialism" concretized in the aesthetic-erotic attitudes of critical young people, especially those involved in countercultural, New Left, student, and minority liberation movements. Without surplus repression, class domination ends and humanity achieves its potential. Eros "absorbs" Thanatos as the pain and tension of repressed bourgeois life—upon which the death instinct feeds—wither away.

One Dimensional Man (1964) and the "Political Preface" (1966) to *Eros and Civilization* describe new sources of repression created by the very affluence which, potentially, will terminate surplus repression. Modern bourgeois society has created technological means of satisfying sexual and aggressive urges that simultaneously prohibit critical thoughts and actions. Through the "scientific management of instinctual needs," technicians can now channel potentially revolutionary situations into consumerism and political reformism. In these conditions, wealth is transformed into "repressive affluence," and the struggle to liberate sexuality and realize Eros requires "a reversal in the direction of progress."[19] Capitalism, it seems, now actually manipulates and defuses proletarian revolutionary impulses, hence political progressivism is associated with an antimodern, critical perspective not yet contaminated by the industrialized West's deadening but pleasurable technology. Domestic rebels now share an "instinctual bond" with Third World freedom fighters in the battle against technological rationalism.

Marcuse saw continuity and change in Marx's revision of Hegelianism. Although Marx emphasized the concrete material contradictions lying at history's dialectical core, he also admired Hegel's synthesis of subjectivity and objectivity. Marx wanted to preserve this unity while rejecting Hegel's abstract idealism. History's dialectical movement, Marx and Hegel agreed, reaches toward the unity of subject and object. For Marx, however, the proletariat, not Mind, is history's subject, an economic class that fulfills history by self-consciously rebelling. The dialectical unity of free subjects and objective history is Hegel's legacy to Marx and the basis of Marx's historical materialism. While revolution requires a "certain attained level of material . . . culture," only when these are "seized upon and directed by a conscious activity that has in mind the socialist goal" does the actual transition occur.[20] The feasibility of social change, therefore, depends on workers becoming a class-for-itself, conscious of its revolutionary potential and willing to battle for liberation. Historical materialism describes a political-historical process that is simultaneously cognitive: "true consciousness (class consciousness) of the proletariat is a constitutive factor in the objective dynamic of liberation."[21] Workers have not experienced this consciousness because capitalism occludes their libidinal natures. However, capitalism itself has now matured to the point where surplus repression is so blatant that it will be recognized and purposefully rejected by an enlightened proletariat, in touch with heretofore repressed biological impulses.

Orthodox Marxism, spawned by Engels and epitomized in the Soviet state, has stripped Marx's theory of its Hegelian heritage. The interpenetration of subject and object is replaced by an objective materialist metaphysics that defines cognition impersonally. The dialectic deteriorates "from a mode of critical thought ["the organon of revolutionary consciousness and practice"] into a universal 'world outlook' and universal method with rigidly fixed rules and regulations, and this transformation destroys the dialectic more thoroughly than any revision."[22] Soviet Marxism still thinks capitalism will bow to history's objective will and collapse. It twists Marxism, introducing new material variables (for example, imperialism, war, inflation, state capitalism) to explain workers' unanticipated reactionary attitudes. At home, the socialist economy is artificially inflated from "above," to "push" history and secure the revolution—inadvertently grooming a domineering bureaucracy. A "new socialist rationality," pious ideological phrases concerning socialist justice and capitalist exploitation, is frantically reiterated by those promising to end ideology, justifying their self-righteous claim to represent history's kismet. Ironically, this ideology echoes the bourgeois nemesis, defusing workers' libidinal potentials to maximize production by means of self-discipline, patriotism, and elite (Party) rule. By naively stressing history's objective moment, Soviet leaders reproduce the repression traditionally plaguing bourgeois culture.[23]

The "Dialectic of Civilization" expresses humanity's battle against domination, first by the primal father, and later God (that is, the father substitute) and one-dimensional technological society. The first two stages were negated through cognitive critique and revolutionary action, that is, by patracide and the establishment of matriarchy, and by secular bourgeois revolutions. Today, we await liberation from capitalist and bureaucratic socialist domination, both now producing enough material resources to transform what was once basic into surplus repression. Oppressed masses will cognize this injustice because the development of each individual (ontogenesis) recapitulates the history of civilization (phylogenesis): The psyche matures through a repeating process of domination and liberation that mirrors the dialectic of civilization. We now live in a time when cognition (subject) and civilization (object) have matured to the threshold of liberation. Proletariat class consciousness expresses the former; technology the latter. Marxism explains the material forms and processes through which civilization has passed. However, the material dialectic merely echoes the primordial, ahistorical forces of Eros and Thanatos. Only when humanity subjectively manifests Eros will the liberating socialist revolution occur. Although Marcuse synchronizes this cognitive process with the objective laws of historical materialism, Freud's ideal forces are clearly prior: "Freud's theory reveals the *biological de-individualization beneath the sociological core*—the former proceeding under the pleasure and Nirvana principles, the latter under the reality principle. . . . The recurrent dynamic of the struggle between Eros and death instinct, of the building and destruction of culture, of repression and the return of the repressed, is *released* and *organized* by the historical conditions under which mankind develops."[24] Like Reich, Marcuse's Marxism confirms the final triumph of instinctual nature over matter.

Marcuse devoted most of his professional life to formulating feasible

Marxist alternatives to orthodox materialism, including existential ontology, Critical Theory, and Freudianism. The latter represents his final thirty years, when he became a hero to a generation of counterculture activists. Lest one be deluded by the appealing Freudian jargon, as perhaps some unhappy bourgeois students were, Marcuse's blend of Freud and Marx is epistemologically anchored in a priori idealism. Notwithstanding the charm of terms like Eros, love, pleasure, sexuality, polymorphous perversity, and the like, Marcuse's social theory argues the desirability and incontrovertible objectivity of proletarian socialist revolution, based on a transcendent dialectical Reason manifest in the (ontogenetic) maturation of each psyche and (phylogenetic) history of the human race. These psychic and historical patterns congeal, in abundant material conditions, into human essence. Despite unanticipated flexibility and an hypnotic technology, capitalism's material contradictions will eventually generate worker authenticity— expressed in violent revolution, Socialist justice, and nonrepressed libidos. Humanity's freedom presupposes the victory of authenticity. Domination— at least in abundant conditions—comes from ignorance and lies. Hence, revolutionary society will tolerate only the truth. Eros is enforced with a stern disposition and an iron hand: "certain things cannot be said, certain ideas cannot be expressed, certain policies cannot be proposed, certain behavior cannot be permitted without making tolerance an instrument for the continuation of servitude."[25] "True democracy," or "liberating toler- ance," forcibly suppresses nonprogressive ideas and acts. Despite the sanc- tity of authentic, reflective subjectivity, Marcuse's a priorism potentially justifies a dictatorship of right-thinking, sexually liberated scientists. He does not shrink from such a possibility. One wonders whether ardent middle- class supporters attracted by Marcuse's promise of sexual emancipation, eloquent critique of rampant industrialization, and sympathies for oppressed and exploited non-Westerners envisioned this kind of double-edged utopia.

Fromm

Marcuse stretched Reich's libido into a consuming human sensuality that manifests the socially binding force of Eros. Erich Fromm (1900–1980) further diluted the sexuality of Freud's libido. Human essence or nature, for Fromm, is a desexualized need to "assimilate" things and "socialize" with other people. Hence, authentic consciousness generates creative, socially useful labor (in other words, praxis) and an affectionate openness toward fellow men and women, whose requital fulfills a need as basic as eating or drinking. Normally, however, this potential is distorted by an ensemble of cognitively experienced economic and social forces that form the "structure of psychic energy which is molded by any given society so as to be useful for the functioning of that particular society." "Social character" indicates the plethora of ideas and behavior patterns that, when internalized, allow us to live and work successfully in society. The process of internalization occurs in and through socializing institutions (for example, family, church, peer groups, schools, theaters, and so on). However, the quality of social character is determined by economic class: "the fundamental factor in the formation of 'social character' is the practice of life as it is constituted by the mode of production and the resulting social stratification."[26] Social character thus mediates base and superstructure, translating material directives into acceptable, "proper" social behavior.

Capitalism, which produces exchange rather than use value and subordinates general interests to individual profit, represses authenticity through its alienating social characters. Capitalists embody the ideals of self-sufficiency, competition, discipline, and misanthropy. Workers are taught to sublimate real interests into commercially profitable market channels, consuming to compensate for inner emptiness and anxiety. Typical bourgeois personality types—"receptive," "exploitative," "hoarding," and "marketing"—confirm capitalism's debilitating effect on human psyches. The destructive battle between authenticity and repressive capitalist conditions also creates a potentially explosive subconscious bond among the oppressed, a "social unconscious" encompassing the irrepressible forces of creativity and love now occluded by pathogenic capitalist social characters. As capitalism matures, it intensifies the experienced contradiction between authenticity and social acceptability, manifest not only in the relative decline in wages, but also in the increasingly inhuman values that capitalism spawns while frantically driving to increase profits during a period of abnormally high inflation and unemployment. Capitalism struggles to hide the "social unconscious," while its never-ending consumerism intensifies frustrations. The confluence of intensifying material contradictions and a hideous spiritual debasement precipitates revolution. "Social change and revolution are caused not only by new productive forces which conflict with older forms of social organization, but also by the conflict between inhuman social conditions and unalterable human needs."[27] Workers rebel after cognizing the "social unconscious" and rejecting capitalist exploitation. Postrevolutionary society will satisfy real needs for praxis and human affection by supporting mutual respect, cooperation, and equality, while producing goods and services required for authenticity, not profit. We are at the threshold of humanistic socialism: the planned, rational satisfaction of society's real needs.

Freud correctly perceived humanity's instinctive potential, social repression, and the significance of the unconscious. But his pessimism regarding the compatibility of emancipated libidos and civilized behavior unknowingly reflects the economic and social conditions of European capitalism. Freud's antisocial, destructive libido corresponds to prevailing bourgeois attitudes regarding life's competitiveness and the social necessity of balancing self-interested groups. Someone with Freud's bourgeois background and education could not know real instincts, for they depict human openness, love, understanding, self-fulfillment, and the moral community. Human beings, instinctively, are inclined toward organic social union. This frightens the bourgeoisie, who react by obsessively reasserting individualism (for example, Freud) or escaping through the numbing security of totalitarianism (for example, fascism).[28] Neither eliminates the original anguish.

Marx was also correct in emphasizing concrete sources of social oppression and, in the early work, praxis as "those potentialities which are given . . . [man] when he is born."[29] Unfortunately, he left these undefined, and this carelessness had grievous consequences. Beginning with Engels, materialists were obsessed with concrete aspects of alienation, ignoring Marx's esoteric doctrine of human potential. Marx always assumed that workers can, potentially, labor creatively and realize their species-essence in socialist equality. The revolution generates economic and social conditions promoting "creative" personality types. This entire emancipatory process, however, is contingent on exploited, frustrated workers reflectively perceiving essentiality.

Freudian psychoanalysis and orthodox Marxism both naively overemphasize one moment of the dialectic. The former turns into another school of bourgeois idealism; the latter into materialist totalitarianism. However, a Freudian-Marxist synthesis eliminates separate weaknesses and offers humanity a philosophy of social revolution that simultaneously propagates authentic human being. Fromm's idealist Marxism talks to both sides of the iron curtain, promising liberation from vulgar socialism as well as from bourgeois commercialism. His sympathetic connection to Eastern Europe's humanists indicates a shared idealism and a commitment to terminate socialist workers' bondage to materialist apostasy.

STRUCTURAL MARXISM

Not all idealist Marxists are this outwardly concerned with sexuality. Some fear that Marxist philosophers now resemble a consciousness-raising tea group more than revolutionary social scientists—emotionally appealing to "authenticity," "sexual liberation," "humanitarianism," "fulfillment," and the 1960s youth-oriented "do your own thing" mentality of French New Leftism. Structural Marxism *wants* to dehumanize Marxism, purging antiscientific bourgeois ideological categories. Although science has significant practical consequences, it is qualitatively distinct from everyday beliefs. Contemporary Marxism, seeking "relevance" and diving headlong into common attitudes and life-styles, abdicates its revolutionary heritage. It must distinguish itself from, not dissolve into, bourgeois culture by fleeing sensuality, emotionalism, and public opinion. Authentic Marxism establishes and maintains universal justice. Structural Marxism is the voice of cool, objective reason in a radical environment now crudely entangled with bourgeois pop culture.

Ironically, relevant theoretical medicine is drawn from the bourgeois philosophy known as structuralism, particularly the work of Claude Lévi-Strauss, which uncovers essential truths that govern social organization, independent of actors, intentions, or facts. The problematic of modern structuralism was set in the pioneering linguistic studies of Ferdinand de Saussure, especially the *Course in General Linguistics*.[30] For nineteenth-century linguists, spoken words (signifiers) express corresponding mental images (signifieds). Saussure emphasized the priority of signifiers, which are impersonal and suitable for formal analysis. But intentionally spoken words comprise a practical means of communicating that alters with time and place. Science, on the other hand, proposes objective truths that condition verbal behavior. The former—*"la langue"*—are explained diachronically, through historical inquiry. The latter—*"la parole"*—comprises a timeless structure that science generates by synchronic inquiry into universal, static relationships. Saussure substituted eternal linguistic structures for histori-cally concrete languages and derived meaning from a total language struc-ture rather than the speaking subject. Spoken words are meaningful only in relation to other words and the collective total structure, irrespective of subjective intention. The project of systematizing a universal language structure that appears unconsciously through speaking subjects was con-tinued by Jakobson, Hjelmslev, and Benveniste.

Lévi-Strauss applied the insights and findings of structural linguistics to social inquiry, particularly the study of kinship systems and mythologies of primitives. Structural social science establishes a priori systems of symbolic communication meaningful in themselves, apart from manifest actions and motives. Lévi-Strauss's strenuous decoding of primitive tribal myths con-firms that activities of diverse, unrelated tribal communities are conceptu-ally arranged into a series of communicative signs that follow an invariant logical pattern or structure. The real meaning of tribal behavior is its function within the inclusive structure. Obviously, participants are not aware of this because subjective experiences, real enough to involved actors when acting, unknowingly express this precognitive structure. Hence popular notions like free will, consciousness, and intentionality are scientif-ically meaningless. "I claim to show, not how men think in myths, but how myths operate in men's minds without their being aware of the fact."[31] When all myths are known—when social structure is entirely revealed—scientists will understand every aspect of interpersonal communication, as well as the human mind in its fixed, atemporal structure. Science's goal, for Lévi-Strauss and the structuralists, is universal human mind: the precognitive structure that guides cognition and action. History merely shifts these same hypothesized structures, so that terms like "primitive" and "modern" are meaningless and historical "progress" irrelevant. Societies unconsciously adopt a combination of timeless structural components. Social "movement" indicates that some combinations work better than others in realizing a life-

sustaining purpose. Those that fail are replaced by others whose own historical fate is already sealed. For Lévi-Strauss, structuralism is a universal
science of invariant, absolute principles governing all interaction. Structuralist social inquiry describes systems of empirical phenomena manifesting an essential, determining structure.

The shared preconceptions of structuralism and Marxism have generated a lively dialogue. Both are, philosophically, anti-individualist, hence
reject basic principles of modern capitalism such as self-interest, negative
freedom, empiricism, and humanism. The structuralist Gaston Bachelard,
for example, argues in *La Formation de l'esprit scientifique* (1967), that
science must negate extant philosophy and ideology, and construct new
thought patterns. This "epistemological break" generates universal structures to explain common perceptions and facts scientifically. Though not
himself a Marxist, Bachelard's structural epistemology critically confronts
individualist ideas and institutions, hence inspires Marxists like Althusser.[32]
Jacques Lacan structurally "decenters" bourgeois actors into impersonal
structures of culture (ego) and desire (id). With both empirical (cognitive)
and subconscious (precognitive) psyches scattered and disunified, human
subjectivity is essentially incoherent, and standard bourgeois philosophy
and psychology meaningless except in upholding the material interests of a
hegemonic capitalist elite.[33]

Structuralism and Marxism are also totalizing methods of inquiry, perceiving reality as multidimensional and interpenetrating, where particulars
are conditioned by the whole. Both scientifically progress beyond immediate empirical observation into a realm of hidden truths. Roland Barthes's
structural science of signs—"semiology"—examines the role of social myth
in conditioning subjective perceptions of ordinary experiences.[34] Semiology,
like Marxism, demystifies everyday capitalist life by explaining how unconscious mythical structures distort public messages, rationalize the status
quo, and reinforce bourgeois class hegemony. Seemingly innocuous empirical events like advertisements, films, and newspaper headlines are redefined
by the structural totality and transformed into tools of capitalist oppression. Semiology has spawned a group of "new semiotics," including Jacques
Derrida, Julia Kristeva, and Phillipe Sollers, who carry the structural
decentering of language and pop culture to a logical conclusion: Each text
or event has its own structure, which it begets merely by being produced.[35]
They replace structural logic—a priori universals conditioning empirical
life—with "grammatology," that is, a totally destructive hermeneutics that
breaks texts into their own impersonal, determining language structures.
Language becomes autonomous: Words and sentences are defined through
perceived relations with other elements of that text, and with other texts,
generating unlimited interpretations. Known as the "Tel Quel" group,[36] the
new semiotics intellectually negate bourgeois culture by critically interpreting
capitalist texts, elucidating "harmless" cultural phenomena that unintentionally propagate class oppression.

Finally, structuralism, like Marxism, presumes that language and culture are conditioned by objective, interpersonal forces, hence "autonomous" concepts and things—artificially torn from reality—are dysfunctional and inauthentic. When its structures are transformed into real processes, that is, when "observed phenomena are raw material from which concepts are elaborated to describe real structures of the world,"[37] then structuralism assimilates materialism: Both analyze concrete processes by which signifier and signified interrelate, repudiating the bourgeois transcendentalism of nonmaterialist structuralism.[38] Since Marx's historical materialism outlines the economic component of determining structures, structuralists are comfortable predicting the decline of private property and individualism and the necessity of worker rebellion.

The postwar radicalization of Western Europe, culminating in the student rebellions of May 1968, reinforced structuralism's tentative union with Marxism.[39] But no one systematically explains how decentered egos, conditioned by impersonal structures, can or will actively transform oppressive systems that they didn't even create. Structuralism, even the radical version, defines truth independent of action. Impersonal structures are always determining and hence intentional revolutionary activism is meaningless. Moreover, ideologies are irrelevant to structural science. Universal structures, theoretically immune to historical moods, are as likely to be reactionary as progressive: there is no scientific criterion supporting radical structuralism against bourgeois structuralism. The union is politically rather than theoretically motivated.

Michel Foucault, a self-styled radical structuralist, illustrates the problem. Foucault structurally redefined history by using impersonal "*épistèmes*,"[40] atemporal structures that limit the ways we cognitively perceive and define objects. In denying continuity or intentionality to history—he sees it as impersonally conditioned, ruptured, unsystematic, discursive, determined by events rather than actors, "a blank, indifferent space, lacking in both interiority and promise"[41]—Foucault perceived hegemonic bourgeois ideas and institutions as "correct" only in upholding the material interests of capitalists.[42] Hence, he was "Marxist," critically demystifying bourgeois rhetoric. However, the same structural historiography, applied to socialism, would perform the same critical function. Foucault's Marxism is conditional, not scientific, because of the political exigencies of his life and times.[43]

Goldmann

Lucien Goldmann (1913–1970) proffered a structuralist-oriented Marxism rather than a synthesis. Every social phenomenon for Goldmann is simultaneously a structure-in-itself and an epiphenomenon of a larger, inclusive structure. Social science, therefore, considers the same object from two different perspectives, structurally describing the object and then causally explaining its historical genesis.[44] Structural analysis describes the partial structure. Causal analysis explains the partial structure in terms of its encompassing wider structure. While impersonal structures describe human activity, they are products of prior structures, "the results of man's earlier praxis."[45] Social science explains the "genesis" of structures that are created in history, achieve an equilibrium, and then "destructure" to make room for new ones. It is synchronic (describing impersonal structures) *and* diachronic (explaining their historical birth in human activity). Structures, therefore, are not autonomous, nor are actors passively determined. Goldmann's "genetic structuralism" is scientifically accurate without violating the intentionality and meaning of empirical human history.

The structure that Goldmann found irreplaceable for describing individual facts, acts, and texts is social class. Social science describes the structure of empirical particulars in apposite *"Weltanschauungen"* — "the conjunction of aspirations, feelings, and ideas which bring together the members of the group (or more frequently social class) and oppose them to other groups."[46] All texts and acts express a structural class world view or consciousness, and the most talented class members express the "maximum of possible consciousness" of their class.[47] Goldmann adopts Lukács's distinction of empirical and authentic class consciousness: the former contingent on "accidental" or personal factors; the latter actually fulfilling an inherent world view. Reputable philosophical and literary works represent authentic consciousness, hence are primarily products of class rather than personality.[48] Everyday activities, on the contrary, are often less accurate as indicators of true class consciousness.

Social science not only describes structures but explains their genesis. Goldmann argues that world views are evaluated by "which of them permits the understanding of the other as a social and human phenomenon, reveals its infrastructure, and clarifies, by means of an immanent critical principle, its inconsistencies and its limitations." The one "which provides the widest possible form and range of comprehension" is Marxism, that is, authentic working-class *Weltanschauung.*[49] Marxism, particularly Lukács's Hegelian version, explains the historical structuration and destructuration of bourgeois consciousness, hence is scientifically accurate. By genetically explaining the modern class struggle and at the same time grasping the dialectical complexity of partial and total structures, Marxism generates both revolutionary activity and knowledge. Goldmann's revolutionary Party, like Lukács's, guides workers toward authenticity, if necessary by sacrificing their empirical consciousness to its scientific will.

Althusser

Structuralists understandably condemn Goldmann's subsuming objective structural theory in working-class consciousness. Structuralism, they argue, must generate ahistorical universals.[50] By congealing empirical subjectivity and universal objectivity, Goldmann smacks of Hegelianism. Louis Althusser (b. 1918) transforms Marxism from a working-class ideology into structural science, a revolutionary theory valid independent of revolutionary actors.

Despite a politically motivated ambivalence on the topic, Althusser's epistemology is clearly structuralist.[51] He interprets dialectical materialism as a "theory of epistemological history," that is, a theory of the historical unfolding of theoretical truth, and relies on Lévi-Strauss's insights regarding the priority of a priori structures and the methodological imperative to uncover hidden, impersonal knowledge.[52] His major works—*For Marx* (1965), *Reading Capital* (1965), and *Lenin and Philosophy* (1971)—explicate and defend a synthesis of structuralism and Marxism.

Althusser depicts society as four levels or instances of human practice: economic, political, ideological, and scientific. By "practice" he means human activity transforming the world to create needed products, what Marx called "labor." "By *practice* in general I shall mean any process of *tranformation* of a determinate given raw material into a determinate *product,* a transformation effected by a determinate human labor, using determinate means (of production). ... The *determinant* moment (or element) is neither the raw material nor the product, but the practice in the narrow sense: the moment of the *labor of transformation* itself, which sets to work, in a specific structure, men, means, and a technical method of utilizing the means."[53] A practice, then, is analogous to a mode of human production, comprising a laborer, an object of labor, a means of laboring, and a product of labor, all related in a specified manner. Economic practice, the grist for orthodox Marxist theory, is a specific material production process combining with specific relations of production to produce needed material goods. Althusser claimed that society encompasses political, ideological, and scientific modes of production, in addition to an economic base. Each transforms a different type of raw material into different types of products, by means of different types of labor, utilizing different instruments of labor. Whereas, for example, economic practice uses labor power and the means of material production to transform natural or processed materials into socially useful products, political practice uses practical activities to transform given social and political relations into new ones, and theoretical practice uses cognition and the means of theoretical labor (that is, a theory's concepts and method) to produce from extant concepts, representations, and institutions a specific product: knowledge.[54] Each practice is a distinct social structure, and society as a whole, the totality, is a complex unity of the separate practices. Collectively, as they constantly interpenetrate, the practices "constitute the global structure of a social formation belonging to a determinate mode of production."[55]

Althusser reestablishes Marxism's scientificity by defining Marxist philosophy, dialectical materialism, as the theory "in which is theoretically expressed the essence of theoretical practice in general, through it the essence of practice in general, and through it the essence of the transformations, of the 'development' of things in general."[56] Dialectical materialism, in other words, is "the theory of theoretical practice," the mode of human production by which scientific knowledge is produced. Its concepts and methods generate truth from existing modes of thinking, and this takes place "entirely in thought," that is, in scientific practice.[57] The theoretical product is all-encompassing, determining not only the production of knowledge, but also the means of producing material goods, ideology, and politics. Indeed, it unveils society's essential structure as a totality composed of interrelated practices. The raw materials for dialectical materialism, Althusser's cryptic "Generalities I," are bourgeois "scientific" concepts and abstractions. Its means of theoretical production is the "problematic" of dialectical materialism, Marx's theoretical framework for determining what problems can be posed and resolved. This is "Generalities II." We understand this problematic by reading Marx carefully, deciphering his obscure but innovative epistemology, his revolutionary approach to scientific practice. To cognize Marx's problematic, we must already be aware that knowledge is a mode of production, which, paradoxically, is an essential principle of Marx's problematic. Since Althusser's entire structural framework, including its four practices, is generated by dialectical materialism, we must already know the sought-after problematic prior to reading Marx! Hence, Althusser tells us in *Reading Capital* the "correct" Marxist technique for reading Marx so we can understand Marxism. The product of enlightened reading is "Generalities III," the "concrete-in-thought," that is, the intellectual representation of real, concrete truth, which is science. It justifies and validates the process of knowledge production and the overarching social structure it is part of. Science thus exists autonomously in the realm of thought. Dialectical materialism, in sum, begins and ends in thought, although conceptually generating accurate knowledge of, and effective means for transforming, concrete reality.

Althusser's distinction between thought (scientific practice) and reality (economic, political, and ideological practices) is irreducible, confirming, in his mind, the primacy of matter over thought. "The *object* of knowledge ... [is] in itself absolutely distinct and different from the *real object* ... the *idea* of the circle, which is the *object* of knowledge must not be confused with the circle, which is the *real object*."[58] But while a real object is the "absolute reference point for the process of knowledge which is concerned with it," hence explained by this knowledge, nevertheless knowledge is not caused by matter.[59] Knowledge, to repeat, is produced theoretically, independent of matter. Dialectical materialism, a scientific theory that confirms matter and thought are separate, is not matter's epiphenomenon.

Empiricism, capitalism's "science," defines knowledge as indissolubly linked to concrete objects, making it merely another aspect or part of known reality. This is empiricism's "original weakness," its "original sin": by encompassing reality it is unable to explain reality scientifically. Empirical science is therefore theoretically unjustifiable. By mixing truth and reality, it ignores one and distorts the other.

By uniting truth and "real history," historicism similarly transforms science into "the direct product ... of the activity and experience of the masses," that is their praxis, beliefs, and class consciousness.[60] Since theoretical practice is indistinguishable from economic, ideological, and political practices, historicism distorts the social totality. This intellectual "Leftism" produces the "theoretical monstrosity" of a world with two "sciences"—proletarian and bourgeois—neither capable of shaking vulgar reality. What orthodox Marxists call "proletarian science" is really Marx's historical materialism: the science of economic, political, and ideological formation valid only for these three levels of nontheoretical activity. Its use is limited to explaining these practical activities, guiding Party activists interested in *how* to foment a workers' revolution, not *why* the social totality generates one—a scientific question that must be answered theoretically. Historicism mistakenly permits historical materialism (the science of social formation) to absorb dialectical materialism (the theory of science), inadvertently propelling proletarian revolutions toward ignorant ideologues who quickly distort history's authenticity. Althusser challenges orthodoxy with "Kautsky's and Lenin's thesis that Marxist theory is produced by a specific theoretical practice, *outside* the proletariat, and ... must be 'imported' into the working class movement."[61] There is no direct identity between real science and working-class ideology.

Ideology, then, reflects interests, not truth, and is a "system (with its own logic and rigour) of representations (images, myths, ideas, or concepts ...) endowed with a historical existence and a role within a given society." It adapts individuals, through techniques of obfuscation and mystification, to socially imposed responsibilities. Hence, bourgeois ideology legitimizes worker exploitation by concealing it, surreptitiously favoring capitalist interests. Socialist ideology expresses proletarian interests by rationalizing democracy and egalitarianism. Since humanity, in any society, must be "formed, transformed and equipped to respond to the demands of their conditions of existence," ideologies will always be needed, even in communism. Ideology, then, is imposed on everyone by impersonal structures that support social existence, reinforcing the "objectivity" of existing reality, legitimizing the status quo. Society's survival depends on ideological practice as much as any other, including science. Always, however, ideology and science remain distinct. "In ideology the real relation [of people and the conditions of existence] is inevitably invested in the imaginary relation, a relation that expresses a will (conservative, conformist, reformist, or revolutionary), a hope or a nostalgia, rather than describing a reality."[62]

Althusser eventually expands this notion of ideology to resemble Gramsci's "civil society." There are two types of state institutions: the Repressive State Apparatus (RSA) and Ideological State Apparatus (ISA). The former includes military and paramilitary organizations, the latter, schools, churches, media, and other symbols of legitimacy.[63] Since ideology is universally present, so too will be both forms of state control, eliminating any chance of the socialist state "withering away."

Ideological practice designates and rationalizes existing reality. Scientific practice, on the other hand, enables us to know it, exploding the ideological problematic that precedes it. All human interests—economic, political, ethical, religious, or aesthetic—are purged from scientific activity, which is epistemologically valid apart from the perspectives of any social group. This disqualifies empiricism, historicism, and humanism, all naively linked to social facts or interests. Scientific Marxism theoretically describes "hidden structures" and "absent causes" impersonally defining society and explaining concrete capitalist dynamics. It accomplishes what Althusser, borrowing from Bachelard, calls an "epistemological break" ("*coupure epistémologique*"): forging a new scientific world view, different from ideological preconceptions that dominate the preceding era. Marx never conceptualized the epistemological novelty of this analysis, choosing instead to promote worker rebellion actively with the ideologically and politically useful science of historical materialism. Moreover, Marx's early writings, mired in hypothesized human essences and capitalist alienation, are scientifically worthless. *For Marx* dismisses everything prior to *Capital* as idealist or empirical gibberish, unrelated to Marx's "objective" analysis— the "break" with posterity. *Lenin and Philosophy* states that even *Capital* is contaminated; only the *Critique of the Gotha Program* (1875) and *Marginal Notes on Wagner* (1882) are authentically scientific.[64] Althusser wants to establish Marxism as a science by referring only to Marx's writing published after the epistemological break, whenever that might be. Every epistemological break—and there have been three: the Greeks' discovery of mathematics; Galileo's discovery of physics; and now Marx's discovery of social and historical science—corresponds to an emerging new philosophy. Dialectical materialism is the philosophy of Marxism, depicting, in theory, the new science and explaining reality with objective concepts. Actual revolutions occur independently, through political, economic, and ideological practice. Proletarian revolutionary activity culminates an empirical critique of capitalism based on the priority of working-class interests, and hence is not "scientific."

Dialectical materialism, by outlining society's four distinct structures, teaches us that complexity is central to Marxism. Society's "global structure" is actually a "structure of structures": a "decentered" totality of four unique and autonomous structures collectively interacting.[65] Noneconomic structures—comprising what orthodox Marxists call the superstructure— determine, and are determined by, the global structure. No one contradiction, for example, between productive relations and forces, determines everything. Orthodox Marxism's obsession with economics "deviates" from scientific Marxism. There are, in fact, multiplicities of contradictions existing at all levels, making social determination complex and multiple. For Althusser, a "law of overdetermination" determines the quality of social life.

Nevertheless, the superstructure's autonomy is relative, not absolute. Economic practice still dominates "in the last instance" because the economy determines for noneconomic structures the quality of their "specific effectivity," their respective degrees of relative autonomy and dependence.[66] Economic practice determines whether it will itself dominate, or which other structure will dominate. While one structure can replace another in dominance, the social whole is invariant in that it always has a dominant element, a "structure in dominance," which governs other structures by assigning them a place in the totality and issuing them functions.[67] In feudal society politics dominated because the absense of economic practice determined the totality's dependence on politics. However, in early capitalism economics appeared forcefully and became the structure in dominance, determining the quality of social life. The burgeoning growth of technology and its frightening potential for psychological manipulation have pushed ideology to the forefront. Capitalist economic progress now makes ideology the dominant structure, determining social life with an inescapable media-reach. Marxist revolutionaries must accurately perceive the precise relations of domination and subordination in a global structure. Its set of complex contradictions, the reciprocal influences of all structural levels, defines the current "conjuncture" in which political action will occur. Hence, a successful working class revolution is generated by many distinct, irreducible structural contradictions (overdetermination), not inevitably by one set of contradictions (economic determinism).

With society an overdetermined structure of structures, no one essential feature governs the others. Consequently, social structures lack a common history. Each relatively autonomous practice has a relatively autonomous history marked by continuities and discontinuities, rhythms, patterns, revolutionary instances, and so on. These distinct histories are "dislocated" with respect to one another: They cannot be reduced to a common temporality. Instead, a complex historical time is constituted by the "differential times" of different structures. However, social history is not chaotic. The structure of structures is temporally bound together by the structure in dominance. Different time frames are only relatively independent of each other, like the different structures in the overdetermined totality. Economics determines in the last instance, eliminating the chance of history unfolding haphazardly or incoherently. In any historical era, economic practice determines which structure is dominant. The history of a practice, therefore, is only relatively autonomous, its evolution independent and irreducible but also tied directly to the economy and indirectly to politics, ideology, and science.[68]

Here is a new concept of "structural causality," one that Althusser felt existed inchoately in Marx's scientific writing.[69] Western science heretofore recognized two kinds of causality: Cartesian, mechanistic, unilinear, causal relationships between isolated empirical facts; and Hegelianism, where parts are determined by a whole, expressed in a historical essence. Structural causality presumes that a cause is always imminent in, not exterior to, its effects, thereby distinguishing itself from empiricism's naive infatuation with sensually experienced facts. But though a structure exists only in effects, it is not entirely present in any one of them. Therefore, while the whole is manifest in all its structures, the latter are more than mere expressions of the former. Society is a relation of independent practices whose pattern of interaction is a product of the totality. Although it is a structure consisting of four practices, which in the last instance is determined by one of them, the other levels are not its epiphenomena. Hegelian Marxists oversimplify things by assuming an essence, embodied in the totality, which guides social formation and history and introduces historical inevitability. While history, in the last instance, is economically determined, nothing in society is predetermined because social structures are relatively autonomous. By reducing everything to an abstract totality, Hegelian Marxism deprives science of specificity, dissolving it mediately in economic, ideological, and political practice, and immediately in historical essence. Hegelian Marxism is as naive and scientifically useless as materialism and empiricism. None insulate science from the vulgar reality of facts, events, and subjective feelings.

Althusser defines society (feudal, capitalist, or socialist) as a "process without subjects" and analyzes social interaction in terms of objective structures that live autonomously, making men and women helpless bearers of its message.[70] When he talks about relative autonomy and independence, he means structures, not people. These have their own life apart from subjective inclinations, which are necessarily distorted anyway by society's ideological practice. Althusser modified orthodox structuralism only by attributing to economics a final determination over other structures. According to Marx's practical science of historical materialism, economic practice historically progresses through inherent contradictions between forces and relationships of production. Althusser concluded that contradictions are immanent in the social totality, appearing when structures exceed a threshold beyond which change must occur. Even when economics is not the structure in dominance, its determination of the dominant structure means contradictions will appear at all levels in all structures. Forces and relationships of production—even scientific, ideological, and political production—are inevitably antagonistic, although "the reasons and laws . . . [for this] remain to be discovered."[71] Contradictions, therefore, occur both within and between structures, not merely between economic classes. The quality of these contradictions, like the quality of social life generally, is overdetermined. There is no quick reductive formula for measuring the intensity of social contradictions.

Since structural dynamics assure us that there always have been and will be social contradictions, dialectics becomes a structural method. Change occurs, revolutions spot social history, because of society's inherent structural framework. History, then, results from struggles between different groups, classes, ideas, and practices—struggles not initiated by subjects. Though structurally determined in the long run, at any particular moment these struggles are unpredictable. Social change is generated by relatively autonomous structures combining, dissolving, and recombining in time, under the final determination of economic practice. Moreover, this movement occurs inter- and intrastructurally, prompting Balibar's structural interpretation of *Capital,* which emphasizes "the transformation of one structure into another," independent of human intention, in the evolution of capitalist economic practice.[72] Disintegrating economic structures recombine through a process of "bricolage," lacking a "bricoleur," into new structures that generate new contradictions. Human subjects are merely structural "supports," even when sacrificing life and limb for perceived revolutionary ideals.[73]

Structuralism, by definition, separates truth and concrete reality, in Althusser's case rationalizing a vanguard Party of Marxist scientists whose social function is purely theoretical. The masses, who will pay the physical costs of rebellion, are an ignorant lot, perceiving only what ideology permits and doing only what economic and political structures dictate. Scientific Marxism is completely independent of the working class. Party members uncover truth, then create a new ideology based on dialectical materialism to propagate mass rebellion and establish socialist equality. Ideology "connects" science to empirical reality. Economic and political structures are indirectly related to both, with the former determining which of the four dominates. Althusser's conundrum is rationalizing the "materialist" quality of dialectical materialism. Truth is apparently trapped in a semi-autonomous theoretical realm.[74]

In more recent work,[75] Althusser meekly confronts this problem. Without substantively altering his structuralism, he reestablishes a link between science and reality with a new social structure added to the four old ones: "the philosophical instance."[76] Marxism, in the revised formula, is no longer "the theory of theoretical practice," though this practice remains as an autonomous structure embodying scientific truth. Marxism is now a philosophical practice, performed by sentient people living and working in the real world. Marxist philosophy, as Lenin intimated, is the class struggle in theory, rigidly defending the primacy of being over thought and the objectivity of science. Non-Marxist subjectivist philosophy is idealistic. Philosophy is thus entwined with economics, politics, and ideology. Marxist philosophy arises with the economic, political, and ideological ascendence of the working class, and necessitates an epistemological break—a reformulation of traditional idealist theories of science. Consequently, science appears after philosophy has burst the old theoretical problematic and is possible only when working-class interests emerge in the world of practical affairs. It appears historically with the conjuncture of mature economic, political, and ideological conditions. Marxism is a working-class philosophy generating an epistemological break and the emergence of science.

Althusser perceptively recognizes the difficulty of reconciling materialism and structuralism, but the belated response is unconvincing. He never repudiated the notion of science existing independent of concrete reality as theoretical practice.[77] Instead, he brought Marxism down a notch, calling it a philosophy rather than a science, and attaching it to working-class interests. While this eliminates one problem, that is, the idealistic basis of dialectical materialism, it creates another. Now Marxism is no longer scientific because it reflects concrete interests from empirical reality.[78] There is no compelling theoretical reason to choose Marxism over other ideologies and no valid criterion for evaluating the relative worth of bourgeois and proletarian philosophy. Superior numbers and strength determine the philosophical issue. Althusser thus negated his own professional *raison d'être,* which involved removing Marxism from the dirty currents of everyday life onto a higher, scientific plane. Moreover, if Marxism does instigate the epistemological break, as predicted, we still need a party of scientists—a post-Marxian party—to inculcate basic nonideological truths that will guide nontheoretical practices. Truth remains divorced from the working class, only now workers rather than scientists initiate the split. Finally, Althusser's law of overdetermination, the heart of his method, precludes simple reductive connections between philosophy and science. If each structure is relatively autonomous, and any one a possible structure in dominance, it is as likely for science to emerge before as after working-class philosophy, in which case we are back where we started: truth trickling down to workers from an ideal structure.

Like other Hegelian and non-Hegelian idealists, Althusser has vainly searched Marx's writings for an explicit epistemology. Finding only inchoate fragments, he creatively formulates an idealist Marxism embossed with Lévi-Strauss's structuralism. Althusser is not a materialist in the orthodox sense and cannot be one as long as he stands by *Reading Capital* and *For Marx.* The shallowness of recent bridge-mending confirms this.

Althusser's structural Marxism has motivated innovative radical inquiry, especially in anthropology and politics. In particular, Maurice Godelier used Althusserian categories to examine primitive kinship systems and myths, areas that nonstructural Marxism had heretofore avoided.[79] Nicos Poulantzas structurally studied the conjuncture of politics, economics, and ideology in modern capitalism.[80] The relative autonomy of each instance allows Poulantzas to draw subtle inter- and intrastructural distinctions—particularly within and between classes—that orthodox inquiry often obscures in reductive generalizations. Both Godelier and Poulantzas facilely manipulate Althusserian philosophy to frame empirical inquiry.

Mao

Mao Tse-tung's (1893–1976) significance in the history of Marxism is anchored by his contributions to revolutionary tactics. By inserting peasants as the "revolutionary" class in non-Western societies; advocating an anti-imperialist coalition of peasants, workers, petit and national bourgeoisie ("New Democracy"); and outlining a strategy for guerrilla warfare, Mao transformed Marxism-Leninism into an effective Third World revolutionary movement. Fundamental Leninist principles regarding the need for centralized leadership vested in a proletarian party and the importance of permanent, continuing revolution even in immature agrarian conditions are untouched, reinforcing the continuity of Marxism-Leninism-Maoism.

Mao was not a first-rate philosopher. His few theoretical writings are awkward and tendentious, rehashing simple orthodox principles with a mind to justifying the course of Chinese rebellion. He surely considered himself a materialist, and this makes sense, especially when Mao wrote, "the source of all knowledge lies in the perception through man's physical sense organs of the objective world surrounding him."[81] But Mao's practical interests and cultural background at times played havoc with materialism, transforming it into something Mao himself probably did not anticipate. Ironically, Mao's weakness as a philosopher has made the final theoretical product more interesting than it otherwise might have been. Despite the chronological gap between the two and dissimilar motives Mao's Marxism resembles Althusser's in several key respects.

Of Mao's two significant philosophical works, *On Practice* (July 1937) and *On Contradiction* (August 1937), the former represents Mao's unique materialist approach to the theory of knowledge. Leading a struggling revolutionary insurrection in an area most orthodox thinkers would call "unripe," Mao had a vested interest in advocating Leninist activism. However, Mao had neither the inclination nor, perhaps, the ability to swim in Hegelian abstractions. *On Practice* postulates social practice (material labor, class struggle, political, scientific, and artistic proletariat activism) as the only criterion of valid knowledge. "All genuine knowledge originates in direct experience," hence the materialist universe is verified by concrete actions.[82] To know something about reality one acts on an idea, observes the consequences, and then reformulates the idea, to explain effectively what actually occurred. Materialist Marxism is verified only in revolutionary struggle, not through abstractions related to economic development and worker consciousness. Successful struggles are incontrovertible positive proof. Mao's guerrilla movement in China must be measured only by revolutionary success or failure. The former confirms its scientific accuracy, even as Marxism's best philosophical minds howl in disbelief.

Lest this sound too much like old-fashioned American pragmatism or anti-intellectual New Leftism, Mao quickly showed materialist colors. The significance of practice does not mean, empiricism notwithstanding, that truth must be experienced. On the contrary, materialism—Marx's philosophy as well as Engels's and the entire orthodox movement—is a "universal truth."[83] Although knowledge is based on practice, unless the latter reveals universality, it is scientifically unacceptable. Successful actors cognize objective material laws, and act "correctly." On the other hand, actors arrogantly ignoring reality suffer a fate—failure—reserved for self-interested dreamers. In Mao's words, if practice "scientifically reflects objective things, then it is reliable, otherwise it is not."[84] "Correct" theory, therefore, guides social practice. Practical consequences either confirm the theory or, in instances of inadequate preparation, alter the theory to conform with actual conditions. Authentic actors cognitively transform perceptual (empirical) experiences into rational (material) knowledge, without capitulating to either empirical or idealist Rightism or dogmatic, mechanistic Leftism. In understanding and acting correctly, they move fluidly from particular (experience) to general (rationality) and back again, each side reinforcing and/or modifying the other. This is Mao's dialectical materialist theory of knowledge. Through practice we eliminate "falsity," retain "truth," and ultimately realize absolute materialist knowledge.

When Mao, in *On Contradiction,* explicates the quality of knowledge, materialism imperceptively melts into something resembling structuralism. He begins safely enough, echoing Engels with "there is nothing in the world except matter in motion and the motion of matter must assume certain forms."[85] Everything in the universe—natural, human, social—develops according to internal forces that work, as Engels described, to contradict, change, and surpass.[86] "Things . . . [in their] movement and the things round it should be regarded as interconnected and interacting on each other. The basic cause of development of things does not lie outside but inside them, in their internal contradictions." Mao, more than Engels, stresses the absoluteness of contradiction, its influence even in times of relative equilibrium when ripe material conditions produce a unity of opposites. The revolutionary transformation from capitalism to socialism produces an apparent historical equilibrium where popular justice is realized and exploitation extinguished. But even here, Mao emphasized the pervasiveness of contradiction, the one permanent aspect of the universe that, in a sense, transcends periods of rest and change. "Conditional, relative identity, combined with unconditional, absolute struggle, constitutes the movement of opposites in all things." A universal movement of opposites exists from beginning to end, everywhere. "To deny the contradiction in things is to deny everything. This is a universal principle for all times and all countries, which admits of no exceptions."[87]

Mao's dialectic, the ceaseless process of struggle by which the universe evolves, resembles the ancient oriental homily depicting the complementarity of "yin" (negative) and "yang" (positive) in the workings of the cosmos. Mao did not shrink from this comparison: "We Chinese often say 'Things that oppose each other also complement each other.'"[88] The dialectic as absolute contradiction implies an a priori interconnectedness of opposing elements that forms the rhythm or structure of material life, as well as knowledge of it. Orthodox theory, on the contrary, ties the dialectic directly to matter, which, when historically mature, carries society to a qualitatively new developmental stage where social antagonisms disappear. In orthodox materialism conflict and contradiction are an aspect of matter, not the intelligible structure within which matter develops. Mao became progressively aware of this distinction. By 1964 he rejected Engels's laws of the transformation of quantity into quality and the negation of the negation.[89] The message is now clear: A universal structure exists that neither qualitatively alters nor turns into its opposite. Contradiction is the distinguishing and defining trait of the universe, the basis of natural, human, and social being. If it qualitatively changed, so would the universe, and life as we know it would end. Moreover, the universal constancy of contradiction means, again contrary to orthodoxy, that history's dialectical movement is indeterminate. Though society evolves dialectically through antagonisms and social struggle, it doesn't always evolve in a predictable fashion toward a predictable goal. Even the idea of social harmony or unity is absurd, an "unreal" concept. The universe is an unending process of contradiction, so in the long run everything that exists—including communism—will negate itself and disappear. European history, progressing from feudal to capitalist to socialist productive modes, is arbitrary and uncertain, arbitrary because if life ever begins anew either on earth or elsewhere, it is problematic whether this particular process will repeat itself, and uncertain because socialism is not the final word in human history. "There is nothing in the world that does not arise, develop, and disappear. . . . [I]n the end, the whole human race will disappear, it may turn into something else, the earth itself will also cease to exist. . . . I don't believe that men alone are capable of having two hands. Can't horses, cows, sheep, evolve? Can only monkeys evolve?"[90] Mao, in sum, ontologizes the dialectic, turning it from a material process into an autonomous structure. The universality of contradiction leaves matter, including humanity, helplessly conditioned. We will become something different from what we now are, irrespective of intention. The future is uncontrollable.

The structural analogy can fruitfully be stretched further. Since everything is governed by a universal process of contradiction, all events and phenomena evolve autonomously through inner tendencies. Society consists of relatively autonomous contradictory levels or instances, any one of which can dominate social life.[91] Like Althusser, Mao discovered a rational order to this heterogeneous, multidimensional picture. There is a basic or principle contradiction whose existence determines the existence and development of other contradictions, in other words, is determining in the last instance. This principle contradiction is inherited from the built-in antagonisms of the material productive apparatus, and in capitalism is represented by the conflict between workers and owners. This foundational conflict dominates contemporary society. Over time, as different aspects of the principle contradiction change (as workers evolve first into unions and then into revolutionary parties), the quality of social life will change as well. Hence, to evaluate a situation correctly, one must be aware not only of the principle contradiction but also of its historically dominant aspect — a particular, empirically verifiable quality. Furthermore, nonprinciple contradictions coexist and change as the principle contradiction develops. In some historical periods, nonprinciple contradictions may play more significant social roles than in others, depending on the form and quality of class antagonism. The class struggle in Third World nations, as Mao writes, accentuates the nonprinciple contradiction between Western Imperialists and all local classes, including metropolitan bourgeois and workers. A particular aspect of the principle (economic) contradiction in effect elevates the superstructure to priority. Similarly, in postrevolutionary socialism the advanced stage of class struggle may turn superstructural contradictions dominant, necessitating cultural revolutions or purges that cleanse the government and bureaucracy of reactionary forces and reinspire the masses. Mao saw no mechanistic or unilinear links between sub- and superstructures. Although the principle contradiction is economic, the aspects or quality of substructural contradictions may increase the social significance of cultural contradictions, perhaps necessitating policies that orthodox materialists might term subjectivist, reformist, or voluntarist.[92]

Once the principle and nonprinciple contradictions are located and we perceive the relative social significance of each, we must then distinguish between antagonistic and nonantagonistic forms of struggle within a contradiction. Mao perceived relative degrees of contradiction.[93] The severe, antagonistic types are resolved by forcibly eliminating reactionary elements, and involve contradictions between masses of workers and capitalists, Imperialists, or reactionary bureaucrats. Nonsevere, nonantagonistic contradictions are eliminated peacefully, administratively and educationally. These usually mark contradictions among working people in the process of organizing everyday affairs. Like everything else, antagonistic and nonantagonistic contradictions are neither stable nor permanent. As conditions change, so will the quality of a contradiction. Workers and capitalists, for example, may relate antagonistically when capitalism begins, nonantagonistically during the anti-Imperialist New Democracy period, and antagonistically again after independence. In the 1960s, Mao apparently regarded postrevolutionary Communist Party bureaucrats as antagonistically related to peasants and workers, despite shared roots in capitalist oppression. He therefore opposed bureaucratic demands for a mechanized army, pay differentials, educational specialization, and an increase in the white-collar labor force on the grounds that these would negate workers' progressive revolutionary interests. The severity of this antagonism is illustrated by antibureaucratic violence and chaos perpetrated by "red-guard" revolutionaries. "Correct" practice requires accurately perceiving not only the conjuncture of principle and nonprinciple contradictions, but also the quality of relevant contradictions. Negotiating with an enemy is as fatal as killing a misguided ally.

Mao's dialectics resembles Althusser's principle of overdetermination.[94] Both presume a structural unity within which matter evolves historically. Both call society a composite of semiautonomous levels or instances linked by a structure in dominance. Both are anti-Hegelian, antiempiricist, and antihistoricist, and define causality structurally. And both see the class struggle as mediately decisive, even though possibly nondetermining in an immediate sense. Obviously, the analogy is not perfect. Mao could not, in 1937, have been influenced by structuralism to the extent that Althusser was in the 1960s when Lévi-Strauss's reputation was glowing. Hence, Mao always considered himself a materialist, oblivious to the salient contradictions between his orthodox preconceptions (for example, *On Practice*) and his dialectics (*On Contradiction*). Despite an incipient structuralism, Mao did not intentionally seek a scientific realm removed from the practical world of action, prompting Althusser to accuse him of an ideological, Leftist obsession with the superstructure. Mao, in fact, was preeminently a man of action. His theoretical writings are pragmatically motivated, justifying his own and his Party's revolutionary policies. This makes *On Contradiction* more anomalous, with its bleak implications for human influence on a universe governed by a priori structures. Althusser, the philosopher, never adequately connected his epistemology to the concrete needs of a revolutionary working class, although he tried. Mao was apparently unaware of the theoretical implications of his epistemology, as he tended the revolution. Neither proffered a convincing structuralist epistemology that simultaneously motivates and justifies revolutionary action.

MYSTICAL MARXISM: BLOCH

Humanist, Freudian, and structuralist Marxism vividly illustrate the potential compatibility of traditional nonradical Western philosophy and idealist Marxism. Ernst Bloch (1885–1977) carried this project to what most Marxists agree is an inexcusable extreme, creating a revolutionary theory one sympathetic observer calls a "mystical, teleological cosmology."[95] Bloch postulated a neo-Platonic essence, or perfection, toward which humanity and the universe are reaching. This perfect state will appear in the future, when humanity cognizes—and the universe empirically expresses—what is now a hidden truth. But no objective, autonomous laws will guide us. Each intentional actor must surmount the barriers of ignorance, despair, and a seemingly inhospitable environment to achieve perfection. A necessary precondition for this enormous task is a positive attitude toward the future, or what Bloch calls "hope": a kind of knowledge revealing the world as it can be. Philosophy provides this hope, realizing the latent possibilities in humanity and the universe by teaching actors to fulfill, in free actions, cosmic destiny. Philosophy, in other words, should be utopian. It either reaches into the future for absolute truth, or alternatively stagnates in the past or present, assuring civilization's absolute destruction. Western philosophy has traditionally emphasized perfection or salvation as a return to a lost reality, or a reality repeating in history. Hence, it unknowingly rallies forces of human destruction and death. We either go forward toward truth, or we perish. There is no middle ground. Bloch's personal experiences with nazism inject an urgency into what complacent young Westerners might consider an overly apocalyptic inspiration.

Bourgeois philosophy's obsession with "facts" and reified attitudes renders it incapable of grasping truth as a not-yet-realized utopia. Marxism, in contrast, is future-oriented, a theory of utopia and a praxis to bring it about. It satisfies Bloch's criterion for philosophy: offering knowledge of a classless, liberated, nonalienated, "perfect" reality of the future and also the will to create it. Marxism is, therefore, an act of hope. Almost as an afterthought, Bloch pays his dues to orthodoxy by affirming the materiality of the universe and declaring that matter evolves, through an inner dynamic, toward perfection. The historical path is strewn with outmoded and surpassed modes of production, each destroyed by the revolutionary will of those seeking a better future. Capitalism's oppressed workers are harbingers of the socialist utopia. The very survival of humanity depends on their success in seizing the productive apparatus and realizing humanity's essence in societies based on cooperation and equality. Anything less (such as reformism) compromises the future and eventually destroys everyone.

The Marxist utopian must actively lead workers toward history's truth, but there is no inevitability to social progress. The Party must decisively create apposite conditions for the task at hand. Bloch's abstract, mystical metaphysics at first directed him to support Leninist Parties and Stalin's "future-oriented" trials, purges, and mobilizations. During this period he was tolerated by East Germany's orthodox hierarchy, despite a vast theoretical gap separating them. In 1956, convinced that communism—East Germany style—was not the utopia he had anticipated, Bloch crossed the western border and lived his remaining years as a philosopher of utopian

Marxism, more comfortable with the Romantic traditions of classical German thought than the sharp-edged materialism of Eastern Europe.

CONCLUSION

Idealist Marxism presumes several interrelated propositions: Truth takes an abstract form which either unfolds historically or transcends temporality as an ahistorical absolute; it is historically and socially realized by cognizant human beings acting authentically; in mature capitalism workers are uniquely capable of authentic thought and action; capitalism generates a revolutionary seizure of the productive apparatus and its replacement by socialist institutions. Although Marx rejected philosophy, he was aware that consciousness is part of reality and cannot be ignored. The ultimate source of revolutionary praxis is an idea, and ideas are meaningless unless cognized. Marx's post-1846 work defines the material processes that accompany inseparable historical acts of enlightenment and revolutionary action.

While materialism and idealism respect the dialectical unity of thought and action, they are separate, independent theories. Materialists define thought as an epiphenomenon of matter, which, through an inner movement, determines when and where people think critically and rebel. For idealists, revolutionary acts dialectically express authentic cognition, which is prior because of truth's abstract form. The unity of critical thought and revolutionary action is generated by oppressed workers' conscious, subjective thought processes. Materialism is a closed, air-tight world view leaving little logical room for individual initiative. Idealism, sharing with non-Marxian philosophy an emphasis on subjective cognition and ideas, is more flexible, capable of justifying proletariat revolution from a variety of perspectives. Idealist Marxism is uncomfortable with the elite cadres of Party-scientists ruthlessly repressing creative subjectivity, claiming to represent material truth. It challenges materialist Marxism both philosophically and politically. This two-pronged opposition is probably what Zinoviev had in mind when he claimed, at the Fifth Congress of the Comintern (1924), that the revisionism of the "two professors" (Lukács and Korsch) threatened the "existence of the international communist movement."[96] The orthodox reaction to idealism has, generally speaking, remained sharp and uncompromising, and for good reason: The two revolutionary theories represent potentially divergent approaches to social life.

However, idealist and materialist Marxism see truth existing prior to either subjective or empirical verification. For idealists, it is consciously recognized by active subjects; for materialists, it impersonally determines cognition. Both Marxisms can potentially justify the authoritarianism of authentic "scientists." Despite idealism's emphasis on active subjectivity, it, too, in power, can be dictatorial.

NOTES

1. They include G. Petrović, M. Marković, S. Stojanović, R. Supek, L. Tadic, P. Vranicki, D. Grlić, M. Kangrga, V. Korać, and Z. Pesić-Golubovic.

2. Veljko Korać, "In Search of Human Society," in *Socialist Humanism,* ed. Eric Fromm (New York: Anchor Books, 1966), p. 5. See also Ivan Sviták, "The Sources of Socialist Humanism," in ibid., pp. 16–28; Marek Fritzhand, "Marx's Ideal of Man," in ibid., p. 177; and Gajo Petrović, *Marx in the Mid-Twentieth Century* (New York: Anchor Books, 1967), pp. 14 and 31–51.

3. G. Petrović, "Man and Freedom," in *Socialist Humanism,* pp. 273 and 274.

4. V. Korać, "In Search for Human Society," in ibid., pp. 4–6.

5. Fritzhand, "Marx's Ideal of Man," p. 177.

6. Mihailo Marković, *From Affluence to Praxis* (Ann Arbor, Mich.: University of Michigan Press, 1974), p. 56. Emphasis added. See also pp. 139–45.

7. Petrović, "Man and Freedom," p. 16.

8. Adam Schaff, *Marxism and the Human Individual* (New York: McGraw-Hill, 1970), pp. 143–44.

9. Wilhelm Reich, *The Function of the Organism* (New York: Farrar, Strauss and Giroux, 1970), p. 79. See pp. 66–79. See also *Reich on Freud,* ed. M. Higgins and C. Raphael (New York: Farrar, Strauss and Giroux, 1967), p. 15.

10. A complete list of Reich's Marxist writings (1927–1936) is in Wilhelm Reich, *Sex-Pol, Essays, 1929–34,* ed. L. Baxandall (New York: Vintage Books, 1972), p. xii.

11. Wilhelm Reich, "Dialectical Materialism and Psychoanalysis," in *Sex-Pol,* p. 66. See also pp. 21f and 27–48, as well as "The Importance of Sexual Morality," in ibid., pp. 235ff.

12. See the 1934 edition of "Dialectical Materialism and Psychoanalysis" (1929), in *Sex-Pol,* pp. 46, 56, and 59–74.

13. Wilhelm Reich, *Character Analysis* (New York: Farrar, Straus and Giroux, 1970), pp. 146–49. The following quote is on p. 44. See also: "The Importance of Sexual Morality," in *Sex-Pol,* pp. 237 and 240ff; "Politicizing the Sexual Problem of Youth," in ibid., esp. pp. 253–74; "What is Class Consciousness," in ibid., pp. 277–358, esp. p. 297; *Mass Psychology of Fascism* (New York: Orgone Institute Press, 1946), pp. 25f; and *People in Trouble* (Rangely, Maine: Wilhelm Reich Foundation, 1953), p. 46.

14. Reich, "Dialectical Materialism and Psychoanalysis," p. 4; and "Psychoanalysis in the Soviet Union," in ibid., pp. 77–88.

15. See Reimut Reiche, *Sexualité et lutte de classes,* trans. [into French] C. Parrenin and F. J. Rutten (Paris: Gallimard, 1971); and Herbert Marcuse, "Political Preface," *Eros and Civilization* (Boston: Beacon Press, 1966), p. xiii.

16. Marcuse, *Eros and Civilization,* p. 239.

17. Ibid., pp. 37 and 35.

18. Ibid., pp. 49 and 81.

19. Marcuse, "Political Preface," pp. xiv, xvi, and xxv. See also idem, *One Dimensional Man* (Boston: Beacon Press, 1966), pp. 247–57.

20. Herbert Marcuse, *Reason and Revolution* (Boston: Beacon Press, 1960), p. 318.

21. Herbert Marcuse, *Soviet Marxism* (New York: Vintage Books, 1961), p. 126.

22. Ibid., p. 122. See also pp. 23–103.

23. Nevertheless, the Soviet emphasis on community ("res publica") puts them

closer than the West to liberating individuals from sexual and other repressions. See ibid., part II.

24. Marcuse, *Eros and Civilization,* p. 106. Emphasis added.

25. Herbert Marcuse, "Repressive Tolerance," in *A Critique of Pure Tolerance,* ed. Robert Paul Wolff (Boston: Beacon Press, 1967), p. 102.

26. Erich Fromm, "The Application of Humanist Psychoanalysis to Marx's Theory," in *Socialist Humanism,* p. 231. See pp. 228–45. Fromm's significant works include *Escape From Freedom* (1914), *Man for Himself* (1947), *The Sane Society* (1955), *Zen Buddhism and Psychoanalysis* (1960), *Marx's Concept of Man* (1961), and *Beyond the Chains of Illusion* (1962).

27. Fromm, "The Application of Humanist Psychoanalysis to Marx's Theory," p. 234.

28. See Erich Fromm, *Escape From Freedom* (New York: Holt, Rinehart & Winston, 1941).

29. Erich Fromm, *Beyond the Chains of Illusion* (New York: Simon & Schuster, 1962), p. 30.

30. Ferdinand de Saussure, *Course in General Linguistics,* (New York: McGraw-Hill, 1959).

31. Claude Lévi-Strauss, *The Raw and the Cooked* (New York: Harper & Row, 1969), p. 12. See idem, *The Savage Mind* (Chicago: University of Chicago Press, 1966), p. 252.

32. See Dominique Lecourt, *Marxism and Epistemology* (London: New Left Books, 1975), pp. 110 and 130–37.

33. See Jacques Lacan, *Écrits* (Paris: Éditions du Seuil, 1971), 2: 190; idem, "Some Reflections on the Ego," *International Journal of Psychoanalysis* 34 (1953): 12; Edith Kurzweil, *The Age of Structuralism* (New York: Columbia University Press, 1980), p. 142; and Rosalind Coward and John Ellis, *Language and Materialism* (London: Routledge & Kegan Paul, 1977), pp. 93–121.

34. See Roland Barthes, *Elements of Semiology* (New York: Hill & Wang, 1968), p. 9, and Coward and Ellis, *Language and Materialism,* pp. 1 and 25–44.

35. Useful secondary sources include: Jorge Larrain, *The Concept of Ideology* (London: Hutchinson, 1979), p. 165; Jan M. Broekman, *Structuralism: Moscow-Prague-Paris* (Dordrecht, Netherlands: Reidel, 1974), pp. 72–94; Coward and Ellis, *Language and Materialism;* and Kurzweil, *The Age of Structuralism,* p. 183.

36. The name "Tel Quel" indicates a group of radical Left intellectuals, a journal that publishes their material, and an extensive series of published monographs.

37. Miriam Glucksmann, *Structuralist Analysis in Contemporary Social Thought* (London: Routledge & Kegan Paul, 1974), p. 139.

38. See Coward and Ellis, *Language and Materialism,* pp. 3–7 and 93–121; Octavio Paz, *Claude Lévi-Strauss: An Introduction* (Ithaca, N.Y.: Cornell University Press, 1970), p. 113; J. Simon, "A Conversation with Michel Foucault," *Partisan Review* 2 (1971): 201; and Maurice Godelier, *Rationality and Irrationality in Economics* (London: New Left Books, 1972), p. 91.

39. Even Lévi-Strauss called himself "Marxist." See *Tristes Tropiques* (New York: Antheneum, 1968), p. 61; *The Savage Mind,* pp. 130–31 and 246; *Structural Anthropology* (New York: Basic Books, 1963), pp. 332–33.

40. See Michel Foucault, *The Order of Things* (New York: Pantheon, 1970), pp. 364f.

41. Michel Foucault, *The Archeology of Knowledge* (New York: Pantheon, 1972), pp. 38–39.

42. See Michel Foucault, *Madness and Civilization* (New York: Random House, 1965), *The Birth of the Clinic* (New York: Pantheon, 1973), and *The History of Sexuality* (New York: Pantheon, 1978).

43. Soviet structuralism is equally guilty. See Jurij M. Lotman, *Struktura chudo zestvennogo teksta* (Providence, R.I.: Brown University Press, 1971).

44. Lucien Goldmann, *Marxisme et sciences humaines* (Paris: Gallimard, 1970), p. 21; and "Introduction Générale," in *Entretiens sur les notions de 'Génèse' et de 'structure'* (Paris: Mouton & École Practiques de Hautes Études, 1965), p. 10.

45. Lucien Goldmann, "Ideology and Writing," *The Times Literary Supplement*, 28 September, 1967, p. 904.

46. Lucien Goldmann, *The Hidden God* (London: Routledge & Kegan Paul, 1964), p. 17.

47. Ibid.

48. Authentic bourgeois class consciousness is represented by the "tragic vision" of its best literary works. See Lucien Goldmann, *The Hidden God,* p. 8; and *The Human Sciences and Philosophy* (London: Cape, 1969), p. 65.

49. Goldmann, *The Human Sciences and Philosophy,* pp. 52 and 56.

50. See M. Glucksmann, "Lucien Goldmann: Humanist or Marxist?" *New Left Review* 56 (July–August 1969): 49.

51. Althusser condemns structuralism in his Introduction to the English edition of *Reading Capital* (New York: Pantheon, 1970), and praises it in *Éléments d'Autocritique* (Paris: Hachette, 1974), p. 56n and 57n. See Glucksmann, *Structuralist Analysis in Contemporary Social Thought,* pp. 167–77.

52. Louis Althusser, *For Marx* (New York: Pantheon, 1969), p. 38.

53. Ibid., pp. 166–67.

54. See Althusser, *Reading Capital,* pp. 42, 59, 170–77, and 212–16; and *For Marx,* pp. 167 and 173.

55. Althusser, *Reading Capital,* p. 42.

56. Althusser, *For Marx,* pp. 168–69. See also pp. 177, 173, and 256; and *Reading Capital,* p. 8.

57. Althusser, *Reading Capital,* p. 42. See pp. 41ff, 87–90, and 189–90; and *For Marx,* pp. 183–93.

58. Althusser, *Reading Capital,* pp. 40f. See p. 87.

59. Ibid., p. 156.

60. Ibid., p. 134.

61. Ibid., p. 141.

62. Althusser, *For Marx,* pp. 231, 191, and 233–34. See also *Reading Capital,* pp. 58, 141, and 177.

63. Louis Althusser, *Lenin and Philosophy* (London: Monthly Review Press, 1971), pp. 127–88.

64. See Althusser, *For Marx,* pp. 155–60; and *Lenin and Philosophy,* p. 90.

65. Althusser, *Reading Capital,* p. 17.

66. See Althusser, *For Marx,* p. 111.

67. Ibid., p. 255; *Reading Capital,* pp. 220–24 (Balibar's essay); and Nicos Poulantzas, *Political Power and Social Classes* (London: New Left Books, 1973), p. 14.

68. See Althusser, *Reading Capital,* pp. 99–109.

69. Ibid., pp. 180–93.

70. Althusser, *Lenin and Philosophy*, p. 201. See also *Réponse à John Lewis* (Paris: Receuil, 1977), p. 94.

71. Maurice Godelier, *Perspectives in Marxist Anthropology* (London: Cambridge University Press, 1977), p. 6.

72. See Althusser, *Reading Capital*, p. 242.

73. Ibid., p. 180.

74. Typical Marxist critiques include: Geras, "Althusser's Marxism," *New Left Review* 71 (January–February 1972): 262–72; P. Hirst, "Althusser and Philosophy," *Theoretical Practice* 2 (April 1971); Alex Callinicos, *Althusser's Marxism* (London: Pluto Press, 1976), esp. pp. 72–77; and Adam Schaff, *Structuralism and Marxism* (New York: Pergamon Press, 1978), pp. 90ff.

75. See Althusser, *Lenin and Philosophy, Philosophie et Philosophie Spontanée des Savants* (Paris: Maspero, 1974), and *Éléments d'Autocritique.*

76. Althusser, *Éléments d'Autocritique*, p. 98.

77, See, for example, Althusser, *Réponse à John Lewis*, p. 56.

78. Lucien Sebag, an anthropologist whose work parallels Althusser's, admits this. See *Marxisme et structuralisme* (Paris: Payot, 1964).

79. See Maurice Godelier, *Rationality and Irrationality in Economics, Perspectives in Marxist Anthropology*, and "Fétichisme, religion et théorie général de l'ideologie chez Marx," *Annali* (Roma: Feltrinelli, 1970): 30–35.

80. See Nicos Poulantzas, *Political Power and Social Classes, Fascism and Dictatorship* (London: New Left Books, 1974), *Classes in Contemporary Capitalism* (London: New Left Books, 1975), and *State, Power, Socialism* (London: New Left Books, 1978).

81. Mao Tse-tung, *On Practice*, in *Mao Tse-tung: An Anthology of His Writings*, ed. Anne Freemantle (New York: Mentor Books, 1962), p. 205.

82. Ibid.

83. Ibid., p. 210.

84. Ibid., p. 205.

85. Mao, *On Contradiction*, in *Mao Tse-tung: An Anthology of His Writings*, p. 220.

86. Mao confirmed his belief in Engels's three dialectical laws of matter in "Sixty Articles on Work Methods," trans. S. Schram, *China Quarterly* no. 46, p. 229.

87. Mao, *On Contradiction*, pp. 216, 238, and 229.

88. Mao, *Selected Works* 4 vols. (Peking: Foreign Languages Press, 1961–65) 343. See also Benjamin I. Schwartz, "The Philosopher," in *Mao Tse-tung in the Scales of History*, ed. Dick Wilson (New York: Cambridge University Press, 1977), pp. 9–34.

89. Mao, "Talk on Questions of Philosophy" with K'ang Sheng and Ch'en Po-ta, 18 August 1964, in *Mao Tse-tung Unrehearsed*, ed. S. Schram (Harmondsworth, England: Penguin Books, 1974), p. 226.

90. Ibid., pp. 110–220.

91. See Mao, *On Contradiction*, pp. 229ff.

92. See, for example, F. V. Konstantinov and M. I. Sladkovsky, *A Critique of Mao Tse-tung's Theoretical Conceptions* (Moscow: Progress Publishers, 1972); and M. Altaisky and V. Georgiyev, *The Philosophical Views of Mao Tse-tung: A Critical Analysis* (Moscow: Progress Pubs., 1971).

93. Mao, *On Contradiction*, pp. 234ff. See also "On the Correct Handling of

Contradictions Among the People," in *Mao Tse-Tung: An Anthology of His Writings,* pp. 264-97.

94. See Alain Lipietz, "D'Althusser à Mao?" *Les Tempes Modernes* (November 1973), pp. 749-87; Philippe Sollers, *Sur le matérialisme* (Paris: Seuil, 1974), esp. pp. 135-36; and Godelier, *Rationality and Irrationality in Economics,* p. 90.

95. The quote is in Alfred Schmidt's "Afterword" to the German edition of Henri Lefebvre, *Le Matérialisme dialectique* (Paris: Félix Alcan, 1939). See Ernst Bloch, *Man on His Own* (New York: Herder & Herder, 1970), and especially *Das Prinzip Hoffnung,* 3 vols. (Frankfurt: Suhrkamp Verlag, 1954-1959).

96. Quoted by M. Watnik, "Relativism and Class Consciousness: George Lukacs," in *Revisionism,* ed. L. Labedz (London: Allen & Unwin, 1962), p. 146. See also Furio Cerutti, "Hegel, Lukacs, Korsch," in *Aktualität and Folgen der Philosophie Hegels,* ed. O. Negt (Frankfurt: Suhrkamp Verlag, 1970), pp. 130ff.

5.

Empiricism

A priori Marxism cognizes universality and its influence over an unsuspecting public. Specific facts, neither ignored nor rejected, are part of a greater reality whose meaning is more than a mere sum of available data. A priori science interprets the particular as an aspect of the absolute, relegating the former to an epistemologically inferior position.

Idealists and materialists are thus backed into an awkward position. The most distinctive feature of modern civilization, its extraordinary productive and technological achievements, spring from a scientific method based on the priority of specific, particular facts. The popular Marxist argument that proletarian science will eventually surpass and sublate bourgeois science comes dangerously close to admitting that social progress hinges on abandoning the spirit of empirical inquiry and with it dreams of additional miraculous accomplishments in industrial, medical, and space technology. Since these will potentially improve the quality of working-class life, these Marxists shamelessly ask workers to sacrifice their own practical interests to realize a workers' utopia.

For many reasons, undoubtedly related to upgrading workers' lives as well as meeting international political and economic commitments, orthodox Marxist states zealously pursue a policy of intense research and development in the empirical sciences. Marxist socialism today subsidizes the odd confluence of two distinct kinds of science: bourgeois empiricism, which, though reified and antihuman, is invaluable for survival; and authentic dialectical materialism, with universal concepts transcending and defining empirical data. The latter protects socialism and advocates history's inherent potential for proletariat revolution. On the other hand, empirical science harnesses the specific, measurable physical laws governing nonhuman matter. Conflicts can occur. When, for example, a fact is deemed "nonprogressive" by Party leaders, dialectical materialists must "correct" empirical scientists by ignoring factual evidence. The Lysenko controversy illustrates the potentially absurd consequences.

In response, some theorists have synthesized dialectical materialism and empirical science. Marx himself was a historian and social scientist guided solely by facts, never meaning to establish a priori truths, abstract "keys" for understanding history, that could fictionally reconstitute empirical reality. Marx's science is valid only when actually explaining the empirical life-world of real human beings. When postulating universal nonempirical principles, it is obscure and mystifying, mimicking the bourgeois philosophy it replaces. Scientific historical materialism generates logical, predictable laws that are manifest in actual empirical conditions. Empiricism is a theory of knowledge focusing solely on this experienced reality, hence is exact and demystifying, exploding bourgeois myths and scientifically establishing the necessity of proletariat revolution and institutionalized egalitarianism. Marxist epistemology uses the same concrete, particular facts that capitalists tap in modernizing the technological apparatus and creating incipient attitudes of rebellion among oppressed workers.

PHILOSOPHICAL EMPIRICISM

Empirical scientific explanations reveal regular patterns of dependence between phenomena and situate these in a net of determining relationships providing a basis for effective pre- and postdiction. Scientific method consists of a set of rules that guarantee objectivity. What is real, or factual, consists only of what we observe, describe, and measure according to universally recognized, impersonal criteria of verification. Scientists generate explanatory theories from collected data and understand the real world as a determined product of repeating patterns of events. From one general theory is deduced the behavior of a whole species of identical objects. Since sentient human beings are part of the real world, perception materializes from received and interpreted external stimuli. For example, my perception of a building is caused by my inner sensory response to the stimulus, which is caused by the building itself. Generalizations regarding human attitudes and behavior are deductively applicable to all identically situated human beings.

Empirical social science approaches the difficult task of explaining subjectively meaningful human behavior by including as research variables subjective factors (for example, feelings, moods, desires, preferences) operationalized and verified according to accepted principles of empirical method. Behavioralism, in other words, packs the full force of empirical science because its basic assumptions and procedures are identical.

To empiricists, social knowledge comprises interpersonal behavior that is scientifically verified. Social science disciplines, then, are generated by whittling social reality into distinct realms, each encompassing an explicit scope of objectively determined behavior. This structurally divides data into compact, self-contained units that correspond to specialized branches of scientific inquiry. Specialization and division of labor streamline social research, creating swarms of experts clustering around distinct disciplines, each producing valid knowledge. The criteria for valid inquiry is constant irrespective of the observed phenomena's scope.

Empirical science is originally derived from bourgeois philosophical preconceptions, the most fundamental being Descartes's dichotomy of mind and matter, his belief that human reality is qualitatively different from matter. The logical corollary, which becomes the linchpin of bourgeois philosophy, argues that human subjects exist apart from, and independent of, external surroundings. In other words, the universe is divided into two realities: the "subjective," human world and the "objective" world of non-human phenomena. The former encompasses values and feelings and is entered indirectly through the vicarious insights provided by art. The latter, factual reality, is cognized by an empirical method based on universally accepted impersonal criteria of verifiability. Science is limited to this objective, factual world. Normative concepts, dealing with essentially non-empirical, evaluative qualities like justice, love, beauty, happiness, and so on are not scientifically explainable. Empirical science is concerned only with what "is," not what "ought" to be.

These seminal thoughts—man as an autonomous, nonsocial animal, the separation of fact and value, and the nonpolitical quality of science—generate bourgeois empirical science. They philosophically justify empirical social science but are not empirically verifiable. Hence, bourgeois science, ostensibly "neutral," "objective," and "impartial," represents philosophical values justified only by subjective commitments of practitioners. Moreover, they embody the material interests of capitalist entrepreneurs and their intellectual representatives, and rationalize bourgeois institutions. Empirical science originates, therefore, as an aspect of capitalism and a tool for perpetuating bourgeois values and institutions. As empirical scientists modernize the productive apparatus and explore the natural universe, these core values gradually dissolve into naively accepted, precognitive attitudes permeating the life-worlds of both empirical scientists and lay people. In this universally shared naiveté, which persists to this day, everyone unquestioningly assumes that individuals are autonomous and unique, values are separate from facts, and science is politically neutral. These assumptions determine what social phenomena are scientifically examined and what variables are relevant. The supposedly value-free compilation of facts unknowingly expresses foundational values that artificially divide social reality into a series of isolated, autonomous phenomena.

These bourgeois principles are critically rejected by all Marxists, who assert the social character of individuality, the indissoluble unity of fact and value, and the desirability of history's movement toward proletariat revolution. What distinguishes empirical Marxism is its unwillingness to fall back on a priori or experiential justifications, which are "nonprogressive," resuscitating theories that empiricism has already historically and analytically surpassed. Moreover, they are unnecessary. Empiricism has the innate potential of negating the class interests it now represents. But a critically revised examination of reality is needed: Unquestioned myths regarding individuality, science, and politics must be pierced by factual evidence. Empirical data, in other words, can disprove common bourgeois preconceptions. Scientists must surpass capitalism's rules, critically rejecting dominant interests and values, to strip the illusions from what passes today as social science. Empiricism, then, is not *necessarily* a tool of bourgeois interests, although it is today and has been historically.

Empirical Marxism resembles "formalist" empirical science, which seeks incontrovertible, formal principles governing the underlying logical order of things, independent of everyday contingencies. A formal structure is true "only insofar as the real world imitates the formal structure—in other words, only insofar as something approximating the formal structure exists in the real world," determined by empirically comparing the real world to the model.[1] If formal principles adequately explain the everyday, factual world, they are valid.

What distinguishes mainstream bourgeois formalism from empirical Marxism, of course, is the unquestioned commitment to capitalism. Non-Marxist formal models are uncritical, incapable of smashing through the veneer of bourgeois rhetoric. One notable consequence is the inability of bourgeois social science—formal or not—to achieve the successes of natural science, where philosophical biases more nearly reflect the actual quality of nonhuman phenomena. There are no universally accepted and empirically verified laws of social behavior whose utility in explaining reality come anywhere near the established laws of physics. Marxists, on the other hand, draw formal theories from Marx's critical insights, hence neither support capitalism nor perpetuate bourgeois myths. Marx's theories are valid because they explain empirical reality, and are verified by specific facts rather than abstractions. When empirically tested, they are confirmed and universally accepted, reflecting the integrity and utility heretofore reserved for the laws of physical science. Most Westerners remain ignorant because of the stultifying social pressures of capitalism which discourage critical science.

Materialists also claim to depict empirical reality accurately, arguing that empiricism and Marxism are supplementary techniques for social inquiry whose findings are mutually supportive: "in philosophy, the materialistic standpoint cannot be combined with any other position than the empiricist one."[2] Indeed, materialism *is* concerned with concrete phenomena, the basic, empirically verifiable matter of nature and society. But materialist theory is valid prior to the act of empirical verification. For materialism, each empirical "fact" artificially isolates a minute quantity of matter from its social and natural context. What distinguishes this context, however, is complexity and irreducibility. Matter evolves dialectically. What we sensually experience as autonomous elements are, in fact, defined by the entire material totality. The interpenetration of all aspects of reality invalidates a method that seeks only cause-effect relationships between a limited number of artificially extracted variables. Materialists seek empirical illustrations of an a priori point of view, not empirical verification, and deny the "uncritical" acceptance of facts as true in themselves. They interpret the universal in the particular, theoretically combining facts to comprehend the a priori laws of nature. Although matter is sensually perceived, it is not accurately explained by a method that ignores underlying, nonempirical truth. "Narrow empiricism . . . confines itself to collecting and coordinating facts, is not interested in discovering the underlying laws of motion and interconnection manifested in those facts, and is sceptical about all bold generalizations and theories. Like dogmatism, empiricism cannot see beyond the limited experience of the present moment."[3]

Materialists believe that modern empirical science, lacking this insight, is in "endless confusion" (Engels) and "travail" (Lenin). By failing to recognize an inclusive, determining dialectical universe, it dooms itself to eventual annihilation. Empirical scientists have accepted bourgeois values without glimpsing capitalism's tragic historical fate, obvious to anyone looking past the empirically obvious. History guarantees that empiricists will eventually practice the real science of dialectical materialism. It is this "real" (that is, a priori) quality of dialectical materialism that empirical Marxism denies. Marx's ideas regarding materialism, history, and revolution are generated from extensive empirical research and are valid only when explaining a constantly increasing corpus of empirical data. The notion that Marxism is true "in itself," prior to evidence, is tautological—useless to serious social scientists.

MARX'S EMPIRICISM

Marx's interest in the empirical life-world was established when he was a law student at the University of Bonn (1835), when he rejected the Left Hegelian belief in an absolute standard of Reason. Although revolutionary thought must be critical, it cannot unthinkingly violate the integrity of the everyday world. Marx defended empirical reality *and* critical reason, mediating the Left Hegelians (especially Bauer and Ruge) and the Conservative Hegelians (especially Savigny). *The Critique of Hegel's Doctrine of the State* (1843) argues that Hegel mistakenly identified being and thought, the real and rational. Hegel's method involves a double inversion or exchange. First, it postulates the priority of an abstract Idea and interprets specific facts as derivative. By reducing (factual) being to (abstract) thinking, empirical reality is negated: being is not being, but thought. Second, Reason becomes self-sufficient, unjustified by the factual world of actual being. Hegel's abstract Idea is a nonsubstantiable myth, irrelevant to the particular, corporeal forms scientists use. He attends empirical reality almost as an afterthought, "not to discover the truth of empirical existence but to discover the empirical existence of truth." Hegel expunges being and replaces it with a nonreal abstraction.

Hegel makes the predicates, the objects, autonomous, but he does this by separating them from their real autonomy, viz. their subject. The real subject subsequently appears as a result, whereas the correct approach would be to start with the real subject and then consider its objectification. The mystical substance therefore becomes the real subject, while the actual subject appears as something else, namely as a moment of the mystical substance.[4]

This fetish for abstraction, not a personal compromise on Hegel's part, doomed Hegelianism to a reactionary world view. The Left Hegelians, and even Engels, did not recognize that the internal logic of Hegel's philosophy generates a biased, reactionary theory of the state. As the dialectical sublation of the antagonism between individual and community, Hegel's state is the incarnation of Mind. He again reverses the order of things: what is real (individuals, families, and civil societies) merely expresses the abstract Idea. Myth obliterates reality. Hegel's hypostatized inversion of reality reflects capitalism's dismemberment of the world into autonomous realms, and its belief that statehood represents a pure freedom independent of economic and social conditions. The *Critique* and *On the Jewish Question* (1843) condemned Hegel for his typically bourgeois interest in the state as a symbol of universal "general interests." In the real world, the bourgeois state, claiming universality, actually upholds an institution (private property) that protects the individual right to pursue self-interest independent of—or against—society. Hegel's epistemological reversal reflects the inverted logic of capitalism: "general will" rationalizes individual caprice; society sanctifies asocial interests; abstract equality is preserved so real inequality remains absolute. Moreover, Hegel's argument is internally unreasonable, naively supporting dominant institutions and values rather than exposing them to Reason's negating force. Hegel's abstractionism turns Reason away from the actual facts of history and toward a self-contained logical pattern that is true regardless of empirical consequences.

Thus empirical reality is accepted as it is; it is even declared to be rational. However, it is not rational by virtue of its own reason, but because the empirical fact in its empirical existence has a meaning other than itself. The fact which serves as a starting point is not seen as such but as a mystical result. The real becomes a mere phenomenon, but the Idea has no content over and above this phenomenon.[5]

The Holy Family (1845) similarly vilifies Left Hegelianism for unquestioningly adopting Hegel's inversion. Despite critically examining aspects of the German state, people like Bruno and Edgar Bauer unjustifiably believed in universal "Spirit." Historical progress, they contended, emanates from the self-contained evolution of an idea, not concrete forces that people actually experience. Left Hegelians, like Hegel, are done in by favoring abstractions over the real needs of real people.

The Critique of Hegel's Doctrine of the State and the introduction to The Critique of Hegel's Philosophy of Right (1843–1844) contend that Hegel failed miserably in scientifically comprehending the political institutions of his time. On the Jewish Question extends the critique from politics to religion. Theology is another form of mystification, enveloping reality in a rush of abstractions justified only by more abstractions. To understand Christianity and Judaism effectively, we must observe the practical, empirical forms of religion, that is, the way that actual Christians and Jews live and work in civil society. This shows, unequivocally, that both religions function smoothly in capitalism while remaining "spiritual." Hence, their empirical essence is individual need and egotism, the worship of what Marx calls the "secular God 'money.'" The opprobrious qualities commonly associated with "Jewishness," such as greed, haggling, usury, money-hoarding, and so on, survive because Western Christian society institutionalizes them. Jews and Christians are victimized by these lascivious forces. Indeed, any successful citizen in capitalism epitomizes what the naive and bigoted call "Jewishness." Anti-Semitic public laws should be abolished not because Jews are better or worse than Christians. Both religions mystify rather than enlighten. However, the complete secularization of society brings us closer to the real source of what is despised: the inhuman values and institutions of capitalism. "It is the immediate task of philosophy . . . to unmask self-estrangement in its unholy forms once the holy form of human self-estrangement has been unmasked. Thus the criticism of heaven turns into the criticism of earth, the criticism of religion into the criticism of law, and the criticism of theology into the criticism of politics."[6]

The 1844 Manuscripts, despite its reputation, epitomizes Marx's early commitment to the priority of empirical facts. The inchoate critique of political economy marking all three manuscripts is empirically motivated and verified: "It is hardly necessary to assure the reader who is familiar with political economy that I arrived at my conclusions through an entirely empirical analysis based on an exhaustive critical study of political economy." Hence the Manuscripts is Marx's first systematic attempt to operationalize a concrete approach to social inquiry. Only the actual, observed aspects of capitalism are examined, independent of bourgeois myths. Marx concluded that life in capitalism is isolated, lonely, and frustrated. Alienated citizens objectify themselves and neighbors, are passively conditioned by abstractions that nourish incessant competition, growing poverty, thankless work, and pitilessness. The sources of this human depravity are actual social relationships.

Man's estrangement, like all relationships of man to himself, is realized and expressed only in man's relationship to other men. . . . The relationship of man to himself becomes objective and real for him only through his relationship to other men. . . . Every self-estrangement of man from himself and nature is manifested in the relationship he sets up between other men and himself and nature.[7]

The sources and quality of alienation are verified empirically, characterizing actual interactions and the ensemble of social relationships in which these occur. Idealists interpreting Marx to mean that humanity has somehow abandoned a creative potential, or "essence," reintroduce the abstractions that Marx earlier condemned. Alienation is a real, verifiable trait of actual people interacting in specific capitalist conditions. Alienation is understood and critically surpassed only by confronting myth with reality, superstition with science, abstraction with fact. And this is the distinctive social function of dialectics. A priorism, ideal or material, like Hegelianism, reestablishes the antihuman hegemony of an Idea.

Marx emphatically denied the existence of, and need for, abstract human essence. He redefined human nature in the sixth *Thesis on Feuerbach* to encompass the empirically verifiable "ensemble of social relations." The second thesis affirms that "objective truth" is verifiable only "in practice," in real phenomena that, contrary to thought, are confirmed empirically. In rejecting the "internal, dumb generalit[ies]" of a priorism, Marx separated himself from abstract bourgeois idealism and metaphysical materialism, both interpreting facts as expressions of abstractions. Because each human being is real and factual, humanity in general is not adequately explained by vague generalities. "[M]an is no abstract being squatting outside the world. Man is the world of man, state, society."[8]

The German Ideology abandons "empty phrases about consciousness" altogether, substituting "real knowledge" and "positive science." The "unity of man with nature" that idealists mistakenly identify as an essential human quality is carefully defined in terms of actual relationships. Humanity is open to nature in actively producing its means of subsistence. This is verified by tracing its actual recorded behavior throughout history. Marx refused to go beyond empirical evidence and postulate preempirical causes or motives. The facts alone confirm that humans satisfy needs with self-created instruments, which in turn influence new needs. These instruments comprise modes of production, each corresponding to a specific social division of labor, that is, the way people cooperate to produce needed goods. There is a causal link between the aggregate of productive forces and the quality of society. "There exists a . . . connection of men with one another, which is determined by their needs and their mode of production, and which is as old as men themselves." Humanity, then, is social because it is always thrown into productive relationships with others. The quality of society is conditioned by the quality of these productive relationships.

Human attitudes and ideas are socially produced, reflecting our relationships to others and nature—hence are conditioned by the productive apparatus. Since reflective cognition stimulates new social, political, and artistic institutions, Marx concluded that the mode of production governs culture. This theory, however, is valid only in explaining the actual historical and social behavior of individuals: "Empirical observation must in each separate instance bring out empirically, and without any mystification and speculation, the connection of the social and political structure with production." Historical materialism is neither "arbitrary" nor "dogmatic." It is based on real evidence, "real individuals [and] their activity," and verified "in a purely empirical way."[9]

The Poverty of Philosophy (1846–1847) reiterates Marx's critique of Hegelian abstractionism and refines the theory of historical materialism. Marx finds Proudhon's ideas weak and unconvincing because, like Hegel's, they are based on mystical a priori abstractions. Proudhon's radicalism is an unrealistic ideal, a utopian dream serving the very practical function of perpetuating bourgeois mystification and oppression. Real knowledge must pierce this shell of obfuscation with concrete terms related to actual activities. Authentic social inquiry negates capitalism by distinguishing rhetoric from self-destructive reality. The central premise of Marxism is inductively drawn from observed history and argues, "a change in men's productive forces necessarily brings about a change in their relations of production." As a theory explaining historical progress, it is useful and valid when verified empirically. However, it is "anything but [an] eternal law . . . "[10] because it encompasses only man's everyday activities, "as he comes and goes, eats, drinks, and clothes himself."[11]

After 1847 Marx's project of explaining and transforming the real world generated historical and economic studies that are fiercely loyal to empirical reality. The former include *The Class Struggles in France* (1850), *The Eighteenth Brumaire of Louis Bonaparte* (1851), and a series of journal articles; the latter, *Wage-Labour and Capital* (1849), *Grundrisse, Capital,* and *Theories of Surplus Value* (1862–1863).

The Class Struggles in France consists of articles examining the upheavals in France during 1848, that Marx contributed to the radical monthly journal he edited called *Neue Rheinische Zeitung-Revue* (originally entitled *1848–49*). *The Eighteenth Brumaire of Louis Bonaparte* analyzes the class relationships behind Louis Napoleon's ascension in December 1851. Together, they were Marx's first attempts at explaining contemporary events in Europe with his theory of historical materialism. Marx documented the political upheavals of 1848 in terms of opposing class interests of workers and petty bourgeoisie. Since French workers lacked political experience and competent leadership, the petty bourgeoisie assumed control of the movements, asking and receiving worker support. However, with a spineless middle class standing by helplessly, the petty bourgeoisie eventually threw their support to Louis Napoleon. Demoralized and factionalized by an inability to shape events significantly, the workers' movement was decimated. In the early 1850s a period of open reaction ensued, when the petty bourgeoisie tried to snuff out the proletariat's revolutionary potential with a social reform program called "Socialist-Democracy." This was socialism in name only, for its prime goal was to preserve wage labour. By increasing salaries, the petty bourgeoisie succeeded in blurring the real issues separating workers and class enemies. The revolutionary workers' movement was dealt a severe blow that no amount of wishful theorizing could alter. Marx alienated the Communist League by withdrawing his support for immediate worker uprisings. Branded a "counterrevolutionary" and "reactionary" by radical leaders, Marx nevertheless refused to compromise the facts, which clearly indicated that French capitalism had not yet reached the threshold of active proletarian discontent. After barely managing to convince the London office of the Communist League, Marx withdrew from political activity into the British Museum, where he studied further the dynamics of capitalism and the necessary preconditions of a successful workers' revolution. To support his family, he continued writing about contemporary politics, especially events in Britain, and his articles eventually were published in the *New York Daily Tribune* and the *New American Encyclopedia*. The events of these years confirmed in his own mind the danger and self-destructiveness of abstract revolutionary theories distorting reality with preconceived categories. Marx, especially at this time in his life, was constantly aware of the chasm dividing theory and reality. Meagerly rewarded for his articles, living in one of London's poorest districts, hounded continually by creditors and landlords, and plagued by illness, Marx commented sarcastically, "Never has anyone written about 'money in general' amidst such a total lack of 'money in particular.'"[12]

The results of Marx's years of inquiry into political economy are voluminous and complex. *Wage-Labour and Capital* demonstrates "empirically, on the already existing historical data which were emerging everyday anew," the relative and absolute immersion of workers in capitalism.[13] Through an analysis that would be extended and perfected in *Capital,* Marx accompanied us through the economic stages of capitalist development, beginning with capitalist birth in exchange value and culminating in the lowering of wages and the worsening of living and working conditions. *Grundrisse* analyzed capitalism in terms of two interrelated phenomena, "Money" and "Capital." Money signified not merely paper or metal, but an entire system of relationships—social, political, legal, psychological, and artistic. Marx described different functions of money and exposed the contradictions between and within them. He placed the entire scope of these social relations in historical perspective, describing its origins and intimating its final destination. Capital is also a system of social relations but one based on incessant accumulation and exploitation and driving toward its own negation. Money, in other words, is a process by which economic values are socially exchanged fairly and equally (the "law of equivalence"), while capital works to extract an extra, or surplus, value from workers. Capitalism embodies an inner tension between its major constituent forces. *Grundrisse* outlines how these inherent contradictions become manifest in the economy and the gamut of capitalist social relationships.

After brief indecision, Marx reasserted the priority of concrete reality over abstraction.[14] Dialectical method begins, said Marx, with empirical facts characterizing a given society, not with abstract historical laws. In studying capitalism, we do not posit universal laws of contradiction inherent in any material productive apparatus, but instead begin with specific phenomena (for example, commodities) and explain how they embody opposing tendencies working to abolish the social conditions from which they arose. The inevitability of this process is demonstrated by starting from the concrete particular and progressing to the abstract universal. Marx reasserted this program in *Capital* and *Theories of Surplus Value,* arguing that bourgeois and utopian socialist political economy naively reverse the proper relation of abstract and concrete, carrying Hegel's error into the realm of economics.[15] The two schools reduced a specific form of labor performed in capitalism (that is, wage labor) to labor "in general," a pure, universal concept that we might find in a dictionary. Abstract labor, in this idealist sense, is "the everlasting Nature-imposed condition of human existence, and therefore is independent of every social phase of that existence, or rather, is common to every such phase." In the hands of political economists, this concept occludes the actual facts of capitalist life: "as the taste of porridge does not tell you who grew the oats, no more does this simple process tell you of itself what are the social conditions under which it is taking place."[16] Such nonempirical arguments, like that which defines "capital" as a generalized "instrument of production" presumably necessary whenever and wherever goods are produced, mystify rather than enlighten. But this is, in fact, the ultimate purpose of bourgeois and utopian economics. *Capital* succinctly answers the seminal questions that have always perplexed bourgeois political economists: What is the common feature enabling us to reduce all commodities to a single measure? What, therefore, is the fair or "just" price for each commodity? What, finally, is a commodity's "real" value? These were vital issues for bourgeois intellectuals explaining and justifying the market economy's pricing mechanism. Their greatest thinkers, Adam Smith and David Ricardo, searched the heavens for absolute principles. Marx unearthed answers in the dynamics of capitalism, the actual human relationships that signify a market economy. *Capital,* then, is more thoroughly soaked in the realities of bourgeois life than any previous economic study. Marx was, in this nonideological sense, the last of classical political economy's front-line thinkers.

In the *Inquiry into the Nature and Causes of the Wealth of Nations*

(1776), Adam Smith described the sources of, and offered an objective method for measuring, national wealth. He distinguished two forms of value: "use value," a product's utility in satisfying a human want; and "exchange value," a product's attractiveness in the marketplace. The former generates philosophical speculation and is reserved for abstract thinkers; the latter is a topic for economists. Actual commodity prices are not equal to exchange value because each commodity also embodies a "natural" value equal to the amount of actual labor that produced it, the so-called "labor theory of value." The ancient practice of bartering illustrates how raw human labor influences exchange value, for here the two are identical. With our more elaborate division of productive labor and developed technology, two other factors are involved in determining a commodity's price: capital and land. Hence a commodity's "natural price" includes the values of labor, capital, and land involved in production. In a particular case, it is a sum of workers' wages, the return on capital used in production, and the rent changed for the land on which the commodity is produced. Thus, a commodity's price is distributed between workers, capitalists, and landowners. Since everyone benefits in each market transaction, it is natural and beneficial for national productivity and wealth to increase. Moreover, the marketplace rectifies its own temporary imbalances, inexorably pushing market price toward natural price. An unjustifiable increase in wages, price, or rent, for example, will, in a competitive economy, reduce consumer demand, abrogating the increase. The "invisible hand" of the marketplace—not government policy—guarantees that market and natural price will correspond and enriches all segments of society.

Ricardo's *Principles of Political Economy and Taxation* (1817) questioned the utility of the labor theory of value. Ricardo reminded us that if a commodity's true value is based on the total amount of labor involved in production, it must then also include the labor embodied in the machines that workers use. Two difficulties arise. First, in a technological, mass-production economy, it is extremely difficult to calculate a commodity's true value. Second, although the amount of capital per unit of labor varies in different sectors of the economy, rates of profit tend to be the same. If prices are determined by labor only, profit should fall in highly industrialized sectors. Hence, Ricardo was less sanguine than Smith about the labor theory of value. Similarly, he recognized that technological development increases the rate of unemployment, driving wages down and increasing social disaffection. Even if altruistic entrepreneurs raise wages, better conditions will generate larger working-class families, which will eventually push wages down again. As Ricardo saw it, subsistence wages are a "natural" imprint of the market's invisible hand.

Capital argues that, like all bourgeois scientists, Smith and Ricardo are naively biased toward liberal preconceptions: It is "natural" for capitalists and landowners to be rewarded for their roles in production; the market is governed impersonally by "natural" forces, which govern the economic behavior of buyers and sellers; government economic intervention is not only wrong but "unnatural." Marx utilized the labor theory of value, which he adopted and modified, to subvert these myths of classical political economy, marshaling factual evidence to prove that capitalism is inherently exploitative.

Commodities, according to Marx's revised labor theory of value, embody two distinct values: a utility in satisfying human needs (use value), and one derived from their crystallized labor time. When products are exchanged, they are evaluated solely on the basis of the latter, what Marx called "exchange value." Thus, a useful product made by one worker laboring in specific circumstances in a particular manner is—when exchanged—given an abstract exchange value representing the total of general labor time involved in production. General labor time determines exchange value, which is not equal to the actual time used in making a product, for productive inefficiency and delay will not lower a product's general labor time.[17] Rather, general labor time is the average time required by a skilled worker to produce a specific product at a specific stage in the development of the productive apparatus. Goods sharing the same general labor time have equal exchange value, regardless of use or quality. To acquire an exchange value, a product must have a use value and become a commodity, entering into a process of exchange. Hence, exchange value is based on the social process of circulation and exchange, not a commodity's intrinsic nature. Products become commodities and get exchange values only when a particular social condition prevails; when individuals are private owners of products and wish to exchange them with each other. Exchange values appear only in capitalism.

Although Marx accepted Smith's idea that labor produces value, he perceived labor as having a dual character: concrete, specific activity producing a socially useful product; and abstract, generalized, homogeneous activity, producing a commodity with exchange value. Capitalism produces commodities, products of abstract labor, hence equates the activities of plumber and chef as exertions of labor power for a measurable time. The amount of time determines the exchange value of the plumber's bathtub and chef's duck à l'orange. An increase in productive efficiency will raise social use value because it increases the number of available products. But the total of social exchange value will remain unchanged, because each product will embody less abstract labor than before.

Exchange value is transformed into price after a universal standard of value is established. Gold is chosen because of its physical properties, for example, its uniformity, divisibility, resistance to corrosion, and so on, even though, in itself, it is no different from any other product. Money represents specified amounts of gold. A product's exchange value is converted into a price by establishing a quantitative relationship between each unit of exchange value and money. Value and price can differ, however, and Marx admits that the money form encourages fluctuations above and below actual exchange value, which is like an axis around which prices revolve. Although hesitantly inferring some factors influencing the practical imbalance between price and value, the gist of *Capital* is its explanation of how real value is determined solely by socially necessary labor time.[18] Marx wanted the determinants of value, not price. In this sense, *Capital* indicts our everyday, bourgeois attitudes. Like Hegel, we have naively reversed the roles of abstract and concrete, assuming that commodities are the source of value and equating them to success and virtue. In the process, we become commodities ourselves, selling labor power to the highest bidder and ignoring the real source of value: our own concrete labors. This reversal, where commodities, not people, become autonomous and controlling, is the source of fetishized interpersonal relationships. *Capital's* "fetishism of commodities"—what Marx earlier called "alienation"—is a specific behavioral pattern of men and women in capitalism that hides concrete economic reality. *Capital* interprets bourgeois dehumanization in neutral, nonevaluative terms depicting real human relationships.

The source of capitalist profit is this process of workers being transformed into commodities by selling their labor power to employers. Labor creates values, but does not itself possess value. The worker becomes a commodity by selling labor power, not labor. Labor power is, therefore, a commodity whose value is determined by the labor time necessary to keep it active and resupplied. In other words, the value of labor power equals the value of the products necessary to keep worker and family alive and reproducing. The definition of subsistence changes in history, although the physical minimum, necessary to keep workers alive, always marks the lower limit of wages. Living workers will always sell labor power for equivalent wage value. What makes labor power unique is its ability to create exchange values greater than the products necessary to maintain it. The excess of value created by labor power over the value workers are paid is "surplus value." In equivalent exchange (when value equals price), capitalists get more exchange value from workers than it costs to maintain them. For example, if in one-half of a day a laborer produces commodities whose value is equal to his wages, the value produced in the second half is surplus value, that is, profit, which is realized only in the circulation of commodities in the marketplace. The total of surplus value Marx called "absolute surplus value." The ratio between surplus value and the amount expended by capitalists on wages is called "relative surplus value." Capitalists are in business only to maximize surplus value and are acutely aware that only human labor creates it. Other forms of capital (money, land, machines, and so on) can acquire surplus value but cannot create it. For capitalists, workers are commodities bought at the lowest possible price and tapped for every bit of working energy. The subjective aspect of workers' lives is relevant only as a potential limit on working capacity. Alienation is a process marking empirical relationships between people involved in a particular mode of commodity production. The worker sells himself to produce wealth for another, perpetuating his own dehumanization and providing the grist for capitalism's productive mill. The imbalance in these relationships—the fact that workers don't receive the full value they create, which accrues to those who don't labor—is what Marx meant by "exploitation." The social forms of capitalist exploitation, the alienated ideas and institutions that workers establish, rationalize the actual patterns of interaction required by conditions of production.

A capitalist's rate of profit is the ratio of surplus value gained in production to the entire capital expended, including "constant capital" (value of raw materials, rent, equipment, and so on) plus "variable capital" (workers' wages). Although constant capital is necessary, only variable capital creates surplus value. Consequently, exploitation is measured not by rates of profit but by relative surplus value. The most profitable industries are not necessarily the most exploitative. Capitalists and utopians who argue that capitalism can be reformed simply by limiting the rate of allowable profit are fighting reality with myth. Capitalism is defined by human exploitation, regardless of the relative success, wealth, or concern of particular entrepreneurs.

To realize surplus value, capitalists must sell their products, which in a market system lacking a rational distributive plan can enormously complicate things. The second volume of *Capital* examines how the circulation of commodities affects an entrepreneur's rate of profit. One conclusion: The longer it takes for commodities to be sold, the more capital is left inactive (that is, unsold goods, stocks of matériel, and so on), the less realization of surplus value. An entrepreneur's prime goal, therefore, is to change commodities into money as quickly as possible in conditions where supply and demand are not centrally coordinated. The spontaneity of this process increases the possibility that prices and values will not correspond. Moreover, rates of profit vary in different branches of production, depending on the ratio of variable to constant capital (or, the "organic composition" of capital) and the time it takes to market the product (some industries have high constant capital costs and slow circulation of products, and some don't). Capital will flow to segments of the economy with the highest rate of profit. Competition among capitalists levels rates of profit while simultaneously causing severe fluctuations in commodity prices. Finally, once a commodity is sold and a profit realized, it does not accrue entirely to the entrepreneur. The merchant who markets the product gets part of it for his important role in realizing the entrepreneur's surplus value; moneylenders (banks) receive interest on loans made to the entrepreneur to purchase constant capital; and landowners receive rent payments for the land used in production. Payments to merchants, banks, and landlords consume a percentage of entrepreneurial profit. However, they merely provide the capital and land that workers must turn into marketable commodities producing a surplus value.

Entrepreneurs in capitalism strive to maximize high rates of surplus value and profit. Capitalism, therefore, has an inherent, empirically verifiable tendency toward the accumulation of wealth and unlimited growth. On the surface, there are positive consequences: Accumulated wealth is reinvested into research and capital expansion, prompting technological development and an increase in productive capacity and jobs. However, the actual history of capitalism, examined in volume 3 of *Capital,* includes unanticipated events that bourgeois political economists, ignoring the real sources of value and profit, disregard. As capitalist accumulation raises the level of technology, it drastically alters the productive process, modernizing it by introducing labor-saving devices to streamline production. This increase in the quantity and quality of constant capital means that less human labor is required to produce the same volume of goods, that is, the rate of variable to constant capital decreases. Since surplus value is realized only from variable capital, the technological growth of capitalism results in a gradual decrease in average rates of surplus value and profit. This, for Marx, is an empirically verifiable law of capitalist development, with devastating implications. Capitalism, over time, subverts its prime reason for existing: the maximization of surplus value relative to used resources. Entrepreneurs react by increasing worker exploitation (lengthening the workday, lowering wages, neglecting working conditions—all tolerated because there is a "reserve army" of unemployed labor waiting to supplant the dissatisfied) and increasing foreign trade (gaining access to inexpensive resources and an expanding market for manufactured goods). Both stem the falling rates of surplus value and profit, but neither suffices. Historical evidence indicates that profits continue declining until small businesses are forced to close, concentrating productive capacity in a dwindling number of large corporations. To recoup financial losses, successful entrepreneurs increase production, oblivious to the waning purchasing power of workers. The ensuing crisis inevitably destroys even more small and medium-size businesses, further concentrates production, and produces a new "stability" from which the entire cycle begins anew.

These constant economic crises, which Marx traced historically, express a contradiction between capitalist forces of production and social conditions. The actual principles of capitalist production, in other words, are progressively worsening the quality of social life for most people. Entrepreneurs, whose thirst for profit is the impetus for economic and technological development, helplessly watch the chaos. They meekly respond by leaving production decisions to managers, who mobilize workers into more efficient and productive units of labor. Ironically, the increasingly social character of capitalist production only hastens the process of capitalist disintegration, as workers start recognizing their united power and abilities. The continuing private appropriation of surplus value becomes increasingly anachronistic. Capitalism prompts workers to experience both the inequities of bourgeois life and their own practical powers. "Centralization of the means of production and socialization of labour at last reach a point where they become incompatible with their capitalist integument. Thus integument is burst asunder. The knell of capitalist private property sounds. The expropriators are expropriated."[19]

The underlying cause of worker rebellion is the entrepreneur's exchange of variable capital for human labor power, and the real tendency of capitalism to multiply exchange value and endlessly increase the exploitation of labor. Capitalism cares little for use value, that is, the utility or quality of its products, or workers' living conditions. An incessant drive for exchange value energizes capitalism, generating newer, more efficient ways of producing commodities to increase the percentage of surplus value. The historical function of capitalism, therefore, promotes progress in technology and the organization of labor. Despite enormous suffering, capitalism is a necessary phase of economic and social development, establishing the conditions for its own abolition.

These, like other aspects of capitalism, are based on empirically verifiable relationships between workers and capitalists. Marx's equivocation was probably due to a scarcity of enough hard evidence to draw definite conclusions. *Wage Labour and Capital* (1849) and the *Communist Manifesto* surmise that capitalist accumulation drives wages to the physiological minimum—only enough to keep a supply of workers alive and active. Workers are, in other words, absolutely impoverished as they grow in size but receive a shrinking sum of total social value. *Grundrisse* and *Value, Price and Profit* (1865) contended that the absolute needs of labor (that is, the physiological minimum) are conditioned by cultural factors. Capitalism produces new needs, satisfied only by higher wages. Rising wages coexist with a progressive deterioration of social conditions. Capitalism, then, causes the relative impoverishment of workers who receive a decreasing proportionate share of socially created values—even as wages rise on an absolute scale. *Capital* supports this last version of impoverishment.[20] The evidence of unionized workers exerting pressure on capitalists for higher wages and the actual increase in salaries after 1850 prompted Marx to adapt his theory to the facts. Criteria of impoverishment include not only wages, but also an intensifying human degradation expressed in the continually deteriorating quality of noneconomic life that most workers experienced. Capitalism's real internal contradictions lead to class struggle and revolution regardless of the exact level of workers' wages. Impoverishment is eliminated by socialism because the sale of labor power will be abolished and production devoted exclusively to use rather than exchange value.

Marx's "laws" of capitalist accumulation and the falling rate of profit are valid only in relation to observed facts of capitalist development. Marx never postulated an absolute, a priori principle making capitalism inherently unfeasible and revolution an inevitable moment of a transcendent material or ideal totality. Discussions of demography, geography, climate, and the so-called "Asiatic mode of production" introduce new variables that make no sense from such reductive, totalistic perspectives.[21]

Unanticipated new factors have proliferated in this century: imperialism provides new markets and inexpensive resources; inflation raises profits; advertising increases demand; unions raise wages; and government economic intervention rescues many industries. We often forget that Marx wrote well before these phenomena began retarding capitalism's predicted demise. He observed the real world in which he lived. The countertendencies even then apparent—for example, maturing technology decreases the value of each unit of constant capital; overproduction is temporarily muted by new overseas markets for industrial goods—did not appear significant enough to alter Marx's prognosis permanently. Even today's countertendencies, Marx would surely argue, do not alter the long-run predictions, despite their underestimating bourgeois flexibility and ingenuity. Contemporary economic policy creates unforeseen problems and contradictions which, unless revised techniques buy more time, even now prove lower rates of profit and higher rates of unemployment will again show their wicked figures. Facts have circuitously confirmed Marx's theories.[22]

Marx continued writing until his death in 1883. Illness and a series of exhausting political controversies sapped his energies and ambition to complete the scientific project outlined in *Grundrisse*. Most of his work during this period dealt with controversial political events of the day. But Marx continually rejected attempts to twist his ideas into an "historic-philosophic theory of the general path every people is fated to tread, whatever the historical circumstances in which it finds itself . . . the supreme virtue of which consists in being super-historical."[23] He soberly evaluated his own work and was impressed only by its usefulness in explaining observed phenomena. In commenting on the likelihood of revolution in Russia, for example, Marx explicitly disclaimed the universality some attach to his historical and economic theories, arguing "the western precedent would not prove anything at all concerning the 'historical fatality' of this [capitalist] process."[24] Marx demanded that his own work be evaluated by its utility in explaining the behavior of real people in specified circumstances. The spirit of critical empirical inquiry survives untarnished throughout his professional life.

Empirical Marxists trace their heritage to Marx's enlightened science. Their "faith" in the revolutionary workers' movement and the necessity of socialism is purely secular and empirical, resembling a physicist's expectation as he watches the temperature of pure water approach 212° F., rather than an ideologue's mystical confidence in the future. But by questioning the physicist's unquestioned assumptions, it escapes bourgeois empiricism's self-imposed prison of the status quo. Empirical Marxism is revolutionary without being utopian. It "recovers . . . the hypothetic-experimental structure of thought . . . the causal-objective foundation . . . of the world and of society. . . . In short, Marx's dialectics do not regress science to philosophic reason, but introduce philosophic reason into scientific intellection."[25]

EMPIRICAL MARXISM
Empirio-Criticism

Even as Engels's a priori materialism was congealing into orthodox Marxism, voices were raised at the end of the nineteenth century questioning its overreliance on abstract, nonverifiable theories. Empirio-critical philosophy, especially in Russia, was the first systematic Marxist critique of orthodoxy that was loyal to empirical method. The ideas of Ernest Mach and Richard Avenarius became quite popular among Russian Marxists and were denounced by orthodox scions like Plekhanov, Akselrod, and Lenin— whose *Materialism and Empirio-criticism* immortalized the movement even as its critique ruined its credibility.[26]

Empirio-critics rejected Engels's and Plekhanov's naive materialism, which was burdened with the abstract epistemology that Marx, in criticizing Hegel, had rejected. Human perception is entirely free of mystery. The experienced world is defined by objects, things, and people empirically present, not by a hidden reality. Engels's fallacy was assuming perceived images are in some way "subjective," distinct from the phenomenon's "objective" essence. Metaphysics is an illusion. Perceived phenomena have no independent, nonempirical significance. "In themselves" they are neither mental nor material; in relation to the perceiving human body they are merely sensations. No absolutes survive beyond active subject and perceived object. Reality, purified of abstractions, is the experience of self and object interacting on equal terms. Consequently, empirio-critics dismiss the epistemological authenticity of terms like "truth," "falsity," "good," "beautiful," and so on. Objective definitions depend on the unverifiable and mistaken presumption that a nonperceptual reality exists by which experiences are evaluated. But truth merely describes empirical reality.

Cognition is a biological reaction of subjects to a stimulus disturbing their equilibrium. In attaching words to perceived phenomena, we interpret experiences based on actual biological needs. Knowledge and ideas, then, appear when we satisfy needs by interpreting experiences appropriately. The criterion of truth depends on the biological needs that we bring to each perceiving act. Science selects, classifies, and records experienced objects according to the human species' biological needs, enabling us to manipulate and predict. Philosophy, on the other hand, generalizes actual experiences and establishes their instrumental significance to humanity. Scientists and philosophers must actively organize reality, not passively receive abstractions. Truth is determined by the dominant life needs of the human species. The world, then, is a meaning created by humanity through collective efforts. In this universal project, only empirical description, based on actual experiences, is useful.

By eliminating the dichotomy of mind and matter, empirio-critics avoid metaphysics. Sensations represent an ambiguous unity of subject and object, neither existing independent of the other, but the latter implicitly guiding the actual perceiving activity. Two subjects, therefore, identically perceive the same object. There is neither an ultimate, nonempirical source of knowledge nor an independent reality to guide action. We act to satisfy needs, and attach the term "truth" to useful sensations. It is imperative that we receive an accurate reading of empirical reality to formulate scientific principles and live a more satisfying existence. Marx's own work settles rather comfortably into this framework. It is scientific and activist, while rejecting a metaphysics of matter or mind. Individuals struggle to satisfy species needs via creative labor. Behavior is guided by exigencies and biological needs, and actors formulate a strategy of effectively modifying empirical reality in their own interests. Ideas and concepts facilitating this process are true, constituting science. Needs are met by creating required products. Hence, the mode of production, based on a division of labor, becomes the crucial form of social life, determining how biological needs are expressed and satisfied. Each productive apparatus, however, brings with it a social cleavage paralleling the economic relationships of production. The needs of each class are not equally satisfied. In capitalism, the dominant class formulates a science satisfying its own needs. It modernizes production through technological innovation and efficiency, simultaneously increasing profits and the population of an awakened working class, whose needs will be satisfied through a proletariat science espousing worker revolution and socialist equality. Bourgeois and proletariat sciences perceive and shape empirical reality in terms of a particular group's needs. Neither is "true" in an "objective," nonempirical sense. The "necessity" of socialism is generated by the pragmatic needs of workers critically evaluating the facts of bourgeois society from their own interests. Metaphysical laws—idealist, materialist, or religious—are unnecessary and irrelevant.

Although empirio-critics supported empirical science, they did not sacrifice Marxism's revolutionary impact. At the turn of the century it appeared that needs of European workers and capitalists were colliding. Empirical evidence apparently confirmed Marx's theories of class polarization and the inevitable radicalization or workers. Empirio-criticism, in the hands of the Russian Bolsheviks, Bogdanov, Lunacharsky, and Bazarov, emerged as a fanatic doctrine espousing the revolutionary destruction of all vestiges of bourgeois arts and sciences—literally razing bourgeois paintings, novels, and sculpture, as well as its technology and instruments of production. The new proletarian culture was built from scratch, reflecting workers' needs and purified of the bourgeois past. Empirio-critics perceiving proletarian needs in less extreme terms and evaluating the facts of bourgeois life less critically (for example, the Mensheviks Yushkevich and Valentinov, and Viktor Chernov, a socialist revolutionary) advocated relatively modest social reforms. The strategic disagreements between radicals and moderates were resolvable through more accurate research into actual working-class conditions and needs, clearly dilineating the extent of worker oppression and the scope of required social change. Since empirio-critics were fact-oriented, strategic quarrels must have been caused by confusion regarding the actual facts of social life.

Bernstein

Eduard Bernstein (1850–1932) terminated this confusion by examining Marx's theories in the light of historical and economic facts surrounding Europe's working-class movement. Bernstein was originally an orthodox materialist so closely associated with Engels and Kautsky that he was chosen executor of Engels's will. However, a forced emigration to England in 1888 transported him from the tight network of German orthodoxy to a more heterogeneous atmosphere, where utopian and Fabian socialists openly debated materialists on key doctrinal points. The new environment dramatically influenced Bernstein's thinking, for in 1899, three years before returning to Germany, he published *Die Voraussetzungen des Sozialismus und die Aufgaben der Sozialdemokratie* (literally, *The Presuppositions of Socialism and the Tasks of Social Democracy;* English translation, *Evolutionary Socialism*), the seminal text of what is called Marxist revisionism.

Bernstein remained a Marxist in believing that Marx's theories correctly explain the broad tendencies of human history. Each historical mode of production has produced opposing classes whose conflicts push history toward the present, where the dominant class of owners economically exploits workers while rationalizing oppression in bourgeois institutions and values. When historical materialism effectively explains actual history, it embodies the scientific spirit which ennobles Marx's best work. Unfortunately, Marx was irreconcilably torn between science and Hegelian a priorism, the belief in objective forces impersonally generating revolutionary violence as the preordained path to socialism. Although Marx never entirely abandoned science, his mature work was, ultimately, "a slave to a doctrine" that is empirically nonconfirmable. Hence, Marxism is flawed and contradictory, "proving a theory laid down before its drafting; a formula lies at the basis of it in which the result to which the exposition should lead is fixed beforehand." Since the utopian, metaphysical Marx inspired Europe's orthodox workers' parties, Marxism had lost all touch with reality, "lagging behind the practical development of the [workers'] movement" they represent. Bernstein abandoned abstract orthodoxy, adopting a method that does not force facts into preconceived categories. He courageously repudiated *Capital,* for example, when it was "falsified by the facts."[27] Kautsky, he noted, arrogantly denied such facts when they contradict Marx's a priorism, a classic instance of what Marx had correctly described in the early work on Hegel as a mystifying reversal of priorities.

Bernstein empirically refuted orthodoxy's material laws of history. For instance, while industrial mergers, which increase the economic role of giant companies, take place, the actual distribution of wealth is expanding, not contracting. The apparent discrepancy is explained by the growth of joint-stock systems, where ownership is dispersed among thousands of investors, dramatically increasing the number of property owners. Maturing capitalism, in fact, disperses wealth and encourages the emergence of small capitalists. Moreover, as capitalist technology matures and efficiency spreads, there is an enormous increase in the number of technical, bureaucratic, and service-oriented jobs, while traditional blue-collar factory work comprises a falling percentage of the total labor force. When combined with the putative growth in small-scale rural landowners, this evidence disproves Marx's theory of the inevitability of class polarization. A rising middle class, neither proletarian nor capitalist, is muting the social effects of worker-capitalist antagonism, decreasing the likelihood of violent proletarian rebellion. Furthermore, an elaborate system of credit, cartels, protective duties, and military conquest, as well as growth in international trade, now guarantees to capitalism inexpensive resources and ready markets. International economics, contrary to Rosa Luxembourg, reinforces capitalist stability. The indicators of proletarian rebellion are rapidly disappearing.

Other events also invalidate Marx's reductive hypotheses. Worker socialization of the productive process is not occurring, as social functions become increasingly differentiated and autonomous. Capitalist exploitation of workers is declining as wages rise and conditions improve. Marx's ominous warning in the *Manifesto* that in capitalism workers have no nation, family, property, or freedom entirely misconstrues the actual character of a mature working class: families prosper; the number of property owners grows; workers are increasingly integrated into public decision-making processes through political reforms; and as World War I would disarmingly illustrate, workers willingly die for their country even in an imperialist-inspired conflict. In sum, workers are not about to erupt in one violent revolutionary conflagration, and it is plainly "utopian to imagine that the community could jump into an organization and manner of living diametrically opposed to those of the present day. . . . "[28]

Bernstein also questioned the utility of Marx's theory of value, which is unmeasurable and abstract, a mystification of economic reality. Since no reliable means exists to measure the intensity and quality of human labor, a commodity's price is more effectively explained by empirically verifiable factors. But Marx's economics is incapable of explaining real, empirically defined concepts. Moreover, Marx's theory that exploitation is positively correlated to the rate of surplus value is not factually justifiable, there being verifiable instances when the former declines even while the latter increases. Using surplus value as a measure of exploitation is, consequently, misleading and factually incorrect.

Bernstein's political strategy is tailored to the real-life situation of workers in mature capitalism, not an a priori *"Weltanschauung."* While believing in the desirability of socialist equality, he argues that it is self-defeating for Marxist parties to impose, from above, a deterministic metaphysics: "Even where socialist parties have originally taken the same hypotheses for the starting point of their work, they have found themselves obliged in the course of time to adapt their activity to the special conditions of their country. . . . [No] program of action applicable for all countries is possible." Marxists, therefore, must accept the world as it is, not as they wish it to be. Orthodox tactics promoting violent revolution, dictatorship of the proletariat, total nationalization, working-class purity, and so on are neither supported by the character and beliefs of modern workers nor warranted by the actual quality of bourgeois institutions: "The question is not whether certain institutions 'ought' to exist, but rather, the reality dictates that it '*is*,' whether Marxists want it or not."[29]

The quickest path to socialism in contemporary Europe, given these realities, is from within established political institutions. By extending and perfecting liberal freedoms with piecemeal Parliamentary reforms, workers can reconstruct and eventually take over the economy. The power of unions will grow, as will the number of workers in secure, well-paying jobs. Over an extended period of gradually accumulating needed political reforms, workers will become socialized by degrees, working cooperatively while enjoying the possessions and freedoms of their steadily improving social positions. The actual transfer of ownership will be procedural, without the violent disruptions that Marx anticipated. Although social change is evolutionary, spontaneous revolutionary insurrections might occur and should be supported. Bernstein opposed abstractionism from either Left or Right. Marxist parties must be committed to the real needs of workers. In contemporary Europe this translated to political and economic reforms as well as pursuing parliamentary alliances with groups heretofore spurned including peasants and petty bourgeoisie. The orthodox alternative, myopically advocating violent revolutions, "would only result presumably in reckless devastation of productive forces, insane experimentalizing and aimless violence, and the political sovereignty of the working class would, in fact, only be carried out in the form of a dictatorial, revolutionary, central power, supported by the terrorist dictatorship of revolutionary clubs."[30]

Bernstein's personal life did not fit the typical Marxist pattern. From 1902 until 1928, with one brief two-year hiatus, he was a deputy to the German Reichstag, where he promoted liberal reforms and prounion legislation, helped write the program for the German Social Democratic Party (SPD), and was established as a major theorist of European social democracy. Bernstein performed the miraculous feat of integrating Marxism and liberal democracy, providing a safe and undefiled haven for nonviolent Marxists seeking a peaceful road to socialism. His revisionism attracted many German workers who were recipients of steadily increasing wages, welfare benefits, and improved working conditions, and were already organized into powerful and effective political organizations. The plight of these workers was not hopeless, nor did revolution seem inevitable. Revisionist Marxism legitimizes their comforts without sacrificing Marxist principles. British workers, with their traditions of peaceful reformism and Fabian socialism, were also highly receptive. As capitalists raised wages and improved working conditions throughout France and central Europe, Bernstein's Marxism became a lightning rod for workers' changing aspirations. Bernstein's legacy, in addition to the historical and scholarly works published in these years, is the reformist mentality adopted by all of Europe's Social Democratic Parties.

Bernstein is not entirely convincing even on his own terms, for many assertions are not empirically substantiated. A growing corpus of data indicates that mature capitalism was, as Marx forecasted, increasing the concentration of wealth, diminishing competition, and aggravating endemic business cycles.[31] On the other hand, some of Bernstein's points, though empirically correct, were theoretically shortsighted. For example, the number of middle-size businesses has indeed remained constant. But Marx's theory concerning the concentration of capital is not thereby disproved, for evidence also indicates that successful middle-size firms are regularly swallowed by large ones and replaced by others. The constant number of middle-size firms does not negate the growing percentage of wealth and productive capacity concentrated in the giant industrial conglomerates. Similarly, wages, in an absolute sense at least, are rising. But Marx was probably also aware of this tendency. In *Grundrisse,* and again in *Capital,* he clearly implied that exploitation is not measured solely by a relative decline in wages, but also by capitalism's appropriation of humanity's physical, intellectual, and emotional well-being. Even as wages rise, Marxists measure the growing exploitation of workers in the deteriorating quality of social and personal relationships. In this sense, Marx's theory is still empirically valid.

However, a more fundamental problem exists, eclipsing Bernstein's inefficacious approach to data collecting and analysis. In choosing empirical criteria of verification, Marxists use a bourgeois-inspired method to negate bourgeois society, primarily by posing critical questions and hypotheses. By emphasizing facts, however, empirical social scientists—bourgeois or Marxist—focus primarily on existing conditions. In the case of Bernstein, this tendency occludes his critical Marxist function. Facts slowly consume the revolutionary hypothesis. Bernstein lost Marx's historical totality with its dialectical interpenetration of subject and object. Marx established non-empirical hypotheses whose utility depends on understanding and explaining empirical reality. But Bernstein's method, based on accumulating social data, assumed a life of its own—independent of Marx's theories. Static empirical correlations overwhelm the concern for dialectics and totality. Bernstein inadvertently slid back into Cartesianism by accepting empirical data at face value, implicitly defending the radical uniqueness and autonomy of reality's separate parts: cause-effect relationships are unilinear and deterministic; individuals are isolated entities influenced by preceding variables; economics is independent of society and politics. Thus, wage increases uplift and save humanity because Bernstein ignored the broader, alienating social and political qualities that define the economic reforms. From a Marxist perspective, the significance of wage increases is conditioned by relevant noneconomic factors. The same facts Bernstein used to indict Marx (for example, the rise in wages, the growth of middle-size business, the expansion of stock systems, and so on) are not nearly so damning when interpreted by Marx's dialectical hypotheses—which empirical Marxists must do. Empirical Marxism requires a methodological commitment to critical theory *and* empirical verification, with neither preponderant. If facts nullify revolutionary theory, then Marxism—as Marx understood it—dies. Explaining Bernstein's reformism solely in terms of his "Kantianism" misses the point.[32] Bernstein admired Kant's critique of intellectual orthodoxy, and used it in combatting materialist "cant," that is, its unacceptable ethics and mystical longing for a socialist utopia. But Kantianism is a consequence of Bernstein's empirical critique, not its source. If empirical facts had confirmed Marx's determinist hypotheses, then Bernstein would not have questioned orthodoxy in the first place, and Kant would be superfluous.

Bernstein's immediate reception by European Marxists was mixed. Predictably, he was excoriated by the orthodox movement, particularly Russian Bolsheviks. Lenin claimed he represented an elite corp of workers, whose rapidly rising wages and standards of living obscured the hideousness of bourgeois society. The long-run tendencies of capitalism, Bernstein notwithstanding, would cleanse the working class of this small group of sycophants. Reformist Marxism, therefore, represented a reactionary elite whose numbers and influence would soon dissipate. Orthodoxy dismissed Bernstein as a reactionary in scientist's garb. Nonorthodox Marxists, however, were not as severe. They admired his project of demystifying orthodox materialism, even while shuddering at his quietistic political strategy. Marxism had indeed become an obscure metaphysics, requiring a strong dose of empirical critique. Bernstein and the empirio-critics took the first step in a long overdue expurgation.

Austro-Marxism

The term "Austro-Marxism" was coined first by the American socialist Louis Boudin to describe a group of theorists living and writing in Vienna after 1904. Originally founded by Max Adler and Rudolf Hilferding, the group also included Otto Bauer, Karl Renner, Otto Neurath, and others. Most of its major work had already appeared by 1914, although it survived and exerted some influence in Austria until 1934.[33] Their writings appeared regularly in the monthly journal of the Austrian Social Democratic Party, *Der Kampf,* and their own daily, *Arbeiter-Zeitung.*

The project of Austro-Marxism was to formulate Marxism as an empirical social science. Carl Grünbêrg, the "father of Austro-Marxism" because of his enormous professional influence on Adler, Hilferding, and Bauer, termed the movement a systematic, empirical, historical discipline, which spurned the metaphysical obscurities of orthodox materialism. Like positivism—whose popularity grew simultaneously—Austro-Marxism defended the epistemological priority of empirical data,[34] and like Bernstein, it concretized Marx's theories of social change. But Austro-Marxism, at least prior to World War I, upheld the revolutionary character of Marxism even while justifying it empirically. This commitment to empirical facts and revolution, we have seen, can produce unmanageable strains. Austro-Marxism first splintered, then dissolved entirely in the philosophical turbulence.

Most of the published work associated with Austro-Marxism is case studies measuring one of Marx's theories against available relevant data. Comparatively little effort was devoted to methodology. Most Austro-Marxists considered the theoretical work of the Vienna School sufficient for establishing the rules of their own science. The notable exception was Max Adler, a philosopher perhaps more sensitive than the rest to the bourgeois principles naively supporting empirical method. Eagerly embracing empirical inquiry, Adler nevertheless repudiated its Cartesian foundation, which historically rationalized the material needs of the bourgeoisie. His methodological writings formulated non-Cartesian principles to justify Marxist empirical social science. Since he could not find these in Marx's own work, he turned to Ernest Mach and especially Immanuel Kant for philosophical inspiration. From Mach he derived a penchant for empirical critique of both materialist and idealist abstractionism, and from Kant, ideas generating a positive theory of human sociability, the theoretical foundation of nonbourgeois empirical social science.[35] Adler believed that historically materialism lacks theoretical first principles. As a critique of knowledge, rather than a metaphysics, Kantianism can negate positivism without overwhelming Marx's concern for concrete empirical facts. By outlining the transcendental foundation of Marx's science, Kantianism complements empirical Marxism. Adler thus sought transcendental justification of a purely empirical, nondogmatic Marxism. His success is indicated by the extent to which his work was taken for granted by the data-oriented Austro-Marxists he legitimized.

Adler wanted categorical principles and a priori concepts necessary to comprehend and explain social phenomena empirically. He realized that social analysis presupposes universal, subjectively relevant categories through which actors experience the world. These categories organize actual experiences in the same sense as Kant's a priori categories of space, time, and cognition and hence are derived from reason, not experience, and are the precondition of empirical science. Despite repudiating philosophy, Marx implicitly recognized the epistemological necessity of universal forms in terms (for example, "species-essence" in the *1844 Manuscripts* and "socialized humanity" in the *Theses on Feuerbach*) that orthodoxy hopelessly misinterpreted. Marx believed in a universal form of sociability manifest in each ego, which Adler calls "socialized humanity" or "social a priori." He accurately depicted man as a social being because he knew that unique subjectivity embodies universal qualities that generate a shared reality. These are "transcendentally given as a category of knowledge," prior to sensual experience. Every reflective individual is also a social actor: empirical subjectivity is "social" simply by existing. Marx recognized that humanity is necessarily "a mutual involvement and interrelationship of men continually created by themselves through their activity," and society an inevitable consequence of the "necessary solidarity of man in a labour process in which the work of every individual is not only directed to every other man, but is inconceivable without them."[36] There are, in sum, a priori ties that bind outwardly autonomous individuals into a social unity.

Adler rejected capitalism's Cartesian, psychologistic theories of social life, epitomized at this time by positivism, Austrian economists like von Mises, and legal purists like Hans Kelsen. The "social a priori" provides a new, nonbourgeois justification for empirically investigating social regularities, transforming what bourgeois scientists call "mental" activities into subjective expressions of social phenomena. Since "everything mental, even though it concerns the individual, is always . . . social," we can examine intentional activity in terms of verifiable social variables. Adler's a priori categories equalize social and natural science: both explain phenomena in terms of their positions in a net of relevant, empirically verifiable facts.[37] Although social actors are conscious participants, hence different from the inanimate elements of natural science, the "social a priori" of empirical consciousness legitimizes the search for impersonal causal social laws. There are empirically valid explanations of human and nonhuman phenomena. On the other hand, by admitting the reality and significance of consciousness, Adler avoids the vulgarity of mechanistic materialism. Social scientists seek causal explanations but also recognize diverse types of causality. Causal relations in society, mediated by consciousness, are not as mechanical as those in insensate nature. All social phenomena—including economic behavior—are mental, not material, and the causal patterns depict relations between intentional human minds. Hence, social scientists must uncover relevant subjectively meaningful motives. Humanity's a priori categories transform these from unique psychological phenomena into social forces equally affecting everyone in identical conditions. Subjectivity, in other words, encompasses the external world. Social action is "caused" by subjectively meaningful, but also empirically verifiable, factors.[38]

The orthodox notion that matter exists in itself, apart from transcendental forms of consciousness, is an absurdity that obliterates the real distinctions between human and nonhuman phenomena.[39] Adler's transcendentalism, on the other hand, is "metaempirical" only in providing a nonbourgeois justification for empiricism, whereas materialism replaces empirical reality with metaphysics. Moreover, Adler's categories—depicting humanity's essential sociality and the reciprocity of conscious motives and concrete forces—perfectly complement Marx's major scientific theories. Hence, Adler is a revolutionary as well as an empirical social scientist elevating specific facts over materialist abstractions. He envisions Austro-Marxism as "the science of the laws of social life and its causal development. Consequently it aims to deduce the development of socialism from capitalism as a matter of causal necessity."[40]

Austro-Marxism's nondogmatic, empirical method generates case studies which are quite remarkable, given the stodgy inflexibility of extant Marxist inquiry. By critically rejecting materialism, they escape the base-superstructure formula that regards politics and ideology as mere reflections of economics. Instead, they depict a whole, dynamic social process consisting of interrelated economic, political, and ideological elements. Although Adler pays his dues to the movement by approving Engels's ambiguous maxim regarding the priority of economics "in the last resort,"[41] he also emphasizes the significance of noneconomic factors, and Austro-Marxism generally—guided by facts rather than ideas—implicitly recognizes the complex reciprocity of all social levels.

One consequence is the broad range of phenomena that Austro-Marxism examined, ranging from written law to nationalism, imperialism, and the class struggle. Orthodoxy considered some of the findings outrageous. Bauer and Renner, for example, in separate works concluded that national and cultural sentiments are an inescapable reality among workers, conditioning their attitudes and behavior. Marxists must tap these for the energy that they can provide the working-class movement. National oppression in Europe had become a function of class oppression. Marxist revolutionaries could work fruitfully with national autonomy movements in fighting bourgeois hegemony, for only in complete socialist freedom will thorny problems of nationalism and cultural autonomy be resolved. In *Finance Capital* and the *Austrian Revolution*,[42] Austro-Marxism openly confronted post-Marxian capitalist trends, including the growth of white-collar workers, the separation of ownership and management, the increasingly significant role of industrial managers, and the growing alliance between finance capital and the state in propagating imperialism and government-sponsored domestic programs that increase consumer demand. Austro-Marxism believed that Marx's theories measure up to the factual reality of capitalist development. Capitalist "flexibility," examined critically—something Bernstein neglected—provides a new dimension to Marxist economic theory and supports the long-term trends that Marx foresaw. The close cooperation of capital and government is creating an organized, centralized economy which, like a ripening fruit, becomes easier to pluck. Objective class interests are still irreconcilable, although immediate class antagonism has been muted. Marxists must recognize that workers are no longer a homogeneous group. The rise in wages and the growth of white-collar employment have pushed skilled laborers into a growing middle strata. Marxist strategy must overcome this division by stressing the real benefits accruing to all workers when class rule ends and, beyond this, encouraging alliances between workers and sections of the middle class and peasantry. Moreover, the increasing growth and independence of the capitalist state exaggerates its vulnerability. When workers gain a clear majority of the noncapitalist population, they can easily control the political process and legislate a workers' revolution. In sum, contemporary economic and political developments have modified the form that class struggle takes and the strategy that revolutionary Marxists must follow but not Marx's bleak prognosis for capitalism or the historically progressive role played by the workers' movement. New possibilities and opportunities exist for perceptive Marxists willing to examine reality factually, free of metaphysical dogma. These facts verify Marx's theories regarding the inevitability of socialism.

Prior to World War I, Austro-Marxists, except for Bauer, believed that these unanticipated changes, while supporting Marx's major hypotheses, diminished the likelihood of violent proletariat revolution. History's march toward socialism would end with workers peacefully expropriating capitalism's bloated, concentrated economic apparatus. By gaining control of bourgeois political institutions, workers can procedurally socialize the means of production and quietly transform society into a socialist democracy. This significant turn from orthodoxy is justified, we have seen, by the evolving empirical character of capitalism. Such evidence, however, doesn't convince orthodox materialists. Confronted by sophisticated empirical Marxists like Adler, Hilferding, Bauer, and Renner, someone like Trotsky is left gaping confusedly: "But very soon I grew puzzled. These people were not revolutionaries."[43] They *were* revolutionaries, of course, but they felt the revolution would be shaped by empirical surroundings rather than run a preordained course. While obvious similarities mark the political strategies of Bernstein and the Austro-Marxists, there are also differences. Bernstein's obsession with facts atrophied his critical faculties, generating a reformist strategy that became an end in itself. In response, Austro-Marxists consciously accepted Marx's critique of capitalism and socialist vision as hypotheses to be measured against the real world. They are revolutionaries guided by reality rather than dogma. Austro-Marxist reformism is a revolutionary strategy for the times, a scientifically correct catalyst for capitalism's tendencies toward self-destruction. It willingly advocates proletarian violence, but only in propitious conditions, for example, when the bourgeoisie annul parliamentary reforms that benefit the working class. Austro-Marxism thus occupies a position midway between Bernstein's noncritical reformism and orthodoxy's dogmatic, metaphysical critique.

The delicate Austro-Marxian balance of reformist tactics and revolutionary theory did not survive World War I. Faced with cataclysmic destruction and political uncertainty, Austro-Marxism split into Right and Left wings, the former favoring peaceful reformism as the only feasible alternative to war's unavoidable atrocities; the latter defining capitalism as war's final cause and advocating an active, revolutionary workers' movement. Although both groups marshal factual evidence, people like Hilferding, for example, who became minister of finance in two governments of the Weimar Republic, responded—like Bernstein—to changing conditions by de-emphasizing the heuristic function of Marx's revolutionary theories. On the other hand, Adler continually emphasized the revolutionary quality of Marxist science while editing a leftwing journal of German Social Democracy.

Della Volpe

Galvano Della Volpe (1895–1968), an Italian philosopher who joined the Communist Party of Italy (PCI) in 1944, made a significant contribution to Marxist theory during the years 1947–1960. His writings, few of which are translated into English, are often obscure, pedantic, and idiosyncratic— Marxist intellectualism at its worst. Nevertheless, Della Volpe was heir to the empirical Marxist tradition and aimed to establish Marxism as an empirical social science of the highest order, without sacrificing its revolutionary potential. This iconoclastic project, however, was clouded by Della Volpe's sycophantic personality, which unfailingly mirrored the orthodox line—even lionizing Stalin. Della Volpe was capable of the most obsequious kind of scholarship, for example, lauding the Stalinist legal system as a "progressive" synthesis of bourgeois liberty and socialist equality which guarantees citizen participation, the inviolability of law, and the absolute independence of judges.[44] Lucio Colletti, a student and colleague, rationalized Della Volpe's life as critical scholar and naive activist by gently reminding us that he was an old-line intellectual who separated politics and theory and willingly obeyed Party directives. More detached observers point to his opportunistic compromise with fascism during World War II and interpret later docility as either a purgative or an attempt to build credibility in the Party. Of course, there are also numerous examples of philosophers whose character withered more than the paper they wrote on, and this is also a plausible explanation. In any case, Della Volpe's theoretical significance is undeniable, even if we withhold judgment on the man.

The *Logica come Scienza Positiva* (1950) traces Marx's philosophical heritage through the critical, empirical work of Aristotle, Galileo, and Hume. Della Volpe interpreted Hegel as an idealist who justified both Christianity and the German nation-state. The Hegelian connection to Marx, which people like Lukács and Gramsci traced through the mediating work of the Left Hegelians, is dismissed outright. Hegelianism is an idealist metaphysics that Marx categorically rejects. Hegel's reversal of priorities, the use of abstraction to explain particulars, cannot be scientifically justified. Marxism, as scientific critique, reverses Hegel's reversal. It is nondogmatic, nonmetaphysical, and fact-oriented—a total critique of bourgeois myth.

When empirical science is cleansed of Cartesianism, however, it is merely an unfocused, static compilation of data, with no criteria for theory formation and no basis for limiting the scope of relevant data. Empirical scientists, in this situation, are helplessly bombarded by an entire universe of disparate, meaningless social facts that must be theoretically arranged and categorized. Della Volpe seeks nonbourgeois preconceptions to guide scientific inquiry. In similar predicaments, Bernstein regressed to noncritical reformism and Adler turned to Kant. Spurning both reformism and transcendentalism, Della Volpe found the answer in "deterministic abstractions."[45] Granted, empirical phenomena are explained by means of conceptual abstractions or theories. The choice, for Della Volpe, is between generic, a priori theories, which squeeze reality into abstract categories, or historically determinate theories that accept things as they are. In other words, the theories that we use to organize and explain empirical reality must be part of that reality. This is what Marx meant by historical materialism: each historical era marked by unique ideas, values, and institutions from which social scientists draw the hypotheses required to begin empirical inquiry. Marx's theories regarding the tendencies of capital, the nature of labor power, class polarization, revolution, and so forth are drawn from his experiences in capitalism. Their utility for collecting data is based on their historical concreteness: They recognize things for what they are, rather than for what they are not. The same hypotheses are scientifically irrelevant and superfluous when lifted from the historical era of capitalism.

Della Volpe's theory of deterministic abstractions is materialist and historicist. Within any historical period, the quality of life and thought is conditioned by matter in motion. Each society satiates material needs through a unique productive apparatus marked by particular relationships of production. Because these are the tools for meeting basic irrepressible material wants, they mediate citizens and cultural institutions, molding the latter's form and content. The economic base, therefore, has a determining influence on social ideas. For Della Volpe, the alternative to materialism is idealism, and as the critique of Hegel illustrates, this deforms reality by imposing unverifiable subjective abstractions on objective, concrete phenomena.

Notwithstanding the theoretical primacy of matter over thought, however, Della Volpe is equally critical (in his writings) of mainstream orthodox materialism. Engels erred by adding to Marx's materialism a metaphysical dialectic, an objective view of the universe ahistorically valid. Marxism heuristically explains capitalism, but is not an objective a priori truth. It is historically determinate, emerging from and reflecting capitalist society and facilitating empirical inquiry. It is verified only by supporting facts, not by abstract reasoning. If verified, Marx's theories are scientifically valid only for the historical era from which they are originally drawn. They are not pat formulas valid universally and transhistorically. Orthodox Marxism, like idealism, forfeits scientificity when it abstractly interprets concrete factual reality, in effect denying reality's concreteness. Stalinism, by implication, epitomizes an irrational dictatorship of abstractions, a belief that truth must triumph even if, in the process, it mercilessly destroys reality. In sum, after stripping empirical science of bourgeois preconceptions, Della Volpe substitutes a philosophy of "historicist materialism," which performs the same function as Adler's social individual: rationalizing Marx's major hypotheses, which then guide empirical inquiry.

Because Marxism is historically determinate and data-oriented, there is a methodological unity to natural and social science. Both modes of experimental inquiry require induction (in other words, the recognition of matter as something outside thought and the accumulation of relevant material facts) and deduction (that is, positing reasonable theories as the framework within which facts are gathered and interpreted). Deduction (reason) must prove itself inductively. Facts are inextricably connected to what Della Volpe calls an "hypothesis-idea," or are insignificant. Orthodox materialism is guilty of overemphasizing reason, assuming its utility and truth independent of factual verification. Bourgeois empirical science, on the other hand, loses its philosophical *raison d'être* (which in any case cannot, today, be factually supported) and aimlessly flounders in an endless flow of data. As Marx and Galileo recognized, science needs both theory and facts. The logic of natural and human science is therefore identical. In utilizing thought to explain the interrelationships of things, that is, formulating hypotheses, the logical "principle of tauto-etherology" as the unity of opposites (the "same" and "other" united into one) is involved. On the other hand, when inductively measuring theories against actual facts, the latter are recognized as independent phenomena. Here, the logical "principle of identity" is needed. Scientific logic, therefore, is a composite of both principles, which Della Volpe painfully called the principle of "tauto-etherological identity." It expresses simultaneously the significance of empirical facts as well as unifying ideas, both necessary aspects of reality.

Marx's unique contribution to scientific theory is recognizing that, within a historically determinate locale, material phenomena that appear isolated are actually dynamically linked in a grand social totality that is, in the last resort, shaped by the economic base. Moreover, the observed pattern is one of negation and progressive sublation, that is, capitalism shapes a culture that annuls and surpasses its own determining productive apparatus. Marxism thus fits neatly into the logic of science. It is a series of theoretical hypotheses regarding the interpenetration of matter (the principle of tauto-etherology) drawn from a specific historical milieu whose concrete facts inductively confirm the original theory (the principle of identity). Marx's dialectical theory, including all the separate hypotheses outlined in *Grundrisse* and *Capital,* is "at once, a theory of both the unity and the exclusion of opposites. It is a theory that tries to guarantee at the same time both the moment of knowledge . . . and that of reality itself."[46] Empirical social scientists, accumulating evidence according to universally accepted methods of empirical inquiry, will substantiate Marx's portentous suggestions concerning capitalism's demise and simultaneously provide explosive fuel for the simmering class struggle. Sociology will become an empirical science that is also materialist and revolutionary.

Colletti

As the foremost postwar philosopher in a party whose rich intellectual heritage extends to Labriola and Gramsci, Della Volpe influenced many younger PCI members, including Pietranera, Rossi, Merker, and Cerroni. However, Lucio Colletti (b. 1924) was the most popular—and perhaps the most gifted—of his protégés. Colletti's work follows the general outline of Della Volpe's in interpreting Marxism as an empirical science which inductively validates Marx's formal theories. Colletti, however, was more concerned with resuscitating the revolutionary aspect of Marxism. He, therefore, supplied a theoretical dimension noticeably lacking in Della Volpe: the interpenetration of science and action, the revolutionary implications of Marxist social science. Whereas Della Volpe could hide in an isolated world of Marxist theory while Party officials dictated courses of action, Colletti saw an indissoluble linkage between theory and action. It is not surprising, then, that Colletti's critique of orthodoxy led him to quit the PCI in 1956 and pursue empirical Marxism outside an organizational framework.

Like Della Volpe, and for the same reasons, Colletti felt that Hegel's influence on Marx has been exaggerated. Colletti traced Marx's philosophical heritage to Kant. Without really being aware of it, Marx was significantly influenced by Kant's insistence on both the independent reality of objective phenomena and science as the only intersubjectively valid form of knowledge. These two aspects of Kantianism—an autonomous objective world and a science to cognize it—are pivotal to the bourgeois systematization of natural science, which Colletti admired. They are also the inchoate origins of Marx's science of historical materialism. Hegel, on the other hand, connected the domains of science and morality and dismissed empirical science as inaccurate. Kant, then, was closer to materialism than Hegel. Hence "from a strictly epistemological point of view, there is only one great modern thinker who can be of assistance to us in constructing a materialist theory of knowledge—Immanuel Kant."[47]

Philosophically, Marx's roots go to Kant. In terms of political theory, Colletti traced Marxism to Rousseau. The major political themes that occupied Marx in his *Critique of Hegel's Doctrine of the State,* the basis of Marxist political theory to this day, are from Rousseau's critique of representative government. These include the state's dependence on society, a critique of parliamentarism, a countertheory of popular sovereignty, and a general critique of the capitalist state. Marxist political theory has never surpassed these, though of course Marx's innovative economic and historical discoveries introduced the missing factor of scientific credibility. Whereas Kantianism inspired Marx's materialist approach to science, "so far as 'political' theory in the strict sense is concerned, Marx and Lenin have added nothing to Rousseau. . . ."[48]

Neither philosophically nor politically did Hegelian idealism play any role in Marx's professional development. While admitting that Marx never explicitly acknowledged the debt to either Kant or Rousseau, it is indirectly affirmed in Marx's prolonged battle with abstractionism. Marx's critique of Hegel's inversion of subject and predicate inspired a lifelong project of making social theory concrete. All of Marx's assertions—from the theory of alienation to the analysis of commodity production—explain real, empirically verifiable phenomena, and therefore are predicated on the epistemological priority of facts. The *Critique of Hegel's Doctrine of the State* proves Marx's commitment to facts, and the 1844 theory of alienation is based only on humanity's actual, distorted relationships with others in capitalism. Responding to the *Manuscripts'* occasional disregard of these empirically verifiable relations, Colletti remarked "if the words are not there, the concept is, though admittedly in a still tentative and half-obscured form." In 1844 Marx still lacked the conceptual equipment necessary to explain perceived facts of capitalist life adequately. This short-lived technical problem—not a lapse into a priorism—produced the *Manuscripts'* enigmatic terminology. Marx's substantive critical thought "moved along a single line of development stretching from reflection on philosophical logic to a dissection of the form and content of bourgeois society. His discussion

of the subject-predicate inversion in Hegel's logic, his analysis of estrangement and alienation, and (finally) his critique of the fetishism of commodities and capital can all be seen as the progressive unfolding, as the ever-
deepening grasp of a single problematic."[49]

Colletti's target was not idealism but a priorism. He was aware that
orthodoxy underemphasizes Marx's early writings, which he felt encapsulated
the germ of Marxian science. The materialist metaphysics posing, since
Engels, as Marxism misconstrues historical materialism by ignoring its
origins in Marx's early critique of abstractionism. Hence "given that most
contemporary Marxism has dismissed the *Critique* without serious consid-
eration, what can be the level of its comprehension of even the first few
pages of *Capital?*" Marx studied not society "in general," but one particular
society: capitalism. And he did it scientifically, spurning ideal or material
abstractions. Echoing Della Volpe, Colletti felt that science requires theories relevant to the phenomena they explain. "So long as men did not know
how to approach the study of the facts, they invented *a priori* general
theories which always remained sterile. In other words, they *substituted* or
superimposed a *generic* or *ideal* object for the *real* object to be explained.
Orthodox Marxism has retrogressed to this pre-Marxian stage, ignoring
Marx's emphasis on factual real processes." Orthodoxy absurdly formulates
reality as simultaneously "being" and "not-being." Contradictions can exist
only between propositions. Real phenomena, on the other hand, are defined by an empirically verifiable existence. Verified contradictions are
"contradictions in reality, and for that very reason particular or historically
determinate ones," anchored in objective historical facts rather than a
priori rationality. "Dialectical materialism is a scholastic metaphysic whose
survival merely indicates the deep inadequacy hitherto of the attempts by
the working class movement to come to terms with the great problems of
modern science. It is an evening class philosophical pastiche." Colletti's
dispute with orthodoxy, this last sarcastic remark indicates, is indelible. If,
as one orthodox Marxist remarked, Colletti's epistemology "smacks more
of positivism . . . than Marxism," Colletti would quickly interject: "against
the dangers of . . . spiritualist idealism I personally would prefer to incur
the opposite risks of neo-positivism."[50]

Colletti's methodology reflects and extends his mentor's. Knowledge
takes two forms: a process occurring in nature, and one born in logical
mental activity. The first places real limiting conditions on thought. The
second "cancels out" empirical reality in the interests of logical purity,
transforming it into thought's consequence or effect. Colletti, like Della
Volpe, explicitly recognized materialism as the philosophical point of
departure for scientific inquiry. Either reality exists in a concrete material
sense or intersubjectively verifiable science is impossible. But even though
matter is a condition for the existence of thought—thought's "cause"—we
cognize reality only by thinking about it. Although objective matter makes

science possible, knowledge is also the product of a subjective thought process that categorizes perceived matter, defining "fact" and "fiction." Thought is, in this sense, the "cause of its cause." "Just as reality is anterior and independent, and thought in relation to it is something on which limiting conditions are placed, so it is also true that we can only arrive at a *recognition* of that reality *deductively*, i.e. through a process from which reality emerges as a result of a sifting and a selection carried out by thought." The concrete material world is expressed and realized in thought. True knowledge, therefore, "is the congruence *between* thought and reality."[51]

Colletti perceived two types of Marxist theory, neither scientifically adequate. First, there is metaphysical materialism, based solely on the heterogeneity of thought and being, and the latter's priority. Impersonal laws characterize matter and shape all human phenomena, including thought. Second, idealist Marxism ignores the heterogeneity of being and thought, emphasizing a dialectical thought process that determines history by successively negating matter. Materialist Marxism artificially separates knowledge and reason; idealist Marxism isolates knowledge from the concrete factual world. Both distort society's subtle and complex blending of objectivity and subjectivity by cutting the (objective) material means of production from the (subjectively) experienced relations of production. The unity of matter and thought, structure and ideology, is obliterated. "Clearly we cannot have a concrete society without taking both together."[52]

Colletti's method is factually accurate but simultaneously explains facts in terms of the logical categories by which they are experienced. Like Della Volpe's method it combines the deductive application of general hypotheses and the inductive compilation of empirical data: facts verify hypotheses. Scientists extract from a specific, concrete world a series of meaningful explanatory concepts that are verified empirically. Empirical verification confirms a concept's objectivity: "from the scientific viewpoint . . . science's task is to explain 'facts' or 'sure phenomena' and nothing else."[53] Like Adler and Della Volpe, Colletti rejected the Cartesian foundations of modern social science, substituting a materialism based on the interpenetration of subject and object. These foundational ideas justify Marx's historical and economic theories, just as Cartesianism justifies bourgeois formal theories.

Colletti labeled Bernstein a man ahead of his time in acknowledging the altered empirical state of capitalism. Bernstein, however, lost Marx's formal deductive theories, an integral component of empirical science. Helplessly facing a plethora of facts, Bernstein lacked the conceptual skills needed to understand them, hence naively adopted bourgeois preconceptions. Bernstein forgot that Marxism is both a science, studying the factual dynamics of capitalism, and a revolutionary theory seeking socialist equality.

Matter places limits on subjectivity, but only through consciousness can we identify both the limits and the reality itself. Consciousness thus "causes" us to understand the objective "cause" of consciousness. "The subject is *part* of the object, a moment within the object, and hence is itself *objective*. Both subject and object are part of an *objective* object-subject process." Conscious subjectivity is a reflective moment of objective social being. "Hence what makes it a *part* is precisely what *distinguishes* it from the totum to which it belongs." Consciousness, therefore, is the only aspect of social life capable of reflecting on, and cognizing, the objective totality. Colletti established two points: (1) objective matter exists, but (2) it consists of a dynamic synthesis of disparate elements, a "unity of heterogeneous parts."[54] While his materialism confirms the fundamental priority of being over thought, being itself is a dynamic totality of matter *and* creative thought.

Since society's superstructure reflects the base and is part of it, Colletti defended the unity of sociology and economics, and rejected economism. By dichotomizing matter into autonomous, impenetrable categories of production (objectivity) and ideology (subjectivity), orthodox Marxism smothers the real world with impersonal abstractions. Authentic deductive theory, echoing subjectively meaningful perceptions, is an integral aspect of objectivity. It is hypothetically drawn from reality, and empirically verified with real evidence. Hence, it is as real as the explained social phenomena, expressing concepts actually experienced by cognitive actors. Stripped of this hypothesized meaning, facts are random, unfocused, and confusing. Just as ideas are an irreducible moment of material reality, theory is a necessary component of scientific inquiry.

Social actors are objective entities whose unique trait is their subjective, reflective thought processes. Scientifically valid hypotheses outline objective patterns of behavior actors reflectively experience. "The objective terms of analysis must also themselves be seen as *active*, as objects capable of referring theoretically to one another, and hence as objects susceptible to description in purely *physical* terms on the one hand and also as social agents on the other. The process is a natural one, but this nature is *socio-historical*." Marx's empirically valid "laws," described especially in *Capital*, are by themselves incapable of explaining why men and women consciously unite into classes and rebel. They refer only to quantitative economic relations, and thus remain "within the limitations of capitalist understanding." Such objective, empirically verified tendencies make sense only as part of a meaningful emancipatory struggle; "alone, they have no decisive value."[55] No mechanistic pattern exists in history leading automatically to revolution, independent of conscious decisions. Each valid theory expresses, potentially, the subjective beliefs of observed actors. Marx's deductive hypotheses are, therefore, calls to revolutionary action, factual truths that actually express workers' growing discontent. Their scientificity is confirmed by empirical (objective) evidence and the actual (subjective) commitment of those studied.

Empirical science is therefore subjective and objective. In the case of bourgeois social science, the former is represented by Cartesianism and the liberal values flowing therefrom. Scientific inquiry in capitalism implicitly expresses this subjective world view and explicitly supports liberal principles and institutions. On the other hand, Marxist social science takes off from Marx's revolutionary deductive theories. It presumes a multifaceted, multidimensional, interpenetrating totality, and explicitly advocates proletariat revolution. Science and values are forever inextricably connected. Orthodox Marxist materialism and bourgeois empiricism radically separate objectivity and subjectivity, hence ignore their own abstract, unrealistic philosophical and political values. The issue is *which* values shall support scientific inquiry, determining the scope of relevant phenomena and the significance of empirical data. "Value judgements are inevitably present in scientific research itself, but as judgements whose ultimate significance depends on the degree to which they stand up to historical-practical verification or experiment; and hence on their capacity to be converted ultimately into factual judgements."[56] Empirical science alone, divorced from revolutionary theory, generates a Bernstein-style acquiescence to the status quo. Revolutionary theory, isolated from empirical verification, is both unrealistic and dogmatic, a real danger to freedom and human (subjective) integrity. Authentic Marxism is empirical and revolutionary, a social science that explains and alters reality.

In Marx, theory and practice are "closely connected so that each is supported and reinforced by the fact that it follows as a consequence of scientific analysis." Marx's mature work, particularly *Capital,* illustrates the subtle blending of science and revolution. As a scientist, he discovered objective relationships, laws governing the development and demise of capitalist production. In this role he makes only "judgments of fact": empirically verified and universally valid. As a work of science, *Capital* is objective and impartial, generating economic laws "external to classes and independent of our wills just like the laws of nature." But Marx also acknowledges matter as a dialectical unity of opposites, an objective totality nurturing creative subjects. The determinate whole, a unity of heterogeneous parts, consists of empirically valid economic laws explaining intentional acts. Objectivity and subjectivity join in economic class, the objective consequence of the productive apparatus but also the subjective political agent for realizing history's laws. Marx's science embodies "objective factors of production . . . simultaneously presented as subjective agents or social classes."[57] When empirical laws are manifest in working-class consciousness, then reality will be transformed in a manner consistent with scientific evidence. This, however, is not an automatic process; Marx was not a determinist. Workers congeal as a revolutionary class because of determinate economic factors *and* authentic political consciousness. Without a revolutionary working-class ideology, factual data indicating capitalism's demise remain unfulfilled. Empirical science is simply not enough.

The scientist's social role involves an active commitment to empirical facts and the working-class revolutionary movement. Marxist empirical scientists must actively oppose the phenomena they study.

Colletti refused to be cowed by Marxist a priorism and eventually was estranged from the revolutionary Party he once supported. Moreover, his nondogmatic empiricism implies that at some point he must come to terms with Marx's nonempirical words and the factual nonexistence of the workers' revolution. By 1974 Colletti candidly declared of Marx's theoretical work, "there are critical areas of uncertainty and confusion about the dialectic" and bluntly acknowledged the unscientific quality of *Capital*. "The result is that Marxism is in crisis today, and it can only surmount this crisis by acknowledging it. But precisely this acknowledgement is consciously avoided by virtually every Marxist, great or small."[58] This sounds reminiscent of Husserl's description of the "crisis" of natural science, a prelude to his critical reconstruction. Whether Colletti continues to rehabilitate the "real," empirically oriented Marx intellectually or abandons Marx as unrealistic will probably depend on the facts of European capitalist development in the coming years.

Analytic Marxism

Analytic philosophy believes traditional discourse—including Cartesianism—haphazardly explicates grand ideas while logical and linguistic tools go unexamined. Meaning is generated by basic elements of theoretical discourse: the words, logic, and syntax that ideas hang on. Worthwhile philosophy is contextual definition, or analysis, which unpacks linguistic complexes into more comprehensible units. In Wittgenstein's *Logical Investigations,* and the work of Wisdom, Ryle, Ayers, Strawson, Austin, and others, contemporary analytic philosophy broadens meaning to include the rules, regulations, conventions, and habits governing the actual uses of linguistic expressions. It remains primarily a descriptive philosophy of language, but language as a means of social interaction, not an ideal code.

No necessary connection exists between analytic philosophy and empiricism. One seeks meaning through contextual definition, the other via factual confirmation. However, both repudiate metaphysics and hence oppose idealism and materialism. The two movements congeal in the work of logical positivists like Carnap, and analytical philosophers like Ayers. Analysis cleans linguistic assertions but makes no factual claims. Science empirically verifies meaningful theory, determining its social usefulness. Despite differences, there is a natural division of labor that encourages active cooperation.

Two remarkably similar books—G. A. Cohen's *Karl Marx's Theory of History* and William H. Shaw's *Marx's Theory of History*—analytically examine Marx's theory of historical materialism, rigorously defining terms, exposing syntax, and linking both to the real capitalist world. They share the heuristic goal of formulating meaningful theory that will generate empirical inquiry.

As is the wont of analytic inquiry generally, method and style outweigh substantive conclusions. In this case, both authors supported old-fashioned economism, particularly the "technological" version, which places final priority in the technical productive forces. They, especially Cohen, provided an extraordinarily detailed definition of relevant terms, for example, "productive forces," "productive relations," and "social relations," referring to Marx, other analytic studies, and actual social rules. Both works are precise, academic, and logically structured and claim to be "reasonably clear statement[s] of what . . . [Marx] thought."[59] Significantly, both authors defined science empirically, as regularities and laws confirmed by factual data.[60] Cohen's more sophisticated treatment delved into the intricacies of "functional explanation" as an empirically useful technique for theory formation. Finally, both felt that their analytically unpacked theory of historical materialism was logical and meaningful, scientifically useful as formal theory, and confirmed by available data.

Analytic Marxism chooses linguistic precision over the loose philosophical hypotheses of Adler, Della Volpe, and Colletti. It also avoids entirely the problem of assimilating dialectics and empirical method—the motivating problematic of nonanalytic empirical Marxism. On the one hand, Cohen and Shaw deny vulgar economic determinism, recognizing the "interacting totality" of base and culture.[61] On the other, "this labyrinthine [philosophical] terrain" is out of bounds; hence, technology dominates in some undefined "nonvulgar" sense.[62] Moreover, politics and theory are unattached. Analytic Marxism seeks only theory formation, is relevant only to academics and philosophers. For Marxists, linguistic clarity, thus far, has a high cost: avoiding any issue that cannot be adequately framed by nondialectical logic and confirmed empirically.

Gurvitch

Empirical Marxism presumes the heuristic worth of deductive theory for scientific inquiry. Marx's major hypotheses guide data collecting. Marxist social science consists of deductive revolutionary theories confirmed or denied by factual evidence. A notable exception to this deductive approach is George Gurvitch (1894–1965), a French sociologist comfortable with theory only when arising spontaneously from rigorously compiled data. Gurvitch was not a Marxist as this term has thus far been used. He approached scientific inquiry devoid of theoretical preconceptions regarding the historical and social functions of economic classes. As a scientist, he was committed to facts, not revolution, and he separated value judgments from the process of scientific inquiry. Moreover, the categories he developed to facilitate data collecting reflect an extraordinarily diverse group of thinkers, ranging from Richert, Windleband, and Weber to Bergson, Scheler, Fichte, and Husserl. This eclecticism did not sit well with Marxists, who dismissed his unorthodox empirical method with disdain and confusion. Non-Marxists, on the other hand, did not know quite how to label Gurvitch, though proffered choices include "empiricist," "Marxist," and "phenomenologist." Several compelling reasons exist for linking Gurvitch and empirical Marxism: He viewed reality as a dialectically interconnected totality, believed in the priority of empirical facts, and perceived the likelihood of proletarian rebellion. Gurvitch created an inductive Marxist method. Empirical Marxism, in this sense, mirrors bourgeois empirical science, which has also spawned inductive and deductive methods.

Like other empirical Marxists, Gurvitch critically rejected Cartesianism. Reality is a totality of interacting, heterogeneous factors. Terms like "subjectivity" and "objectivity" are volatile, constantly created and recreated as individual existence interacts with and is defined by social existence. Naively separating actors and environments hides this linkage. All aspects of social life—from a citizen's consciousness of himself and others, to the structures of political and social institutions, class formation, and the global features of civilization itself—dynamically interact. The specific form each takes is conditioned by the totality, the collectivity of interrelated factors. Since there is no dominant factor, orthodox Marxism is as abstract and unrealistic as Cartesianism. The former gestates a hegemonic party of scientists ruthlessly "perfecting" reality; the latter, a society of "free" homunculi who helplessly watch mystical economic laws guarantee inequality.

A dynamic reality needs a dynamic method. Only dialectics eliminates abstractionism and explains society as it really is. Dialectics encompasses five interrelated processes also exhibited by social phenomena, hence authentically reflects reality.[63] It accounts for the movement of social totalities and exposes their tensions, oppositions, and conflicts, without squeezing these into preconceived categories. In sum, dialectical method accurately and nondogmatically depicts objective social relationships. Social scientists must use it to accumulate data impersonally according to accepted empirical procedures. Science describes, not interprets, reality. Gurvitch's dialectical method is therefore "hyperempirical" in depicting observable facts and eschewing reductionism.[64]

Gurvitch perceived hyperempirical dialectics in Marx's pre-1846 work, where society is an irreducible collective activity, a whole constituting the factors comprising its content. Marx's dialectic, then, is part of humanity's purposive involvement with nature. The interpenetration of subject and object defines life's real movement; intentionality occurs within, and reflects, objective being. For the early Marx, the dialectical totality is prior to subject and object, hence materialism and idealism are equally misconceived. Marx's mature work, however, equivocates. A reductionist material metaphysics is gradually frozen in the work of Engels, Kautsky, Plekhanov, and Lenin. "Dialectical materialism," a term that Marx never used and at least prior to 1846 would have found repugnant, occludes reality with abstractions. Orthodox, reductionist Marxism had lost the true meaning of dialectics.[65]

The social totality, a whole determining and expressing its parts, is irreducible. Social science renders these complex interrelationships intelligible through observation and description. Hence the totality lives, scientifically, in isolated empirical facts. However, this endless barrage of data is meaningless unless heuristically categorized. Gurvitch therefore acknowledged the artificiality *and* the necessity of compartmentalizing the social sciences. His own solution for organizing a dynamic, multidimensional reality into manageable categories that facilitate data collecting is "depth sociology." Gurvitch sliced reality into a series of "horizontal" and "vertical" categories: the former categorizing forms of social life (ranging from spontaneous sociability, through groups and classes, to organized and structured global societies); the latter, depth levels marking the structure and intensity of social interaction (ranging from the spontaneous and mystical "collective mind," which indelibly imprints the collective on each individual consciousness, to increasingly structured forms of social behavior such as revolutionary action and social roles, to society's most structured organizations and institutions). Vertical and horizontal constantly intersect while internally levels interpenetrate. Each level on both poles, therefore, is a moment of the whole, indissolubly linked to other levels and the totality. The categories are thus heuristically useful rather than real, functioning to structure empirical data before self-destructing when evidence is in and complex interconnections established. They represent a "dynamic framework of reference adapted to the total social phenomena and called on to promote explanation in sociology," convenient racks to hang his own multifaceted research, including sociologies of knowledge, law, time perception, and morality.[66]

Hyperempirical dialectical inquiry generates social science. Factual data unfold regularities among various aspects of the totality, illustrating correspondences between groups of social phenomena. The entire factual ensemble indicates social patterns or movements, not unilinear causal relationships. Scientific evidence generates "a pluralism of limited, relative, and varying partial determinisms which are distinctly different in each concrete universe, each specific world studied by a particular science."[67] This evidence, embodied in Gurvitch's empirical studies, confirms the basic principles of historical materialism.

Gurvitch was uncomfortable not with the substance of Marxism, but with its dogmatic materialist reductionism. Moreover, he admired Western empirical research despite its idealist Cartesianism. Like other empirical Marxists, Gurvitch's social science was factual. But he did not deductively apply Marx's hypotheses. Hyperempirical inquiry, which accumulates quantities of dialectically linked facts, constituted its own theory. Valid social theory is inductive rather than deductive, cumulatively drawn from perceived facts rather than applied to organize and explain them.

Gurvitch's hyperempiricism inductively verifies most of Marx's historical hypotheses. Speaking factually, capitalism collapses because it cannot mute inherent class-related contradictions, but not before a spasmodic "fascist techno-bureaucratic" adventure that brutally destroys bourgeois liberties while claiming to save them. Although evidence is not yet entirely in, Western civilization leans historically toward cooperative, nonalienated socialism, a society of direct working-class hegemony. Economic self-management radically diminishes the state's legitimate role, turning it—on the domestic front, at least—into the "administrator of things" that Marx anticipated.[68] Personally, Gurvitch evaluated this transition from capitalism to socialism as both desirable and highly likely, given available evidence. However, the hyperempirical inductive method prohibits moral or deductive generalizations. Thus, after admitting that "it would seem difficult to avoid social revolutions," the cautious scientist diligently avoided evaluating observed facts: Scientists "must only ascertain the effect of their presence, combination, and effective function."[69] Gurvitch, in other words, rejected the unity of facts and values. Scientists impersonally accumulate data and generate hypothetical theories. Once the dialectical conceptual framework replaced Cartesianism, Gurvitch insisted on the absolute integrity of factual evidence. It would be inconsistent to advocate a revolutionary politics when scientifically committed to empirical facts, wherever they lead. Gurvitch's dilemma resembles that of bourgeois inductive scientists, who as scientists must also squash interpretive generalizations, activities, and preferences. Of course, their unquestioned Cartesianism safeguards capitalist institutions by preserving the putative isolation of observed social facts. Capitalism's unsolvable economic and social contradictions are immune to nondialectical science. Gurvitch, on the other hand, factually crams the dialectical grid. Both Marxist and bourgeois inductive methods are fact-oriented, "hyperempirical." But only Gurvitch's dialectical perspective strips capitalism to its self-destructive core and coolly surmises the immanence of a socialist future.

CONCLUSION

What distinguishes Gurvitch from other empirical Marxists is his unwillingness to declare authentic, dialectical social science an activity that, in factually describing reality, must simultaneously change it. With the exception of an inchoate analytic Marxism, the project of turning empirical science revolutionary dominates post-Bernsteinian empirical Marxism. Adler, Della Volpe, and Colletti managed the synthesis by replacing Cartesianism with dialectics and then deductively applying Marx's theories to empirical inquiry. Revolutionary activity and empirical verification are complementary aspects of the material totality. The empirical validity of Marx's theory of proletariat revolution scientifically justifies its advocacy. Hence social roles of empirical scientist and revolutionary activist coalesce. Gurvitch's anomalous inductionism precludes this synthesis, guaranteeing—paraphrasing Hobbes's epithet—the triumph of empirical logic over revolutionary common sense. He was a nonrevolutionary Marxist whose lifework empirically confirmed Marx's theory of working-class revolution.

NOTES

1. Paul Diesing, *Patterns of Discovery in the Social Sciences* (Chicago: Aldine, 1971), p. 39. See also pp. 29–47, 101–7, and 124–33.

2. Adam Schaff, *Structuralism and Marxism* (New York: Pergamon Press, 1978), p. 77.

3. Maurice Cornforth, *The Theory of Knowledge* (New York: International Publishers, 1963), p. 146. Susan Stebbing, *Philosophy and the Physicists* (New York: Pelican Books, 1944), p. 7, makes this same point from a non-Marxist perspective.

4. Karl Marx, *Critique of Hegel's Doctrine of the State,* in *Early Writings* (New York: Vintage Books, 1975), pp. 98 and 80. Hereafter cited as *KMEW.*

5. Ibid., p. 63. See pp. 90, 127, 145, and 149; *On the Jewish Question,* in *KMEW,* p. 233; and the "Introduction" to *Grundrisse,* ibid., pp. 101–2.

6. Karl Marx, *Introduction to A Critique of Hegel's Philosophy of Right,* in *KMEW,* p. 244–45.

7. Karl Marx, *Economic and Philosophical Manuscripts,* in *KMEW,* pp. 281 and 330–31.

8. Karl Marx, *Introduction to A Critique of Hegel's Philosophy of Right,* p. 244.

9. Karl Marx and Friedrich Engels, *The German Ideology* (Moscow: Progress Pubs., 1976), pp. 43, 45, 49, 41, and 36–37.

10. Karl Marx, *The Poverty of Philosophy,* in *Selected Works,* ed. D. McLellan (London: Oxford University Press, 1977), p. 210. Hereafter cited as *KMSW.*

11. Marx and Engels, *The German Ideology,* p. 59.

12. Letter, in Marx and Engels, *Werke,* 39 vols. (Berlin: Dietz Verlag, 1974), 8: 385.

13. Karl Marx, *Wage Labour and Capital,* in *KMSW,* p. 248.

14. Marx, *Grundrisse* (New York: Vintage Books, 1973), p. 881.

15. See especially the first chapter of Karl Marx, *Capital* 3 vols. (New York: International Publishers, 1975), vol. 1. *Theories of Surplus Value* 3 vols. (Moscow: Progress Publishers, 1969–72) is a three-volume critique of classical and socialist economic theory, focusing on Adam Smith (vol. 1), Ricardo (vol. 2), and the British socialist followers of Ricardo (vol. 3).

16. Marx, *Capital,* 1: 184. See also *Theories of Surplus Value,* in *KMSW,* pp. 393–414.

17. Natural things—for example, waterpower, land, trees, and so on—have no exchange value, even though they have a price. This will be explained by the notion of surplus value. See *Capital,* 1: 35–71.

18. Ibid., 3: 105–41.

19. Ibid., 1: 763.

20. Ibid., p. 645.

21. Ibid., pp. 508–18, and Karl Marx, *Pre-Capitalist Economic Formations* (New York: International Publishers, 1964).

22. At the turn of the century, a lively debate unfolded concerning the empirical usefulness of Marx's economic theories. Defending their empirical utility was Rudolph Hilferding, opposing it, the Austrian economist Eugen Bohm-Bawerk. See Bohm-Bawerk's *Geschichte und Kritik des Kapitalzinstheorien* (1884) and *Zum Abschluss des Marxschen Systems* (1896); English translation, *Karl Marx and the Close of His System* (1898). See also Hilferding, *Bohm-Bawerk's Marx-Kritik* (1904).

23. Karl Marx, "Reply to Mikhailovsky" (1877), in Lewis S. Feuer, ed., *Marx & Engels — Basic Writings on Politics and Philosophy* (Garden City, N.Y.: Doubleday, 1959), pp. 440–41.

24. Karl Marx, "Letter to Vera-Sassoulitch" (1881), in *KMSW,* p. 577.

25. Umberto Cerroni, "Socialist Humanism and Science," in *Socialist Humanism,* ed. Erich Fromm (New York: Anchor Books, 1966), pp. 134–36.

26. See George L. Kline, "Changing Attitudes Toward the Individual," in *The Transformation of Russian Society,* ed. C. E. Black (Cambridge: Cambridge University Press, 1960), pp. 618–23.

27. Eduard Bernstein, *Evolutionary Socialism* (New York: Schocken Books, 1965), pp. 210 and 209; Vicktor Adler, *Briefwechsel mit August Bebel und Karl Kautsky* (Vienna: Wiener Volksbuchhandlung, 1954), p. 289; Bernstein, *Evolutionary Socialism,* p. 210.

28. Ibid., p. 125.

29. Ibid., pp. 166 and 186.

30. Ibid., p. 155. See also pp. 200–22. Bernstein's efforts to turn Marxism into a reformist ideology were paralleled, to a significant degree, by the so-called "Legal Marxists" in Russia, who wrote primarily in the last decade of the nineteenth century.

31. See for example, W. Leontiev's incisive analysis in the *Proceedings of the Fiftieth Annual Meeting of the American Economic Association,* 1937 (*American Economic Review Supplement,* March 1938), pp. 5–9; Joseph Schumpeter, *History of Economic Analysis* (New York: Oxford University Press, 1954), esp. p. 883; Lucio Colletti, *From Rousseau to Lenin* (New York: New Left Books, 1972), pp. 97–102; and James O'Connor, *The Fiscal Crisis of the State* (New York: St. Martin's Press, 1973). There is a useful bibliography in Ira Katznelson and Mark Kesselman, *The Politics of Power* (New York: Harcourt Brace Jovanovich, 1975), pp. 489–96.

32. See George L. Kline, "Kolakowski and the Revision of Marxism," in *European Philosophy Today* ed. Kline (Chicago: Quadrangle Books, 1965), pp. 131–32; and Colletti, "A Political and Philosophical Interview," *New Left Review* 86 (July-August 1974): 10.

33. For a bibliography of the major works of Austro-Marxism see Tom Bottomore and Patrick Goode (eds.), *Austro-Marxism* (Oxford: Oxford University Press, 1978), pp. 292–300.

34. Otto Neurath, "Empirical Sociology: The Scientific Content of History and Political Economy," in *Empiricism and Sociology* ed. M. Neurath and R. Cohen, (Dordrecht, Netherlands: Reidel, 1973), pp. 319–421. For a time Neurath belonged to both schools.

35. See Max Adler "Mach und Marx. Ein Beitrag zur Kritik des modernen

Positivismus," *Archiv für Sozialwissenschaft und Sozial politik* 33 (1911): 348–400. Adler integrates Kant and Marx in *Kant und der Marxismus* (1925). See also Karl Vorlander, *Kant und der Sozialismus* (Berlin: Reuther und Reichard, 1900). Other Kantian Marxists include L. Woltmann, C. Schmidt, and F. Staudinger.

36. Adler, *Kant und der Marxismus,* in *Austro-Marxism,* pp. 65–66; and *Der soziologische Sinn der Lehre von Karl Marx,* ibid., p. 59.

37. Ibid., p. 60.

38. Adler was aware of the enormous complexity of the issue and his inadequate formulation. His views vacillate from an early emphasis on the uniqueness of subjectivity (*Kausalität und Teleologie im Streite um die Wissenschaft* (1904), to stressing the epistemological priority of causal explanation (*Der soziologische Sinn der Lehre von Karl Marx* (1914), and back again (*Lehrbuch der materialistischen Geschichtsauffassung* (1930–1932). See Robert A. Gorman, *The Dual Vision* (London: Routledge & Kegan Paul, 1977).

39. Adler criticized Engels and the entire orthodox movement for ignoring the a priori categories of consciousness in *Lehrbuch der materialistischen Geschichtsauffassung.*

40. Adler, *Kant und der Marxismus,* p. 64.

41. Adler, "Zur Soziologie der Revolution," *Der Kampf* 21 (1928): 570–76. English translation, "The Sociology of Revolution," in *Austro-Marxism,* pp. 136–46.

42. Rudolf Hilferding, *Das Finanzkapital* (Vienna: Wiener Volksbuchhandlung, 1904), and Otto Bauer, *Die Österreichische Revolution* (Vienna: Wiener Volksbuchhandlung, 1923). See also Karl Renner, "Problems of Marxism," in *Austro-Marxism,* pp. 91–101, and *Wandlungen der Modernen Gesellschaft* (Vienna: Wiener Volksbuchhandlung, 1953); and Max Adler "Wandlung der Arbeiterklasse?" *Der Kampf* 26 (1933): 367–82; English translation, "Metamorphosis of the Working Class," in *Austro-Marxism,* pp. 217–48.

43. Leon Trotsky, *My Life* (New York: Scribners, 1930), p. 213.

44. Galvano Della Volpe, "The Legal Philosophy of Socialism," in *Socialist Humanism,* pp. 425–40.

45. See Galvano Della Volpe, *Logica come Scienza Positiva* (Florence: G. d'Anna, 1956); "Introduction to Della Volpe," *New Left Review* 59 (January–February 1970): 97–100; Mario Montano, "The 'Scientific Dialectics' of Galvano Della Volpe," in *The Unknown Dimension* (New York: Basic Books, 1972), pp. 342–64; and Lucio Colletti, "A Political and Philosophical Interview," *New Left Review* 84 (July–August 1974): 3–28.

46. Galvano Della Volpe, "Dialettica Scientifica e Teoria del Valore," Preface to E. V. Il'enkov, *La Dialettica dell'Astratto e del Concreto nel Capitale di Marx* (Milan: Feltrinelli, 1961), p. viii. See also *Logica come Scienza Positiva,* pp. 167ff. After the *Logica,* Della Volpe abandoned methodology. In *Rousseau e Marx* (1957) he favorably compared Rousseau's egalitarian freedom with the civic liberties of Locke and Kant, tracing Marx's critique of bourgeois law (from the *Critique of the Gotha Programme*) to Rousseau. The *Critica del Gusto* (1960), which some call his most sophisticated work, develops a Marxist aesthetics.

47. Colletti, "A Political and Philosophical Interview," p. 10. See also *Marxism and Hegel* (London: New Left Books, 1973), pp. 113–38, esp. p. 122.

48. Lucio Colletti, *From Rousseau to Lenin* (London: New Left Books, 1972), p. 185. See also "A Political and Philosophical Interview," pp. 14f; and Introduction to *KMEW,* pp. 40–46.

49. Ibid., pp. 56 and 47.

50. Ibid., p. 40; *From Rousseau to Lenin*, p. 4; *Marxism and Hegel*, p. 135—his emphasis; "A Political and Philosophical Interview," p. 16; Novack's remark in his *Polemics in Marxist Philosophy* (New York: Monad Press, 1978), p. 200; and "A Political and Philosophical Interview," p. 20.

51. Colletti, *Marxism and Hegel*, pp. 119 and 127—emphasis is his. See also pp. 104ff and *From Rousseau to Lenin*, pp. 10ff and 66ff.

52. Ibid., p. 7.

53. Lucio Colletti, "The Theory of the Crash," in *Towards a New Marxism* (St. Louis, Mo.: Telos Press, 1973), p. 183.

54. Colletti, *From Rousseau to Lenin*, pp. 10 and 14.

55. Ibid., p. 12; "The Theory of the Crash," p. 188.

56. Colletti, *From Rousseau to Lenin*, p. 76.

57. Colletti, "The Theory of the Crash," p. 177; *From Rousseau to Lenin*, pp. 229 and 16. See ibid., pp. 229-36.

58. Colletti, "A Political and Philosophical Interview," pp. 13 and 21.

59. G. A. Cohen, *Karl Marx's Theory of History* (Princeton, N.J.: Princeton University Press, 1978), p. ix.

60. Ibid., pp. 265-83; and William H. Shaw, *Marx's Theory of History* (Palo Alto, Calif.: Stanford University Press, 1978), pp. 69-70 and 160.

61. Ibid., pp. 70-72; and Cohen, *Karl Marx's Theory of History*, pp. 166-69.

62. Shaw, *Marx's Theory of History*, p. 68.

63. Including "complementarity," "mutual implication," "ambiguity," "polarization," and "reciprocity of perspectives." See Georges Gurvitch, *Dialectique et sociologie* (Paris: Flammarion, 1962), pp. 5-28, 179-88, and 193-218. English translation in George Balandier, *Gurvitch* (New York: Harper & Row, 1974), pp. 66-72 and 79-84. See also Pitrim A. Sorokin, *Sociological Theories of Today* (New York: Harper & Row, 1966), pp. 464-96; and Phillip Bosserman, *Dialectical Sociology* (Boston: Porter-Sargent, 1968), esp. pp. 227-39. Gurvitch compared his own dialectic to orthodox dialectical materialism in *Dialectique et sociologie* and *La Vocation actuelle de la Sociologie* 2 vols. (Paris: Press Universitaires, 1950), 2: 32.

64. See Georges Gurvitch, "L'hyper-empirisme dialectique, ses applications en sociologie," *Cahiers Internationaux de Sociologie* 15 (1953), pp. 3-33. English translation in Balandier, *Gurvitch*, pp. 73-79. See also Gurvitch, *The Social Frameworks of Knowledge* (New York: Harper & Row, 1971), pp. 106-8.

65. Gurvitch, *La vocation actuelle de la sociologie*, 1: 55. See also *Dialectique et sociologie*, and *The Social Frameworks of Knowledge*, pp. 105ff.

66. Georges Gurvitch, *The Spectrum of Social Time*, (Dordrecht, Netherlands: Reidel, 1964), p. 13. See also *La vocation actuelle de la sociologie*, 1: 63.

67. Bosserman, *Dialectical Sociology*, p. 240. See Gurvitch, *Déterminismes sociaux et liberté humaine* (Paris: Presses Universitaires, 1955), pp. 9-40.

68. Gurvitch saw Western society evolving from "democratic liberalism" to "managerial organized capitalism," to "fascist techno-bureaucratism," to "centralized state collectivism," and, finally, to "decentralized pluralist collectivism"—each marked by antagonism between hegemonic and oppressed classes. See *The Social Frameworks of Knowledge*, pp. 96-228, and *The Spectrum of Social Time*, pp. 86ff.

69. Gurvitch, *The Social Framework of Knowledge*, p. 10. Gurvitch's personal preferences are in ibid., pp. 220 and 228; and *La déclaration des droits sociaux* (Paris: Vrin, 1946).

6.

Experientialism

Marxism is the theory and practice of human liberation. After its orthodox materialist version inspired a dogmatic dictatorship of Party-scientists, purists reread Marx and reinterpreted the epistemology of dialectical materialism. Idealism, emphasizing thought and intentionality, resembles materialism epistemologically. Both presume that an a priori truth determines either the quality (materialism) or significance (idealism) of experience. As a guarantor of human liberation, idealist—like materialist—Marxism is defective. While revivifying subjectivity enlivens the dormant promise of worker freedom, its a priorism simultaneously slams the door on self-government. Immature or inauthentic class consciousness is also objectively incorrect. In situations where criteria of objectivity oppose consciousness, the former will prevail: What revolutionary would willingly forfeit victory for a lie? Humanity must be served, but not at the cost of truth.

Empirical Marxism counters a priorism with concrete, verifiable evidence. But this shifts scientific criteria from one impersonal reality to another, leaving human subjects vulnerable. Empirical social science, bourgeois or Marxist, depersonalizes human phenomena by ignoring subjective factors not observed, described, and measured. Its social theories depict causal relationships that are valid, in specific circumstances, for any actor—irrespective of subjective particularities. Self-determining action is therefore impossible. Moreover, empirical social science is philosophically justified only via a priorism, either Cartesian or dialectical. In sum, empirical science, like a priorism, presumes an objective, impersonal reality imposed on actors. This means liberation is once again in the hands of scientists, who create social conditions that generate true freedom, which is determined by a priori preconceptions. Empirical social science breeds technocratic dictatorships. In capitalism, technocrats hired by corporations and the state reinforce private property, liberal institutions, and consumerism. In socialism, Party control is technologically reinforced through a propaganda apparatus. In neither is self-determining freedom a viable prospect.

After examining the historical consequences of a priorism and empiricism, some Marxists see truly emancipatory social theory—manifest in liberating actions—growing only from a radical subjective critique of encrusted values and institutions. One disturbing fact must be faced by capitalists and Marxists: Reflective subjects decide for themselves what to believe. Truth lives only in cognition, which impersonal social theory will inevitably mute. A priorism and empiricism, therefore, deceptively rationalize the transferring of actual decision-making power from subjects to an elite cadre. The emancipatory rhetoric of a priori and empirical Marxism screens a real commitment to autonomous truth, which in appropriate conditions is crammed down the throats of unenlightened citizens— irrespective of numbers or working-class credentials. Only by redesigning Marxism, eliminating "objective" realities that rationalize dictatorship, will it survive as a workers' movement. Marx's socialist utopia is manifest in the reflective experiences of its beneficiaries. As scientific theory and revolutionary praxis, Marxism must be philosophically justified experientially.

PHILOSOPHICAL EXPERIENTIALISM

This is no easy task. How does one evolve an objective social science from a subjectivist epistemology? The knowledge I reflectively constitute is no more convincing for you than yours is for me. While a priori knowledge reflects a transcendental truth and empiricism generates artificial disciplinary boundaries to accumulate valid data, experientialism apparently repudiates the "objectivity" of society and the possibility of ever discovering scientific social knowledge.

The philosophical gestation of experientialism began with Martin Luther's heretical theology, which situates divinity in the conscious perceptions of God's flock and advocates faith through personal fulfillment rather than an overbearing Church hierarchy. Radical individualism germinated in sixteenth- and seventeenth-century social theory, and finally blossomed in the unlikely person of Thomas Hobbes. Hobbesian man is alone and isolated, living as a self-interested ego. The validity of everyday knowledge is measured solely by its practical utility in increasing the life chances of competitive subjects vying for society's limited resources. The implications, unintended by an author entrenched in seventeenth-century rationalism, are revolutionary: Human nature is irretrievably cut from transcendental moorings, leaving truth at the mercy of self-interested subjects. Social, political, and ethical theory are no longer compelling in themselves. Their emptiness means some cruder force must keep us peacefully together, one whose rationale is the experiential need of each citizen daily threatened by death. Knowledge now meekly serves subjectivity.

John Locke's reaction is unequivocal. Experientialism serves almost no one's needs, least of all the social class sponsoring the original break with spiritualism in the name of individual liberty. Though medievalism is irreparably shattered, the concrete economic, social, and political needs of a growing middle class make some form of a priorism indispensible. Self-interest must somehow be fused with objectivity. The synthesis is manufactured by a natural truth, based on self-evident "reason," which guides egotistical individuals to peaceful, cooperative interaction. This ideal knowledge replaces the brute force of Hobbes's Leviathan, without sacrificing self-determining freedom. We assume, therefore, that experiential knowledge coincides with absolute truth, subjectivity and objectivity overlap. Society exists objectively, reflecting the natural order of things, but also guarantees each citizen the right to determine how serious participation and commitment will be.

This optimistic retreat from experientialism frames later speculations. Nineteenth- and twentieth-century liberals reiterate the bimodal world view, though phrases like "enlightened self-interest" or "basic rights" replace the increasingly antiquated "natural laws." The intent remains: human autonomy tempered by a cool, inviolable truth protecting personality and property. This promethean task distinguishes the evolution of philosophical liberalism from John Stuart Mill to Green, Hobhouse, and Rawls.

Liberals uncomfortable with a priorism are easily seduced by empiricism. Hobbes's isolated actor is a self-interested subject floating in hostile surroundings. Empiricists objectify these, and develop a method for impersonally, factually describing them. Ironically, subjectivity is also part of empirical reality, so it, too, loses its autonomy. Empiricists methodologically consume their parent, eliminating the experiential moment that inspired them, without, however, adversely affecting liberal institutions established as peons to "responsible" human freedom, hence honoring the departed by refraining from critical (subjective) comment. A transition from the liberal brand of experientialism to empiricism is painless and even respectable, affirming institutions of "enlightened," propertied freedom even while denying its syncretistic philosophy.

By the second decade of this century experientialism is known only in the mutilated forms of liberalism and empiricism. Purists like Kierkegaard and Nietzsche are dismissed by serious thinkers as romantic nihilists, inspiring some artists and unprincipled rogues, but irrelevant to the methodology of social inquiry. Significantly, subjectivism is muddied primarily by a profound fear of its economic implications, not by philosophical antipathy. Edmund Husserl strives to rescue subjectivity from a priori and empirical captors and milk existentialism for that universality it flagrantly snubbed.

Husserl's early writing probes subjective perception from a nonempiricist perspective. The problem is perplexing, for Husserl's emphasis on consciousness isolates him in a rather blatant solipsism.[1] If knowledge is actually universal, Husserl must demonstrate how objectivity occurs within consciousness and remains intersubjectively verifiable.

His account is enlightening. Because contemporary science is empiricist, scientific disciplines are now in a state of crisis, their "genuine scientific character, the entire manner in which they have posed their problem and have devised their method for [solving] it . . . becoming questionable."[2] Scientific knowledge is still attainable, but not with a method distorting the quality of subjective experiences and isolating consciousness from the perceived world. Knowledge is scientific only when scientists, and anyone else willing and capable, perceive its universality. We uncover scientific knowledge in the realm of subjective consciousness, where all we can and do know originates, not in the natural world of nonhuman phenomena. Philosophy must delve into consciousness in search of an apposite method, ultimately in search of knowledge itself. Genuine science is synonymous with philosophy, and scientific method coincides with a body of rules or procedures facilitating the ascent into reflective subjectivity. Primarily because contemporary science starts from unclarified and ambiguous premises, philosophy, to be truly, "rigorously" scientific, must leave nothing unsolved. By carefully explicating conceptual presuppositions, they are reflectively cognized, hence epistemologically valid. Philosophy is rigorously scientific by exposing universal knowledge, the nonempirical framework for empirical inquiry.

Since science is philosophically constituted, and philosophy focuses on consciousness, scientific knowledge is derived from, and verified by, consciousness. Science, in other words, is not independent of the consciousness of reflective subjects. Scientific method comprises a multiplicity of independent cognitions, all unified in the transcendental phenomenological reduction. The truths of science are linked together at their source: the universality of transcendental subjectivity. The subjective experience of universal knowledge is then communicated to others. However, communicated scientific knowledge must be identically reconstituted in each separate individual through similar reflective procedures. The method by which scientific, or "eidetic," knowledge is subjectively constituted is thus an integral part of a phenomenological philosophy of science.[3]

Husserl's quest for objectivity emphasizes individual initiative and intellect. By performing a series of intellectual procedures known as reductions, observers are elevated to successively purer states of consciousness, culminating in the universal subjectivity of the transcendental ego—the purest possible state of reflective awareness, a transcendental merging of subjectivity and objectivity. The transcendental ego encompasses universal consciousness, from where we constitute absolute knowledge, the fertile source of contingent empirical facts. Such knowledge takes the form of "*eidé,*" or essences: apodictic truths manifested in, and giving meaning to, particular factual phenomena perceived in the everyday world. Knowledge of these essences, what Husserl calls "eidetic" science, is the only means of attaining the universality traditionally associated with scientific inquiry. Transcendental phenomenology probes directly into the essential invariants comprising science's real subject matter, which live in a nonempirical reality.

Husserl's science is thus complete and unambiguous. Scientific laws are valid only when intentionally constituted by reflective egos. Universal knowledge is an aspect of the subjective constituting process. Science and phenomenology are inseparable. However, ironically, *eidé* exist prior to subjective constituting acts, somehow determining or guiding intersubjectively valid perceptions—hence defeating their own *raison d'être*. Experiential science thus has an inherent tendency towards a "supersubjective" a priorism, something sympathetic social theorists must come to terms with.[4]

Experientialism, it seems, grasps helplessly for a lifeline to intersubjectivity that will, also, nourish self-determining subjects. Marx, especially in his theory of alienation, has provided theoretical tools for a solution.

MARX'S EXPERIENTIALISM

Marx, of course, is not a phenomenologist. Neither did he struggle philosophically with the complex issues related to subjectivist social inquiry. There is evidence, however, that he believed in humanity's irreducible freedom and autonomy. Civilization, determined neither by God, history, nor impersonal market forces, progresses by free humanity shaping the future. Marx's lifework, even the later economic writings, generated a society where human initiative flourishes, unencumbered by debilitating capitalist institutions. Marxism, therefore, is really predicated on indeterminism, although Marx was also sensitive to humanity's ironic enslavement by its own institutions. In perceiving capitalism as oppressive and dehumanizing, Marx confirmed humanity's potential for self-determining freedom. If we really were, inherently, the products of impersonal forces, freedom would be unachievable, humanity's only remaining choice being which social structure to be chained to. Marx's optimism regarding the socialist future could not, logically, emerge from this bleak viewpoint. Human beings have freely created the conditions now enslaving them, and can potentially create new, emancipatory social forms. Marxism explained how and when this occurs. The putative contradiction between free humanity enslaved by its own products is nullified by Marx's concept of alienation.

Though the theoretical origins of alienation are ancient, Marx was immediately and directly influenced by Hegelianism. For Hegel, we recall, reality is absolute Mind unfolding in history, gradually becoming conscious of externalizing itself in and through productive activity. Human essence is this self-consciousness. Throughout history, humanity externalizes itself by laboring productively. Human labor, therefore, mediates a world falsely polarized into subjective and objective realms. Cultural evolution is necessarily a history of human alienation, for it records human subjects ostensibly battling objective reality—hence is also the record of human enslavement to the myth of polarized reality. True freedom depends on actors self-consciously realizing that productive activities are Mind's own creations, that is, the manipulated "external" world is not external to Mind. Authentic self-consciousness cognizes Mind's ubiquity and merges with it, simultaneously abolishing external reality and alienation. Culture and nature are aspects of Mind; hence, willful action is also objective.

Marx rejected Hegel's idealist sublation of nature. External reality is real and undeniable, an "inorganic body" sustaining organic life. "Man *lives* from nature, i.e. nature is his *body,* and he must maintain a continuing dialogue with it if he is not to die. To say that man's physical and mental life is linked to nature simply means that nature is linked to itself, for man is a part of nature."[5] Rather than abolishing externality, Marx ascertains humanity's proper natural function. Labor, our connection to nature, is not alienating if it expresses self-determining freedom. Authentic labor confirms life's objective and subjective realms, and embodies a healthy relationship between actors and environments. Humanity is not omnipotent in the sense of autonomously controlling nature, a reality that must be respected by human and nonhuman inhabitants. But neither is it a passive, determined product of impersonal laws. Within nature's objective limits, humanity intentionally transforms the world to satisfy basic physical, emotional, and intellectual needs. Although freedom occurs within nature's objective constraints, it is no less real for that, for these merely funnel creative energies into fruitful activities. Labor, creative praxis, is the quintessential human attribute, distinguishing us from nature's other, nonhuman creatures. It turns alienated only when dehumanized, that is, when devoid of freedom and creativity, and satisfying artificial needs. This occurs when humanity unintentionally produces an oppressive, dehumanizing environment that instills fallacious images naively internalized by actors who have freely forfeited their freedom.

In sum, labor is naturally intentional and self-determined, but alienated by conditions that humanity itself creates. Hegel mistakenly attributes alienation to uncontrollable a priori forces. Marx's alienation is neither inevitable nor irreversible. When humanity freely reasserts itself, it can and will creatively negate dehumanization.

All Marx's writings are basically experiential, although his strategy gradually changed. The early work describes humanity's innate, natural freedom and capitalism's inhibiting, alienating influence. Later, Marx described the actual dynamics of alienating capitalism, implicitly presuming that an enlightened working class will forcibly reestablish hegemony. The potential conflict appears only when these two are artificially separated, which was not Marx's intent. The theoretical unity of Marxism, the power of human subjects to define and shape their futures, inspired each specific work.

The *Critique of Hegel's Doctrine of the State* and *On the Jewish Question* show the bourgeois political state mythically symbolizing the general public interest while actually preserving private property, clearly favoring private over social interests. Since capitalism protects private property, the natural relationship between humanity and its world is reversed: property, ostensibly an attribute of man, becomes subject; man, by nature a free subject, becomes the object of private property. Things take on human qualities, and humanity is reified, that is, transformed into nonthinking objects, a process Marx later called "alienation" or "fetishism." The implicit assumption, more blatant in the *1844 Manuscripts,* is humanity's inherent—but ignored—freedom to define and determine its own fate. "The whole character of a species, its species-character, resides in the nature of its life activity, and free conscious activity constitutes the species-character of man." Living things act in nature to satisfy needs, hence are defined by that activity: each living thing "is . . . its life activity." Life-preserving and defining labor is determined by "species-character," which in the case of humanity is "free, conscious activity." Reflective, self-defining activity "directly distinguishes man from [other] animal life." When humanity labors creatively, it lives its potential. "Only because of that is . . . [man] a species-being. Or rather, he is a conscious being, i.e. his own life is an object for him, only because he is a species-being. Only because of that is his activity free activity." Though nonhumans also labor productively, they do so only to meet immediate physical needs. Humanity, on the other hand, labors even when free from physical need. "Animals produce only according to the standards and needs of the species to which they belong, while man is capable of producing according to the standards of every species and of applying to each object its inherent standard; hence man also produces in accordance with the laws of beauty." These laws, existing only for humanity, are intellectually created by reflective actors to guide their own activities. Hence we actively shape nature according to self-developed plans. The object of labor, then, is "the *objectification of the species-life of man;* for man reproduces himself not only intellectually, in his consciousness, but actively and actually, and he can therefore contemplate himself in a world he himself has created."[6]

Alienation appears when the freely created environment annuls inherent creative capacities. In this situation man's autonomy is negated, his "own creation confronts him as an alien power . . . his power over objects appears as the power of objects over him; in short, he, the lord of his creation, appears as the servant of that creation." Man's proper relationship with the world is reversed. Whereas he should shape reality to suit his own needs, alienation creates "an inhuman power [that] rules over everything." Humanity no longer controls its destiny. When labor is separated from species-character, humanity's natural advantage over nonhuman animals is eliminated. We are, in other words, living subhuman existences, with freedom subordinated to mere physical survival, the goal of all living creatures. Consciousness, humanity's basic life activity, turns into "a mere means for . . . existence,"[7] and the human creators of commodity-society are transformed into commodities—controlled and traded like any other manufactured item, their value decided by impersonal market forces, which treat men and women no differently than apples or automobiles.

Alienation has no preordained beginning or end. It appears when humanity suspends critical consciousness by passively accepting oppressive conditions. It will end in liberated self-consciousness and revolutionary praxis, two complementary aspects of human authenticity. Consciousness must reflectively negate its depraved, inhibiting surroundings. "The reform of consciousness consists *entirely* in making the world aware of its own consciousness. . . . It will then become plain that the world has long since dreamed of something of which it needs only to become conscious for it to possess it in reality." Reformed consciousness cognizes "tasks which can only be solved in one way—through practice." Liberated thought accompanies liberating labor, thoughtful social actions creating a more satisfying environment. "To be radical is to grasp things by the root. But for man the root is man himself. . . . The criticism of religion ends with the doctrine that *for man the supreme being is man,* and thus with the *categorical imperative to overthrow all conditions* in which man is a debased, enslaved, neglected, and contemptible being . . . ." In sum, revolutionary action is born in reflective cognition. It expresses and culminates enlightened self-consciousness, not impersonal laws. Revolution, therefore, is a self-conscious protest against perceived inhumanity, beginning from "the point of view of the particular, real individual," rather than from a magic moment when an economic class congeals.[8] It is, in other words, a self-determined, reflective project based on workers' subjectively experiencing an intolerable situation.

Like other human projects, history is determined by reflective actions, not a priori laws, and is not rumbling toward an objective impersonal destination. It is, in Marx's words, "a conscious process, and hence one which consciously supersedes itself." Social science offers no deductive formulas, for "the science of man is . . . itself a product of the self-formation of man through practical activity."[9] A priori and empirical social sciences, by establishing validating criteria independent of actual experiences, are remnants of bourgeois obfuscation, perpetuating the myth of human helplessness in the face of autonomous laws—even laws guaranteeing proletariat revolution. Marx's concept of alienation presumes, first, that actors are inherently capable of self-determined action; and second, capitalism generates servile, passive, routinized behavior. By these criteria, a priori and empirical Marxism are symptoms of an alienated life-style, not its revolutionary critique. Neither defines human freedom as self-determining action, and both see history moved by objective forces that are cognized and actively expressed—but not substantively altered. Marx's social science is knowledge of humanity's self-formation in time, analyzing events in terms subjectively meaningful to free, reflective social actors. It is revolutionary in connecting reflective cognition with a creative act establishing humanized socialist institutions. It is indeterminate in rejecting a priori or empirical timetables for capitalism's demise. While unlikely that humanity will remain forever in its current state of unthinking apathy and while capitalism grows more blatantly exploitative, still we can never be certain precisely when—or even if—emancipatory action will occur. "History does nothing. . . . It is men, real, living men, who . . . possess things and fight battles. . . . History is nothing but the activity of men in pursuit of their own ends."[10]

The German Ideology marked a tactical turning point. Although experientialism had not substantively diminished, Marx was less concerned with humanity's inability, in capitalism, to control its destinies intentionally.[11] Alienation became the unadvertised background for a more empirical examination of capitalism. Economics provided a new perspective on the same human reality. Prior to 1846 Marx philosophically measured everyday experiences in capitalism, finding them deformed and inauthentic. Now Marx translated philosophical critique into a science that factually substantiates humanity's fall into inauthenticity. But Marx presumed that economic phenomena are crystallized forms of human praxis. His concrete analysis demystifies classical political economy by establishing the material substance of abstract market principles. Human activities, Marx implied, have economic consequences, which in capitalism obscure the human activities. Marx froze and dissected capitalist economic processes to reaffirm their human origins and, correlatively, humanity's ability to transform what it created. The objective, factual, nonphilosophical style of Marx's mature work tricks orthodox disciples who ignore the early writings. Capitalism's essential feature is not poverty, oppression, or class struggle—all verifiable aspects of bourgeois life—but the loss of authenticity. By explaining how capitalist production dehumanizes, humanity actively mobilizes a society of "freely associated men . . . consciously regulated by them in accordance with a settled plan."[12]

Major economic concepts outlined in *Grundrisse* and *Capital*—the labor theory of value, money, constant and variable capital, surplus value, profit, and so on—are actually forms of social praxis. These scientific works demystify reified, fetishized activities with concrete empirical analysis. Marx, in other words, did to classical political economy precisely what he had done earlier to Hegel: purged abstractions that obscure the human origins of society and emasculate humanity's potential. The early philosophical anthropology is implicit in the later scientific critique. Marx's description, in *Grundrisse,* of labor as "the self-realization and objectification of the subject, therefore real freedom," could as easily have been written in the *Manuscripts.* The former, however, analyzes actual dynamics of alienated labor, while the latter describes the theoretical dimensions of authenticity. They are complimentary approaches to the same human subject matter.

Only man, among all forms of life, "starts, regulates, and controls the material reactions between himself and Nature," appropriating Nature "in a form adapted to his own wants. . . . [W]hat distinguishes the worst architect from the best of bees is this, that the architect raises his structure in imagination before he erects it in reality."[13] History is made first in the reflective minds of human actors and then in self-determining praxis. A priori and empirical Marxism perverted Marx's central, truly revolutionary insight.

EXPERIENTIAL MARXISM

Although experientialists can argue that Marx reestablished the social hegemony of free actors, it is ludicrous to contend that he was a phenomenologist or even would have been one had he known what phenomenology was. Marx was more interested in deflating bourgeois society by exposing its debilitating influence on workers and hence dealt primarily with objective social forces rather than subjective experiences. Moreover, by shunning philosophy, Marx managed to ignore the putative contradiction between self-determining freedom and science, two principles he squarely supported. Consequently, despite a sincere and lifelong concern for human emancipation, Marx would have considered subjectivism a bourgeois fantasy. Indeed, non-Marxian subjectivism—cynical, irreverent, but basically quietistic—fits neatly into bourgeois social life. Experiential Marxists, however, sublate a quintessential bourgeois philosophy, deriving an intersubjectively meaningful subjectivist approach to social inquiry and action. They strive, in other words, to resurrect Marx's unacknowledged subjectivism, drawing its heuristic potential for socialist revolutionaries.

Phenomenology and Existential Phenomenology

Husserl believed that we subjectively perceive objects and events by cognitively "opening" toward them, intending them with conscious awareness. Everything associated with the "external world" originates in this perceptual process. "Reality" is thus generated by consciousness; hence, we cognitively filter it through socially derived values and feelings. Individuals experientially define the world and determine their futures. Scientific "objectivity" is an illusion, a product of observers' estrangement from their own perceiving processes. Whatever exists has its "being" in consciousness. Nevertheless, valid intersubjective knowledge exists, but must be constituted individually by a purified consciousness—the transcendental ego—whose universality transcends subjectivity. Science encompasses nonempirical essences that in the everyday world are perceived as contingent facts. Husserl's analysis of the common, nonpurified, lived-in world—the *"Lebenswelt"*—clearly presumes this philosophy of science. Logically, *"eidé"* are the only conceivable criteria of objectivity in a philosophy based on the primacy of consciousness. However, these also transform transcendental phenomenology into idealism. Experiential Marxism carefully prunes a priori concepts that contradict the spirit and intention of a subject-oriented epistemology.

It begins by defining terms. The subtle but important distinctions between existential and Husserlian brands of phenomenology reveal new and potentially fruitful avenues to social theory.

Whereas Husserlian phenomenologists focus solely on conscious experiences, existential phenomenologists believe that existence, not consciousness, is the proper subject matter of phenomenology. Human beings do consciously perceive reality, but consciousness is generated by a more foundational realm: existence. Phenomenology, dealing only with consciousness, is a key unlocking hidden essential structures of existence. In brief, orthodox Husserlian phenomenology seeks accurate philosophical knowledge of conscious, sentient human beings. Existential phenomenology wants to know what being is and how we consciously philosophize within it.

Husserlian phenomenology, emphasizing consciousness, risks solipsism without justifying the scientificity of its findings. Hence, it generates a philosophy of science and a problem logically solved only through transcendentalism. Existential phenomenology, on the other hand, argues with nonsolipsistic knowledge but does not proffer a social scientific method. By describing how people *can* consciously act, rather than how conscious people act, existential phenomenology escapes the impossible task of finding criteria of objectivity among self-determining subjects. Existential ontology describes the objective being which philosophically accounts for subjectivity, that is, "which makes reflection itself possible."[14] In doing so, it avoids solipsism without diluting the uniquely subjective quality of human existence.

Finally, while Husserlian and existential phenomenology both faithfully describe consciously experienced phenomena, being—the latter's subject matter—is prior to consciousness, hence not susceptible to phenomenological description. It presents itself to consciousness when we reflectively interpret phenomenological facts. Existential phenomenology adopts this "hermeneutic" method to supplement Husserl's strictly descriptive technique.

These existential alterations of Husserlian phenomenology eliminate the latter's irresolute subject-object tension, the cause of Husserl's idealism, without violating principles distinguishing phenomenology from other approaches to knowledge: the epistemological priority of reflective experience in formulating essential—not contingent—knowledge. Most experiential Marxists concur that nonidealistic phenomenological social theory must grow within the ontological borders of existential phenomenology, toward which we now turn.

Existential and Social Ontology

Husserlian phenomenology rejects the traditional Cartesian dichotomy of mind and matter by directly associating consciousness with the object it is conscious of.[15] Existential phenomenologists extend Husserl's idea of intentionality, characterizing structures of existence, not merely mind. Being, in other words, is intentionally positioned toward space and time. This key existential phenomenological thesis, ontologically interpreting Husserl's intentionality, provides experiential Marxism with an alternative, revolutionary phenomenological method.[16]

As Beings-in-the-world, we are open to socially sanctioned values, attitudes, and behavior—an objective pattern that is integrated into our subjective lives. We either automatically obey, sacrificing free actions, or choose a relevant, self-determined response. Empirical method explains only the first category of social behavior, that is, mundane, routinized tasks naively accepted and performed. Existential phenomenology, on the other hand, explains what a particular society means to inhabitants and what each citizen, potentially, subjectively reacts to. Human existence as Being-in-the-world means that actors are inconceivable without social environments. Social ontology reveals the intersubjective world that is part of being and the context for our free actions.

Society consists of people sharing universally approved values, attitudes, and behavior patterns. Although itself insensate, it does consist of actors unified by shared rules, hence reflects the human quality comprising it. Just as individuals are "beyond themselves," ontologically open to time and space, society—many individuals living together in shared conditions—is also "beyond itself." It transcends temporal and spatial limits, living as the reciprocal interaction of several factors: history, current events and behavior; physical resources, institutions, structures, and processes; ideals, values, expectations, and goals for the future; and a world environment where all these take shape. These interacting social dimensions collectively comprise a dynamic totality defining each separate component. Society is now its past, future, and worldly interactions.

Existential phenomenology critically rejects Cartesianism, which dichotomizes reality into mind and matter. Hence, it similarly rejects the contemporary scientific view of society as something spatially and temporally enclosed and fragmented into autonomous behavioral and institutional realms—each studied by a discipline. Society's present is not isolated from its past and future because society *is* its past, present, and future; like citizens, it is temporally open. Since human existence opens spatially as well, we cannot isolate one level of society, for example, the "political," and understand it independent of other levels. Members of society *are* the social worlds they perceive. When behaving "politically," they simultaneously express all the social relationships they encompass: one dynamically expresses and defines the other. The "here" and "now" coinciding with physical bodies does not explain social reality. Particular events cannot be isolated from others present in a shared social world or cut off from the past and future.[17]

An existential phenomenological methodology requires interpretive social disciplines. By reconstructing the social maelstrom from which their particular discipline emerges, perceptive observers depict society's openness to time and space and reciprocally interacting social levels.

Existential Marxism

The spatial and temporal qualities of being support experiential Marxism. Ontologically open to space, human existence is permeated by material social conditions, including the means and relationships of production. Actors are defined by objective positions in economy, society, and polity— by class, status, and power. Society is multidimensional, precluding a linear cause-effect connection between base and superstructure. Experiential Marxism surpasses orthodoxy by stressing the mediations between matter and the quality of social life, a view entirely consistent with existential phenomenology. Moreover, actions take place in a context conditioned by the past, which equally affects all actors sharing a common heritage. Consequently, existence has a distinctly intersubjective flavor, formed by shared material conditions and a common history. The worldly matter to which we are open culminates historical trends, express present conditions, and foreshadow future material forms.

Objective positions in economy, society, and polity determine the quality of experienced life. If, as Heidegger implies, this is dehumanized, alienated, or oppressed, it is because material conditions have become dehumanizing, alienating, and oppressive.[18] Thus, experiential Marxism accepts the class struggle as a significant force in capitalist society, provided we emphasize the complexity and importance of social mediations.

Clearly, existential phenomenology's "interpretive" social inquiry is also "dialectical," not in the reductive orthodox sense, but as a method for uncovering the hidden, but real, aspects of social life lying beyond empirical verification but providing the context for empirical social experiences. Dialectics thus depicts the elaborate network of social mediations shaping every material condition or social phenomenon. In the terminology of existential phenomenology, dialectical method reveals the spatial and temporal multidimensionality of social life, the way social phenomena and temporal modes interconnect. We uncover that ultimate social truth defining each factual cluster of phenomena.

Experiential Marxism, therefore, requires dialectics as a method, even though it is quite different from orthodox dialectical materialism. Experientialists perceive no "truth," no "objective" reality, existing apart from being. The starting point for philosophical inquiry is ontology, where one merely interprets evidence gathered phenomenologically. Existential ontology is not imposed on or against human existence; it is the structure allowing each of us to experience free existence. In orthodox Marxism, subjectivity and freedom are moments of a determining material totality. Phenomenological dialectics is based on existence. Since this is only experienced subjectively, the social and historical dialectic lives in and through the reflective self-consciousness of aware subjects. The totality's "concreteness" is measured and validated by phenomenological criteria. Instead of dogmatic blueprints, experiential Marxism proffers a perception of history that is useful for explaining reflective social experiences, but guarantees nothing.

EXPERIENTIAL MARXISTS

Marcuse

The glamour and controversy associated with later writings should not obscure Herbert Marcuse's prewar German beginnings, where he achieved a certain notoriety by iconoclastically synthesizing Heideggerian existential phenomenology and Marxism. From 1928 until 1933, the period of Marcuse's association with Martin Heidegger in Freiburg, Marcuse published fifteen essays and a book on Hegel intended as his *Habilitationschrift.*[19] This work responded to the "predicament" plaguing European Marxism, that is, its inability, during a period of capitalist crisis and transition, to win the support of workers who, "objectively," are ripe for rebellion. Marcuse attributed this predicament to orthodox dialectical materialism, which belied not only the everyday life experiences of its only potential constituency, but also the authenticity of Marx himself. Marcuse appropriated existential phenomenology to articulate a critical, nondogmatic Marxism that, by reinvigorating history's subjective dimension, would attract mass support. Hence his motives were practical and theoretical. First, he tapped the increasing vulnerability of prewar Western capitalism which, especially in Germany, was experiencing a crisis of authority. A united, reinspired revolutionary workers' movement would fill the public void and establish socialist hegemony. And second, Marxism would be more theoretically compelling when purified by the real-life experiences of sentient human actors.

The most important of Marcuse's early writings is a short essay entitled "Contributions To A Phenomenology of Historical Materialism."[20] The "critical question" preceding Marcuse's examination of the Marxist predicament was "does the theoretical basis whence Marxism arises, that is, the necessity for the historical activity that it recognizes and proclaims, come from a full grasp of the phenomena of historicity?" The mere existence of this predicament indicated, to Marcuse, that materialism ignores human historicity. Marxism must now depict subjectively meaningful existence, whose fundamental quality is historicity, that is, its temporal and spatial openness. "Following Heidegger's fundamental analysis set forth in his work *Being and Time,* we will then attempt a phenomenological interpretation of historicity."[21]

Marcuse adopted existential ontology to revise Marxism critically. Human existence is precognitively open to the world, that is, is "historical through and through" and manifest in a specific "spatio-temporal context."[22] Being-in-the-world, a concept that Marcuse traces in Dilthey as well as Heidegger, embodies "the historical unity of man and world, consciousness and being"—a unity that bourgeois idealism and orthodox materialism destroy. The former presupposes an omnipotent subject, the latter determining matter. Both are a priorist. Neither grasps subjectivity's essential historicity. The temporal and spatial openness of free subjects means reality is a dialectical unity of subject and object. Subjectivity, in other words, is defined temporally and spatially while history and society are meaningless apart from cognitive reflection. Only phenomenology exposes a priorism to the reflective subject's critical glare, revealing the subtle dialectical unity of Being-in-the-world. Moreover, phenomenology renders humanity self-consciously aware of its historical and social worlds, a philosophical self-consciousness that guides meaningful praxis. Philosophy, then, is a force that influences history. Since self-determined action presumes a critical awareness of the world, actors become active historical "subjects" only by reflectively understanding history and society: "true action is again taken in as the ownmost ["*eigenste*"] task of philosophy."[23] In sum, phenomenology uncovers being's historicity, which manifests the unity of subject and object, consciousness and being, theory and praxis.

Marcuse's Marx shared phenomenology's goal of deflating a priorism through self-conscious critique. Marx implicitly recognized being's historicity when he equates "historical existence" and "authentic," "meaningful," or "true" existence. "We know only one science," says Marx, "the science of history." Hence "the world-historical existence of individuals" is "closely tied to history."[24] Historical materialism unknowingly systematizes phenomenology's belief in the historicity of being and society. Human civilization records subjects self-consciously altering material surroundings in the light of reflective cognition. Although Marx never employed the term "historicity," he certainly acknowledged it conceptually. It is humanity's temporal and spatial openness that allows societies to form. Primitive peoples shared what Marcuse calls a "living space" with historical dimensions, where individuals satisfy existential needs by laboring cooperatively. Society, therefore, exists because historical man shares a common living space and common needs that are satiated collectively. The "primary mode of historical existence"—the distinguishing activity of social man open to history, nature, and neighbors—is productive labor. The historical appearance of divided labor, intended to streamline production, fragments society into classes which "exist in, and are determined by, the primary mode of historical existence, i.e. by the mode of production." Existence as Being-in-the-world, in other words, is defined by the concrete, observable matter it embodies. The appearance in history of classes means existence takes the form of class society. The material evolution of class society changes the features of historical being, now open to and expressing a new shared material world. "The ontological relationship between existence and the world . . . is constituted in concrete historical events. . . . This we call the material content of historicity. In the last analysis, this determines existence not only factually, but also structurally." This, in Marcuse's view, does not mean base determines superstructure. Although ideology has a material content, neither exists independently. Being-in-the-world encompasses both domains simultaneously, unifying them in the actual structure of existence: "the old question whether spirit came before matter or consciousness before being . . . turns out to be meaningless. What is actually given is only historical social existence which is *both* spirit and matter, consciousness and being."[25]

Men and women are social because of historicity. While creatively surviving, they form economic classes to perform specific productive functions. Since labor is the "primary mode" of existence, these material classes determine life-styles and beliefs, prompting creative action as class members rather than isolated individuals. Society's material base produces agents of historical progress, classes cognitively perceiving their historical and social roles and acting—often violently—to make society better serve their needs. Historical materialism is based on human historicity: "The analysis of historical man has shown consciousness and its achievements to be aspects of a social and historical totality founded on concrete historical being. Even cognition does not lead human existence beyond historicity."[26]

Marcuse assumes Being-in-the-world irretrievably throws humanity into concrete matter we cannot escape. As historical beings essentially open to worldly phenomena, "everything is an endless sum of activities, one after the other, yet all inextricably interconnected and determined."[27] Since existence is a totality that unifies historical concreteness and subjectivity, it requires a method that leaves the dynamic total whole undistorted. Empirical science artificially dismembers reality and severs each part from history. Orthodox dialectical materialism reduces consciousness to matter, unifying reality with a contrived a priorism. Marcuse, however, integrates phenomenology and dialectics, creating a "dialectical phenomenology" that catches the historicity of existence and hence the evolution of society. Phenomenology depicts humanity's historicity, the concrete interconnections of things, and the material content of existence. History is formed by self-determining agents reflectively perceiving the world and acting. Dialectics, on the other hand, outlines the historical evolution of concrete matter, including the necessity of class antagonisms and the self-destructive impulse of each productive mode. Concrete history is subjectively realized by revolutionary agents whose activity fulfills perceived needs and history's material necessity. Marxist theory and praxis are authentically reunited, mimicking *The German Ideology*'s "purely phenomenological" dialectic. Influenced by Engels, orthodoxy strayed from Marx's early, correct version of dialectics to a dogmatic metaphysics. Today, it is neither Marxian nor phenomenological: It ineffectively explains reality without understanding or uniting a depersonalized working class.

Marcuse established all the basics of experiential Marxism. Existence is spatially and temporally open to the world, hence human beings—including workers in capitalism—are stained by historicity. Capitalism surreptitiously numbs human cognition and makes us servants to an oppressive productive apparatus. This mentality lives in the prereflective, naive, everyday world of capitalist wage labor. Marxism enlivens our reflective awareness of historicity—the historical and materialist quality of social existence—and simultaneously emancipates oppressed, passive workers. Free, reflective praxis culminates history's material evolution toward socialism: "the historical activity that restores authentic existence is necessarily revolutionary activity." Existential phenomenology thus annihilates its bourgeois heritage, becoming "a turning point in the history of philosophy—the point where bourgeois philosophy transcends itself from within, and opens the way to a new 'concrete' science."[28]

But Marcuse never proffered what would have been a heretical and courageous argument establishing the dialectic on subjective criteria, which, logically, is what phenomenology must do. Instead, he continually emphasized history's material inevitability, obviously afraid of straying too far from orthodoxy. "Radical action is essentially *necessary,* both for the agent and for the context ('Umwelt') where the action occurs. By its occurrence it substitutes a necessity for the suffering and for the intolerable. . . . It is neither good nor bad, but only necessary or unnecessary. . . . Nothing happens by itself."[29] While Heidegger temporarily inspires a solution for the Marxist predicament, there is, from the beginning, something abrasive about existential phenomenology's individualism, which Marcuse claimed "by-passes the material condition of historical existence," diluting history's material necessity.[30] Reality is shaped by either reflective cognition—the phenomenological position—or impersonal matter. The dialectical unity of opposites is generated by either a reflective phenomenology of existence or an objective, impersonal material totality. While Marcuse at first pretends to the former, he never really abandons the latter. This ambivalence eventually turns him from phenomenology altogether when he mistakenly argues that existential ontology overwhelms history's subjective dimension.[31] An existential phenomenologist knows that ontology only describes universal structures within which free action takes place. Marcuse, then, is unhappy with materialism but unwilling to accept the existential phenomenological alternative permanently. In the short run, he joined the Frankfurt School, denying positive epistemology entirely, material or subjective. As we know, Marcuse eventually choked on the quiescent social implications of Frankfurt skepticism. He finally settled for Freud, postulating an a priori ideal truth defining concrete matter as well as its historical subjects.

Paci

Enzo Paci's *The Function of the Sciences and the Meaning of Man*, the most important single work in the "Milan School" of radical social philosophy, generated a Marxist philosophy from Husserl's transcendental phenomenology. Paci believed that the Husserlian reduction to pure or transcendental subjectivity is the necessary first step in scientific social inquiry. The transcendental subject is consciousness open to, and indelibly stained by, "temporal irreversibility." People, reflectively living in the present, experience reality as the past reverting into the future. The essential quality of pure subjectivity is "becoming," which is experienced from an internal consciousness of time. Transcendental subjectivity is, therefore, intentional consciousness in time, what Heidegger and Marcuse call historicity. The experienced world—including intermonadic, sensible, perceptual, corporeal, and spiritual aspects—also constitutes itself in time, that is, is historical. In other words, the pure subject and the real, experienced world are both temporally open, marked by historicity. Hence, pure subjectivity generates an authentic, reflective experience of this world, not an ideal metaphysical reality. Although Husserl argues that the pure ego transcends the world, Paci suggests "subjectivity without the world contains it."[32] The authentically experienced world of pure subjectivity is Paci's "*Lebenswelt*." It is separate from the mundane world of everyday life, which occludes authentic consciousness. Only through systematic reflective self-consciousness can we smash naive, common prejudices and experience the "*Lebenswelt*." There is no conflict between subjectivity and the authentic life-world of reflective social actions: Pure subjectivity and pure objectivity correspond.

Life in capitalist society is mundane, alienating, and fetishized. On the other hand, the "*Lebenswelt*" is a reality of cooperation and understanding, where being is spatially and temporally open to all aspects of social life, including fellow humans. The "*Lebenswelt*" is a truly communist society. Historical materialism lives in each subject's desire to "become," to experience reality as the past reverting into the future. Man's "telos" (his subjective orientation toward a not-yet-realized, emancipated "*Lebenswelt*") and history's "telos" (materialism's concrete totality) are expressed in the free praxis of authentic subjects (the proletariat). Phenomenology generates a revolutionary working class. It "is no longer a science of 'eidé' in the sense of logic, but it becomes a science of human praxis whose ideal of 'eidos' is the revolutionary task."[33] Husserl's contemplative epoché is transformed into revolutionary praxis. Transcendental knowledge reveals "the capitalist occlusion of the subject and truth" and propels each subject toward socialism, where human potential can flower.[34] Marx's historical dialectic lives in the practical consequences of the transcendental reduction.

Paci analyzes transcendental subjectivity as if the results were transparently objective. Phenomenologically, the temporal openness of consciousness signifies only Paci's consciousness of the temporal openness of consciousness, unless he has actually experienced an ideal perceptual mode somehow transcending and governing each reflective activity. By throwing the transcendental subject back into society, Paci—like Hegel—presumes an ideal, metaphysical quality defining the *"Lebenswelt."* When he admits his analysis of the *"Lebenswelt"* is "an interpretation or, maybe, a correction . . . but [one] required by the coherent development of Husserlian phenomenology," he underestimates and confuses Husserl's intentions.[35] It is inconceivable, given his pursuit of "things themselves," that Husserl felt that criteria of objectivity are located within society. Moreover, why undertake a phenomenology of the *"Lebenswelt,"* as Husserl did in the *Krisis* lectures, if objectively verifiable knowledge defines social life? Despite Paci's intentions, his argument is based on, and takes us back to, Husserl's transcendentalism.[36] His students, particularly Rovatti, admitted as much in their transcendental phenomenological versions of Marxism.[37]

The two major efforts, after Marcuse, to systematize experiential Marxism were by Sartre and Merleau-Ponty.[38] Both began at existential ontology and phenomenologically constituted the social and historical worlds, deriving a revolutionary social theory from workers' reflective self-awareness.

Sartre

Jean-Paul Sartre's (1906–1980) 1946 essay "Materialism and Revolution" condemns orthodoxy as vulgar, deterministic materialism.[39] Marx's subtle inquiry into the social and historical limits on freedom is corrupted by Engels's heavy-handed metaphysics. By reducing society to an artificial system of determined relationships, Marx's perceptive dialectical blend of human purpose, activity, and institutions is exploded into pieces. Orthodox materialism is a popular social myth that is occasionally useful in creating revolutionary attitudes among oppressed wage labor, but essentially false. Its success is therefore self-defeating. Institutionalized orthodoxy inevitably stifles the revolutionary impulse it originally generated. Creative subjectivity is pummeled into mediocrity by a bureaucratic elite representing the final, absolute, irrefutable Word. An unjustifiable, false system—even one with desirable short-term consequences—ultimately censores real-life experiences, creating an opaque unity of unthinking, fearful servants.

While these ideas were already familiar to readers of Korsch, Gramsci, and the Frankfurt School, they played a significant role in Sartre's own thinking and hence the evolution of experiential Marxism. "Materialism and Revolution" was a turning point for Sartre. Its critique was based on Sartre's existential philosophy of freedom, developed in an impressive array of novels, essays, plays, and philosophical tracts published immediately

before and during World War II. But the impassioned plea to humanize
Marxism also marked an exciting new intellectual adventure. Existential
structures had heretofore hidden the social function of economic classes.
Although as early as 1934, in *The Transcendence of the Ego,* Sartre
guardedly praised historical materialism, his ensuing work moved toward
existential ontology, not economics. "Materialism and Revolution" depicts
Sartre's renewed concern for the social aspects of existence. By lauding
Marx's humanist dialectic, the dynamic unity of subjectivity and historical
necessity, Sartre began the project of synthesizing existential freedom and
working-class justice that culminated in the *Critique of Dialectical Reason,*
undoubtedly the seminal work of experiential Marxism. "Materialism and
Revolution," then, is an end and a new beginning, opening Sartre's past and
future. To understand his experiential critique of orthodoxy, we must know
why humanity is free and how this freedom embodies history's drama of
class struggle and revolution.

Being and Nothingness phenomenologically dilineates two realities: "being"
("*être en-soi*") and "nothingness" ("*être pour-soi*"). The former exists as
physical mass and is adequately observed as the object it is. Being in this
sense is static and concrete. Humanity's being, however, encompasses
consciousness reaching beyond itself toward the perceived world. "Consciousness is consciousness *of* something. This means that transcendence
is the constitutive structure of consciousness; that is, that consciousness
is born *supported by* a being which is not itself." Human being, in other
words, is consciousness, and consciousness is a negation—always reaching
toward what it is not. Consequently, Sartre's definition of consciousness is
also his ontology: "consciousness is a being such that in its being, its being
is in question in so far as this being implies a being other than itself."[40]
Consciousness is "for-itself" because it is a self-initiated movement beyond
itself. The contrast with being in-itself—self-enclosed, static, and physically
determined—is obvious.

Since consciousness is beyond itself, it is self-determining, that is, essentially free to create itself. Morality and meaning are generated from being's
worldly relationships. What one stands for, one's subjectively perceived
self-image, is a function of engaged consciousness, which is always self-
determined. The quality of life is what human beings make it: existence
precedes essence. Freedom "is the unique foundation of values and . . .
nothing, absolutely nothing, justifies me in adopting this or that particular value, this or that particular scale of values. As a being by whom values
exist, I am unjustifiable. My freedom is . . . the foundation of values while
itself without foundation."[41] In *Being and Nothingness,* life is an endless,
dizzying process of intentional self-creation. Neither a priori nor empirical
laws can determine subjective existence.

Autonomous being, however, lives in a social world requiring standard-
ized modes of behavior and thinking. Existential freedom continually

battles social forces that level humanity to a common set of values and behaviors. Everyone must stop at designated corners, wait at bus stops, stamp letters, dress appropriately, communicate in shared languages, and so on. But each willful citizen also chooses values and freely decides how to act. The effect of external reality on free consciousness is what Sartre calls "anxiety." Neither sublime nor easy, life is a constant struggle to remain human in dehumanizing circumstances: "there can be a free for-itself only as engaged in a resisting world." But freedom, though limited, is not necessarily diluted. All conceivable external situations (alternately called "facticity" and "the given") are potentially transcended by reflective, free consciousness that creatively evaluates and responds. "No factual state, whatever it may be (the political and economic structure of society, the psychological 'state,' etc.), is capable by itself of motivating any act whatsoever. . . . No factual state can determine consciousness. . . ."[42] Actors neither determine external situations nor are determined by them. As beings open to the world, they choose projects and intentionally define external environments.

Unfortunately, most of us most of the time embrace the enticing numbness of universal mediocrity. It is easier to follow the crowd passively than constantly blaze radically subjective paths through unsympathetic, suspicious associates. Bad faith is inauthenticity: ignoring one's free potential, willfully denying free existence "to constitute myself as being what I am not."[43] By unthinkingly internalizing social rules we "become" a social role. Being's radical negativity is transformed into a stagnant object, and life's responsibilities are transferred onto impersonal "others," eliminating anxiety-ridden authenticity. This flight from freedom is common, even endemic, to social life, but nevertheless willfully chosen by each fallen actor.

Bad faith is generated by normal social behavior. The negativity of authentic existence is violated by the Other's gaze, which cognitively "grasps" a partner by objectifying his being. An authentic Other, possessing the inherent power to change or negate an entire relationship, is threatening, especially in institutionalized settings where frequent interaction necessitates predictable behavior. By depersonalizing or categorizing the Other, we scotch the prodigious effort normally required to understand a dynamically changing subject, and simultaneously protect ourselves from rejection. "In short, in order to maintain before me the Other's freedom which is looking at me, I identify myself totally with my being-looked-at. . . . To be other to one-self . . . is the primary value of my relations with the Other."[44] Human interaction, loving or not, generates bad faith, as partners strive to dismantle the Other's freedom and negativity.

Inauthenticity conditions the way we relate to inanimate things. After objectifying and being objectified by Others, we begin defining subjectivity with impersonal material goods, which indicates, at bottom, a desire to unite with objects in an "internal relation," a "relation of being." We live inauthentically in society by accumulating things and submerging our personalities in them. "I am what I have," declared Sartre, without clarifying how authentic people, in society, can creatively use (rather than merely have) things, in other words, keep a thing a thing.[45] Except for the "playful" activities of a few artists and scientists, most people will apparently relate to things acquisitively irrespective of historical, social, or economic circumstances.[46] Though bad faith is subjectively chosen, Sartre didn't say which social institutions encourage this choice and which don't, in effect exorcizing history and society. We are potentially free, but in society we choose subservience. Legitimizing social and historical influences on behavior would violate humanity's radical freedom to choose uninhibitedly. Hence Sartre's cursory analysis of institutions. *Being and Nothingness* inadvertantly absolutizes alienated bourgeois consciousness.

Sartre incongruously, but freely, chose a system of thought and action emphasizing objectively determined behavior. On a personal level, there was in 1946 no problem: Sartre's self-determined life project actively promoted workers' liberation from capitalist exploitation. "I know that man has no salvation other then the liberation of the working class. . . . I know that our intellectual interest lies with the proletariat."[47] The difficulty lay in integrating Marxism, his freely chosen project, into a philosophy based on self-determining subjectivity. Since materialism is false, Sartre's problematic, from "Materialism and Revolution" onward, was to redefine Marxism to take account of both existential freedom and distorting social influences, a herculean task that eventually yielded the *Critique of Dialectical Reason*.[48]

Part One of the *Critique,* also published as *Search for a Method,* sketches the relationship between existentialism and Marxism, and proposes an apposite method of social inquiry. Marxism, not existentialism, is now "the philosophy of our time." Historical epochs are marked by sets of defining material conditions that can be scientifically understood, despite being merely partial aspects of a subjectively experienced totality. Social activity, in other words, is economically and socially conditioned in history, but also intrinsic to free agents subjectively perceiving the world. Social inquiry, therefore, is necessarily interpretive, searching for hidden, nonmaterial cognitive meanings generated by objective circumstances. Society, then, is multidimensional, conditioned by dynamic, reciprocal interrelationships between different experiential levels, ranging from the historical and economic to the purely personal. Each is explained on its own terms, not by dogmatic reductionist formulas. Hence existentialism contributes to social science by explaining nonmaterial, nonobjective levels of social experience. These encompass a surprisingly broad range of activities, for Marx's major analytical categories (for example, exploitation, alienation, fetishism, reification, and so on) are "precisely those which most immediately refer to existential structures." Consequently, existentialism—"at the heart of Marxism"—replaces materialist reductionism with an awareness of human reality.[49] When combined with Marxist history and economics, it generates an invaluable scientific method.

By integrating self-determining subjects into objective Marxist categories, Sartre defines what he calls a "progressive-regressive method." While a concern for society's multidimensionality is certainly not new to Marxism, this progressive-regressive method significantly alters the existentialism of *Being and Nothingness.* Our full comprehension of subjective projects now requires inserting them into society's total movement. Existentialism alone omits this, depriving reflective action of historical and social contexts. Reductionist Marxism omits the existential project, the irreducible subjective level of historical and social experience. Humanity's existential projects mediate concrete objectivity and intentional consciousness.

Sartre identifies historical patterns that confirm Marx's hypotheses regarding the inevitability of class struggle and proletariat revolution, but does not attribute these to a priori or empirical laws.[50] History's concrete patterns are constituted only when real subjects project cognitive experiences into action. The dialectic is not enclosed and self-perpetuating. Like existence, it is defined by negativity and change, constantly disintegrating and re-forming as it stays open to the future. Its final destiny is determined by intentional projects occurring in concrete milieus inherited from the past. Sartre challenges orthodoxy to justify itself and responds that it can do so only by introducing a determining, reductive metaphysic. "It is necessary to choose. In effect: either we reduce everything to identity . . . and we make of the dialectic a celestial law which imposes itself in the Universe, or metaphysical force which by itself engenders the historical process . . . or we restore to the individual man his power to go beyond his situation by means of work and action. This [latter] solution alone enables us to base . . . [historical] movement . . . upon the real."[51] History's dialectic is generated by ontological existential structures. Historical data is thoroughly human, a product of situated actions undertaken by conscious actors. Orthodoxy manifests dominating social institutions that pulverize human subjects into a pliable mass. Humanity denies itself by unquestioningly serving a cadre of Party metaphysicians.

Both capitalism and orthodox materialism enslave. Humanity must somehow transcend exploitative free markets as well as totalitarian Parties, a task achieved only when it chooses to transform society radically according to a subjectively relevant emancipatory project. This, of course, was Marx's prime goal, hence revolutionary Marxism fulfills existentialism. A successful proletariat revolution embodies the full realization of each worker's existential freedom.

The *Critique* examines the extent to which dialectical reason makes history intelligible, that is, "the heuristic value of the dialectical method when it is applied to the human sciences."[52] It depicts structural links between individual praxis and the dynamic historical and social totality.

A proposed second volume would trace these structures in history, thereby concretizing the *Critique*'s rather abstract discourse.

Sartre connected *Search For a Method* to the remaining *Critique* with the concept of totalization.[53] To an untrained, insensitive eye, human actions appear to be unrelated events that are satisfactorily explained with unilinear empirical correlations. Analytical reason, epitomized by the empirical sciences, does, in fact, explain a limited scope of nonreflective social phenomena, in which actors passively react to external stimuli. But it is pitifully useless in explaining conscious, reflective social action, or describing why social behavior turns inauthentic. Individuals act socially to realize a project *and* produce a "totality," that is, a collective, "inert" social product. Totalization, therefore, is the process by which subjects purposefully manipulate environments to produce collective consequences. As individuals totalize their actions, these are totalized by others' acts. Each subjective project, then, lives in a social field of others' totalizations. Actors, ontologically open to the world, are aware of this field and reflectively use it to guide behavior. Hence, social action blends subject and totalized object. An existential project, which in *Being and Nothingness* occurred *within* a "situation," now *includes* that situation as a necessary aspect of itself. The action "means" more than either existentialism or materialism, separately, can fathom. Moreover, empirical facts are meaningless apart from the empirically nonverifiable existential projects organizing them. These, in turn, are defined by the perceived totality. Dialectics alone captures these volatile interconnections between a purposeful totalizing act and its arena of totalizations. Dialectics also confirms and expresses the openness or negativity of existence: Subjects are "active" products of the world, as well as "passive" totalizers. The world, history, and others are all manifest in free projects.

In *Being and Nothingness,* anyone, even a monarchist, could be authentic. The *Critique* dispels this relativism by binding each totalized project to history, where intersubjective patterns unify the multiplicity of subjective projects into a single global tendency. History is immanently moved by a single totalization that connects separate projects. "Better," "progressive" projects support this tendency. Observers discern truth from falsity by engaging history, assimilating its "totalization in process." All totalizing projects, even those producing "science," are inextricably connected to and influenced by the social fields they totalize. Social scientists insulated from history's unifying tendencies cannot experience them, hence are incapable of understanding or explaining them as well. They produce inauthentic, naive, nondialectical knowledge, analogous to the nonreflective ideas of inauthentic everyday actors. Worthwhile science is neither value-free nor "objective." Theory and praxis, knowledge and action, dialectically interpenetrate, whether we are aware or not. Sartre felt that engaged social inquiry confirms Marx's hypotheses, thereby justifying a revolutionary working-class ethics.

Totalization, in sum, links individual actors to history without abolishing the self-defining subjective aspect of the global whole. Sartre strips the flashy veneer from bourgeois individualism by rejecting its falsely romanticized vision.

The critical experience will start out from the immediate, that is, from the individual attaining himself in his abstract praxis, to rediscover, through deeper and deeper conditionings, the totality of his practical links with others, and thereby the structure of the diverse practical multiplicities and through the contradictions and struggles among these, the concrete absolute: historical man.[54]

The *Critique* examines the structure of these mediations, starting with subjective praxis and progressing through groups, organizations, institutions, history, and the historical dialectic.

The original totalization symbolizes the structure of all future social acts and is generated by need. Elementary, precognitive physical needs to eat, breathe, drink, and find shelter throw us into nature. The human organism is precognitively "attached" to external natural things that challenge it for survival. Human need is described in *Being and Nothingness* as a "lack": a negation that living organisms must surpass. Praxis—creative labor transforming matter to satisfy needs—is a negation of the negation, the primordial dialectical movement, externalizing the human organism as it internalizes exteriority. Solitary individuals act in nature to satisfy needs, because nature has acted on them making their survival problematic: "man is 'mediated' by things to the extent that things are 'mediated' by man."[55] At first, two solitary actors act independently, isolated from each other. However, a third person, faced with similar needs to be satisfied via praxis, grasps the intentionality of the two isolated laborers, organizes the world into a coherent whole, and acts. This "totalizing third" defines the earlier disconnected acts. He "totalizes" them, acting to turn them into collective phenomena that others nearby will have to reckon with in filling their own needs. His unifying actions, therefore, guide all future social acts. The totalizing third symbolizes society. Individual actions are mediated by the social "third," which has already defined and structured the surroundings. Our openness to the world means that society is part of subjective existence. Reflective subjects are inextricably attached to society, even when they choose to negate or ignore it. Society necessarily mediates individual action.

From the primordial dialectical connection to nature emerges the inescapable fact of scarcity: There is simply not enough for everyone. In consuming needed objects, human beings threaten each other by competing for limited resources. Scarcity, in other words, pits individuals and groups against each other to avoid death, and permeates history from its beginnings. It makes the Other appear an enemy, "inhuman" and "expendable," an "Excess Third." The primordial hunt for limited goods also distorts human relations. Individual praxis is "stolen" by the Other, and its meaning modified in the competition to survive scarcity. My creative baking, for example, is noticed, financed, and eventually coopted by an Other who will use my praxis to serve his own needs—transforming my labor into dry, menial work. This process is not necessarily intentional. When several farmers, acting singly, clear their respective lands of trees to maximize productive capacity, they unintentionally create flood conditions that pervert the original acts. Scarcity is "the abstract and fundamental matrix" of the "alterity" that defines interpersonal relations and transforms active subjects into acted upon objects. By internalizing the fact of scarcity we plant the human impulse toward violence. Scarcity's negation of man encourages each life-seeking actor to (violently) negate Others. "Nothing—not even wild beasts or microbes—could be more terrifying for man than a species that is intelligent, carnivorous, and cruel, which can understand and outwit human intelligence, and whose aim is precisely the destruction of man. This, however, is obviously our own species as perceived in others by each of its members in the context of scarcity."[56]

Scarcity, then, is a basic and inescapable fact of life, not a product of capitalism. Similarly, violence is endemic to all societies—capitalist, socialist, whatever—until scarcity ends. The *Critique* focuses exclusively on society as it is, tainted with all the atrocities plaguing humanity through history. Scarcity and violence are overpowering external forces, "standing behind" or "conditioning" historical evolution, not merely two of many factors (for example, distribution of resources, economic development, and so on) that collectively contribute to history. Sartre is thus burdened with their bleak consequences regardless of hegemonic economic, social, and ideological systems. His analysis of socialism, as we shall see, lacks the utopian optimism that usually marks Marxist theory. In a later work, Sartre tentatively speculates on life in a "socialism of abundance," where authority structures dissolve because "each individual [will have] full possession of himself. . . . [R]evolution . . . is a long movement in which power is dismantled."[57] In abundance, alterity disappears, individual and collective praxis overlap, and politics whithers away.

Classes appear in society when individuals, faced with certain scarcity of needed resources and imminent death if left to fend for themselves, collectively perform required social work and agree to limit consumption. Scarcity, of course, conditions history as the struggle of opposing classes. Historical materialism adequately describes social evolution despite ignoring scarcity's role in shaping humanity's incessant existential struggle against Others. This battle of wills, not a priori or empirical abstractions, forms classes, determines the quality of social life, and introduces the possibility of revolutionary change. Historical materialism, therefore, extends Sartre's existential analysis of social interaction in scarcity. Economic exploitation, which Marx accurately perceived, unbeknownst to Marx "establishes itself against a background of scarcity."[58]

Historical materialism emphasizes the objective component of capitalist exploitation, the unfair maldistribution of resources that produces unjustifiable scarcities within an already scarce milieu. Workers are denied the rewards of labor, while capitalists reap unearned profits. Available material goods and services, even in scarcity, frequently go unused because the market maximizes exchange rather than use value. Overproduction generates depressions rather than human relief. Potentially, capitalist production can alleviate humanity's material needs and promote the reciprocal awareness of common humanity. Instead, it maximizes competition, throwing Self and Other into a whirlpool of mutual antagonism and conflict.

Why do free actors, capable of creative praxis, passively submit to a dehumanizing social structure? Capitalism is not simply "objectively exploitative." Its citizens have "interiorized" material scarcity, generating antisocial attitudes and behavior. The consequences of willfully emphasizing the Otherness of fellow men and women are alienated, reified relationships marked by fear, anxiety, and an unwillingness to see Others as anything but objective antagonists. In the mad capitalist race to produce and consume material wealth, we lose our own humanity as well, living *for* commodities rather than using them to live authentically. Inorganic products penetrate psyches and condition actions. Although workers productively manipulate machines, the machines actually determine what and how we produce.

Individuals in history interiorize scarcity, creatively produce goods needed to survive the battle against objectified Others, and eventually are obsessed with these products—negating their own humanity. The multiplicity of actors' praxis is transformed into an anonymous crystallized collective praxis, beyond the planned control of any particular actor. Such collectively produced processed matter—material and intellectual—is called the "practico-inert." As a residue of praxis it epitomizes humanity's inherent existential freedom. Ironically, however, it transforms free people into passive, determined cogs. The practico-inert is "the domination of man by worked matter," making him "a product of his product." "His free activity, in its freedom, takes upon itself everything that crushes him. . . ."[59] Free humanity is imprisoned by its own products, which are created by everyone and no one. By impersonally dictating appropriate behavior, the practico-inert reinforces the alterity of isolated, fearful subjects. Actors become interchangeable, atomized things defined by reified groups, or "series." Hence a series is a passively unified group of actors, rationalized by the external object that conditions it. When queueing at a bus stop, for example, passengers are interchangeable, for everyone's isolated behavior is unthinkingly determined by the same social rule that, ironically, originated as a creative, subjectively meaningful response to a real need. Listening to the radio, buying a newspaper, driving to work, laboring at a desk or assembly line, marrying, starting a family: each conditioned action performed identically by relevant series members. The practico-inert lives in the vast scope of predictable behavior characterizing members' everyday life experiences and is gestated by any nonabundant society—capitalist or socialist. What distinguishes capitalism's practico-inert is its quality of reinforcing unjustifiable scarcities and overemphasizing antagonistic, fearful human relationships.

Marxist history and economics correctly discern history's rationality. Class struggles and revolutions have always occurred, and ample evidence now exists that capitalism, too, is a means of production that will not survive the contradictions between its classes. Orthodox Marxism wrongly believes that this rational pattern reflects immutable material laws. Actually, actors are willful and free but also wed to a totalized social milieu. Proletariat revolution becomes immanent when workers cognize their self-determining potentials and project this freedom into revolutionary acts. Revolution lives as negativity, that is, as unfulfilled human freedom—the same freedom that once built capitalism on the ashes of medievalism. By ignoring the historical function of praxis, orthodoxy misinterprets the origins and nature of capitalist oppression, and defuses a potentially disruptive situation.

The rebirth of individual freedom occurs only in a group. Beings open to the world live inauthentically as isolated, autonomous individuals in alienated capitalism. Only when they willfully act in a shared reality do they live the truth of existence. Our ontological openness to Others and the world means that real freedom occurs in and through humanity and manifests collective praxis. Serialized groups, however, institutionalize passivity. As alienated collectivities they only reinforce human atomism. Groups, on the other hand, are organically solid, members identifying with victimized Others and sharing a common project.[60] When individuals find the mechanical structure of the series intolerable, they coalesce into a sudden fraternity of self-conscious actors—a "group-in-fusion." Its projects are collectively synchronized but not passively obeyed. Individual praxis is nourished by group praxis. Actors creatively partake in a united collectivity realizing a shared project, comparable in some ways to a well-coached, disciplined, motivated football squad. Such common action dissolves the Otherness of the series: every Other becomes the same in and through the group's shared efforts; each individual is free in and through the action of everyone. In a series, the totalizing third—society—is outside the individual, mediating his particular actions. But in genuine groups the third is internal, perfectly synchronized with each participating praxis. Every actor consciously wills the Other's reflective project.

This is the domain of authentic freedom, and appears only when actors self-consciously reject the serialized environment and labor together for meaningful change. Groups-in-fusion collectively tear down an institution-alized milieu and its hegemonic elite, replacing it with a self-governing group whose interests and goals are unique to itself. Normally, an economic class is a collection of serial groupings externally constituted in the practico-inert. Though in close physical contact, workers are naively isolated from Others and the social totality and passively directed by exploitative eco-nomic and social forces. When discontent spreads, however, they discover themselves as a class-in-action, a fusing group, and work collectively—in total individual freedom—to eliminate capitalism's unjustifiable scarcity. A socialist revolution is a free act by a fused collectivity seeking more humane living conditions. Workers' Parties are the totalizing third for a united revolutionary proletariat. They must precipitate the transition from a serialized to a fused working class. History's rational dialectic is restored with working subjects reflectively expressing and defining objective matter.

Groups-in-fusion live only in members' free actions and regress into seriality as these atrophy. Ironically, this potential dissolution of authentic-ity always lurks in fused groups because of each member's ontological freedom to choose—the same freedom which dissolved the original series. To avoid disintegration, the group-in-fusion may institute an "oath," or pledge, establishing a collective force with juridical-like powers to prevent a breakdown of individual commitment: a negation of individual freedom which preserves the common, authenticating praxis. With the oath comes "fraternity-terror," the enforcement power exercised by each over all and all over each to maintain the group's commonality.[61] It replaces the group's fear of a common enemy that had originally congealed them in a shared revolutionary praxis. The fraternity-terror is a violent refusal to be subjected to the violence of external scarcity and the threatening return to seriality. Groups need such protection because members can voluntarily negate the group by withdrawing. Group freedom is dialectically transformed into a liberating, violent reign of terror.

In an age of scarcity, the group's battle against seriality resembles Don Quixote's contest with the windmill. Material goods must still be produced, and members gradually realize that their separate long-term survival is threatened by the Other. To survive, the group must perform necessary economic and social functions that, in a technological milieu, require specialization and division of labor. Specialized subgroups are organized, each ignorant of others' actions and divided by ominous conflicts of inter-est. Group members desperately reassert their collective unity by creating a totalizing "sovereign" (for example, a state or leader) who coordinates and unifies the specialized subgroups. Directing an increasingly complex and divided group, the sovereign turns into a domineering and alienating external third. "Under the pressure of exterior circumstances, the common individual tries to become a thing which is held against other things by the unity of a seal; the model for the institutional group is the forged tool." The sovereign, enamored with new-found power and fearing the fused group's impulse for self-direction, guarantees their obedience and powerlessness by reinforcing social atomization. A governing bureaucracy sprouts. Alterity and fear return. The group-in-fusion's success guarantees the reappearance of a new practico-inert, with new serialized living experiences. The historical stage is thus set for a revival of fused groups and revolutions. Through it all, one depressing truth lives: Although the fused group is the only true model of self-governing democracy, it cannot survive for long in scarcity. Orthodoxy's "dictatorship of the proletariat" is an absurdity, "a bastard compromise between the active, sovereign group and the passive seriality."[62]

Despite history's putative circularity, an inherent historical trend does exist leading to ever higher degrees of economic and social equality even within serialized society. Sartre also uses the dialectical categories as tools for deciphering the historical totality's intelligibility, "set[s] of formal contexts, curves, structures, and conditionings which constitute the formal milieu in which the historical concrete must necessarily occur." The categories dialectically interpenetrate. Concrete social problems are complex interactions of groups and series, leaders and masses. The progression from serialized to fused back to serialized groupings does not necessarily occur in successive chronological stages. They may coexist simultaneously on different social levels, each comprising a partial totalization that, with others, eventually coalesces into the total whole. The working class, for example, unites many different series, each with its own subjectively internalized practico-inert. Unskilled workers, perhaps in only one industry or area, may fuse while skilled workers remain passive. Black workers may rebel and whites stay complacent. The proletariat is not a homogenized group: Every social collectivity consists of complex overlays of groups and series. Each distinct collectivity must be understood in itself before we can generalize about history, which totalizes all its partial totalities. Marxism's declaration that history is objectively "ripe" for a workers' revolution is generated from a "regressive" analysis of society's synchronic structures (that is, an analysis of concrete series occurring simultaneously in one historical period or phrase) *and* a "progressive" examination of diachronic patterns (that is, an analysis of class phenomena as they evolve through time). Marxism must justify itself by examining dialectically how and why historical subjects have acted creatively in dehumanizing material conditions. When workers are constituted as a unitary group-in-fusion, and only then, can they initiate emancipatory social change. Dialectics explains the social and historical tendencies in which praxis has previously organized itself, hence encourages today's proletariat to realize itself and history in reflective action. Dialectical Marxism thus restores the "double synchronic and diachronic moment through which history is unceasingly totalizing itself."[63]

The *Critique* tells us how human beings interact socially in conditions of scarcity and evolves a social ontology encompassing basic social structures such as series, groups-in-fusion, organization, institutions, and collectivities. Like the early Marcuse, Sartre's experiential Marxism springs from existential phenomenology, that is, it outlines the social consequences of being-in-the-world. Although he admits the *Critique* "cannot in any way ... [hope] to re-construct real History in its development," Sartre also argued that Marx's "essential discovery" is "that work, as an historical reality and as the utilization of specific tools in an already determined social and material situation, is the real foundation of the organization of social relations."[64] Sartre, in other words, outlined an experiential historical and social dialectic and claimed that history's residue of free praxis generally corresponds to Marx's doctrine of historical materialism. Reflective praxis takes place within and is shaped by that actor's participation in the class struggle. When the proletariat revolution occurs, it will be a product of free action that is also predictable given history's inner material tendencies. Sartre assumed, and promised to prove in the nonexistent second volume that progressive-regressive inquiry will confirm Marx's insights regarding the ultimate priority of the class struggle.[65]

Merleau-Ponty

Sartre's desire to redefine Marxism experientially was shared by his colleague and arbiter in postwar France, Maurice Merleau-Ponty (1908–1961). Both were existential phenomenologists nurtured on Husserl and attracted to Marx, especially the early writings on alienation. Prior to 1950, Merleau-Ponty was more closely aligned with French communism than Sartre, whose pre-*Critique* existentialism made such an alliance inappropriate. From 1950 to 1955, as Sartre inched toward authentic social theory, their interests and activities merged, and they jointly edited a counterestablishment journal, *Les Tempes Modernes*. Unfortunately, Merleau-Ponty never wrote a grand philosophical synthesis of existentialism and Marxism, and tragically died before Sartre's *Critique* was published. Near the end, he grew increasingly pessimistic about experientially reformulating Marxism and critical of Sartre's pre-*Critique* pointers in this direction. On the eve of Sartre's boldest synthesis, Merleau-Ponty had abandoned Marxism, though not the desire to emancipate oppressed peoples. His lifework, especially sensitive to the potential dangers of all ideologies, also testifies to the enormous theoretical chasm between pure experientialism and orthodox Marxism. By acutely perceiving both sides of a complicated issue, Merleau-Ponty appeared, in the short run, immobilized and eventually dissuaded from continuing the synthetic project. Here is a case where an unusual combination of intellect and sensitivity was counterproductive in terms of the evolution of social theory. After perusing Merleau-Ponty's intellectual biography, one is prone, sympathetically, to ignore Sartre's dogmatic style and admire the steely resolve that is probably required to see this kind of problematic through to the theoretical end.[66]

There is no telling how much of Merleau-Ponty's acidic critique of Sartre is the result of personal animosity, his own growing disillusion with Marxism, or basic philosophical differences.[67] Sartre's ontology, in Merleau-Ponty's opinion, is overly Cartesian, identifying human existence entirely with subjective consciousness. By hiding in Descartes's "cogito," he was unable to join effectively existential freedom to a Marxist—or, for that matter, any other—social theory. Consequently, Sartre's (pre-*Critique*) social philosophy is nonexistent. His Marxism has no rationale other than Sartre's existential freedom to choose an illogical life project. In the long run, there aren't compelling philosophical reasons for *not* capitulating to arbitrary Party dictates and vulgar determinism. Hence, the final consequences of Sartre's free choice deny freedom altogether and inexcusably forget human creativity. Merleau-Ponty wanted to revitalize Marxism with a non-Cartesian philosophy of existence, driving a middle course between Sartre's absolute freedom and orthodox dialectical materialism, legitimizing both subjective freedom and the objective conditions within which this occurs. The *Phenomenology of Perception* (1945) outlines these new existential categories.

Emphasizing neither subject nor object, Merleau-Ponty instead examined the bond connecting subject and object, the ambiguous "inter-world" ("*entre-monde*"). Sartre's ontology was unjustifiably subjectivistic. Heidegger's universal "Being" ("*Dasein*") was overly abstract. Merleau-Ponty sought existential structures falling somewhere in between. The *Phenomenology of Perception* locates these in the human body, whose structure supports Being-in-the-world. Bodies are not the passive things most philosophers have ignored. They are active subjects—"body-subjects"—always reaching into the world. When communicating, for example, one body expresses meaning and experiences the meaning of another's, confirming the Other's existence by perceiving his body. The body's precognitive movements, expressions, positions, and activities (for example, perspiring, vomiting, convulsing, tensing, relaxing, and so on) prove it is a perceiving, as well as perceived, subject. It is open to the world, acting and reacting even before I am conscious of its being part of me.

My subjective self-perception is necessarily incomplete because it cannot grasp my body's precognitive openness. But the Other's perception of me, limited only to my body's appearance, ignores my unique consciousness. The unity of my body's precognitive connection to the world and my cognitive awareness of Self and Others, constitutes existence. Each individual is a complex unity of conscious ego and objective world. While some reify the ego and artificially detach it from reality, for example, Sartre in *Being and Nothingness,* authentic philosophy must confront life's inescapable ambiguity: Conscious beings can never fully control their identities. We are precognitively thrown into a foreign world, hence are partially unknown and unknowable to ourselves. Yet objectivism, the total and naive denial of human subjectivity, is unjustifiable. Reflective beings can, indeed, subjectively choose their actions. Ontologically, we are free. But freedom is situated and real, not entirely intentional, having "the power to commit me elsewhere, [but] . . . not the power to transform me instantaneously into what I decide to be."[68] Moreover, the body's precognitive openness means we necessarily live intersubjectively. Society is part of us even before we are aware of it, offering us objective meanings just as we inject subjective meanings into it. Humans are social subjects because our bodies are in the world perceiving and being perceived, acting and being acted upon.

Although no "historical truth" exists independent of reflective projects and meanings, these subjective phenomena manifest an "average and statistical significance." "[F]reedom modifies history only by taking up the meaning which history *was offering* at the moment in question." Actors in history are neither uncontrollably determined by conditions, nor uninhibitedly free. Always living the body-subject's ambiguity, humans can never be certain of the relative force of project and environment: "In this exchange between the situation and the person who takes it up, it is impossible to determine precisely the 'share contributed by the situation' and 'the share contributed by freedom.' . . . We are involved in the world and with others in an inextricable tangle. . . . " Freedom is in and through the world, hence in "passing from objective to subjective, it is impossible to say just where historical forces end and ours begin, and strictly speaking the question is meaningless since there is history only for a subject who lives through it, and a subject only insofar as he is historically situated."[69]

The methodological consequences of existential ontology—Heideggerian (via Marcuse), Sartrean, or Merleau-Ponty's—are similar. Actors in the world are open to history and society. Existence, therefore, encompasses historical and social factors interpenetrating in a dynamic totality. Social "levels"—economic, political, social, aesthetic, legal, and so on—are artificial, meaningless abstractions that come alive only when reinserted into their life-giving social whole. Hopelessly and irrationally attached to capitalist's material interests, empiricism ruptures reality and reifies each discipline. Empirical social science is thus unjustifiable. Marx, on the other hand, was aware of the unbreakable unity of unique subjectivity and material objectivity, and struggled, especially in the early writings, to bind them into a viable social method acknowledging the internal connection of economics and ideology. Marx's historical materialism sublates bourgeois reification, explaining "not only the economic subject, man as a factor in production, but . . . man as creativity. . . . It does not bring the history of ideas down to economic history, but replaces these ideas in the one history which they both express, and which is that of social existence."[70]

History, then, is a meaningful, dialectically interconnected totality where each aspect or level is defined by its interactions. What this meaningful totality actually means is problematic for at least two reasons. First, historical actors intentionally select projects in the context of a world in which they are precognitively immersed. As individuals, they can never be certain why and how they chose to act. It is highly unlikely that observers—removed temporally and spatially—can vicariously experience both the subjective experiences and objective conditions that would explain the free behavior. Second, each historian's freedom means that "what he calls the course of events is never anything but its course as he sees it."[71] Historiography alters periodically as history changes the way we perceive and define prior events. "There is no one meaning of history."[72] It is as ambiguous as life itself. Methods reducing history to one universal formula or reconstructing a bygone social milieu with accumulated empirical data alone are at best partial explanations and at worst pure fiction.

Expanding "economics" to include mental and ideological motives and acknowledging history's ambiguity, Merleau-Ponty was now hard put to account for Marx's economic writings, particularly the unique role that Marx accorded society's material base. Merleau-Ponty somehow had to distinguish his own Marxist method from others originating quite independent of Marxism, such as Gestalt psychology. In a similar fix, Sartre hypothesized the ultimate priority of economics but postponed verification, leaving that for the *Critique*'s mysterious second volume. Merleau-Ponty worked harder but left the problem unsolved. Every cultural phenomenon, he claimed, is economically as well as politically, socially, legally, and morally significant. "[H]istory by its nature never transcends, any more than it is reducible to, economics." The relative importance of economics, in the *Phenomenology,* is determined factually. In every era, one order of significance dominates, and historians must espy which "fits the facts more perfectly." Marx conclusively proved economics becomes decisive only at moments of revolutionary transition—just as a sick patient is spasmodically conditioned by the "vital rhythm of his body." Hence, economics is always historically significant, occasionally determining, but usually not decisive.[73] This painfully complex formula was diluted somewhat by a more radical Merleau-Ponty, who in *Sense and Non-Sense* defined the social totality "mainly through the intermediary of the activities by means of which it assures its survival and transforms surrounding nature,"[74] that is, the dominant productive mode. While production obviously conditions history and society, Merleau-Ponty equivocated on its relative importance within the dialectical totality. He apparently interpreted historical materialism to mean that social change is economically caused but only at specified times and places—when production becomes what Althusser later called a "structure in dominance." Normal, everyday, nonrevolutionary life is defined by the totality, where economics is merely one partial, determined fragment.

Although history has no final cause, the base occasionally rises to guide us into the future. It determines, and has been determined by, history.

Dialectics exposes this complex interpenetration. *The Structure of Behavior* examines the dialectical union of the physical (physiology), vital (biology), and mental (psychology) as a unified, irreducible totality constituting the "human order" and determining behavior. Nondialectical empirical science accumulates cause-effect relationships that ignore entirely the whole's complexity, hacking behavioral studies into physicalism, biologism, and mentalism. Socially, dialectics is "a unity rich in final convergence and not a unity by reduction to a single order of reality or a single genetic schema." Social meanings are enmeshed in an irreducible, open-ended unity. Society is à dialectical complicity of opposing principles, an interplay of visible and invisible, subjective and objective, human and natural, self and other, values and facts, theory and praxis. History, we know, is neither determined by, nor determines, consciousness. The seeming opposites sustain each other in their opposition. Their "reciprocal interpenetration" provides a "field of experience wherein each element opens onto the others" in a dynamic, open world that has no final or preconceived destination.[75] "The 'subject' is no longer just the epistemological subject but is the human subject who, by means of a continual dialectic, thinks in terms of his situation, forms his categories in contact with his experience, and modifies this situation and this experience by the meaning he discovers in them."[76] The elements in each putative opposite—for example, love-hate, fact-value, thought-action, subject-object—are internally linked to each other and externally attached to other antagonistic pairings. What results is an incredibly complex series of interactions that simultaneously constitute the whole and are conditioned by it. Dialectics "is in principle a thought with several centers and several points of entry," assimilating real individual, social, and historical processes.[77]

Though society is dynamic, open-ended, and ambiguous, it is not a chaotic world lacking rules or system, "where at any moment angels become devils and allies friends." Merleau-Ponty, at least before 1955, carefully disentangled dialectics from relativism. Trained dialecticians situate themselves historically and choose values and policies freely rising to history's surface. History's inherent logic, Sartre's "tendency," is the criterion of ethical behavior and social progress and hence must be obeyed: "It is this absolute within a surrounding contingency which constitutes the difference between Marxist dialectic and vulgar relativism." Though all law terrorizes because it excludes and punishes certain activities, all terror is not justifiable. Only historically "progressive" terror—terror that eliminates terror by advocating humanist revolution—is ethical. Merleau-Ponty presumably accepted Marx's analysis of class antipathy, revolution, and the broadening base of social power and human fulfillment. In 1947 Merleau-Ponty assumed that a successful workers' revolution will initiate a "truly human coexistence" and is strongly indicated by observed patterns of feudal and capitalist evolution. Revolutionary Marxism "is *the* philosophy of history and to renounce it is to dig the grave of Reason in history. After that there remain only dreams or adventures."[78]

Neither Sartre nor Merleau-Ponty historically verified Marxism, illustrating how free actions, in specified conditions, have always taken the universal forms of class struggle and revolution. Sartre was increasingly confident of its plausibility, hence eagerly participated in the French working-class struggle, occasionally even cooperating with a philosophically primitive Communist Party. Orthodoxy advocates "correct" goals, though for the wrong reasons. Merleau-Ponty, on the other hand, magnified the potential conflict between a nondeterministic existential dialectic and orthodox dialectical materialism.

His cynicism evolved gradually. Like Sartre, he castigated Soviet communism as a devious, unending, reductionist, dictatorial nightmare, a regime that kills all semblance of individuality.[79] Contrary to orthodoxy, revolution is contingent on human cognition and praxis, its expected date "written on no wall nor any metaphysical heaven."[80] "I am never in my heart of hearts a worker or a bourgeois, but a consciousness which freely evaluates itself as a middle class or proletarian consciousness. . . . Revolt is, then, not the outcome of objective conditions, but it is rather the decision taken by the worker to will revolution. . . . "[81] Revolutionary parties must respect reflective individuality, which encompasses "a network of human will and economic fact." They must acknowledge spontaneous life experiences and reflect popular will, for "the sense of the masses is always true."[82] Orthodoxy, reductionist and nondialectical, is unwilling and incapable of achieving these goals. It requires a life-giving infusion of existential phenomenology.

By 1955, however, a less sanguine Merleau-Ponty wearily admitted "the politics of philosophers is what no one practices. . . . [Philosophers] simply do not know what politics is all about."[83] Truth and humanitarianism dissipate quickly in the vicissitudes of practical politics. History's dialectic thrives on opposition and freedom. As the aura of revolutionary excitement paled under Stalin's bloody boot, Merleau-Ponty opined that political success, not just philosophical vulgarity, perverted Marx's dream. Revolutions solicit total loyalty from every participant. Opposition is terminated as patriotism settles heavily on everyone, shrouding free thought and actions. "It is no accident that all known revolutions have degenerated: . . . [A revolution] betrays and disfigures itself in accomplishing itself. . . . Revolutions are true as movements and false as regimes." Only the impractical and naive continue hoping for a revolutionary regime that cultivates subjectivity: This thoughtless humanism inhibits political success in the first place. Successful Marxist regimes, predictably, are reductionist. As political movements, they "respond to adversity either by means of terror exercised in the name of a hidden truth or by opportunism; in either case, the dialectic wanders from its own line."[84] Though heuristically useful for academics, Marxism "is certainly no longer true in the sense it was believed to be true." It is now "a truth that failed," one "bursting apart" under totalitarian regimes. Philosophy must segregate theory and praxis and avoid playing "at passions, politics, and life."[85] Marxist theory requires strong doses of subjectivity and humility to resuscitate a free, open, and ambiguous dialectic. Then, perhaps, workers will recognize history's logic and act jointly for justice and freedom, not merely power. This is unlikely in the foreseeable future. Merleau-Ponty rested his immediate political hopes on a liberal parliament and the new, short-lived anti-Communist Left (*"La Nouvelle Gauche"*). Like the elder Plato, Merleau-Ponty clearly settled for the best practical regime: "thus the question arises whether there is not more of a future in a regime that does not intend to remake history from the ground up but only to change it and whether this is not the regime that one must look for, instead of once again entering the circle of revolution."[86] Philosophically, Merleau-Ponty reverted to phenomenologically discerning the mysterious *"entre-monde."*[87] On the eve of his untimely death, Merleau-Ponty praised Max Weber's "heroic" liberalism and diligently examined and perfected Weber's ideal-typical method. Revolutionary visions motivate dreamers and fanatics.

CONCLUSION

Sartre and Merleau-Ponty experientially reinvigorated orthodoxy, but neither recognized Marxism as dynamically evolving theory and praxis, lacking a materialist home base. Hence, each measured his own work by an artificially objective orthodox standard and reacted differently to the perceived gap.

Sartre made two problematic assumptions aligning his experiential Marxism with orthodoxy. First, scarcity is an ahistorical given needlessly grafted onto history's dialectic. The *Critique* ignores advanced industrial society's technological potential of eliminating scarcity or at least satisfying its citizens' minimal needs. In plentiful conditions, Sartre's depressing predictions of serialized socialism could turn into promises of mutual cooperation, affection, and fulfillment. As it now stands, the *Critique* continually flirts with Stalinism even while rhetorically upholding subjectivity. Despite ridiculing orthodoxy's "dictatorship of the proletariat," Sartre also warrants a strong sovereign to preserve the social fruits of worker rebellion with an institutionalized bureaucracy. Workers must pliantly condone such centralized direction by naively following orders. Though a transitory phase preceding the collective action of a new fused group, Soviet dictators now exonerate Party hegemony with similar promises of a brighter, liberating future.

Sartre's implicit antisubjectivism feeds on the second assumption: that history's inner tendency confirms Marx's hypotheses concerning the priority of the base. A significant dilemma is untouched. If "the only practical and dialectical reality, the motive force of all, is individual action," how can the dialectic be based, "in the last resort," on objective matter?[88] The issue is crystallized when he admits that without its a priori foundation the dialectic "promptly disappears," for it is "a reality . . . in which nobody can completely recognize himself; in short a human work without an author"— and then warns dialecticians to avoid "dogmatic metaphysics" by continually referring to "the comprehension of the living man."[89] When the potential ability to surpass matter cognitively is also part of an a priori dialectic, we can choose only what we must do anyway; we could not do other than what we chose. If subjects are necessary moments of an inclusive object, then Sartre's entire progressive-regressive method is random intellectual foreplay preceding the inevitable, predictable culmination. Who can stop a prospective "totalizing third" from enforcing objectively prescribed rules that are—or at least "should" be—subjectively meaningful and truly "free"? Paradoxically, this danger originally prompted Sartre to reevaluate Marxism. The predicament evolves from Sartre's ambition to totalize a diverse set of subjectively determined social acts concretely. He assumed that this can be accomplished without distorting the uniqueness of praxis. Hence, in practice his theories resemble orthodoxy.

Merleau-Ponty, on the other hand, so conscientiously protected experientialism that he eventually forgot the original synthetic project. The obvious fissure separating Eastern Europe's dictatorial orthodox regimes and his subjective humanism soured Merleau-Ponty's taste for Marxism. History's incomplete, ambiguous dialectic is artificially capped by extant "revolutionary Marxism"; hence, experientialism and Marxism don't mix. By naively accepting the dominant materialist version of Marxism, he capitulated before the battle was fully engaged.

While Sartre overzealously sacrificed the subjective kernel of experientialism to concretize his Marxism, Merleau-Ponty humbly rejected the revolutionary critique and became an apolitical phenomenologist. The victim in both cases is experiential Marxism, whose discernible features are a reasonable alternative to orthodoxy.

Experiential Marxism postulates the free, reflective self-consciousness of beings spatially and temporally open. A priori and empirical Marxism paint subjectivity as one moment within a determining historical object. Phenomenology defines historical progress with the free praxis of creative social actors acting in, not determined by, multidimensional environments. History's "telos" awaits the authenticating social consequences of liberating reflection. A priori and empirical Marxism equate historical and individual "telos," the necessity of free praxis and the inevitability of its historical appearance. The implications of experiential Marxism for social inquiry and action are unique.

Experiential Marxism isolates one phenomenon—capital—and probes an entire dynamic totality, imparting one possible meaning to current institutions and processes in the light of the past and future and in terms of interrelated, non-"economic" phenomena. Actors are historically conditioned by concrete material relationships, dialectically expressed in institutions, "normal" behavior, values, and ideas. To the extent that institutions, values, and behavior occlude humanity's potential for self-realizing, free social action, they are oppressive. Revolutionary liberation humanely transforms these inhuman conditions. But experiential Marxism is not objective or scientific, numbingly applied everywhere. It suffices only after surviving a rigorous examination of relevant societies, including self-consciously aware subjects creatively modifying material surroundings. Marxist analytical categories such as "capital," "class struggle," "surplus value," and so on (though not the irreplaceable dialectical method) offer one possible explanatory framework. Though it is, today, an invaluable propaedeutic to social inquiry, its usefulness may, in time, be surpassed. Moreover, the exegetical potency of these categories may fluctuate, depending on the quality of extant self-awareness and the subjective motives of significant social actors.

The validity of experiential Marxism is determined by whether aware citizens really did, do now, and will perceive and act socially as described, nonempirical factors never verified absolutely.[90] But far from turning scholars insignificant in an essentially ambiguous human condition, experiential Marxism forces them, as social educators, to "awaken" citizens to hypothesized social reality, cultivating revolutionary theories in the self-conscious perceptions of an informed public. Here, thought and action merge. Creative scholars are not isolated to insure objectivity when compiling data. They validate a theory by getting involved in the common quest, prompting naive social actors to perceive their malaise self-consciously, ultimately sculpting the future with the ideas and actions of liberated men and women. Theorists are important practically, unleashing forces of critical knowledge where they have a real material effect: the reflective perceptions of actors in oppressive material conditions. These will be democratized as the social totality is conditioned by reflectively perceived human needs. Revolution, in other words, is organically linked to liberated self-awareness, not externally implanted by a Party to mobilize naive workers. How else can one make sense of Marx's own words on the priority of human subjectivity?

NOTES

1. See Edmund Husserl, *Logische Untersuchungen.* The revised English translation is *Logical Investigations* trans. J. N. Findlay (London: Routledge & Kegan Paul, 1970)

2. Edmund Husserl, *Phenomenology and the Crisis of Philosophy* (New York: Harper & Row, 1975), p. 1.

3. Edmund Husserl, *Ideas, General Introduction to Pure Phenomenology* (New York: Humanities Press, 1931), sections 67-71 and 75.

4. See Robert A. Gorman, *The Dual Vision* (London: Routledge & Kegan Paul, 1977), pp. 108-41.

5. Karl Marx, *Economic and Philosophical Manuscripts,* in Karl Marx, *Early Writings* (New York: Vintage Books, 1975), pp. 327-78. Emphasis is his. Hereafter cited as *KMEW.*

6. The preceding quotations are in ibid., pp. 328-29. See also *Excerpts from James Mill's Elements of Political Economy (1844),* in *KMEW,* pp. 269-77.

7. Marx, *Excerpts from James Mill's Elements of Political Economy (1844),* p. 266; idem, *Economic and Philosophical Manuscripts,* pp. 366 and 328.

8. Karl Marx, "Letters from the Franco-German Yearbooks" (1843), in ibid., p. 209; *Critique of Hegel's Philosophy of Right, Introduction,* in ibid., p. 251; and "Critical Notes on 'The King of Prussia and Social Reform,' " in ibid., p. 419.

9. Marx, *Economic and Philosophical Manuscripts,* pp. 391 and 375.

10. Karl Marx, *The Holy Family,* in *Selected Writings,* ed. D. McLellan (London: Oxford University Press, 1977), p. 125. Hereafter cited as *KMSW.*

11. See Karl Marx and Friedrich Engels, *The German Ideology* (Moscow: Progress Publishers, 1976), pp. 464-65. Cf. the third *Thesis on Feuerbach.*

12. Marx, *Capital* 3 vols. (New York: International Publishers, 1975), 1: p. 80.

13. Ibid., pp. 177f.

14. Maurice Merleau-Ponty, *The Visible and the Invisible* (Evanston, Ill.: Northwestern University Press, 1968), p. 65.

15. See René Descartes *The Philosophical Works of Descartes,* trans. and ed. Elizabeth Haldane and G. R. T. Ross (New York: Macmillan, 1955), pt. I, art. xxxii, p. 346, and art. xxiv, pp. 260-82. Also pt. I, art. xxxiv, p. 347, and pt. III, arts. ccxi-ccxii, pp. 425-427.

16. Heidegger's ontology is based on structures of Being ("*Dasein*"), Sartre's on structures of conscious existence, and Merleau-Ponty's on structures of a precognitive "body-subject."

17. See Maurice Merleau-Ponty, *The Adventures of the Dialectic* (Evanston, Ill.: Northwestern University Press, 1973), p. 31.

18. Martin Heidegger, "Letter on Humanism" (1947), trans. Edger Lohner in *Philosophy in the Twentieth Century,* ed. William Barrett and Henry D. Aiken 4 vols. (New York: Random House, 1962), 3: 287.

19. The best commentary on Marcuse's early work is Alfred Schmidt, "Existential Ontologie and historischer Materialismus bei Herbert Marcuse," in Jürgen Habermas (ed.) *Antworten auf Herbert Marcuse* (Frankfurt: Suhrkamp Verlag, 1968), pp. 17-49, which describes and criticizes the usefulness of existential ontology to explain history. A more biased critique of the early Marcuse is Paul Piccone and Alexander Delfini, "Herbert Marcuse's Heideggerian Marxism," *Telos* 6 (Fall 1970): 36-46.

20. This article first appeared in *Philosophische Hefte* 1 (July 1928), "Special edition on Heidegger's *Being and Time,"* pp. 45-68. It is reprinted in *Telos* 4 (Fall 1969): 3-34.

21. Ibid., pp. 3 and 4.

22. Marcuse, "Das Problem der geschichtlichen Wirklichkeit: Wilhelm Dilthey," *Die Gesellschaft* 8 (1931), pt. I, p. 362; and "Contributions to a Phenomenology of Historical Materialism," *Telos* 4 (Fall 1969), p. 25. See also ibid., p. 7.

23. Marcuse, "Das Problem der geschichtlichen Wirklichkeit: Wilhelm Dilthey," pp. 365 and 367. See also Martin Heidegger, *Being and Time* (New York: Harper & Row, 1962), p. 449.

24. Cited by Marcuse in "Contributions to a Phenomenology of Historical Materialism," p. 7.

25. Ibid., pp. 30, 25–26.

26. Ibid., p. 10.

27. Ibid., p. 6.

28. Ibid., pp. 20 and 12.

29. Ibid., pp. 17–32.

30. Ibid., p. 21.

31. See Marcuse, "On the Problem of the Dialectic," trans. Morton Schoolman and Duncan Smith, *Telos* 27 (Spring 1976), esp. pp. 23–24

32. Enzo Paci, *The Function of the Sciences and the Meaning of Man* (Evanston, Ill.: Northwestern University Press, 1972), p. 35. This entire argument is contained in pt. 1, pp. 3–40. See also pp. 93–94, 118–20, and "Sul problema della interosoggettivitá," *Il Pensiero* 3 (1960): 291–325.

33. Pier Aldo Rovatti, "A Phenomenological Analysis: The Return to the Subject and to the Dialectic of Totality," *Telos* 5 (Spring 1970): 161.

34. Paci, *The Function of the Sciences and the Meaning of Man,* p. 323. This argument is derived primarily from pt. 3, pp. 289–450, though Paci's analysis of the nature and function of the sciences is on pp. 41–288.

35. Ibid., p. 37.

36. Fred R. Dallmayr, "Phenomenology and Marxism: A Salute to Enzo Paci," in *Phenomenological Sociology: Issues and Applications,* ed. George Psathas (New York: Wiley, 1973), pp. 328–30, concurs. Numerous quotations could be cited here as evidence. See, for example, Paci, *The Function of Sciences and the Meaning of Man,* pp. 88, 98, 100, 122, 130–36, 354, 383, 442, 445.

37. See Rovatti, "A Phenomenological Analysis: The Return to the Subject and to the Dialectic of Totality," p. 171; and Paul Piccone, "Dialectical Logic Today," *Telos* 2 (Fall 1968): 65–66.

38. Tran Duc-Thao's "Marxisme et Phénoménologie," *Revue Internationale* 2 (1946), esp. pp. 176–78, phenomenologically analyzed the superstructure, tentatively requesting a subjectively revitalized Marxism. He recanted in *Phénoménologie et materialisme dialectique* (Paris: Minh-Tan, 1954), calling phenomenology an abstraction and reverting to materialist orthodoxy.

39. Jean-Paul Sartre, "Materialism and Revolution," in *Existentialism Versus Marxism,* ed. George Novack (New York: Dell, 1966), pp. 85–109.

40. Jean-Paul Sartre, *Being and Nothingness* (New York: NYU Press, 1966), pp. lxxiii and lxxiv.

41. Ibid., p. 46.

42. Ibid., pp. 591 and 532.

43. Ibid., p. 81. See pp. 7 and 69.

44. Ibid., p. 446.

45. Ibid., p. 724. See pp. 706ff.

46. Ibid., pp. 513ff.

47. Sartre, "Materialism and Revolution," p. 107. Cf. his assertion: "Every man is political. But I did not discover that for myself until the war, and I did not truly understand it until 1945." "Self-Portrait at Seventy," in *Life/Situations: Essays Written and Spoken* (New York: Pantheon Books, 1977), pp. 44–45.

48. Jean-Paul Sartre, *Critique de la raison dialectique.* English translation by Alan Sheridan-Smith, *Critique of Dialectical Reason* (Atlantic Highlands, N.J.: Humanities Press, 1976).

49. Jean-Paul Sartre, *Search for a Method* (New York: Vintage, 1969), pp. 30 and 175.

50. Sartre, *Critique of Dialectical Reason,* pp. 20 and 15–41.

51. Sartre, *Search for a Method,* p. 99.

52. Sartre, *Critique of Dialectical Reason,* p. 66.

53. See ibid., pp. 45–76.

54. Ibid., p. 52.

55. Ibid., p. 79. Sartre's definition of praxis is more convoluted, but essentially the same: "an organizing project which transcends material conditions towards an end and inscribes itself, through labor, in inorganic matter as a rearrangement for the practical field and a reunification of means in the light of the end." (ibid., p. 734).

56. Ibid., p. 132.

57. Sartre, *Life/Situations,* p. 84. See also Thomas R. Flynn, "An End to Authority: Epistemology and Politics in Later Sartre," *Man and World* 10, no. 4 (1977): 448–65.

58. Sartre, *Critique of Dialectical Reason,* p. 739.

59. Ibid., p. 184.

60. See Ibid., p. 51. See pp. 345ff. Cf. Sartre's distinction in *Being and Nothingness* between the "we-subject" (that is, the fused group) and "us-object" (that is, the serialized group).

61. See Sartre, *Critique of Dialectical Reason,* pp. 405ff.

62. Ibid., pp. 606 and 661–62.

63. Ibid., p. 671.

64. Ibid., pp. 39–40 and 152.

65. Jean-Paul Sartre's *L'Idiot de la famille: Gustave Flaubert de 1821 à 1857,* 2 vols. (Paris: Gallimard, 1971), applies his method to one individual's actions in history. By itself this work does not even approach the task Sartre set for the second volume of the *Critique.*

66. Which is quite lengthy. See A. Rabil, *Merleau-Ponty, Existentialist of the Social World* (New York: Columbia University Press, 1967), pp. 75–115; John F. Bannan, *The Philosophy of Merleau-Ponty* (New York: Harcourt, Brace & World, 1967), pp. 198–228; and Mark Poster, *Existential Marxism in Postwar France* (Princeton, N.J.: Princeton University Press, 1975), pp. 145ff.

67. See Merleau-Ponty, *Adventures of the Dialectic,* pp. 95–201, and *The Visible and the Invisible,* pp. 50–104.

68. Maurice Merleau-Ponty, *Phenomenology of Perception* (London: Routledge & Kegan Paul, 1967), p. 447.

69. Ibid., pp. 450, 453–54, and 173n. See also idem, *Humanism and Terror*

(Boston: Beacon Press, 1969), pp. 95–96.

70. Merleau-Ponty, *Phenomenology of Perception,* p. 171n.

71. Merleau-Ponty, *Humanism and Terror,* p. 64.

72. Merleau-Ponty, *Phenomenology of Perception,* p. 173n. See also "The Yogi and the Proletarian," in *The Primacy of Perception,* ed. J. Edie (Evanston, Ill.: Northwestern University Press, 1964), pp. 213–14; and *Humanism and Terror,* pp. 40–44, 64–65, 94–96, and 153–54.

73. Merleau-Ponty, *Phenomenology of Perception,* pp. 173n, and 172n.

74. Maurice Merleau-Ponty, *Sense and Non-Sense* (Evanston, Ill.: Northwestern University Press, 1964), p. 113. See also p. 112.

75. Merleau-Ponty, *Adventures of the Dialectic,* pp. 69 and 203.

76. Merleau-Ponty, *Sense and Non-Sense,* pp. 133–34.

77. Merleau-Ponty, *Adventures of the Dialectic,* p. 203. See also *Phenomenology of Perception,* pp. 167–68.

78. Merleau-Ponty, *Humanism and Terror,* pp. 120, 121, 112, and 153.

79. See ibid., pp. xxiff, 14ff, 98, and 111–48, esp. p. 123n.

80. Merleau-Ponty, *Sense and Non-Sense,* p. 81.

81. Merleau-Ponty, *Phenomenology of Perception,* pp. 442–43. See p. 445.

82. Merleau-Ponty, *Humanism and Terror,* p. 112.

83. Maurice Merleau-Ponty, *Signs* (Evanston, Ill.: Northwestern University Press, 1964), pp. 5–6.

84. Merleau-Ponty, *Adventures of the Dialectic,* pp. 207 and 95. Cf. Robert Tucker, *The Marxian Revolutionary Idea* (New York: Norton, 1969), pp. 181–214.

85. Merleau-Ponty, *Signs,* pp. 9, 10, 12, and 13.

86. Merleau-Ponty, *Adventures of the Dialectic,* p. 207.

87. See Merleau-Ponty, *Signs,* pp. 14–22, and *The Visible and the Invisible.*

88. Sartre, *Critique of Dialectical Reason,* p. 361. See also "Existentialism is a Humanism," in *Existentialism Versus Marxism,* p. 82, and "Materialism and Revolution," pp. 105ff.

89. Sartre, *Search for a Method,* pp. 100, n.5, and 181. This apparent contradiction is the theme of Aron's critique of Sartre. See Raymond Aron, *Marxism and the Existentialists* (New York: Simon & Schuster, 1970), esp. p. 168, and *History and the Dialectic of Violence* (New York: Harper & Row, 1975).

90. Cf. Merleau-Ponty's observations that "as long as there are men, the future will be open and there will only be a probabilistic calculation and no absolute knowledge. Consequently, 'the dictatorship of truth' will always be the dictatorship of a group and to those who do not share it, it will appear purely arbitrary." (*Humanism and Terror,* p. 92).

7.

Marxism's "Agnostics" and "Atheists"—Critical Theory and the New Left

Truth, for a priori, empirical, and experiential Marxists, does exist and can, in appropriate circumstances, be subjectively acknowledged. They are "believers," basing theory and praxis on irrefutable, universal principles. Truth is harnessed by capable and willing subjects who become living gods, discerning reality and actively making the future.

Religions elevate doctrinal purity, truth, above life itself, justifying holy crusades that destroy life so that God's message of love and mercy can survive. Agnosticism (a doctrine asserting the relativity and uncertainty of religious principles) and atheism (the unequivocal denial of divine truth) make humanity responsible for its own behavior, reasserting the priority of human life. Some radical theorists now argue that Marxism—a priori, empirical, and experiential—has become a quasi religion. Whether objectivity lives in matter, ideas, facts, or perceptions, is less important than hypothesizing its positive existence. Marxism, like more traditional religions, evolves in history by apotheosizing revealed truth. Stalin's purges and slaughters illustrate how a hallowed doctrine ossifies and then torments nonbelievers. Totalitarian Marxist regimes have heretofore been doctrinally materialist but could as easily sprout from idealism, empiricism, or experientialism: Objective truths invariably deteriorate into reigns of "justifiable" terror. Moreover, an emancipatory, egalitarian theory has been transformed into a human hell where physical survival is its own reward. Real emancipation survives only by spurning positive truths that menacingly promise absolute fulfillment.

Marx was, for a time at least, aware of this. Marxist "nonbelievers" take seriously his injunctions against epistemology and philosophy and his emphasis on concrete processes. Philosophy mystifies and confuses, effectively blocking meaningful social change. "Truth" is not expressible in abstract systems. Thought processes generating need-satisfying activities are "true"; those inhibiting human fulfillment, "false." Since humanity's needs change in history, so will criteria of valid knowledge. At any one time, needs are conditioned by society's productive capacity, which determines how we labor and what is produced. Oppressive societies emphasize particular interests rather than general needs, generating "false" ideas; democracy productively fulfills genuine public needs, generating true, "scientific" knowledge.

Marx's logic repudiates absolute, objective, ahistorical standards of understanding and evaluating societies. But Marx was also a revolutionary heatedly advocating proletarian insurrection and hegemony. This contradiction necessitates epistemology's back-door entrance, never acknowledged but thoroughly exploited. Thus, Marx talked about "essences," material "laws" of history, the priority of historical and economic "facts," and self-determining "praxis," always seeking criteria for distinguishing "falsity" from "truth," that is, defining *what* human needs are, *how* to satisfy them, and *why* history favors socialist revolution. Notwithstanding Marx's warnings, Marxism has turned into not one but several competing doctrines, each universalizing a positive epistemology.

The Frankfurt School of Critical Theory, Marxism's "agnostics," resurrected Marx's admonitions against philosophical systems. Granted, truth may exist and social change is often justifiable. But after its "discovery" and operationalization, it ossifies and invariably bludgeons human beneficiaries. Reality is reduced to absolute theory. Marx, on the other hand, sought to pierce capitalism's artificiality and rhetoric, exposing the exploitation its workers experience daily. Dialectics catches the hidden social interconnections that, when perceived, sublate bourgeois freedom, justice, and equality. Authentic Marxism is critique, not a source of doctrinal purity, liberating humanity from false doctrines without imposing new ones. If critical relativism and impassioned passivity are the fruits of purified Marxism, then these are the least of possible evils. Authentic revolutionaries reflectively reject tired formulas that, throughout history, have exposed humanity to untold sufferings inflicted by Truth's noble armies.

New Leftists, Marxism's "atheists," accept Marx's injunctions against epistemology literally: no "truth" exists independent of, or embodied in, concrete historical behavior. Knowledge is manufactured only to serve the material needs of hegemonic interests, hence is itself meaningless. History, Marx perceptively recognized, is an incessant battle of conflicting classes, where thought is merely one more weapon. If strategically effective, it is valuable; if not, it is worthless and expendable. Orthodox dialectical materialism, the "old" Left's philosophy, is "true" only when preserving and expanding the power of Communist Party officials—and then only for them. Its reductionist materialism purposively immobilizes workers and reinforces the Party's privileged social, economic, and political niches.

New Leftists argue, on the contrary, it is less important what workers think than that they liberate themselves from bourgeois or Party oppression. Most of Marx's work is valueless, intellectual trash. Only his insights into the class struggle and the necessity of worker rebellion have any practical worth. History's endless theoretical justifications and explanations only strengthen intellectuals and their sponsors, those responsible for this profusion of nonsense. Action is what counts, not reflection. Words, ideas, or actions that encourage mass revolution are justified, regardless of content. We must fight for, not think about, freedom. The revolution will eventually be justified after it is won, with ideas that propagate proletariat hegemony.

Critical Theory and New Leftism embody the cynicism of radicals who have witnessed fascism, Stalinism, Hiroshima and Nagasaki, the cold war, the threat of nuclear annihilation, and socialist and capitalist bureaucratism. They are sensitive to the dangers of precipitate action and the hypocrisy of ideas, hence are understandably wary of universal movements promising absolute fulfillment. The Frankfurt School, having experienced firsthand Hitler's and Stalin's atrocities, absolutize caution, fearing above all the bloody excesses that always accompany revolutions. The New Left, composed primarily of young, post–World War II middle-class intellectuals who caustically acknowledge the repressive rhetoric and stagnant institutions of capitalism as well as socialism, throw caution to the winds in a frenzy of self-justifying action.

CRITICAL THEORY

Horkheimer and Adorno

Modern critical theory originated with the Frankfurt School, established in 1923 as the Institute for Social Research ("*Institut für Sozialforschung*") in Frankfurt-am-Main. Several founding members—including its first director, Carl Grünberg, as well as Friedrich Pollack and Franz Neumann—were also associated with Austro-Marxism, so there were at the very beginning overlapping interests and methods. When Max Horkheimer became director in 1931 and people like Theodore Adorno, Leo Lowenthal, Walter Benjamin, Eric Fromm, and Herbert Marcuse joined, critical theory gradually took its own identity as a distinctive and original restatement of Marxism.[1] Even today, however, no single work encompasses critical theory's major principles, methodology, and findings systematically and completely.[2] Although its meaning is the published writing of representative thinkers—which is rich, plentiful, and extraordinarily diverse—the seminal work of Horkheimer and Adorno, the only members affiliated with the institute for their entire professional careers, accurately denotes critical theory's unique approach to social inquiry and action. Their sad biographies symbolize the conundrum that critical theory became as it aimlessly followed its critical logic.

Still influenced by Austro-Marxism in 1931, Horkheimer's institute explored the complex connections of economic base, psychological development, and culture, emphasizing interdisciplinary cooperation and empirical research. The early Frankfurt School used value-free empirical research to confirm Marx's historical and economic hypotheses.[3] During the following eight years, however, in Germany and exiled in New York City, Horkheimer clearly distinguished what he called "critical" theory from "traditional" bourgeois theory and all extant interpretations of Marxism, including orthodox materialism and Austro-Marxism.

Traditional social theory incorporates the empirical sciences' Cartesianism, presuming that living and nonliving phenomena are enmeshed in a net of causal relationships deciphered by analytically fracturing reality into unilinear deductive sets and accumulating data. Horkheimer noted that scientific theorizing is always historically conditioned.[4] Empirical science is derived from and reflects contemporary social values. Science is never independent and a priori. Dominant scientific frameworks reproduce existing socioeconomic systems by alleviating or eliminating their dysfunctions. Traditional theory is thus a reified ideological category limited to empirical evidence, fueling capitalism with an expanding technology and obscuring the link between economic exploitation and bourgeois procedural democracy.

But critical theory is not historicism, which also reflects hegemonic socioeconomic forces by refraining from negative critique. Since social theory can never be neutral, critical theory advocates radically transforming existing social arrangements. Hence the term "critical" is used "less in the sense it has in the critique of pure reason than in the sense it has in the dialectical critique of political economy." Critical theory desires a society of free actors which "transcend[s] the tension and . . . [abolishes] the opposition between the individual's purposefulness, spontaneity, and rationality, and those work-process relationships on which society is built," a society, in other words, where subjective freedom flourishes in cooperative and efficient social units, where rationality replaces senseless aggrandizement.[5] Critical theory, contrary to historicism, implicitly acknowledges a universality which in some vague and indeterminate manner inheres in our dismal, exploitative reality. By postulating the existence and plausibility of a potentially more "perfect" society, this absolute generates critical theory's anticapitalism.

Equally significant, however, is critical theory's admission that truth is basically unknowable as pure doctrine. With each imagined discovery, reality is transformed from a dynamic process, where "elements continuously change in relation to each other so that they are not even to be radically distinguished from each other," to an artificial, static, reified substance reduced to abstractions.[6] Critical theory indicts closed philosophical systems, whatever they say, and hence relinquishes the "presuppositions of philosophy" and humbly admits "it can neither furnish the rational grounds for its own origin, nor can it realize its own fulfillment by itself."[7] "Truth" is an indeterminate potential allowing one to understand and evaluate society critically without capitulating to extant philosophical myths. Consequently, early Critical theorists stress ethics, that is, the obligation to examine critically and actively transform reality. Without a guiding epistemology, however, positive action becomes unjustifiable, for it advocates "better," "truer" states, and these require universal social visions. Positive social action, in other words, presumes more than critique. Critical theorists are eventually compelled either to abandon the movement (for example, Marcuse, Fromm, Habermas) or wearily acknowledge the impossibility of meaningful social change.

Though reality is sensually experienced, Critical theory, unlike traditional empirical theory, does not reduce knowledge to sensation. In a human world characterized by movement and interpenetration, neither subject nor object dominates. Sensations are therefore extremely complex phenomena, combining social forces and consciousness into a cognized unity. *What* we perceive is historically and socially conditioned, that is, generated by past actions and reflecting dominant values and institutions. *How* we perceive it depends on a subjective process that is established and reinforced by all the complex cultural forces that normally affect a situated actor. Hence "the facts which our senses present to us are socially performed in two ways: through the historical character of the object perceived and through the historical character of the perceiving organ." Perception is "a product of society as a whole."[8] While we understand history and society sensually, we also recognize the limitation this imposes on us and labor diligently to surpass it. Critical theorists accomplish this by creatively transcending sense experiences toward a multidimensional reality. They work effectively, therefore, in nonbureaucratic, nonpressured surroundings, which unleash creative and critical intellects.

Critical theory's epistemological agnosticism means that it defends neither the primacy of matter over consciousness (materialism) nor consciousness over matter (idealism). Both mistakenly absolutize a partial fragment of reality. Materialism is concerned only with concrete, objective conditions in which people suffer, not the suffering itself as cognitively experienced in daily activities. This purges reality of its soul, substituting reified categories that interact impersonally. "The principle that the materialist doctrine designates as reality is not fit to furnish a norm. . . . Matter in itself is meaningless: its qualities cannot provide the maxims for the shaping of life either in regard to the commandments or to the ideal. . . . [Material] knowledge . . . yields no models, maxims or advice for an authentic life."[9] Materialism naively reduces subjectivity to its opposite, hence is inhuman. Idealism, on the other hand, plays with cognition like an autonomous, self-perpetuating toy, immune to surroundings. By absolutizing consciousness— or, in the case of empiricism, sensations—idealism ignores the concrete forces conditioning cognition. Whereas materialism, which fetishizes concreteness, is inhuman, idealism is mystical and unreal. Western social theory gravitates between inhumanity and irrelevance, neither substantively altering a bleak human condition. Proposed syntheses—for example, Lukács's *History and Class Consciousness,* Austro-Marxism, Lenin's *Philosophical Notebooks*—are inevitably deposited in one of the initial categories because, like materialism and idealism, they support epistemological absolutes. The logic of any positive philosophical system pulls magnetically toward one of these poles. Moreover, the "truth" of materialism and idealism is really the social interests they serve: bureaucratic parties or corporate elites. Both distort reality to enhance the prestige and power of one small group. Only critical theory absolutizes nothing. By acknowledging reality's dialectical complexity as an irreducible totality, it stands for critique and change rather than a narrow interest.

Critical theory's evaluation of Marx and the orthodox movement generally is ambivalent. Horkheimer, for example, posited the heuristic utility of Marx's theories of class, surplus value, profit, pauperization, and the historical inevitability of capitalism's breakdown.[10] However, since critical theory rejects philosophical absolutes, it does not unequivocally support either Marx or any Marxist "school" and ridicules distortions and reifications wherever they occur. In general, critical theory argues that Marx understated, at times abandoned, the historical dialectic's nonphilosophical quality. There exist no first principles to reduce validly reality's dynamic, interpenetrating processes into static, universal principles. No facet of reality is independent or complete. Obviously, then, Marx and Engels's suggestions that economics is in some sense prior to thought is false.[11] Sub- and superstructures interpenetrate, and while economics obviously conditions hegemonic values and institutions, these are subjectively experienced rather than "caused" and also independently influence the totality. Indeed, the *Dialectic of Enlightenment* (1944) reversed the traditional Marxist hypothesis by arguing bourgeois ideas irreducibly condition alienation, exploitation, and liberal democracy's transition to fascism. Freedom and progress, as subjectively meaningful ideas, evolve on their own into human domination.

Early in his career Horkheimer—like Lukács—evidently believed authentically self-conscious workers were history's agents of revolutionary transformation.[12] But events like the 1939 Nazi-Soviet Treaty reinforced nonreductionism and generated a critical theory belonging to no one particular class. With base and superstructure internally linked, and neither prior, no "objective" revolutionary tendency exists. Exploited workers will not necessarily rebel merely because of their position in the productive apparatus. Critical theory appeals to all perceptive, critical minds and foresees a rational revolutionary transformation emancipating everyone. Horkheimer and Adorno, in fact, were increasingly cynical of workers' so-called revolutionary potency as they sadly note the masses' noncritical acceptance of whatever system they live in. Horkheimer arrogantly speculated that critical theorists, not workers, may be history's revolutionary catalysts, for "truth may reside with numerically small groups of men . . . [who] may at the decisive moment become the leaders because of their deeper insight."[13] As capitalism's exploited majority, workers obviously will participate in, and benefit from, rationalizing social change—but not necessarily initiate it. Hence, bureaucratized, hierarchic, and secretive orthodox Parties are reviled for several reasons. First, their materialism is dogmatic and reductive, rationalizing social interests but epistemologically useless. Second, their dictatorial structure stifles imagination and creativity, the heartbeat of critical theory. Third, as a "Workers' Party" they unfairly isolate manual workers and nonworkers, ignoring the latter's rational potential, hence needlessly postponing meaningful change. Finally, they coopt critical theorists' authentic historical and social roles as revolutionary leaders.

The broadest chasm separating critical theory from both Marx and other schools of Marxism is mood. Marxism normally overflows with exuberant optimism. Their critique of capitalism is self-assured and hopeful, born in universal principles promising emancipation and fulfillment. Political activity has a moral purpose, realizing a desirable and/or necessary collective goal. Even revolutionary violence is engaged hopefully as a means of purging history's insidious antihumanism, cleansing civilization's spotted past with universal peace. Such optimism reflects the confidence that often accompanies revealed truth.

Critical theory doubts that truth will ever be satisfactorily revealed. One must merely criticize and work for change while humbly fleeing unjustifiable oppression. Moreover, even this is problematic. Critical theory stays in business, so to speak, because institutions and ideas invariably turn nondialectical, assuring reflective critique a rational historical role. Perfect justice, in practice, always deteriorates into its opposite. Consequently, human misery, once experienced, is never balanced or undone by dramatically new life forms. Critical theory is what Adorno calls a "sad science" ("*traurige Wissenschaft*"), hopelessly evaluating the human condition: "it might seem a wonderful objective that future generations will live a happier and more intelligent life on earth than today's generation does under the present bloody and stupefying conditions. But ultimately even those future generations will disappear and the world will continue in its orbit as if nothing happened."[14] In such circumstances violence, revolutionary or not, is certainly not worth its horrible cost in human lives. Why spend blood needlessly when the adventure goes nowhere we haven't already been? Horkheimer pushes this reasoning to an awkward extreme, praising those who quietly perished in Hitler's concentration camps as "martyrs . . . the symbols of humanity that is striving to be born."[15] Critical theory's pessimism eventually overwhelms common sense. Since only critique is justifiable, all political activity—not merely the violent kind—is senseless. Contemplation replaces action. Critique becomes purely intellectual, a reflective negation that dares not soil itself by engaging others in the public arena. Actions require positive goals, and these, history proves, enslave actors. Authentic revolutionaries flee what transformed Marxism from enlightened critique into totalitarianism; they rebel without acting—hence Horkheimer's Marxist critique of bourgeois economics, which grows intellectually "without transgressing the principles of the exchange economy . . . ," by theoretically drawing economic and social antagonisms. "Unlike the operation of modern specialized science, the critical theory of society remains philosophical even as a critique of economics. . . . "[16] Critical theory "negates" capitalism intellectually, without active resistance. Practically, its revolutionary critique leaves capitalism untouched.

The term "rationality" is never carefully defined by critical theory, though presumably it meant humanity asserting itself, abolishing exploitation and profit, and establishing freedom. Intellectually, it distinguished critical theory from socially supportive critiques such as historicism. Workers, however, are not infallible and cannot be trusted to initiate authentic action, that is, are "irrational." By 1940 critical theory's evolution into a contemplative, pessimistic rebellion eliminated even the theoretical need for positive concepts. When later eulogizing Adorno, Horkheimer argued that "the absolute" is never depicted, only yearned for. It is "the Other" from which we evaluate present society. Its function is purely intellectual, justifying reflective critique. Attempts at postulating a positive doctrine or encouraging concrete actions are, if history can be trusted, doomed.

Critical theory spent the ensuing decade applying these principles to Nazism and the Holocaust. Predictably, critical theorists were dissatisfied with the standard orthodox view that fascism is "the highest stage of capitalism," a natural and inevitable corporate fling at salvaging economic power. The Frankfurt School collectively, and Horkheimer and Adorno in particular, broached topics that for orthodoxy are unthinkable: Economics alone cannot effectively explain fascism; fascism is not entirely a bourgeois artifact; and, finally, workers, too, are severely infected with the fascist mentality. Fascism, in fact, embodies extraordinarily complex historical and social processes expressed in, and reinforced by, family relationships, religion, language, social values, and other aspects of what philosophers and sociologists call "everyday life." While economic contradictions condition capitalism's metamorphosis into fascism, they neither cause nor adequately explain it. The values a child learns from parents and siblings, analyzed empirically in *The Authoritarian Personality,* can mature into authoritarian, fascistic ideologies. Reducing this long and intimate process of family socialization to economic factors distorts the actual life experiences of those marching Nazi mobs and, paradoxically, replicates their perverse distortions of reality. All the interpenetrating economic and noneconomic aspects of European liberal democratic capitalism have congealed into an incomprehensibly brutal dictatorship. Liberalism dialectically transforms itself into its bloody opposite, by an inner developmental logic that transcends the personal wickedness of a Hitler or Mussolini.

Even the most glorious of humanity's dreams, for example, the "most general sense of progressive thought . . . aimed at liberating men from fear and establishing their sovereignty," becomes a nightmare.[17] Horkheimer and Adorno trace Hitler's irrationality directly to the eighteenth-century Enlightenment, which annihilated church and aristocratic hegemony with the simple appeal to emancipated reason and individual autonomy. For feudalism's oppressive world view, which buried individuality in Christian myth and landed economic power, one appeared guaranteeing each subject's uniqueness and freedom. Christianity's holistic and dominating universe was fragmented, and individuals—like atoms—floated indeterminately in self-created social environments. Government protected and served individual freedom, and self-interest was materially realized in a free-market economy based on the sanctity of private ownership. Here is "enlightened" human thought, promising a democratic utopia. But here also is a world view that obliterates nature's unity and selfishly exploits its resources. Enlightenment philosophy nurtured empirical science, which would eventually reify both subjects and nature itself. Moreover, the Enlightenment generated economic, social, and political systems potentially dominated by corporate elites. These inchoate tendencies matured in the nineteenth and twentieth centuries, and crystallized into fascism. A bloated capitalist technology is now uncontrollable, manipulating nature as well as humanity with an insidious "culture industry." Workers are isolated, afraid, and anomic, ideal victims for dominating fascist bureaucrats. Capitalists frantically grasped Hitler's coattails, hoping to weather an incipient workers' threat to their hegemony. The dialectic of Enlightenment carried humanity over the brink. But carried them in style, with plush democratic jargon and luxurious promises of freedom and equality. Enlightenment rationalism, born 200 years ago in the myths of individual autonomy and humanizing reason, is buried in myth as well, only these depict "*Lebensraum,*" "Arian supremacy," "*der Führer,*" and the "Final Solution."

Dialectic of Enlightenment signaled a change in direction. Instead of focusing exclusively on human domination, particularly of workers by capitalists, critical theory now explored its inherent quality. Domination itself, not a particular economic or social system, is now the final cause of human enslavement. Historically, it has taken different forms, including that of man by man, man by nature, and nature by man. Since it is never justifiable, bourgeois domination is morally indistinguishable from those that precede and will follow. Modern technology, capitalist or socialist, depersonalizes humanity and transforms nature into an instrument, a means to an "unnatural" acquisitive end. Domination is therefore endemic to technological civilization. Capitalism complicates things by permitting those exploiting nature to similarly exploit their fellow humans in search of profit. In theory, socialism will abolish only this last form of exploitation, not domination itself. Utopian socialist fantasies will be brutally expunged by the same technological weapons that Hitler perfected in Nazi Germany. In practice, the revolutionary socialist movement, with its reductivism and hierarchic bureaucracy, has merely replaced capitalist exploitation of workers with an equally horrible party that unmercifully destroys subjectivity. Domination, therefore, is not merely economic and is not just found in capitalism. The concept of economic class became irrelevant and, with the exception of one posthumously published article written in 1942 by Adorno, was purged. Transcending Marx's class struggle is the ubiquitous conflict between humanity and nature that shapes our dismal history.

Domination, in sum, is born in humanity's artificial polarization of subject and object, and will end only when we cognize the interpenetration and inseparability of all people with each other and with nature. But this is not accomplished with positive philosophical systems or concrete revolutionary acts, for in practice both pervert their irrational founding myths. But is civilization itself possible without such systems, acts, and myths? Horkheimer and Adorno sadly intimate that civilization and horror are coexistent: "It is not the portrayal of reality as hell on earth but the slick challenge to break out of it that is suspect. If there is anyone today to whom we can pass the responsibilities for the message, we bequeath it not to the 'masses,' and not to the individual (who is powerless), but to an imaginary witness—lest it perish with us."[18]

As German men and women inexorably sank into a "new kind of barbarism," critical theory compulsively reiterated its pessimism and fear of political activity. Horkheimer contended that activities such as overthrowing governments, nationalizing factories, and organizing workers are feasible only at some future, unspecified date. With domination flourishing and philosophy naively coopted, authenticity now entails reflectively negating social reality, not foolishly acting. "The real social function of philosophy lies in its criticism of what is prevalent.... By criticism, we mean that intellectual ... effort which is not satisfied to accept the prevailing ideas, actions, and social conditions unthinkingly...."[19] In an irrational world, authentic revolutionaries fantasize a better future even when existing madness precludes meaningful change. Revolutionaries are nonattached and critical. Fantasy *is* their reality.

The Eclipse of Reason describes fantasism as "objective" or "emancipatory" reason, reflectively acknowledging history's dialectical unity of empirical opposites, hence the harmony of subjects with Others and objective Nature. Emancipatory reason is the necessary precondition for abolishing domination. "Instrumental" or "technical" reason, on the contrary, stresses means rather than ends, technical efficiency rather than critical evaluation. It lives in modern philosophies, like positivism and pragmatism, that mindlessly find technical means to realize any naively accepted social purpose, hence function smoothly in any system of domination—capitalist, socialist, or fascist.

By 1950 critical theory was publically debating well-known empirical scientists, the so-called "*Methodenstreit.*" Though certainly not innovative, this dialogue solidified critical theory's antiempiricism and established Theodore Adorno as its major spokesperson.[20] In distinguishing between what Horkheimer now called "facade" sociology and a more authentic social method stressing "structural interconnections" ("*Verstrickungszusammenhang*"), critical theory resurrected Lukács's notions of totality and mediation. Empiricism factually dissects reality, verifies causal relationships, and proffers this knowledge to manipulative technocrats who support hegemonic economic interests. Hence, empirical social science generates domination ("*Herrschaftswissen*"), not pure knowledge ("*Bildungswissen*"). By ignoring the historical and social fabric nurturing and defining each empirical fact, contemporary social science obliterates its subject matter. It is a "sociology without society."[21] Authentic society is a dynamic totality, where particular and general interpenetrate, and the whole expresses and conditions each of its empirical parts. "Totality has no life of its own beyond that which it comprises. It produces and reproduces itself through its particular moments . . . and no particular element can be understood merely from its functioning without insight into the whole, which has its essence on the movement of the particular."[22] Reliable social science depicts the total essence underlying immediate, sensually given facts.

Instrumental social inquiry generates practical knowledge, that is, performs an ideological function antithetical to pure science. By reifying one aspect of reality and rationalizing supportive social actions, it merely sponsors a hegemonic group. Pure science, on the other hand, generates critical reflection and interpretation, not concrete action. Critical theory therefore lumps empirical science and orthodox Marxism in the same instrumental category. "Correct" praxis, "liberating" action that supports humanity as a whole, presupposes a free, autonomous actor. But freedom means purging oneself of reified, reductive ideologies and acknowledging reality's dynamic complexity. Critical theory frees us but only by abjuring concrete actions. While evaluating the present in terms of essence and possibility, it purposefully refrains from arrogant, pseudoscientific, action-oriented assertions, hence avoids duplicating the horrors of contemporary life. Freedom and concrete action are incompatible. "The aim of correct praxis would be its own elimination."[23]

Adorno's *Negative Dialectics* (1966) epitomizes the best and worst of critical theory. A work of genius and sensitivity, it artfully depicts a non-reductionist dialectics. However, it is also pretentious, condescending, and often virtually incomprehensible. These contradictions are part of the book's meaning. Adorno's revolutionary message is that truth cannot be substantively communicated through the covers of a book or the tenets of a philosophical system.

One useful way to attack an uninviting academic monograph is to find its philosophical identity, the objective presuppositions generating each hypothesis or chapter. But in *Negative Dialectics,* Adorno eliminates this identity. Every concept or hypothesis interconnects with its opposite, leaving no solid basis for building a philosophical system or organizing a book. Hence, philosophy itself is impossible, and reliable, truthful books cannot be written. But philosophy is both necessary and unavoidable for thoughtful people because nonreflective praxis—the alternative—perpetuates conformity and injustice. Faced with the practical need for philosophy and its theoretical impossibility, critical theory favors philosophy as pure negation. The dialectic, so conceived, is not a method or an objective description as it is for other Marxists. It persistently opposes all theoretical schemes, all universal methods, by describing reality's complexity and history's interconnectedness without reducing these to simplistic formulas. "Dialectics is the self-consciousness of the objective context of delusion; it does not mean to have escaped from that context. Its objective goal is to break out of the context from within. . . . It lies in the definition of negative dialectics that it will not come to rest in itself, as if it were total."[24]

Dialectics is therefore destructive and constructive: destroying popular myths regarding the "separateness" of historical epochs and empirical facts; and reflectively constituting what Adorno calls "force-fields" and Walter Benjamin "constellations," that is, historically and spatially open configurations surrounding particular acts. A responsible dialectician "stops telling the sequence of events like the beads of a rosary. Instead, he grasps the constellation which his own era has formed with a definite earlier one."[25] Constellations are critical, not affirmative, concepts, illustrating the falsity of modern life and thought but not establishing reductionist patterns. Dialectics unfolds reality's contradictions and interconnections and exposes the totality's indeterminate priority over its parts. This dialectical knowledge, not exaggerated promises or naive acts, emancipates humanity.

Perceived dialectically, society eludes definition, being neither the sum total of individual subjects nor an objective being. As a totality, it constitutes the reciprocal interaction among human subjects and material objects. Society simultaneously expresses authentic subjectivity and objectivity but is also independent of both and—ultimately—determining. Positive definitions for terms like "freedom" and "causality" are impossible without reducing the totality to a hollow identity theory. The very notions of "free will" and "determinism" are false because they embody epistemological starting points, that is, they assume the priority of subject or object. Freedom's only meaning is negative: reflectively repudiating a concrete instance of enslavement. "Freedom can be defined in negation only, corresponding to the concrete form of a specific unfreedom. . . . [It] turns concrete . . . as resistance to repression. There has been as much free will as there were men with the will to be free." Similarly, causality is meaningful only as a critique of naive free-will theories. The concept is heuristically useful, expressing one aspect of the totality. However, its economistic reification is as unjustified as capitalism's rhetorical commitment to freedom. "Eventually the [social] system will reach a point . . . where the universal dependence of all moments on all other moments makes the talk of causality obsolete. It is idle to search for what might have been the cause within a monolithic society. Only that society itself remains the cause."[26] Art and science, like freedom and causality, are interpenetrating aspects of the same dynamic whole. Art and the artistic mentality are therefore valuable tools of scientific social inquiry, a passage to rational fantasy. Adorno "cannot accept the usual mode of thought which is content to register facts and prepare them for subsequent classification. . . . [The social scientist's] essential effort is to illuminate the realm of facticity—without which there can be no true knowledge—with reflections of a different type . . . which diverges radically from the generally accepted canon of scientific validity."[27]

Adorno, too, became increasingly despairing and pessimistic. Technological society is inherently domineering and oppressive, but any conceivable revolutionary praxis would only generate one equally horrible.

Whatever an individual or a group may undertake against the totality they are part of is infected by the evil of that totality; and no less infected is he who does nothing at all. This is how original sin has been secularized. The individual who dreams of moral certainty is bound to fail, bound to incur guilt because, being harnessed to the social order, he has virtually no power over the conditions whose cry for change appeals to the moral "ingenium."

Marx's injunction to "change" the world, not merely interpret it, is "archbourgeois" hypocrisy. By making the objective world into a subjective image, Marxist-inspired revolutionaries mimic capitalism's principle of identity even though outwardly reversing the relationship of subject and object. Adorno retreats to critical thought because "the practice that would matter is barred." Theoretically challenging reality, going "as much against the facade as possible . . . as far as it is capable of moving," provides us "a breathing spell it would be practically criminal not to utilize."[28]

Adorno lived a secluded, scholarly old age, aloof from everyday struggles of a new breed of radical bent on confrontation politics. Eventually, he was verbally lambasted by German activists, who also scolded the entire Frankfurt School for their nonrevolutionary demeanor. Stunned by this reprimand from the same radical intellectuals with whom he identified and based what little hope he could forage, Adorno met an untimely death in 1969. On the other hand, Horkheimer's despair sweetened his evaluation of capitalism and turned him toward a nonsectarian God. His warning to New Left activists is straight and to the point: "Thoughtless and dogmatic application of the critical theory to practice in changed historical circumstances can only accelerate the very process which the theory aimed at denouncing. . . . Social theory [not revolutionary praxis] therefore forms the main content of contemporary materialism." Horkheimer now treasured the social system that protects his privacy, allowing him to fantasize. Critical thought is an end; any society that delivers is a justifiable and desirable means. Authentic revolutionaries must critically evaluate surroundings, but also wholeheartedly support them if they permit such evaluation. "[T]he free world is at the moment still an island in space and time, and its destruction . . . would also mean the destruction of the culture of which the critical is a part."[29]

Horkheimer's new-found patriotism colored his reading of Marx. Still a "Marxist," Horkheimer reinterpreted Marxism to mean the "freedom of the entrepreneur which is limited today to a small group, . . . be extended to the whole society."[30] Moreover, critical inquiry justifies the "still insufficiently noted . . . fact that the development of man is bound up with competition, that is, with the most important element of the liberal economy."[31] Horkheimer rejected all identity theories—all positive philosophical systems—including his own rejection. Pure critique consumes itself, as capitalism's vested interests complacently watch.

Critical theory is radical in a very peculiar sense, resembling Benjamin's description in 1920 of two German Leftists who "stand not left of this or that orientation, but simply left of everything that is possible."[32] Certainly there are psychosocial factors rationalizing the Frankfurt School's castrated radicalism. Any sensitive intellectual transported into Hitler's Germany and experiencing the Holocaust firsthand would probably absolutize depression and fear. Orthodox Marxism's response, even to professed Marxists, is blemished when, to the east, Stalinism openly pollutes Russian workers' dreams of emancipation. For educated, upper-middle-class intellectuals—Germany's "bourgeois Marxist intelligentsia"—revolutionary critique is surely more respectable than dirty organizational work or bloody rebellion.[33] As Jews, most Frankfurt members are probably comfortable with a secular philosophy rejecting metaphysical blueprints and positive symbols of absolute truth but also incorporating a strong sense of history, ethics, and social justice. Such factors, however, do not resolve critical theory's dilemma: How can Marxist critique remain authentic after rejecting, philosophically and practically, concrete revolutionary action? Critical theory's truncated Marxism "has all the vices and virtues of an indiscreet person with a stunted sense of respect."[34] It levels enemies—capitalist and bureaucratic socialist—with brilliant arguments, evocative images, and prosaic obfuscations but then withdraws fearfully before its advantage is translated into action. Hence it is "revolutionary" only in closed societies that blatantly inhibit subjective self-expression. In these circumstances intellectual negation is the only feasible critical activity. But success generates failure. As reflective critique successfully transforms social values, critical theory turns impotent and reactionary: These new attitudes are also negated, negating the original negation. Successful revolutions require a positive vision justifying concrete demands and actions, not merely a negative critique of the status quo. While, potentially, these too may turn domineering, they also introduce hope and opportunity where there are none. Critical theory, justifiable or not, opts for hopelessness. The ultimate benefactors are society's extant hegemonic elites.

Habermas

At Adorno's death and Horkheimer's ideological and religious conversions, Critical theory displayed the trappings of mystical, neo-Romantic intellectualism. Jürgen Habermas (b. 1929), an obvious heir to the Frankfurt legacy, wants to reestablish links between theory and practice without violating Critical theory's rigorous antireductionism. *Theorie und Praxis* (1963), *Erkenntnis und Interesse* (1968) and "Technik und Wissenschaft als 'Ideologie' " (1970) all display the postwar Frankfurt School's antipositivist bias but with a new twist. For Habermas, scientific frameworks justify and rationalize practical human interests. Positivism, the dominant contemporary mode of scientific inquiry, is based on nontheoretical real interests, in relation to which it is objective. No transcendental grounding exists for positivism or any other science. Habermas thus echoes critical theory's rejection of absolutes. However, this revised formula assumes that knowledge (theory) is verified through the practical activities of concerned actors (praxis), hence a glimmer of optimism regarding the human condition. Though interests alone determine a science's "objectivity," critical theorists can now ascertain practical interests appropriate to reflective critique, and act to satisfy them—thereby justifying critical theory. However, in concretely satiating reflective, critical interests, these are easily transformed into a positive doctrine, that is, a philosophical system—albeit a "negative" one—encouraging believers to act concretely. This conundrum, endemic to critical theory, can be cosmetically disguised with clever words and phrases, but is debilitating when angry demonstrators in the streets demand support for violent actions. Habermas is convincing, but perhaps irrelevant.

Human interest "establishes the unity between . . . [each] constitutive context in which knowledge is rooted and the structure of the possible application which this knowledge can have."[35] Science justifies and operationalizes practical interests. Each science, therefore, generates knowledge having a pragmatic function. Habermas examined three possible sciences representing three distinct human interests, each with a unique meaning, object, and method that collectively comprise its criteria of objectivity.

In everyday activities, actors encounter bodies, things, events, and conditions that are intentionally manipulated. The technical knowledge required to manipulate phenomena successfully toward desired ends is supplied by empirical-analytical science, theoretically rationalized by positivism.[36] Empirical science provides knowledge for controlling the universe, satisfying a "technical human interest" through an instrumental technology. Empirical methods are open, flexible, and inductive, qualities popular in social systems based on individual liberty and governmental restraint. Empirical science also proclaims the epistemological priority of isolated facts, reinforcing societies already split into seemingly unrelated categories such as politics, economic, jurisprudence, art, religion, and so on. It generates technically complex commodities that are profitably sold to consumers conditioned by technology to buy. Finally, empirical scientists unquestioningly accept existing economic and social institutions, hence are smoothly integrated into capitalist utility structures. By implication, empirical science supports bureaucratic socialist systems as well, given the necessary political room to grow. Empirical science, in sum, generates technical knowledge used by powerful social interests.

But in living socially we also encounter intelligent, sentient actors whose use of language, knowledge, and consciousness resemble ours, but whose irreducible subjectivity makes them unique and different. To survive, human beings must communicate with other symbol-using actors by using language and everyday processes of symbolic interaction. Our "practical human interest" of communicating with and understanding fellow human beings creates the need for hermeneutic or cultural science, manifest in myth, religion, nonspiritual idealism, historicism, pragmaticism, and so on.[37] Hermeneutic science provides a symbolic foundation for intersubjectivity, a means for cognizing the complexes of meanings that others experience, and a basis for working cooperatively. Throughout history, until the present, hermeneutic science was the legitimating social ideology, underlying "objective" inquiry as well as justifying ancient and medieval institutions. Now, however, empirical science has replaced hermeneutics. Contemporary technological society emphasizes manipulation and control rather than cognitive understanding and communication. Empirical science objectifies humanity by stressing structural similarities between human and nonhuman phenomena and then developing techniques of domination. Technological humanity neither thinks morally nor perceives others as qualitatively unique. It seeks technical efficiency, not the good life, hence impersonally manipulates human life. "The moral realization of a normative order is a function of communicative action oriented to shared cultural meaning and presupposing the internalization of values. It is increasingly supplanted by conditioned behavior . . . [in] the industrially most advanced societies. . . ."[38]

Technological society eliminates symbolic communication and interaction, abrogating the social aspects of individuality. Actors live as isolated, manipulated units, oblivious to cognitive symbolic connections bonding humanity. These anomic lives are dominated by ignorance and helplessness. "Domination," then, means social interaction exhibiting "distorted communication," the inability to communicate effectively and intersubjectively.[39] Humanity thus has a residual need to reestablish communicative links with others, what Habermas calls an "emancipatory human interest." Critical science cognitively negates technological society. Its method is critical and reflective, questioning both naively internalized technological structures and empirical reasoning. Practical consequences of emancipatory science include the elimination of restrictions on communication. "Public, unrestricted discussion, free from domination, of the suitability and desirability of action-orienting principles and norms ... such communication at all levels of political and repoliticized decision-making processes is the only medium in which anything like 'rationalization' is possible." Emancipatory science, in practice, ends social repression and rigidity, permitting "progressive individuation."[40] By establishing intersubjective communication, humanity takes the necessary first step toward social justice. A step that self-consciously negates positivism, and acknowledges the reciprocal connections between and among individuals and institutions, the interpenetration of Self and Other, subject and object, theory and praxis. Emancipatory science, in other words, is critical and dialectical.

Emancipation requires new reflective forms of intersubjective knowledge and communication; hence, Habermas used hermeneutics to mediate domination and liberation. We can negate technology with new reflective answers to practical problems, which we communicate intersubjectively. Hermeneutic science is reborn in the human need to transmit liberating knowledge to others. Habermas feels that Freudianism is useful to this process of communicating and understanding critical knowledge. Psychoanalysis liberates oppressed personalities who have subconsciously internalized and hidden a seminal childhood conflict. Neurotic symptoms like slips of the tongue, deviant linguistic practices, compulsive repetition, confusion between communicative levels, and so on, indicate that the original repressed conflict has inhibited effective communication, in extreme cases generating an incommunicable private language. Freudian psychoanalysis, in other words, is based on a theory of linguistic failure, Habermas's "distorted communication." By self-consciously contemplating relevant symptoms and acknowledging repressed sources, analysands restore the primal conflict to open, public communication. Reflection liberates by facilitating free communication among nonrepressed, critical thinkers rationally shaping the future. Critical social science "socioanalyzes" social systems as Freudian psychoanalysis does individuals, opening up "the hidden pathology of collective behavior and entire social systems."[41] Habermas assumes that "normal" societies and individuals—exhibiting free, unin-

hibited understanding and communication—are not conditioned by subconscious primal conflicts. Hence socioanalysis and psychoanalysis are
useful only in oppressive, dominating circumstances.

In evaluating Marx, Habermas, like Horkheimer and Adorno, offers luke-
warm, equivocating praise. As a critic of bourgeois political economy,
vividly contrasting assumptions and reality, Marx is without equal.[42] But
this is not critical social science, for it leaves unanswered important epistemological and practical questions concerning criteria of validity, the nature
of freedom, and the meaning of authentic praxis. "The critique of political
economy was simply a theory of bourgeois society as a critique of its
ideology," and hence doesn't surpass the bourgeois system it condemns.[43]
When Marx did struggle with foundational theoretical and practical issues,
he abandoned the critical perspective. Metaphysical materialism plagues
much of Marx's work, a remnant of eighteenth- and nineteenth-century a
priorism. "Revolutionary" materialism hides, but does not eliminate,
traditional epistemological assumptions. Just as non-Marxist a priorism
rationalizes the hegemony of one small group (the bourgeoisie), Marxist a
priorism performs an identical social function, although Communist Party
bureaucrats have replaced capitalists.

Moreover, when Marx wrote, economics and government served common
interests but performed different functions. Marx's views on the causal
priority of base over superstructure reflect this dichotomy. Early capitalism's productive apparatus significantly conditioned its steady movement
toward a dominating, depersonalized technical rationality. Consistent with
classical liberal theory, the state's economic and social roles were minimal.
What Marx could not foresee was the capitalist state's gradual expansion
into nonpolitical realms. Today, the laissez-faire bourgeois state has been
replaced by one actively involved, via its own technological apparatus, in
all segments of social life, streamlining social organization and upgrading
productive efficiency. The state, like the capitalist economy, now actively
supports technical interests. Since human domination feeds on instru-
mentalism, the capitalist state as well as its productive apparatus play equal
roles in oppressing workers—and neither is autonomous. Consequently,
technical rationality is reinforced economically, socially, politically, and
ideologically, saturating every aspect of social life and infecting every
citizen, worker and nonworker alike. While a capitalist economy dialectically
expresses and reinforces technical rationality, Marx's theory that it causes
oppression is outdated. Similarly, class antagonism only partially explains
contemporary domination. As sophisticated technology streamlines material production, and an increasingly active bourgeois state eliminates its
gross social malfunctions, workers' living conditions will likely improve,
complicating the meaning and consequences of class struggle. Marx's
theory of the proletariat's progressive immiseration—relative or absolute—is
irrelevant in modern capitalism, where class struggle is no longer the prime

instigator of meaningful social change. Economism reflects traditional, noncritical epistemologies and only dresses domination in new clothes. Capitalism's working class is not necessarily a revolutionary vanguard, though authentic change will emancipate everyone, including the working class.

Marx's latent a priorism obfuscates human freedom.[44] Despite some tantalizing early suggestions of a revitalized subjectivity, Marx finally opted for a definition depicting society's impersonal productive patterns. Socialism becomes the necessary and sufficient condition for human emancipation. The mature Marx made critical subjectivity an epiphenomenon of concrete matter, ignoring the obvious similarities with empirical causality. Both treat subjects instrumentally, as pliable objects serving a preconceived, naively accepted truth. Marx's notion of emancipation, which ignores critical, self-conscious reflection, only perpetuates capitalism's technical mentality. The quality of experienced domination is not diminished by a change in hegemonic elites.

Habermas thus replaced Marx's objective economic categories, that is, the means and relationships of production, with the concepts of "labor" and "symbolically mediated interaction."[45] Marx believed that productive forces determine the quality of human labor. Habermas defined labor as instrumental behavior: rationally manipulating nature to satisfy material needs. The growth of technological productive forces extends our power of technical control, hence increases the efficiency and effectiveness of labor. Marx also believed objective productive relationships determine the quality of social oppression, that is, the dominant economic class forges supportive social values and institutions. Habermas defines oppression in terms of symbolic communication, the extant norms, institutions, and language by which individuals understand others and communicate interpersonally—that is, hermeneutic or practical knowledge. As technical replaces practical knowledge, the ability to think and communicate effectively atrophies. Instrumental labor, which should be an effective means for realizing a reflective end, becomes an end in itself. Human beings are depersonalized and manipulated by dominating owners of technology. Emancipation requires praxis (instrumental labor) reuniting with theory (symbolic communication), a process that accompanies reflective social critique. Labor is then goal-oriented and purposive; society's productive capacity fulfills reflective human needs, not narrow interests. Marx, finally, believed socialism an inevitable historical product of objective matter. Habermas connects revolution to reflective critique, without speculating on the precise quality of postrevolutionary economics. The latter is born in reflective knowledge, and grows soon enough after human communication is reestablished.

Under Horkheimer and Adorno critical theory had deteriorated into a feeble plea for sanity, a "protest, impotent in practice, against an apocalyptically self-obturating system of alienation and reification, and . . . the spark whose preservation in a self-darkening world will keep alive the memory of something quite different." Habermas accepted their warnings of the essential falseness and inadequacy of identity theory, but struggled to connect critical theory and revolutionary practice. "The truth of critical social theory is a 'verité à faire'; in the last resort it can demonstrate its truthfulness only by successful liberation."[46] Even in Habermas's skilled hands, however, negative dialetics is still a poor guide for those of us wishing to act as well as think. Though emancipated praxis realizes a "general and unforced consensus," precisely what will this consensus be? Habermas argues only emancipated actors can answer this. Fine, but who is emancipated? Should critical theorists support Yippies as they block commuter traffic during rush hour? or an SDS occupation of city hall? or a socialist party's call for a national work stoppage? or a Communist Party's exhortation to revolutionàry violence? Indeed, should critical theorists presume emancipation will manifest socialist institutions? In a nutshell: By what criterion shall we evaluate the quality of critical thinking and the utility of concrete actions? Habermas has no positive answers, even admitting his is a "prepolitical" form of discourse, still incapable of drawing "the consequences of knowledge directed toward liberation."[47] Consequently, Habermas exhorts us to think critically, reflectively negate existing institutions and values, oppose economic, political, and social domination; but also be wary of instigating state violence or falling to ideological dogmatism. "Maoist" revolutionary student activity in Western Europe is condemned as counterproductive "left Fascism" or "actionism," even though, presumably, it practically expresses critical thinking by capitalism's "enlightened," intelligent victims—the very group that critical theory depends on. Though students should "permanently destroy . . . [capitalism's] crumbling achievement-ideology, and thus bring down the already fragile legitimizing basis of advanced capitalism . . . ,"[48] they must also acknowledge "the danger of diversion either into the privatization of an easily consolable hippie sub-culture or into the fruitless violent acts of the actionists."[49] There apparently are no absolute criteria for determining where the former ends and the latter begins, so revised critical theory occasionally flaunts the narrow line separating senseless word games from practical advice.[50] Habermas's critical theory offers hope rather than despair and action, not endless contemplation. But it is created by and for intellectuals.

Although, practically, Habermas barely outpaces his predecessors, even this short distance was too much for Frankfurt purists. Moreover, Habermas's philosophy, they contend, grows pretentious. Outwardly admitting that we cannot, in principle, discover the limits of human nature, Habermas also defines humanity's three basic "interests" as "deep-seated . . . which direct our knowledge and which have a quasi-transcendental status."[51] They are "invariant," "abstract," and "determine the aspect under which reality is objectified. . . . They are the conditions which are necessary in order that subjects capable of speech and action may have experience which can lay a claim to objectivity."[52] Human interests presume that individuals are essentially cognitive, intelligent, and creative, communicating social beings simultaneously identical and nonidentical. They are the "fundamental interests of mankind as such" not merely the limited historical interests of a particular class.[53] All this sounds vaguely idealist. Even Habermas is "embarrassed" with "quasi-transcendental" phenomena, and argues plaintively against "transcendental logics" based on "intelligible egos" or other identity theories.[54] Human interests are a naturally evolving intersubjective framework permitting communicative discourse, allowing humanity to contemplate and discuss technical, practical, and emancipatory issues. They precede praxis and structure valid knowledge in each realm. Habermas cannot turn "interests" into a strictly empirical concept, because this abolishes objectivity, generating a multitude of unique interests and personal sciences. Hence the "quasi-transcendental" terminology, an awkward midpoint between idealism and negativity. Habermas personally resolves the tension by admitting that these are tentative "speculations," not the final word. However, his formal resignation from the Frankfurt School in 1972 indicates the problem's true dimensions.

Habermas's revised critical theory hopefully reattaches theory and praxis. To the extent that it proffers useful guidance to revolutionary activists, it must emphasize humanity's a priori interests and needs, positing a bridgeable gap between empirical life and human fulfillment. To the extent that it recoils from these "quasi-transcendental" interests into critical negativity, it becomes, like its predecessor, impotent intellectualism. Critical theory, revised or not, is trapped between logic and politics. With the triumph of the former comes despair; of the latter, idealism. People like Marcuse, Fromm, and—perhaps—Habermas opt for idealism. Critical theorists, on the other hand, are doomed to a restless and perpetual "*angst.*"

NEW LEFTISM

Political exigency is handmaiden to a heterogeneous, leaderless movement usually labeled the New Left. A young, well-educated, predominantly middle-class cadre of social activists want from Marxism only concrete and immediate action. The "Old Left" resembles a rogues' gallery of intellectual stars. Entirely too much time and effort have gone into radical theory, while generations of oppressed workers come and go. In the rare cases where theory actually coalesced with revolutionary practice, bourgeois hegemony was transformed into Party dictatorship. From the masses' perspective, it is futile endlessly to formulate and justify revolutionary theory. Although the Frankfurt School clearly acknowledged neo-Marxism's blatant hypocrisy, their "solution" capitulated to capitalism by theoretically justifying passivity. Frankfurt Marxism reflected a century of Marxist philosophy, piously depicting bourgeois domination and gazing fearfully at the working class's dormant power. New Leftism sounds the revolutionary alarm. It is tactical, not theoretical, mobilizing the oppressed and instituting strategies heretofore described only in books.

New Leftism seeks only the revolutionary transformation of capitalism. Since revolution *is* action, theory is clearly derivative. Authentic Marxism instigates insurrections and only later develops theories explaining what has transpired. "The important factor, then, is the concrete form which the real movement will assume. If it confirms that which claims to be its own concept, then in truth the theory is a true revolutionary theory. If, on the other hand, it invalidates it, the theory is downgraded to the level of an ideology or utopia...." Theory is an afterthought, an epiphenomenon conditioned by praxis. It is open, unfinished, and relativistic—and bound to successful revolutionary movements. Only strategically useful ideas are "true": "revolutionary consciousness *is* the product of struggle."[55]

New Leftism is therefore defined by the exigencies of proletarian struggle, hence changes in changing circumstances. Three broad tenets, however, explain New Leftism, though not all New Leftists in all circumstances adhere to them individually or collectively.

First, since revolution is self-justifying, it can occur whenever and wherever a properly organized group destroys extant elites and institutions. Hence the European and American New Left fascination with successful Third World revolutionaries like Ché Guevara, Regis Debray, Frantz Fanon, and Mao Tse-tung. These heroes did not, in battle, intellectually debate the quality of postrevolutionary justice. Successful revolutions answer all the hypothetical problems that Marxists traditionally speculate about.

Second, revolutions totally transform the entire network of bourgeois values and institutions. Capitalist domination is reinforced by everything from television commercials, to working conditions, electoral politics, and organized religion. Reformism, separating social levels and working piecemeal to rectify each one individually, disregards the multidimensionality of capitalism. Historically, reformism has altered governments and laws, not the quality of capitalist exploitation, hence is "incorrect." Meaningful social change occurs simultaneously on all social levels or survives in none at all. Revolution transforms not only an exploitative economy but all facets of bourgeois morality, including attitudes regarding sex, drugs, education, interpersonal and family relationships, and work. This last phenomenon is particularly important because it supports capitalist productive relationships. The bourgeois work "ethic"—discipline, honesty, frugality, and forebearance—generates worker alienation. The cult of labor is a bourgeois invention. Revolutionaries substitute fulfilling, satisfying activities, resembling what capitalists might term "play." Obviously such non-repressed actions will fundamentally alter factories as well as society's entire approach to production and distribution. Although the postrevolutionary future is undetermined, new, cooperative institutions will accompany capitalism's demise. Many New Leftists advocate communalism as an apposite, emancipated social form, replacing a decadent work ethic with pleasure, cooperation, and love.[56]

Finally, men and women must determine their own fates. Successful revolutions are spontaneous outbursts of liberated reflective will, completely supported by free and equal participants. History has proven that hegemonic revolutionary parties enslave rather than liberate, that is, are nonrevolutionary and "untrue." Orthodox materialism, the "Old Left," is the radical equivalent of bourgeois idealism: Both intellectually rationalize an exploiting elite. Orthodoxy has no clear goals beyond industrializing and supporting Soviet world hegemony, neither revolutionary. Thus, the "conceptual apparatus of [orthodox] Marxism" no longer fulfills the needs of oppressed peoples.[57] The mantle of human emancipation, first carried by Marx, "is no longer worn by organized Marxism-Leninism."[58] Worker rebellions today manifest spontaneous, nonsupervised or directed wildcat strikes demanding qualitative improvements in working and living conditions, not merely higher salaries. These "contestation strikes" reject wage differentials, authority hierarchies, and trade unionism, and advocate worker self-management. Nonworkers, particularly students—unique in being simultaneously victims and critical observers—engage in leaderless street confrontations with hegemonic forces, including police, government, and big business. These sorties reinforce human spontaneity, freedom, and self-direction, qualities that a successful revolution requires. Postrevolutionary society will institute some form of participatory democracy based on human dignity and self-worth, where actors "do their own thing" without exploiting neighbors.

Although New Left theory rejects formal theory, its tactics are generated by familiar Marxist assumptions regarding capitalist exploitation, alienation, and the desirability of socialism. The implicit belief in subjective freedom, hence the superstructure's autonomy, recalls experiential Marxism. Twenty years before New Leftism, Sartre had advocated replacing disciplined productive labor with artistic free play. Lukács's Hegelian dialectic describes total revolution as history's authentic response to capitalism's interpenetrating hegemonic tentacles. New Leftism's "innovative" critique of everyday life—its oppressive values, beliefs, customs, institutions— was already established in Horkheimer and Adorno's *Dialectic of Enlightenment*. Reich's and Marcuse's analyses of capitalist sexual repression energize the New Left obsession with violating bourgeois sexual taboos. Pannekoek's council communism is its model for spontaneous worker self-management. In brief, the unacknowledged theoretical origins of New Leftism are extensive, even encompassing non-Marxist phenomena like the civil rights, gay rights, and antiwar movements, utopianism, anarchism, dadaism, and surrealism. The point, however, is New Leftism's nonintellectual eclecticism, its mindless mixing of antithetical principles to concoct an effective, though irrational, revolutionary stimulant. Unresolved, ignored contradictions range from their simplistically coupling subjective autonomy (for example, "do your own thing") and cooperative social arrangements, to optimistically assuming that nonmoral activists—and tactics based solely on political expediency, often including brutal physical attacks—will establish postrevolutionary communities upholding universal human dignity. Can society realistically trust individuals who nonreflectively junk ethics and epistemology and advocate any conceivable action—irrespective of consequences—they perceive as tactically useful?

In a real sense, then, New Leftism is heir to a nonrational, mystical revolutionary tradition that includes George Sorel and the "Arguments" philosophers.

Sorel

George Sorel (1847–1922) indicted rational enlightenment philosophy and empirical science for artificially reducing life to simple categories that are incapable of grasping humanity's "dark area": the subliminal forces of tradition, sex, religion, will, and nationality that permeate human history.[59] Rationalism naively believes that injustice is eradicated with empirical knowledge, reformist legislation, and humanitarianism. On the contrary, life is a complex totality of internally linked phenomena. Rational knowledge is ill-suited to such complexity, unintentionally generating weakness and ignorance, not enlightenment. A complex social totality is comprehended not rationally, but through myth, that is, by irrationally acknowledging an essentially irrational dialectical reality. Myth, not bourgeois rationalism, is the foundation of authentic social inquiry. Through myth we experience innate primitive instincts, stripped of history's nonmythical sediment. Myth is therefore pessimistic and critical, spurning easy reductive formulas and negating the rational status quo. Myth, in other words, is simultaneously authentic and revolutionary. We either leave society untouched, living in "rationally" exploitative conditions, or annihilate it totally in a fit of authenticity.

Sorel understood Marx's historical materialism in these terms. It pessimistically explains human history and mobilizes a critical, revolutionary working class. Similarly, it rejects reform and empirical reductionism, exhorting the proletariat to challenge and destroy capitalism. Marxism is myth because it postulates a complex, irreducible capitalist totality and inspires revolutionary insurrection. Moreover, this myth manifests a general workers' strike, which destroys bourgeois civilization in the name of human emancipation. Historical materialism is not a rational blueprint. While inconclusively speculating about socialist cooperation and collective unity, it is primarily negative: glorifying rebellion rather than painting a utopia.

The mythical general strike mobilizes workers into syndicates. Traditional working-class parties and trade unions inhibit our intuiting the revolutionary myth and hence perpetuate rational tyranny. Workers' syndicates, on the other hand, spontaneously organize workers into factory-based, self-managing teams that subvert bourgeois authority structures. They inspire members to intuit the authentic myth of proletariat revolution subjectively, and subordinate practical economic, social, and political issues to this irrational goal. Syndicates, therefore, oppose bourgeois institutions, unite the working class against a common bourgeois enemy, and generate postrevolutionary social forms of self-governing workers and farmers interacting cooperatively (resembling what Marx, in criticizing Proudhon, ironically called a "petty-bourgeois utopia").

Proletariat revolution seeks neither power nor classlessness. Instead, it purges modernity of unnatural oppression and initiates the direct freedom of emancipated humanity. Consequently, it rejects class dictatorship—even of the majority—and debilitating governmental bureaucracies. The myth of the general strike is anti-intellectual, antibourgeois, antihierarchical; its only tactic is success. It doesn't follow theoretical formulas or obey tactical cliques and turns violent for practical reasons. By physically annihilating the capitalist enemy, workers facilitate a swift transition to self-management and rejuvenate the precivilized, irrational instincts that will organize postrevolutionary society.

Sorel, like other Marxists, advocated class war, rejected utopianism, abolished the state, and believed in total revolution. But he also glorified innate, prebourgeois qualities such as heroism, greatness, dignity, and authenticity. Accordingly, he admired and emulated the ancient Christian martyrs and therefore—illogically—respected many of Western civilization's religious, social, and sexual traditions. He believed in voluntarism and self-determining freedom but simultaneously sanctified an irrational myth that propelled humanity into uncontrollable rebellious paroxysms. He was a historical materialist who also advocated anarcho-syndicalism and spontaneous irrationality. He was a proletarian revolutionary who sympathetically cited Vico, Proudhon, Bergson, Nietzsche, Tocqueville, Taine, Renan, and others. In sum, he cared little for theoretical rigor or intellectual system building, picking and choosing ideas that would mobilize the discontented. As an anticapitalist revolutionary who opportunistically said and did anything—eventually supporting even fascist-inspired movements—he was the spiritual Founding Father of New Leftism.

The "Arguments" Group

A more immediate influence on New Leftism is the philosophy and social theory associated with several popular post-Stalinist radical journals, particularly *Arguments*.[60] While much of this work is philosophically mediocre, it does raise important questions and offer bold answers. Consisting almost exclusively of ex-orthodox Marxists liberated by the post-Stalinist intellectual thaw, the Arguments group exploded Stalinism with barbed critique and a loosening of philosophical standards. They daringly referred to Heidegger, Sartre, Freud, Picasso, or any other figure—Marxist or not—relevant to their critique. Their work is philosophically unsystematic, vague, and ambivalent, though socially significant for legitimizing—especially in France—different kinds of Marxist theory. "French revisionism [for example, the Arguments movement] was the direct consequence of de-Stalinization, but at the same time it is the work of one-time Stalinists. Hence its demands (total revision), hence also its limitations. Revisionism adds nothing to Marxism, but . . . was to make its own contribution to the grand enterprise of philosophical liberation."[61] This audacious enterprise also issued pioneering translations of Hegelian Marxist classics, including work by Labriola, Lukács, Korsch, and Gramsci.

Arguments' topics reflect the group's interest in the early Marx and idealist Marxism: the subjectively inspired dialectic, society as an inter-penetrating totality, alienation as an economic and social phenomenon, the social significance of subjective perception and will, and the autonomy of culture. Substantive contributions in these areas are minimal. However, by merely reformulating contemporary Marxism in nonorthodox terms, their influence among disillusioned French radicals ballooned. The most enduring Arguments contribution to French social theory was an eclectic critique of everyday life. Though unoriginal, like all their work, the Arguments group popularized a radical critique of Western Europe's dehumanizing, but attractive, consumer society. Similarly, the Marxist concept of revolution is stretched beyond economics toward fundamentally altering people's feel-ings, life-styles, and social relationships. Authenticity requires critically negating established bourgeois shibboleths regarding work, sex, drugs, the family, art, government, and so on. Hence Marxist revolutionaries are simultaneously avant-garde thinkers, concerned with aesthetics and fully enjoying life as well as instigating rebellion. Play and art negate capitalism by generating feelings of uninhibited self-expression, self-control, and au-tonomy, intimating "a civilization of play."[62] Economically, this translates into worker self-management and public ownership of the productive ap-paratus. However, this is socialism with a difference: Factories will be art studios and workers liberated artists playfully manipulating machines. The aphorism "Don't work ever," written on Parisian walls by young radicals during the 1950s and 1960s, is certainly a peculiar Marxist call to arms.

Unfortunately, Arguments social theory lacks a solid theoretical base. Its outlandish demands illogically presuppose a suppressed human essence straining to escape capitalist enslavement, an inherent self-determining freedom, and a reflective antireductionism. Arguments theory is thus in-debted to ideal, experiential, and critical Marxism, in addition to its implicitly orthodox critique of political economy. These are never separated or ranked, prompting writers to emphasize whatever they find momentarily useful. Theoretically, they negate orthodoxy's reputation as the legitimate representative of Marxism, rather than establish a cogent social theory. Practically, they mobilize oppressed citizens—workers and nonworkers—to rebel. In an anti-Stalinist postwar environment, perhaps dramatic, illogical analysis is deemed an efficient revolutionary tactic. In any case, the Arguments group played a minor role in the theoretical evolution of Marxism, popularizing old ideas rather than creating new ones. But their theoretical sloppiness and revolutionary ambitions influenced New Leftism to abandon philosophical pretense entirely. A popular but eclectic and unconvincing theoretical critique of everyday life generated nontheoretical New Left activism.

New Left Activism

With a legacy of Sorel and the Arguments group, it is not surprising to hear New Leftists condemn radical literature for needlessly "arguing" and "lying"; "in any case . . . [it does] not make much of a difference, only direct experience . . . [is] incontrovertible."[63] Revolution is a practical goal that must not be obscured by needless intellectualizing. Capitalism's masses are "not bound together by an abstract theory of history but by an existential disgust."[64] Revolutionary action has its own justifiable consequences—and they alone comprise revolutionary theory. "The revolution is an indefinite process that has no stages you can break it down into, a process that cannot start out from a demand for socialism but leads to it inevitably when the revolutionary avant-garde sincerely represents the exploited classes." Marxism is theoretically valid only when the consequences of revolutionary action substantiate it. Otherwise it is an intellectual game calculated only to passify the masses. Note the illogical but calculated confluence, in Daniel Cohn-Bendit's importation, of amusement, lovemaking, violence, spontaneous freedom, selfishness, and social revolution:

Now put on your coat and make for the nearest cinema. Look at their deadly love-making on the screen. Isn't it better in real life? Make up your mind to learn to love. Then during the interval, when the first adverts come on, pick up your tomatoes, or if you prefer your eggs, and chuck them. Then get out in the street and peel off all the latest government proclamations. . . . then act. Act with others not for them. Make the revolution here and now. It is your own.[65]

This statement's truth is its mobilizing potential. Since Cohn-Bendit's constituency in this case was predominantly young, middle-class, educated, and disillusioned, he aped their unique values and desires, which were tactically, not epistemologically, significant. Because revolution is self-justifying, New Leftism taps all strategically useful ideas, in this instance including hip, sexy, tough, egotistical rhetoric. The intent is revolution, not intellectual or moral integrity.

New Leftism's intellectual fatuousness often obscures real motives. Originally, New Leftists were revolutionaries, but their flexible tactics and nondogmatic speeches attracted a heterogeneous variety of what Weinstein called "militant interest-group activists," people who support social activities like rent strikes, marches, demonstrations, boycotts, and occupations, not for their revolutionary value but as useful means of reforming social inequities.[66] Particularly in America, with its monolithic liberal tradition, New Leftist "revolutionaries" are often fellow travelers laboring to replace inept officials, change the law, or establish liberal rights and freedoms for political nonparticipants. Their goals leave capitalism untouched, so in this sense they are using, as well as being used by, authentic New Leftism. It is a marriage of convenience with one partner unaware of its own liberal bias and the other unwilling to discuss such esoteric nonsense. New Leftism is thus transformed, in practice, into a nebulous, unfocused social movement, encompassing liberal activists as well as hard-core revolutionaries who reject liberalism entirely. As a result, much of contemporary European and especially American New Left radicalism was nonrevolutionary, even though some New Leftists were certainly revolutionaries. Thus, one Marxist justifiably argued "revolutionary" New Leftism "encapsulate[s] radical politics within the categories of pragmatic and other forms of positivist thought. . . . [Its goal is] the transformation of the content of social life while retaining its ideological and institutional forms."[67]

By subsuming theory in practice, New Leftism receives both more and less than it bargains for. The turbulent 1960s, with their protest movements, riots, and civil violence, were at least partially conditioned by New Left activists who organized and led many young people into the streets of Paris, New York City, Washington, D.C., and Berkeley, California. New Leftists felt that theory inhibits meaningful action. And action is what they got, often among elite social groups and in nonurban areas even they could not have anticipated. New Leftism was a success. But its popularity among dissatisfied people was due to its anti-intellectualism, its antidogmatic tenets which—in the Old Left—had frightened away so many nonrevolutionary dissidents. By welcoming anyone willing to disrupt the status quo, New Leftism transformed itself into a nonrevolutionary activist movement, composed of such unlikely comrads as hippies, ecologists, students, potheads, back-to-the-land naturalists, vegetarians, black activists, liberated women, avant-garde artists, neoconservatives, antiwar professionals, revolutionary Marxists . . . the list stretches endlessly. Each mobilized around perceived issues of immediate concern, issues prompting anti-"establishment" protest. But very few harbored antisystem ulterior motives. With anti-intellectualism rampant, however, basic differences separating revolutionaries and nonrevolutionaries never surfaced. New Leftism thus failed dismally if we judge it by its own original criteria. While instigating social action, from their original revolutionary perspective this action in general was meaningless and insubstantial. As capitalism reformed, most New Leftists were defused, and the coalition disbanded. Former members drifted into corporate and professional positions or sought emotional fulfillment elsewhere, perhaps in religious or cult groups. When political movements lack intellectual substance, when they nonreflectively unite heterogeneous activists, they likely will dissolve as quickly as coalesce. Hence, by spurning theory New Leftism sealed its own disheartening fate.

CONCLUSION

Ironically, the social effects of both New Leftism and critical theory are identical: Neither liberated anyone from capitalist exploitation. History's message seems clear: While political action can perpetuate domination and reflection the status quo, revolutionary movements based solely on either abstract critique or spontaneous action cannot succeed. Praxis must be reflectively inspired, reflection concretely realized in and expressed by action. Although critical theorists and New Leftists condemn orthodoxy's reductive, nondialectical materialism, both eventually succumb to the extirpated devil.

NOTES

1. Under Grünberg's directorship, the institute published the journal *Archiv für die Geschichte des Sozialismus und der Arbeiterbewegung,* commonly known as the *Grünberg Archiv.* Later, it changed to *Zeitschrift fur Sozialforschung,* hereafter cited as *Zfs.* The term "Frankfurt School," which today describes the institute's work and members, was not chosen by them.

2. See Institut für Sozialforschung, *Soziologische Exkurse* (Frankfurt: Suhrkamp Verlag, 1956), Max Horkheimer and Theodore Adorno, *Sociologica II* (Frankfurt: Suhrkamp Verlag, 1956), Albrecht Wellmer, *Critical Theory of Society* (New York: Herder & Herder, 1971), and G. E. Rusconi, *La Teoria critica della Societa* (Bologna: Il Mulino, 1968). See also Martin Jay, *The Dialectical Imagination* (Boston: Little, Brown, 1973) and Zoltán Tar, *The Frankfurt School* (New York: Wiley, 1977).

3. See Horkheimer's inaugural address: "Die gegenwartige Lage der Sozialphilosophie und die Aufgaben eines Instituts für Sozialforschung," *Frankfurter Universitätsreden* (1931): 3-16; and "Vorwort," *ZfS* 1 (1932): iii.

4. See Max Horkheimer, "Traditionelle und Kritische Theorie," *ZfS* 6, no. 2 (1937): 245-92. English translation, "Traditional and Critical Theory," in Horkheimer, *Critical Theory—Selected Essays* (New York: Seabury Press, 1972), pp. 188-243.

5. Ibid., pp. 206, n. 1, and 210. See also Horkheimer, "Philosophie und Kritische Theorie," *ZfS* 6, no. 3 (1937): 630.

6. Horkheimer, *Critical Theory—Selected Essays,* p. 28.

7. Jürgen Habermas, *Theory and Practice* (Boston: Beacon Press, 1973),

pp. 201–2.

8. Horkheimer, "Traditional and Critical Theory," p. 200.

9. Max Horkheimer, "Materialismus und Metaphysik," *ZfS* 2, no. 1 (1933): 31n.

10. Horkheimer, "Traditional and Critical Theory," pp. 213ff.

11. See the postscript to ibid., p. 244, and "Materialismus und Metaphysik," *ZfS*.

12. See Goran Therborn, "The Frankfurt School," in *Western Marxism* (London: Verso, 1978), p. 107.

13. Horkheimer, "Traditional and Critical Theory," p. 241.

14. Horkheimer, "Bemerkungen zur philosophischen Anthropologie," *ZfS* 4, no. 1 (1935): 8.

15. Max Horkheimer, *Eclipse of Reason* (New York: Oxford University Press, 1947), p. 161.

16. Max Horkheimer, *Kritische Theorie* 2 vols. (Frankfurt: Suhrkamp Verlag, 1968), 2: 174 and 195.

17. Max Horkheimer and Theodore Adorno, *Dialectic of Enlightenment* (New York: Herder & Herder, 1972), p. 3.

18. Ibid., p. 256.

19. Max Horkheimer, "The Social Function of Philosophy," in *Critical Theory—Selected Essays*, pp. 264–70.

20. The debate is encapsulated in a series of essays, from both perspectives, included in Theodore Adorno, et al., *The Positivist Dispute in German Sociology* (New York: Harper & Row, 1976).

21. Institut für Sozialforschung, *Soziologische Exkurse*, p. 108.

22. Theodore Adorno, *Gesammelte schriften* 8 vols. (Frankfurt: Suhrkamp Verlag, 1972), 8: 549–50.

23. Theodore Adorno, "Das Ziel richtiger Praxis wäre ihre eigene Abschaffung," in *Stichworte: Kritische Modelle 2* (Frankfurt: Suhrkamp Verlag, 1969), p. 178. Horkheimer criticized Eastern Europe's socialist societies from this perspective in *Kritische Theorie*, p. x.

24. Theodore Adorno, *Negative Dialectics* (New York: Seabury, 1973), p. 406.

25. Walter Benjamin, *Illuminations* (New York: Schocken, 1969), p. 263; and Theodore Adorno, *Zur Metakritik der Erkenntnistheorie* (Frankfurt: Suhrkamp Verlag, 1971), pp. 24–25.

26. Adorno, *Negative Dialectics*, pp. 231–64 and 267.

27. Adorno, *Prismen,* (Frankfurt: Suhrkamp Verlag, 1955), p. 7.

28. Adorno, *Negative Dialectics*, pp. 242–45.

29. Horkheimer, Preface (1968) to *Critical Theory—Selected Essays*, pp. v and ix.

30. Max Horkheimer, *Verwaltete Welt? Ein Gespräch* (Zurich: Die Arche, 1970), p. 28.

31. Interview with Horkheimer in *Der Spiegel*, January 5, 1970.

32. Walter Benjamin, *Angelus Novus, Ausgewählte Schriften* 2 vols. (Frankfurt: Suhrkamp Verlag, 1966), 2: p. 459. Benjamin had a mystical faith in the power of social fantasy, which could—he felt—reveal human domination and also reopen the chance for human redemption.

33. Gerhard Zwerenz, *Kopf und Bauch* (Frankfurt: S. Fischer, 1973), p. 125.

34. Leszek Kolakowski, *Toward a Marxist Humanism* (New York: Grove Press, 1968), p. 35.

35. Jürgen Habermas, *Theory and Practice,* p. 9.

36. See ibid., pp. 8f and 268ff, and idem, *Knowledge and Human Interests* (Boston: Beacon Press, 1971), pp. 308f; and Wellmer, *Critical Theory of Society,* pp. 9–65.

37. See Habermas, *Knowledge and Human Interests,* pp. 309f, and idem, *Theory and Practice,* pp. 7ff.

38. Jürgen Habermas, "Technology and science as 'Ideology,'" in *Towards a Rational Society* (Boston: Beacon Press, 1971), p. 107.

39. Jürgen Habermas, "Towards a Theory of Communicative Competence," in Peter Dreitzel (ed.), *Recent Sociology, Number Two* (London: Macmillan, 1970), pp. 144–48.

40. Jürgen Habermas, "Technology and science as 'Ideology,'" in *Towards a Rational Society,* pp. 118–19.

41. Habermas, "Towards a Theory of Communicative Competence," pp. 117–18. See also idem, *Knowledge and Human Interests,* pp. 214–45. Freud felt that therapy transfers revealed symptoms into some form of "normal" social behavior. Habermas apparently felt that self-understanding is its own therapy.

42. See Habermas, *Theory and Practice,* pp. 195–252.

43. Habermas, "Technology and science as 'Ideology,'" p. 101.

44. See Habermas, *Knowledge and Human Interests,* pp. 43ff.

45. Habermas, "Technology and science as 'Ideology,'" pp. 93ff.

46. Wellmer, *Critical Theory of Society,* pp. 52 and 72.

47. Habermas, *Theory and Practice,* pp. 15–16.

48. Habermas, "Technology and science as 'Ideology,'" p. 122.

49. Jürgen Habermas, "Student Protest in the Federal Republic of Germany," in *Towards a Rational Society,* p. 26.

50. See, for example, Wellmer, *Critical Theory of Society,* p. 122; and William Leiss, *The Domination of Nature* (New York: Braziller, 1972), and *The Limits to Satisfaction* (Toronto: University of Toronto Press, 1976).

51. Habermas, *Theory and Practice,* p. 37.

52. Ibid., pp. 8–9. See also *Knowledge and Human Interests,* pp. 140–60.

53. Habermas, "Technology and science as 'Ideology,'" p. 113.

54. Habermas, *Theory and Practice,* pp. 14–22; and "Preparatory Remarks on a Theory of Communicative Competence," in *Theorie der Gesellschaft,* ed. J. Habermas and T. Luhmann (Frankfurt: Suhrkamp Verlag, 1971), pp. 101–41.

55. Richard Gombin, *The Origins of Modern Leftism* (Baltimore, Md.: Penguin Books, 1975), pp. 130 and 118. The best compilation of significant New Left documents is M. Teodori, *The New Left: A Documentary History* (New York: Bobbs-Merrill, 1969). An extensive bibliography of New Left writings and relevant background material are offered in Lyman T. Sargent, *New Left Thought* (Homewood, Ill.: Dorsey Press), pp. 170–84.

56. See ibid., pp. 35–56.

57. Carl Oglesby, "The Idea of the New Left," in *The New Left Reader,* ed. Carl Oglesby, (New York: Grove Press, 1969), p. 11.

58. Gombin, *The Origins of Modern Leftism,* p. 139.

59. See esp. Georges Sorel, *Reflections on Violence* (Glencoe, Ill.: The Free Press, 1950). See also *The Illusions of Progress* (Berkeley, Cal.: University of California Press, 1969), *Matériaux d'une théorie du proletariat* (Paris: Rivière,

1919), and *The Decomposition of Marxism* (New York: Humanities Press, 1961).

60. The term "Arguments Group" denotes the work appearing in three similar postwar journals: *Arguments, Internationale situationniste,* and *Socialisme ou Barbarie.* Members include H. Lefebvre, E. Morin, J. Duvignaud, P. Fougeyrollas, C. Audry, K. Axelos, D. Mascole, F. Chatelet, and R. Barthes. See Mark Poster, *Existential Marxism in Post-War France* (Princeton: Princeton University Press, 1975), pp. 209–14.

61. Gombin, *The Origins of Modern Leftism,* p. 54.

62. Ibid., p. 74.

63. Oglesby, "The Idea of the New Left," p. 154.

64. Rudy Dutschke, "On Anti-authoritarianism," in ibid., p. 251.

65. Daniel Cohn-Bendit, "The Battle of the Streets," in ibid., p. 266.

66. James Weinstein, *Ambiguous Legacy* (New York: Franklin Watts, 1975), p. 117.

67. S. Aronowitz, "Introduction" to Horkheimer's *Critical Theory — Selected Essays,* p. xi.

8.

A Family Divided

Neo-Marxism lives and grows in history, taking new forms when circumstances judge old ones lacking. The evolution from dogmatic materialism to opportunistic New Leftism covers a theoretical spectrum broad enough to fit such diverse epistemologies as idealism, empiricism, experientialism, and pure critique. Marxism's children have indeed gone separate ways. But they retain a common genetic identity which, for non-Marxists, diminishes intrafamily theoretical disputes. These blood traits are the irreplaceable core of Marxism, the minimum required of any individual calling him or herself a Marxist. Four principles unite an otherwise divisive Marxist family.

First, Marxism is dialectical. Whereas non-Marxist theory fragments reality and emphasizes one component or level, Marxism's universe is a multidimensional, interpenetrating totality. Authentic knowledge—natural, social, personal—encompasses the net of dynamic connections binding particulars to each other and to the collective totality. Social inquiry and action must acknowledge this multidimensionality by linking empirically isolated phenomena. Of course, Marxists disagree when philosophically justifying dialectics. Materialists and idealists posit impersonal dialectical patterns that ultimately determine specific phenomena, rendering history pre- and postdictable. Empiricists verify dialectics with empirical data. The dialectic lives in facts, not in a material or ideal abstraction. Experientialists generate dialectics phenomenologically. Free, indeterminate Beings-in-the-world manifest a spatially and temporally open totality, a multidimensional reality energized by creative praxis. Critical theory's chronic antireductionism eliminates every possibility *but* dialectics. Since objectivity is unknowable, reality must be an interpenetrating totality having no verifiable origin or pattern—an irreducible whole immune to positive explanatory systems. And New Leftism derives dialectics from revolutionary action. Since reformism fails miserably as revolutionary strategy, society must be a dialectical whole with interpenetrating levels. Dialectical theory confirms successful revolutionary action.

Second, Marxism interprets capitalism as alienating and exploitative. Bourgeois society turns humanity toward a de-natured, dehumanized identity. Real needs are disguised by an acquisitive capitalist elite; hence, the public's welfare is sacrificed to private wealth. People are isolated and anomic, competing rather than cooperating, consuming instead of fulfilling inherent abilities. Capitalist oppression is manifest culturally as well as in an exploitative productive apparatus, where workers are denied the full value of their labors. Capitalism thus generates a class of economically and socially oppressed workers, exploited by employers and brainwashed by an alienating bourgeois culture. Materialism argues the determination "in the last resort" of economics and hence sees alienation conditioned by capitalist exploitation, and the latter unfolding—impersonally and dialectically— toward its own negation. Idealism, acknowledging cognition, emphasizes capitalism's subjective component and the priority of "rational," "progressive," "dialectical" ideas in establishing and transforming productive modes. Empirical Marxism defines alienation and exploitation as verifiable facts of capitalist life. Neither abstractly conditions the other; hence, the precise relationship is determined factually by impersonal evidence—evidence, incidentally, that verifies capitalist oppression. For experiential Marxism, social and economic oppression thrives on naively internalized consequences of free action. Capitalism's appearance in history indicates that humanity willfully—if unknowingly—enslaves itself. Critical theory finds any community based on positive beliefs—hence all extant capitalist societies— alienating and exploitative. New Leftism wants to abolish such conditions, not analyze or explain them.

Third, Marxism would replace capitalism with socialism. Bourgeois oppression is surpassed when individual freedom generates a classless, organic social unity, and labor satisfies real human needs. Socialist economies maximize use rather than exchange value, thereby producing only what society requires. Rational cooperation replaces irrational competition. Produced goods are distributed purposefully, supplying everyone with the material means for creative lives. Individual freedom and socialist justice are knit into a seamless union of reflective actors. But Marxists disagree on the quality of authentic socialism and the apposite means of social transformation. Materialism sees class antagonisms propelling humanity into violent, inevitable conflagrations that will end in proletariat hegemony. In the short run at least, the latter manifests a proletarian "dictatorship" representing the Good and True, hence governing authoritatively in the workers' own interests. Idealism senses the incipient danger to subjectivity and postulates a humanist socialism of self-governing "rational" actors— though an "irrational" hegemonic proletariat would require authoritarian "guidance." Revolutions are inevitable and violent but also conditional— awaiting workers' rational cognition of universality. Empirical Marxism is ambivalent. Those, like Bernstein, stressing data accumulation, mute their revolutionary zeal and even hypothesize a peaceful evolution to socialism, which substantively perfects, not destroys, bourgeois procedural democracy. Those emphasizing radical theory and action, such as Della Volpe, are scientists who are comfortable with orthodoxy's cult of violence and revolutionary dictatorship. Experiential Marxism sees revolutions conditioned by the free praxis of reflective victims. They are indeterminate, inevitably neither violent nor peaceful, and in our era manifest self-governing socialist democracies of authentic Beings-in-the-world. Sartre's depressing retreat into Stalinist authoritarianism is not endemic to experientialism as such. Critical theory envisions reflective socialism as desirable but pure fantasy, instantly infected by inauthentic consequences of concrete acts. Though socialism alone can rationally emancipate exploited workers, Stalinism, sadly, teaches us a "liberating revolution" is a contradiction in terms. New Leftism spurns theories of "correct" revolutionary means and ends, leaving these to the retroactive glare of successful socialist revolutionaries.

Finally, Marxism originates in Marx. Competing Marxists bathe together in Marx's paternal "sacred aura," skillfully justifying their own views with his.[1] Motives are practical and theoretical. After Bernstein confessed to "revising" Marx, a storm of crude and hurtful invective brewed in orthodox circles, questioning Bernstein's integrity and loyalty and purging him from the movement. Since then, neo-Marxists emboss their credentials with Marx's own words—carefully edited—to legitimize theories and protect reputations. Consequently, radical social theory matures in this century through a "process of revising Marx by rediscovering him."[2] Practical considerations are aided by Marx's ambiguous philosophy, which, we have seen, on the one hand denies philosophy and on the other hungrily travels in several different philosophical directions. Competing schools of Marxism are inspired by Marx because he does, in fact, inspire competing Marxisms. Perceptive scholars use Marx to justify a priorism, empiricism, experientialism, reflective critique, and revolutionary activism—authenticating each significant meaning of contemporary Marxism.

Marxism, therefore, is dialectical, indicts capitalism, advocates socialism, and knows relevant texts. It also compels each believer to make difficult and complex theoretical decisions having significant practical consequences. Since meaningful inquiry and action necessarily presuppose a set of theoretical principles, these choices can be ignored, not avoided.

Materialism offers hope, confidence, and scientific guidance, but simultaneously denies meaningful subjective freedom to everyone but Party leaders—who also dress spontaneity in universal principles. Strategy is impersonal and absolute, foretelling violent class war. Postrevolutionary society is governed "dictatorially," though in workers' Party-perceived interests.

Idealist Marxism tantalizes revolutionaries who dread materialist dogmatism, melting abstract cognition into concrete material processes. History's inevitable workers' revolution depends on rational subjectivity. But idealism also complicates revolutionary strategy. Marxism now cultivates explosive subjective *and* objective conditions, hence legitimizes the revolutionary role of intellectuals. Moreover, in difficult times idealism invites "rational" scientists to steer the postrevolutionary helm. Subjectivity is negated by the defenders of subjectivity. Orthodoxy travels a more direct path to the same destination, without idealist rhetoric.

Empirical Marxism shares a method with bourgeois social science, hence a means of communicating and laboring cooperatively. However, though "modern," it also criticizes modernity's Cartesianism. It taps the burgeoning supply of empirical research techniques without capitulating to a reactionary bourgeois elite, attracting socially conscious empirical scientists seeking radical change that doesn't annihilate the fruits of modern science. Unfortunately, the pressure to pursue facts can, where baldly empirical indicators of change are few, diminish revolutionary activism. Even Gurvitch's counterfindings subsume action in hyperempirical data accumulating. Conversely, an apposite Marxist concern with rebellion blinds one to infelicitous facts—perverting empirical method—and/or marries empirical Marxism to dominant orthodoxy, mimicking empiricism's servile connection to capitalism. Either alternative sacrifices empirical Marxism's uniqueness. The divergent biographies of Bernstein and Della Volpe and the ideological fractioning of Austro-Marxism illustrate the problem. Colletti's increasing disillusion with both Marxism and bourgeois empiricism indicates the dearth of quick solutions.

Critical theory is an intellectual's safety valve, offering sensitive, intelligent, reticent radicals the choice of not choosing. The evils of reductionism—bourgeois or Marxist; a priori, empirical, or experiential—are immense and inescapable, and negated only by reflective critique. Paradoxically, critical theory's contemplative bromide dehumanizes by denying actors the everyday freedom to act purposefully. Moreover, it is an unanticipated bonanza for entrepreneurs, generating brilliant anticapitalist monographs with profitable markets among disillusioned but complacent Westerners.

New Leftism satiates the radical's compelling need to act decisively for socialist justice. However, its anti-intellectualism invites either excess or triviality—the former from fanatics enamored with revolutionary techniques and responsible only to themselves; the latter from disgruntled citizens seeking nontraditional avenues of political protest and reform. New Leftism, by reviling formal principles, becomes a potpourri of self-seeking activists, united only by shared living space.

Experiential Marxism admits that a science of reflective social action is impossible. Authentic actors are defined by self-determining freedom; hence, no reliable guide, material or otherwise, can foretell the imminence or quality of social change. That the revolutionary legacy formerly held by

Engels and Kautsky should, in an existential phenomenologist's hands, proclaim civilization an irresolute mystery, is for many an unsupportable theoretical twist. To these critics, existential ontology smells of abstractionism, with ahistorical absolutes and egoistic ruminations. Being-in-the-world *is* an ontological and epistemological absolute, depicting human authenticity— the source of valid knowledge. But the only alternative to some kind of positive system is critical theory's despair and helplessness. Moreover, existential ontology retains one advantage over a priori and empirical competitors: It avoids entirely limiting or guiding self-determining human freedom and hence poses no threat to free social action. But neither is it nihilism. Existential ontology, socialized, generates dialectical inquiry, a critique of capitalism, a call for socialism, and a rereading of Marx empha- sizing his concern for real human freedom. In brief, it generates an experi- ential Marxism that is validated only through self-determined, reflective actions. Its tenets are abstract until cognized by capitalism's exploited majority—an educational task for revolutionary activists. Concrete mate- rial change indicates success. Socialism brings authentic institutions and values, manifesting universal freedom and self-government.

Experiential Marxism alone advocates self-determining freedom as well as socialist justice. Although it guarantees only long hours of revolutionary activism, it may be Marxism's best hope in capitalist societies saturated with undelivered promises of subjective autonomy.

NOTES

1. Lucio Colletti, "A Political and Philosophical Interview," *New Left Review* 86 (July–August 1974), p. 13.

2. Sidney Hook, "Introduction" to Edouard Bernstein, *Evolutionary Socialism* (New York: Schocken Books, 1965), p. ix. See pp. vii–xx.

Bibliography

This selection includes only primary sources relevant to the text. Wherever possible, English language editions are listed.

Adler, Marx. *Der soziologische Sinn der Lehre von Karl Marx.* Leipzig: Hirschfeld, 1914.

_____. *Kant und der Marxismus.* Berlin: Laub'sche Verlagsbuchhandlung, 1925.

_____. *Kausalität und Teleologie im Streite um die Wissenschaft.* Vienna: Wiener Volksbuchhandlung Ignaz Brand, 1904.

_____. *Lehrbuch der materialistischen Geschichtsauffassung.* In *Soziologie des Marxismus.* 3 vols. Vienna: Europa Verlag, 1964.

Adorno, Theodore. *Minima Moralia.* London: New Left Books, 1974.

_____. *Negative Dialectics.* New York: Seabury, 1973.

_____. *Prismen; Kulturkritik und Gesellschaft.* Frankfurt: Suhrkamp Verlag, 1955.

_____. *Stichworte: Kritische Modelle 2.* Frankfurt: Suhrkamp Verlag, 1969.

_____. *Zur Metakritik der Erkenntnistheorie.* Frankfurt: Suhrkamp Verlag, 1971.

_____, et al. *The Positivist Dispute in German Sociology.* New York: Harper & Row, 1976.

Althusser, Louis. *Essays in Self-Criticism.* London: New Left Books, 1976.

_____. *For Marx.* New York: Pantheon, 1969.

_____. *Lenin and Philosophy.* London: Monthly Review Press, 1971.

_____. *Philosophie et Philosophie Spontanée des Savants.* Paris: Receuil, 1974.

_____. *Reading Capital.* New York: Pantheon, 1970.

Barthes, Roland. *Elements of Semiology.* New York: Hill & Wang, 1968.

_____. *S/Z.* New York: Hill & Wang, 1974.

Bauer, Otto. *The Austrian Revolution.* New York: Burt Franklin, 1925.

Benjamin, Walter. *Angelus Novus, Ausgewählte Schriften.* Frankfurt: Suhrkamp Verlag, 1966.

_____. *Illuminations.* New York: Schocken, 1969.

Bernstein, Edouard. *Evolutionary Socialism.* New York: Schocken Books, 1965.

Bloch, Ernst. *Das Prinzip Hoffnung.* 3 vols. Frankfurt: Suhrkamp Verlag, 1954–1959.

_____. *Man on His Own.* New York: Herder & Herder, 1970.

Bottomore, Tom and Goode, Patrick, eds. *Austro-Marxism.* Oxford: Oxford University Press, 1978.

Bricianer, S. *Pannekoek et les conseils ouvriers.* Paris: EDI, 1969.

Broekman, Jan M. *Structuralism: Moscow-Prague-Paris.* Dordrecht, Netherlands: D. Reidel, 1974.

Brzozowski, Stanislaw. *Idee.* Lemberg, Poland 1910.

Bukharin, Nikolai. *Historical Materialism.* Ann Arbor, Mich.: University of Michigan Press, 1969.

_____. *Imperialism and the World Economy.* New York: H. Fertig, 1966.

Cohen, G. A. *Karl Marx's Theory of History.* Princeton, N.J.: Princeton University Press, 1978.

Colletti, Lucio. "A Political and Philosophical Interview," *New Left Review* 86 (July–August 1974): 3–28.

_____. *From Rousseau to Lenin.* London: New Left Books, 1972.

_____. *Marxism and Hegel.* London: New Left Books, 1973.

Cornforth, Maurice. *The Theory of Knowledge.* New York: International Publishers, 1963. .

Coward, Rosalind, and Ellis, John. *Language and Materialism—Developments in Semiology and the Theory of the Subject.* London: Routledge & Kegan Paul, 1977.

Della Volpe, Galvano. *Logic as a Positive Science.* London: New Left Books, 1980.

Derrida, Jacques. *Of Grammatology.* Baltimore, Md.: Johns Hopkins University, 1974.

Engels, Friedrich. *Anti-Dühring.* Peking: Foreign Language Press, 1976.

_____. *Dialectic of Nature.* New York: International Publishers, 1940.

_____. *The German Peasants War.* Moscow: Foreign Language Publishing House, 1956.

_____. *Ludwig Feuerback and the End of Classic German Philosophy.* New York: International Publishers, 1941.

_____. *The Origins of the Family, Private Property and the State.* New York: International Publishers, 1972.

_____. *Socialism: Utopian and Scientific.* New York: Scribners, 1892.

Feuer, Lewis, ed. *Marx and Engels—Basic Writings on Politics and Philosophy.* New York: Anchor Books, 1959.

Foucault, Michel. *The Archeology of Knowledge.* New York: Pantheon, 1972.

_____. *The Order of Things.* New York: Pantheon, 1970.

Fromm, Erich. *Beyond the Chains of Illusion.* New York: Simon & Schuster, 1962.

_____. *Man For Himself.* New York: Rinehart, 1947.

_____. *Marx's Concept of Man.* New York: F. Ungar, 1961.

_____. *The Sane Society.* New York: Holt, Rinehart & Winston, 1976.

_____, ed. *Socialist Humanism.* New York: Anchor Books, 1966.

_____, et al. *Zen Buddhism and Psychoanalysis.* New York: Harper & Row, 1970.

Godelier, Maurice. *Perspectives in Marxist Anthropology.* London: Cambridge University Press, 1977.

_____. *Rationality and Irrationality in Economics.* London: New Left Books, 1972.

Goldman, Lucien. *Entretiens sur les notions de 'Génèse' et de 'Structure'.* Paris: Mouton & École Practique de Hautes Études, 1965.

_____. *The Hidden God.* London: Routledge & Kegan Paul, 1964.

_____. *The Human Sciences and Philosophy.* London: Cape, 1969.

_____. "Ideology and Writing," *The Times Literary Supplement,* 28 September 1967, p. 904.

——————. *Marxisme et sciences humaines.* Paris: Gallimard, 1970.

Gombin, Richard. *The Origins of Modern Leftism.* Baltimore, Md.: Penguin Books, 1975.

Gramsci, Antonio. *La Citta futura.* Milano: Feltrinelli, 1959.

——————. *Opere di Antonio Gramsci.* 12 vols. Turin: Einaudi, 1947–1972.

——————. *Selections from the Prison Notebooks.* New York: International Publishers, 1971.

——————. *Selections from Political Writings, 1910–20.* New York: International Publishers, 1977.

——————. *Political Writings, 1921–6.* New York: International Publishers, 1978.

Gurvitch, Georges, *Déterminismes sociaux et liberté humaine.* Paris: Presses Universitaires, 1955.

——————. *Dialectique et sociologie.* Paris: Flammarion, 1962.

——————. *Essais de sociologie.* Paris: Recueil Sirey, 1938.

——————. *La déclaration des droits sociaux.* Paris: Vrin, 1946.

——————. *La Vocation actuelle de la Sociologie.* 2 vols. Paris: Presses Universitaires, 1950.

——————. *The Social Frameworks of Knowledge.* New York: Harper & Row, 1971.

——————. *The Sociology of Law.* New York: Philosophical Library, 1942.

——————. *The Spectrum of Social Time.* Dordrecht, Netherlands: Reidel, 1964.

Habermas, Jürgen, ed. *Antworten auf Herbert Marcuse.* Frankfurt: Suhrkamp Verlag, 1968.

——————. *Knowledge and Human Interests.* Boston: Beacon Press, 1971.

——————. *Theory and Practice.* Boston: Beacon Press, 1973.

——————. *Towards a Rational Society.* Boston: Beacon Press, 1971.

——————, and Luhmann, T., eds. *Theorie der Gesellschaft.* 2d ed. Frankfurt: Suhrkamp Verlag, 1971.

——————. *Legitimation Crisis.* Boston: Beacon Press, 1975.

Heidegger, Martin. *Being and Time.* New York: Harper & Row, 1962.

Hilferding, Rudolf. *Bohm-Bawerk: Karl Marx and the Close of His System.* New York: A. M. Kelly, 1949.

——————. *Das Finanzkapital.* Vienna: Wiener Volksbuchhandlung, 1904.

Horkheimer, Max. "Bemerkungen zur philosophischen Anthropologie," *Zeitschrift für Socialforschung* 4, no. 1 (1937): 620–45.

——————. *Critical Theory—Selected Essays.* New York: Seabury Press, 1972.

——————. "Die gegenwärtige Lage der Socialphilosophie und die Aufgaben eines Instituts für Sozialforschung," *Frankfurter Universitätsreden,* 1931, pp. 3–16.

——————. *Eclipse of Reason.* New York: Oxford University Press, 1947.

——————. *Kritische Theorie.* 2 vols. Frankfurt: Suhrkamp Verlag, 1968.

——————. "Materialismus und Metaphysik," *Zeitschrift für Sozialforschung* 2, no. 1 (1933): 1–36.

——————. "Philosophie und Kritische Theorie," *Zeitschrift für Sozialforschung* 6, no. 3 (1937): 620–45.

——————. *Verwaltete Welt? Ein Gespräch.* Zurich: Die Arche, 1970.

——————. "Vorwort," *Zeitschrift für Sozialforschung* 1 (1932): iii.

——————. and Adorno, Theodore. *Dialectic of Enlightenment.* New York: Herder & Herder, 1972.

——————. *Sociologica II.* Frankfurt: Suhrkamp Verlag, 1956.

Hyppolite, Jean. *Genèse et structure de la phénoménologie de l'esprit de Hegel.* Paris: Aubier, 1946.

————. *Introduction à la philosophie de l'histoire de Hegel.* Paris: M. Rivière, 1968.

————. *Logique et existence: essai sur la Logique de Hegel.* Paris: Presses universitaires de France, 1953.

————. *Marxisme et existentialisme.* Paris: M. Rivière, 1962.

————. *Studies on Marx and Hegel.* New York: Basic Books, 1969.

Institut für Sozialforschung. *Soziologische Exkurse.* Frankfurt: Suhrkamp Verlag, 1956.

Jaurès, Jean. *Oeuvres.* 9 vols. Paris: Rieder, 1931–1939.

Kautsky, Karl. *The Class Struggle.* New York: Norton, 1971.

————. *Die materialistische Geschichtsauffassung.* 2 vols. Berlin: Dietz, 1927.

————. *The Economic Doctrines of Karl Marx.* London: Black, 1925.

————. *Ethics and the Materialist Interpretation of History.* Chicago: C. H. Kerr, 1914.

Kojève, Alexandre. *Introduction to the Reading of Hegel,* edited by Raymond Queneau. New York: Basic Books, 1969.

Kolakowski, Leszek. *The Alienation of Reason.* Garden City, N.Y.: Doubleday, 1968.

————. *Main Currents of Marxism.* 3 vols. London: Oxford University Press, 1978.

————. *Marxism and Beyond.* London: Pall Mall Press, 1969.

————. *Toward a Marxist Humanism.* New York: Grove Press, 1968.

Korsch, Karl. *Marxism and Philosophy.* New York: Monthly Review Press, 1970.

Kosík, Karel. *Dialectic of the Concrete.* Dordrecht, Netherlands: Reidel, 1976.

Lacan, Jacques. *Écrits I.* Paris: Éditions du Seuil, 1966.

————. *Écrits II.* Paris: Éditions du Seuil, 1971.

Lenin, V. I. *Collected Works.* 45 vols. London: Lawrence & Wishart, 1960–1970.

————. *Materialism and Empirio-Criticism.* Peking: Foreign Language Press, 1972.

————. *Philosophical Notebooks.* Moscow: Progress Publishers, 1972.

Lévi-Strauss, Claude. *The Raw and the Cooked.* New York: Harper & Row, 1969.

————. *The Savage Mind.* Chicago: University of Chicago Press, 1966.

————. *Structural Anthropology.* New York: Basic Books, 1963.

————. *Tristes Tropiques.* New York: Atheneum, 1968.

Labriola, Antonio. *Essays on the Materialistic Conception of History.* New York: Monthly Review Press, 1966.

————. *Scritti politici.* Bari, Italy: Laterza, 1970.

Ludz, P., ed. *Georg Lukács: Schriften zur Ideologie und Politik.* Neuwied-Berlin: Luchterhand, 1967.

Lukács, Georg. *History and Class Consciousness.* Cambridge, Mass.: MIT Press, 1971.

————. *Lenin. A Study on the Unity of His Thought.* Cambridge, Mass.: MIT Press, 1971.

————. *The Theory of the Novel.* Cambridge, Mass.: MIT Press, 1971.

Luxembourg, Rosa. *The Accumulation of Capital.* New York: Modern Reader Paperbacks, 1968.

_____. *The Russian Revolution* and *Leninism or Marxism?* Ann Arbor, Mich.: University of Michigan Press, 1976.

_____. *Selected Writings,* edited by D. Howard. New York: Monthly Review Press, 1971.

Mao Tse-tung. *An Anthology of His Writings,* edited by Anne Freemantle. New York: Mentor Books, 1962.

_____. *Mao Tse-tung Unrehearsed,* edited by S. Schram (ed.). Harmondsworth, England: Penguin Books, 1974.

Marcuse, Herbert. "Contributions to a Phenomenology of Historical Materialism," *Telos* 4 (Fall 1969): 3–34.

_____. *Eros and Civilization.* Boston: Beacon Press, 1966.

_____. *Essay on Liberation.* Boston: Beacon Press, 1969.

_____. *Negations.* Boston: Beacon Press, 1968.

_____. *One Dimensional Man.* Boston: Beacon Press, 1966.

_____. "On the Problem of the Dialectic," *Telos* 27 (Spring 1976): 13–29.

_____. *Reason and Revolution.* Boston: Beacon Press, 1960.·

_____. *Soviet Marxism.* New York: Vintage Books, 1961.

Marković, Mihailo. *From Affluence to Praxis.* Ann Arbor, Mich.: University of Michigan Press, 1974.

Marx, Karl. *Early Writings.* New York: Vintage Books, 1975.

_____. *Karl Marx: Selected Writings,* edited by D. McLellan. London: Oxford University Press, 1977.

_____. *Selected Writings in Sociology and Social Philosophy.* edited by T. B. Bottomore and M. Rubel. London: Watts, 1956.

_____, and Engels, Friedrich. *Selected Correspondence.* Moscow: Progress Publishers, n.d.

_____. *Werke.* 39 vols. Berlin: Dietz Verlag, 1974.

Merleau-Ponty, Maurice. *Adventures of the Dialectic.* Evanston, Ill.: Northwestern University Press, 1973.

_____. *Humanism and Terror.* Boston: Beacon Press, 1969.

_____. *Phenomenology of Perception.* London: Routledge & Kegan Paul, 1967.

_____. *Sense and Non-Sense.* Evanston, Ill: Northwestern University Press, 1964.

_____. *Signs.* Evanston, Ill.: Northwestern University Press, 1964.

_____. *The Structure of Behavior.* Boston: Beacon Press, 1963.

_____. *The Visible and the Invisible.* Evanston, Ill.: Northwestern University Press, 1968.

Novack, George, ed. *Existentialism Versus Marxism.* New York: Dell, 1966.

Oglesby, Carl, ed. *The New Left Reader.* New York: Grove Press, 1969.

Paci, Enzo. *The Function of the Sciences and the Meaning of Man.* Evanston, Ill.: Northwestern University Press, 1972.

_____. "Sul problema della interosoggettivitá," *Il Pensiero* 3 (1960): 291–325.

Pannekoek, Anton. *Lenin as Philosopher.* London: Merlin, 1975.

_____. *Workers' Councils.* Melbourne: Southern Advocate for Workers' Councils, 1950.

Petrović, Gajo. *Marx in the Mid-Twentieth Century.* New York: Anchor Books, 1967.

Plekhanov, George V. *Contributions to the History of Materialism.* New York: H. Fertig, 1967.

————. *The Development of the Monist View of History.* Moscow: Progress Publishers, 1956.

————. *Fundamental Problems of Marxism.* New York: International Publishers, 1969.

————. *The Role of the Individual in History.* New York: International Publishers, 1940.

————. *Selected Philosophical Works.* 5 vols. 2d ed. Moscow: Progress Publishers, 1974.

Poulantzas, Nicos. *Classes in Contemporary Capitalism.* London: New Left Books, 1975.

————. *Fascism and Dictatorship.* London: New Left Books, 1974.

————. *Political Power and Social Classes.* London: New Left Books, 1973.

————. *State, Power, Socialism.* London: New Left Books, 1978.

Reich, Wilhelm. *Character Analysis,* New York: Farrar, Strauss & Giroux, 1970.

————. *The Function of the Organism.* New York: Farrar, Strauss & Giroux, 1961.

————. *Mass Psychology of Fascism.* New York: Orgone Institute Press, 1946.

————. *People in Trouble.* Rangely, Me.: Wilhelm Reich Foundation, 1953.

————. *Reich on Freud,* edited by M. Higgins and C. Raphael. New York: Farrar, Strauss & Giroux, 1967.

————. *Sex-Pol, Essays, 1929-34,* edited by L. Baxandall. New York: Vintage Books, 1972.

Rovatti, Pier Aldo. "A Phenomenological Analysis: The Return to the Subject and to the Dialectic of Totality," *Telos* 5 (Spring 1970): 160-173.

Ryazanov, David G. Explanatory Notes to Revised (1922) Russian edition of *The Communist Manifesto of Karl Marx and Friedrich Engels.* New York: Russell & Russell, 1963.

————. *Karl Marx and Friedrich Engels.* London: Martin Lawrence, 1927.

————. *Karl Marx—Man, Thinker, and Revolutionist.* London: Martin Lawrence, 1927.

Sargent, Lyman T. *New Left Thought.* Homewood, Ill.: Dorsey, 1972.

Sartre, Jean Paul. *Being and Nothingness.* New York: NYU Press, 1966.

————. *Critique of Dialectical Reason.* Atlantic Highlands, New Jersey: Humanities Press, 1976.

————. *L'Idiot de la famille: Gustave Flaubert de 1821 à 1857.* 2 vols. Paris: Gallimard, 1971.

————. *Life/Situations. Essays Written and Spoken.* New York: Pantheon Books, 1977.

————. *Search For a Method.* New York: Vintage, 1969.

Schaff, Adam. *Marxism and the Human Individual.* New York: McGraw-Hill, 1970.

————. *Structuralism and Marxism.* New York: Pergamon Press, 1978.

Schumpeter, Joseph. *History of Economic Analysis.* New York: Oxford University Press, 1954.

Sebag, Lucien. *Marxisme et structuralisme.* Paris: Payot, 1964.

Shaw, William H. *Marx's Theory of History.* Palo Alto, Calif.: Stanford University Press, 1978.

Smart, D. A., ed. *Pannekoek and Gorter's Marxism.* London: Pluto Press, 1978.

Sollers, Philippe. *Sur le matérialisme.* Paris: Seuil, 1974.

Sorel, George. *The Decomposition of Marxism.* New York: Humanities Press, 1961.

————. *The Illusions of Progress.* Berkeley, Calif.: University of California Press, 1969.

————. *Matériaux d'une théorie du prolétariat.* Paris: M. Rivière, 1929.

————. *Reflections on Violence.* Glencoe, Ill.: The Free Press, 1950.

Stalin, Joseph. *Dialectical and Historical Materialism.* New York: International Publishers, 1940.

Stojanović, S. *Between Ideals and Reality.* New York: Oxford University Press, 1973.

Teodori, M. *The New Left: A Documentary History.* New York: Bobbs-Merrill, 1969.

Timpanaro, Sebastian. *The Freudian Slip—Psychoanalysis and Textual Criticism.* London: New Left Books, 1976.

————. *On Materialism.* Atlantic Highlands, New Jersey: Humanities Press, 1975.

Tran Duc-Thao. *Phénoménologie et matérialisme dialectique.* Paris: Minh-Tan, 1954.

Trotsky, Leon. *In Defense of Marxism.* New York: Pathfinder Press, 1970.

————. *My Life.* New York: Scribners, 1930.

————. *The Revolution Betrayed.* New York: Pathfinder Press, 1972.

Wellmer, Albrecht. *Critical Theory of Society.* New York: Herder & Herder, 1971.

Index

Robert A. Gorman is Associate Professor of Political Science at the University of Tennessee, Knoxville. He is the author of *The Dual Vision: Alfred Schutz and the Myth of Phenomenological Social Science* and of articles which have appeared in scholarly journals of politics, sociology, history, and philosophy.